Chaos, Madness, and Unpredictability ...

Placing the Child With Ears Like Uncle Harry's

Warren Spaulding
1893—1977

Whose gift of his family home provided the agency with a base for operations and a name.

Chaos, Madness, and Unpredictability ...

Placing the Child With Ears Like Uncle Harry's

(The Spaulding Approach to Adoption)

Christopher Unger
Gladys Dwarshuis
Elizabeth Johnson

Spaulding for Children
Chelsea, Michigan

Library of Congress Cataloging in Publication Data

Unger, Christopher, 1947-
    Chaos, madness, and unpredictability.

    Bibliography: p. 372
    1. Spaulding for Children (Agency)   2.   Adoption—
United States.   3.   Problem children—United States.
4.   Handicapped children—United States.   I.   Dwarshuis,
Gladys, joint author.   II.   Johnson, Elizabeth, 1950-
joint author.   III.   Title.
HV885.C35U53   362.7'3   74-19934
ISBN 0-9600790-1-7

Published by Spaulding for Children

Printed in the United States of America

First edition

Cover photograph by Katherine Jason Butler
Mr. Spaulding's photographer unknown
Family, Ice Cream Social, Tree Trimming Party, and
    Author Photographs by Rick Ridley
Spaulding farmhouse photograph by Kay Donley
Research assistance by Elizabeth Johnson

Ruth Carlton's "A Child is Waiting" columns (pp. 116-118) are
    reproduced from *The Detroit News* with permission

Funds provided by the Children's Bureau-
    Office of Child Development, HEW

To those children
who are
or who should be
available for adoption

and to
Warren Spaulding
who loved them all

The authors wish to thank those people who helped make this book possible.

Wayne Anderson
Bill St. Aubin
Pat Babcock
Jay Ballew
Elwood & Mary Lou Bender
Elizabeth Berry
Roger & Gloria Bessey
Dottie Blacklock
Roger & Barbara Buiten
Walter & Harriet Burge
Shirley Burnett
Ruth Carlton
Dorothy Carter
Dr. William Cave
Charlotte Chadwell
Ed Cobb
Gordon Cook
Jane Costabile
Phyllis Cornell
Helen Cortright
Chuck & Vicki Councilman
Jan Crafton
Bob Daniel
Gerban DeJong
Ted & Mary DeRose
Mary Jane Dettling
Ted DeWolf
Kay Donley
Sydney Duncan
Albert & Nannie Earle
Ron Edmonds
Sharon Eisen
Gretchen Farah
Dr. Pat Ferman
Tom & Susan Fletcher
Peter & Joyce Forsythe
Mary Gaken
Ursula Gallagher
Beth Goebel
Phyllis Gold
Lillian Gordon
Ferman Haas
Clayton Hagen
Mike Hall
Thelma Hartman
Son Hayiland

Dick Higley
Bob & Joan Hoffman
Kathy Johnson
Vicki Johnson
Barbara Kaplan
Jayne Kidney
Sue Kraysler
Vici Leach
John & Susan Lewis
Don & Geneva Lile
Hon. James Lincoln
Jackie Locker
Dr. Harold Lockett
Hon. Richard Loughrin
Marty & Ken McClatchey
William McKinley
Lois March
Mike & Ryley Meagher
Don & Lillian Miller
Clara Noble
Lynn Otzman
Ed Paulette
Mary Peih
George & Joan Perros
Naomi Peters
Dorothea Peilemeier
Mary Pryor
Freda Ramseur
Kathy Ragan
Robert & Nancy Richardson
Rick Ridley
Don Rolph
Dorothy Rose
Fran Sage
Jeannine Sawers
Richard Schneider
Carol Schroen
Sue Schroen
Tom & Patricia Schulte
Arn Shackleford
Rev. Warner Siebert
Warren Spaulding
Hon. John Steketee
Leroy & Mandy Storr
Don & Beverly Struthers
Cecelia Sudia

Gerry Sullivan
Bud Turner
Nancy Unger
Olga Unger
Willy Vandereerden
Elvira Vogel
Debbie Wallis
Fran & Arlene Wanger
Roseann Ward
Dr. Bruce Warren
Barb White
Bill & Ernestine Williams
Gloria Williams
Laura Williams
Fred Wight
Lester & Beverly Yager
Carl Zinn

Table of Contents

Forward

Most people still believe "adoptable" children are babies — orphans living in a big building, lying in a crib unloved and unwanted, without toys, without parents to love them. They envision themselves visiting the orphanage, walking through a ward, and saying, "I want *that* one because she looked at me in a certain way." They take the orphaned baby home and watch her grow into a beautiful and intelligent young woman who marries the President of the United States. That's an old fantasy we must put to rest.

We need to have people talking about what it is like to live with a 12 year old who is reading three years behind grade level, who can be a mouthy upstart, but who occasionally comes through as a *real* kid with needs, desires, frustrations, and rewards attached to him, too. Everyone must understand that adoption isn't something done in orphanages by people walking through and pointing to a crib. There is still a lot of work to be done.

From a conversation with
Kay Donley
Director
Spaulding For Children
February 2, 1977

Introduction

This is the story of Spaulding for Children — a small, voluntary, and specialized adoption program in Michigan established for the sole purpose of finding adoptive families for children whose previous efforts to achieve permanence have been handicapped by their age, race, sibling-ship, educational, physical, or emotional problems. Specifically, it is a description of the philosophies, methods, and techniques which constitute the agency's approach to adoption. More generally, it is an attempt to show, by example, that with enough hard work, determination, appropriate attitudes, and the right choice of techniques, most children legally available for adoption can be successfully placed and maintained in an adoptive family.

Since Spaulding's establishment in 1968, the foundation of the agency's success has been a vigorous commitment on the part of a confident Board and staff that the task they have set for themselves is possible. They believed, and have proven, that parents do exist who are interested in and capable of parenting older and handicapped children.

There are, of course, several children for whom Spaulding has not been able to find families. However, since September 1968, the Michigan staff have found families for about 200 children whom workers from other adoption programs based in private agencies, juvenile courts, or county offices of public welfare agencies had not been able to place.

The successes of Spaulding for Children have played a major role in gradually expanding the working definition of the "hard-to-place" child. In 1968, for example, the Michigan Department of Social Services (MDSS) defined as "hard-to-place" any child who was over age two, of minority race, or who possessed minor handicaps or deformities. Presently, the MDSS uses this label only for those children who are over age ten, if white, and over age eight, if minority race, and for those children who are moderately retarded, severely or multiply handicapped, emotionally disturbed, or terminally ill.

Although similar types of improvements in adoption attitude and practice have been made in a number of states and countries in recent years, there are still many deeply held attitudes and customary behaviors which must be changed. Spaulding is still one of the few adoption programs that has specialized in placing children traditionally seen as hard-to-place or "unadoptable." It is clear that with all of the children in need of adoption (estimated by the Child Welfare League of America to number 120,000 in the United States alone),[1] many other placement programs are needed in which workers have the commitment and skills to find permanent families for these children.

In 1972, in an effort to help meet this need, Spaulding's Board and staff committed themselves to an extensive program of training and consultation and to an active sharing of their philosophies, methods, and techniques with all interested child welfare professionals. As greater numbers of adoption programs in this nation, and even other countries, began looking to the Spaulding approach to adoption as a model for solutions to some of their own difficulties, Spaulding workers began receiving increasing requests to hold or participate in workshops and training sessions. These training and consultation seesions, for both adoption professionals and interested parents, have been presented in many parts of the United States as well as in Canada, Great Britain, and Australia. Spaulding is also currently participating in the establishment of a national "Family Builders" network of specialized adoption programs to serve as placement resources and models for adoption services for older and handicapped children throughout the country.

The success of Spaulding for children is not a miracle or an extraordinary occurrence. It is, instead, the result of putting into practice a common sense approach toward children and parents who are ready to adopt each other. Common to Spaulding and other placement programs sharing its approach is the belief that the primary responsibility of staff is to the *child*, and its principle long-term concern is the effects of placement on an adopted child. Though Spaulding's workers often support different interpretations of the agency's basic philosophy, methods, and techniques, the staff believe that adoption is, until proven otherwise, the best placement choice for every child for whom a living arrangement with his biological family is no longer a real possibility.

It is for this reason that Spaulding workers are so persistent in their placement efforts concerning children who are or should be legally avail-

[1]Child Welfare League of America, 67 Irving Place, N.Y., N.Y. (Personal communication, May, 1977).

able for adoption. Once they have done all they can to determine a specific child's needs, found the appropriate family for that child, and made the placement, the staff try to provide optimal service to the family as a unit. This approach contrasts with that of many other adoption programs which may proclaim the child to be their major interest but continue to act in the best interests of parents who are seeking children.

Although the Spaulding staff is primarily concerned with the child, their interest in his future also means they must work closely with prospective adoptive parents. The staff have, however, rejected the traditional client-worker relationship. Adoption at Spaulding is not a process of rewarding those applicants who successfully negotiate the obstacle course of evaluation. It is, instead, a process throughout which parents are given the opportunity to know and understand the difficulties and rewards of parenting a specific child, to work toward improving their ability to parent that child, and to make the final decision if and when to move toward actual placement.

The Spaulding staff realize that the goals they seek through their common sense approach to adoption can never be perfectly achieved. There are many critical problems for children and families to encounter, and at some time almost every placement has produced significant difficulties and discouragements. There is also always the inevitability of some disrupted adoptions and periods of low worker morale, for working with older and handicapped children and the families who seek to adopt them presents many difficult placement, post-placement, and post-confirmation challenges to placement staff. Spaulding's approach to adoption is an all out effort to meet these challenges head on; an effort which the agency has come to realize requires both the cooperation of staff members who consistently help and support one another and the existence of specialized funding sources capable of meeting the substantial cost of providing these services.

This study of Spaulding for Children was funded by a grant from the Children's Bureau, Department of Health, Education, and Welfare, and was undertaken to help spread the transmittable portion of the now widely recognized success of this adoption agency. It is a description of one agency dismayed by the shuffling of children from one temporary placement to another, concerned about the lack of uniformity of local and state adoption laws, and frustrated by procedures which are different within every referring agency and court. It is a description of an agency that, in seeking to confront these problems and obstacles by working closely with other placement professionals, developed innovative ideas, ran into certain barriers as it struggled to implement these ideas, and subsequently developed strategies to work around and through the problems encountered.

The title, *Chaos, Madness, and Unpredictability . . . Placing the Child with Ears Like Uncle Harry's,* represents the combination of two of the most frequently made observations during the preparation of this study. The first is that parents who adopt older, handicapped, and minority race children often feel comfortable accepting them into their family either because the new arrivals in some way resemble their other children or because they, themselves, have grown up around or had previous contact with similar individuals. Some families, in fact, may focus on, or even be attracted by, the commonalities which they find. They may have a very positive feeling about a child with large, funny ears ("like their Uncle Harry's"), a child who is retarded, or one who has cerebral palsy.

The second observation is that the successful adoptive placement and maintenance of older, handicapped, and minority race children demands that all members of placement staff constantly provide each other with the substantial support necessary to develop the aggressive response required to overcome the chaos, madness, and unpredictability too frequently created or resignedly ignored by those portions of the child welfare and legal systems responsible for the care of children.

Although the format of this book follows the general chronological development of an adoptive placement and each chapter is written as a distinct unit, *Chaos, Madness, and Unpredictability* is not an attempt to present the Spaulding approach to adoption as a precise model for other placement programs to follow. The combination of attitudes, techniques, and philosophies responsible for the agency's success can never be perfectly duplicated, for different sets of problems, each with their own most appropriate solutions, will spring from every different combination of circumstances which exists. Nevertheless, it is hoped that information presented here will enable other adoption professionals, as well as adoptive parents, to appreciate the existence of similar circumstances within their own setting and, thus, offer some help in planning for and providing adequate responses. In knowing what might be faced and what solutions can be found, adoption professionals and interested citizens may be better able to help change adoption philosophy, attitudes, and procedures and so further the goal of a permanent family placement for every child.

C. Unger
G. Dwarshuis
E. Johnson

Ann Arbor, Michigan
Summer, 1977

Creating
a Specialized
Adoption Program

Spaulding's Objectives and Premises

1

OBJECTIVES

The primary motivation behind the establishment of Spaulding for Children was, and continues to be, that of supplementing existing public and private child placement services in Michigan and elsewhere by providing children and parents with a single purpose adoption agency committed to finding permanent families for those children not being placed by other programs. Until Spaulding's creation, child welfare programs within Michigan made no specialized efforts to find permanent adoptive families for children who were not in demand. This is not surprising, for as late as 1967, it was not generally realized that such children constituted a serious child welfare problem.

Spaulding was designed to focus on adoption services, to stay out of the foster care business, and to avoid the "new-born baby business" with its accompanying process of unwed mother counseling and intake. The new agency was designed to avoid the broad spectrum of problems seen by its creators as commonly accompanying the placement of healthy young children. It was designed to fill a gap — to offer what its founders perceived to be a much needed service which had never before been provided adequately on a regular basis.

The intent was to create an adoption agency which would examine the very premises upon which adoption was based, and then implement, as standard practice, workable innovations or reforms which might aid in the expeditious placement of older and handicapped children. At its inception, Spaulding's objectives did not include the aggressive promotion of the belief that adoption, rather than foster care or other forms of temporary placement, was best for the child who is separated from his family. Subsequent Spaulding experience, however, has strengthened this "prejudice" to such an extent that the staff are now convinced that children who are not adopted and who are instead placed in some other form of parent-child relationship are less likely to become independent, caring members of society.

The desire of the founders of Spaulding was not to destroy the agency system, but to supplement it. They believed the placement of such children depended not only upon the kinds of services offered but on the attitudes, skills, and degree of commitment of the staff. They sought a staff that was energetic, articulate and sensitive, and willing to work long and even unusual hours in order to provide whatever services are necessary whenever they are necessary. They believed that it was essential, in adoption, for the child to be prepared to begin living with a family who was ready, willing, and able to care for him.

Many formulas for success look simple at first glance. What is often overlooked is that intentions are easier to state than to implement. At Spaulding, the successful adoptive placement of children traditionally seen as hard-to-place or "unadoptable" results from an all-consuming commitment to the well-being of children. All agency practice, as the agency's name implies, has been built upon the conviction that the welfare of the child is to be considered first and most important in every situation. This active commitment to children — to all children including those who are mentally or physically handicapped, emotionally disturbed, older, minority race, and even terminally ill — is more than just a fundamental attitude. It is an essential dedication.

Everything its founders intended Spaulding should do and all it has accomplished can be viewed within the framework of child advocacy. At Spaulding, child advocacy is a continuous process of aggressively intervening on behalf of children to protect and extend their right to receive those services considered necessary to afford them a secure family relationship. The agency's ultimate task has been to seek more appropriate responses from the child welfare system, in the form of permanent placement with appropriate families, concerning those children who are or should be available for adoption but for whom permanent families were not actively being sought. To accomplish this, the agency not only places children but is actively involved in teaching others; in sharing with professionals in other placement programs the information and experiences needed to enable them to place other older and handicapped children legally available for adoption.

PREMISES

The Spaulding Board and staff have formulated the following premises as the basis for the achievement of their agency objectives:

1. THE WELFARE OF THE CHILD IS TO BE THE FIRST CON-
SIDERATION IN EVERY SITUATION. All children need and
should have the opportunity for a permanent family of their
own to nurture them and offer them a sense of belonging. Staff
are convinced that adoptive placement offers a waiting child
his best chance for a caring attachment.

2. PERMANENT FAMILIES CAN BE FOUND FOR NEARLY ALL
CHILDREN WHO ARE OR SHOULD BE LEGALLY AVAIL-
ABLE FOR ADOPTION AND CAPABLE OF BENEFITING
FROM A FAMILY RELATIONSHIP. There are parents who can
and will provide the love, support, and commitment these
children need, and children capable of bringing rewards to
these families. The same goal is sought for each child: to inte-
grate the child into an appropriate family.

3. MOST INFORMED APPLICANTS ARE CAPABLE OF PAR-
ENTING A CHILD. This conviction allows the agency to work
with potential adoptive parents whose lifestyles and
philosophies of parenting have usually eliminated them as
prospective adoptive parents. Working class parents, single
parents, parents with several biological children, parents who
have re-married, parents of middle age, parents of religious
groups not widely understood or accepted, parents with limited financial resources, and parents with serious medical problems have successfully adopted children from Spaulding.

4. SOCIAL WORKERS' ATTITUDES, SKILL, AND DEGREE OF
EMOTIONAL COMMITMENT TO THE INDIVIDUAL CHILD
ARE THE SINGLE MOST IMPORTANT DETERMINANTS OF
THAT CHILD'S CHANCES FOR ADOPTION. Staff is convinced that failure to find appropriate families for children is
most often due to the absence of worker commitment to placement, for workers unconvinced that a child is adoptable are
likely to abandon their search for a family should applicants not
quickly materialize. As a consequence, Spaulding seeks staff
who have a strong sense of dedication, a large measure of
sensitivity, knowledge of the causes and effects of handicapping conditions, and an ability to talk with children. Successful
staff members also tend to be energetic, articulate, and willing
to work long and unusual hours to provide whatever services
are necessary for the child. Successful workers need not be
superhuman or necessarily in possession of prescribed
academic training.

5. NEWSPAPER PUBLICITY (AND ANY OTHER AGGRESSIVE RECRUITMENT EFFORT WHICH EMPHASIZES A CHILD'S NEED FOR PERMANENT PLACEMENT) SHOULD BE USED TO INCREASE THE CHILD'S CHANCES FOR ADOPTION. It is necessary for children to be *identified* and *visible* before they can be placed for adoption. The probability of a child being appealing to and appropriate for potential parents is greatly enhanced when recruitment efforts clearly describe the child's individual characteristics in understandable terms.

6. THE PROCESS OF PREPARATION FOR ADOPTION IS ESSENTIAL TO THE SUCCESS OF THE ADOPTION. Parents must be adequately informed about a child's special needs and level of functioning. Only in this way can they resolve their concerns before making the decision to adopt. Pre-placement visits are an essential part of this process. It is equally important for placement programs to form trusting relationships with older and handicapped children, as well as the families who seek to adopt them, in order that each may be adequately prepared for the commitment of permanent family living.

7. IF PLACEMENTS ARE TO SUCCEED, THE PLACEMENT PROGRAM MUST COMMIT ITSELF TO ASSISTING FAMILIES ON AN INDEFINITE BASIS. Problems cannot be avoided as an adopted child and an adoptive family attempt to adjust to each other. Workers expect, and regard it as normal, that families request and participate in such services. A significant majority (80 percent) of Spaulding families maintain sporadic to frequent contact with the agency for supportive services beyond the confirmation of their adoption.

   Unless workers remain committed to providing these services and perceiving them as a normal part of working with older and handicapped children, adjustment problems may become intolerable to adoptive families. All families are entitled to post-placement and post-confirmation services until the child has reached at least the age of majority.

8. ADOPTION PROGRAMS SEEKING TO PLACE OLDER AND HANDICAPPED CHILDREN WITH PERMANENT FAMILIES MUST BECOME FAMILIAR WITH THE PHENOMENON OF DISRUPTED ADOPTIONS. There is no way to ensure the success of all adoptions, for there is no way to perfectly predict the future. Changes in circumstances or attitude may alter the course of the adoption. Placements which disrupt constitute

the most difficult part of placing older and handicapped children for adoption. However, even though a disruption does occur, the child and the family can be helped to cope with the experience, and the child can be successfully placed with a new adoptive family. Of those children who experience a disruption, almost all are successfully replaced with another adoptive family.

Spaulding's belief that adoption is best for the child in need of permanence is not weakened by their knowledge that many children's placements will be difficult and that some will disrupt. They do not measure their own success by the absence of disrupted adoptions, but by the fact that children who would otherwise be cared for in foster homes or institutions are being placed in permanent families. Further, workers must realize that the percentage of disrupted placements will increase significantly when the children being placed are older or are handicapped by mental, physical, or emotional problems. When infants or toddlers are placed for adoption, it is most often the inability of parents to adjust to the child which leads to disruption. With children who are older or handicapped, the critical adjustments are not only more difficult to make but must be made mutually by the child and the family.

9. PLACEMENT PROGRAMS WILL NEED TO DEVELOP NEW METHODS OF GROUP SUPERVISION AND MUTUAL SUPPORT IN THE FACE OF NEW CHALLENGES AND THE ENDLESS PRESSURES OF CRISIS SITUATIONS, PARENT-CHILD CONFLICTS, AND DISPUTES WITH COURTS AND AGENCIES. Spaulding uses a teamwork approach to make it possible for workers to struggle together toward solutions to difficult and critical problems. The agency's teamwork approach not only provides mutual support for all workers but shared responsibility for and equal investment in appropriate solutions even when workers are not in agreement with each other. At Spaulding, it is not "my" children or "my" families but "our" children, families, and placements.

10. THE USE OF ADOPTION SUBSIDY FOR HARD-TO-PLACE CHILDREN HELPS FAMILIES FINANCE THE INCREASED COSTS OF PARENTING THESE CHILDREN. Adoption subsidy expands the number of parents who can adopt children and ensures that the most suitable parents can be found.

11. THE COST OF AN EFFECTIVE SPECIALIZED PROGRAM TO

PLACE CHILDREN CONSIDERED HARD-TO-PLACE IS BEST MET THROUGH A PURCHASE OF SERVICE SYSTEM IN WHICH THE REFERRING AGENCY OR COURT DIRECTLY PURCHASES THE SERVICES PROVIDED BY THE SPECIAL-IZED PLACEMENT PROGRAM. Such a system, when a fee is paid only following actual placement, simultaneously rewards results rather than intentions and utilizes specialized staff in full-time, cost-effective programing for the hardest to place children needing adoption.

12. THE SUCCESS OF A PLACEMENT IS JUDGED NOT BY THE ABSENCE OF PROBLEMS BUT BY THE ESTABLISHMENT OF A SOUND PARENT-CHILD RELATIONSHIP AND THE CHILD'S RESULTING PROGRESS. The agency does not use perfection as a criterion for adoptive parents. The staff recognizes that parents will encounter problems and that some will be unable to adjust to their adopted child, but this does not lessen the agency's belief in the basic validity of the adoption.

2

Sources of Funding in Adoption

For Agencies: Purchase of Service and Other Sources

Since its establishment, Spaulding has employed a policy of financial reimbursement for its services which significantly differs from the fee-charging policies of most other adoption programs. To provide for part of its financial needs, the agency relies upon a purchase of service agreement in which the placement programs which refer children pay a set placement fee to the agency for those children placed.

OPPOSITION TO CHARGING PARENTS FEES

Spaulding's Board and staff believe that the responsibility for providing the money required to find families for children and to maintain those placements should not rest with parents adopting the child. No matter what its income level, the family is already providing an expensive and long-term beneficial service to the community by assuming the cost of rearing a child. It is the agency's conviction that adoption exists to serve children but that the presence of fees too often leaves applicants with the feeling that the adoption process exists to serve parents. As a result of this philosophy, the agency regards the charging of applicant fees (traditionally considered to be "the parents' portion of the adoption costs"), not only as an inappropriate means of financially supporting adoption services but as a process equal in absurdity to charging a surgeon to operate on a child.

Spaulding also opposes "waiver policies" whereby placement programs agree to reduce or eliminate fees charged families who consider the "hard-to-place" child. The agency does not consider this strategy to be a healthy and straightforward solution to the placement of these children. In a consumer-oriented economy, it feels a waiver of fees based upon certain characteristics of the child clearly implies a lesser value for some children than for others.

The charging of fees to parents is not just an issue of principle; it is a practice which significantly diminishes a program's ability to find permanent placements for its older and handicapped children. A parental fee structure of any kind is a serious disincentive which effectively discourages applications from many prospective adoptive families. Of equal importance is that such a structure is also often accompanied by applicant misunderstandings and program abuses. By not charging fees to parents, Spaulding has eliminated the four major areas of misunderstanding created by such fees:

1. No matter how frequently placement programs contend that parents' fees are paying for a service, many applicants still understand they are "buying" a child.
2. Many applicants believe agencies will approve their placement only if they pay a fee. Thus, many families capable of parenting a child in need of placement are led to believe they do not have enough money, and they abandon their interests in adoption.
3. Applicants often believe that adoption is a service for couples who have no other means to obtain a child and that, as a result, they must be willing to pay part of the cost of maintaining that placement program. If they have other means of forming a family, the message is that adoption is not meant for them.
4. Many adoption programs see their role as providing services to parents who seek assistance with a problem. They feel parents should pay fees, for parents would then feel the services provided are valuable. Agencies also reason that paying the fee will make the parents more comfortable because they would then be free of a sense of debt to the agency for the services provided. Spaulding feels such rationale is irrelevant in an agency which views its primary role as serving children rather than finding solutions to parents' problems.

Spaulding's Board and staff believe it is the community which must assume responsibility for seeing that all children have permanent families. They believe the community is indebted to the adopting parents for shouldering the financial, physical, and emotional responsibility of rearing these children. As a result, Spaulding elected to transfer the financial responsibility for the placement costs away from the parents and onto the community, specifically to the source of foster care maintenance and services within the agency or court having legal custody of the child.

DEFINING THE PURCHASE OF SERVICE FEE

In order to formally accomplish this transfer, Spaulding has extended the concept of "purchase of adoption service": the policy of requiring referring agencies and courts to pay a fee to cover some of the costs of the placement services requested for and rendered to a child in their care. Although not yet formally applied to the field of adoption, the idea that an agency or court may pay for specialized services for its clients is an extension of a well-established principle long used in medicine, business, and in other child welfare programs. In child welfare, such purchases have been made for children requiring foster care, psychiatric, psychological, dental, medical, and institutional services. When applied to adoption, purchase of service encourages the referring agency or court currently bearing the expense of maintaining the child in a foster care or institutional placement to transfer part of those available funds to meet the cost of making a permanent plan for the child's future.

As used by Spaulding, the purchase of service fee is paid only after the child is actually placed. In this way, the agency is able to guarantee that the money is spent in direct benefit to both the child and the referring program. Also, as noted earlier, the referral agency has tangible proof, i.e., Spaulding's bill, that placement can be accomplished for that child. Payment is for the placement, not for recruiting efforts, unused family studies, or good intentions. If the child is not placed, no fee is charged.

By charging the referring agency or court for part of the cost of adoption, Spaulding feels it is also increasing the awareness of an ever-increasing number of child welfare professionals concerning the significant long-term financial savings of adoption services over all forms of temporary care. Such understanding is a vital part of the agency's total strategy of encouraging other placement programs, who have primary responsibilities for children, to begin measuring their success in terms of meeting the permanent placement needs of the children in their custody.

ESTABLISHING PURCHASE OF SERVICE

The development of a just, reasonable, and affordable purchase of service fee to be charged to referring courts and agencies has been a long and difficult process for Spaulding. The agency originally had no actual experience with which to determine an appropriate purchase fee level.

As a result, its first fee calculations were based upon what it thought to be the most reasonable available measure: the cost of maintaining a child in foster care in Michigan for six months. However, because of the complexity of determining the service and administrative costs which are a part of every foster care placement, Spaulding simply chose to charge the equivalent of the much more easily determined figure of six months of foster care payments to foster parents.

Throughout its history, Spaulding's purchase of service fee has always remained at a level much lower than the total cost of the child's actual placement. The agency has not charged referring courts and agencies the actual cost for various reasons. First, no program expressed an interest in spending more dollars for an adoptive placement than for foster care. Also, in the past, there has been no widely accepted cost-related formula generally accepted within the field of child welfare which would facilitate full-cost determination on a case-by-case basis. The amount Spaulding charged referring programs (between $360 and $450) was based on a 1968 equivalent of foster care payments and was a sum recognized by most adoption workers as equivalent to the cost of care for a child if he remained unadopted.

The existence of relatively low purchase fees creates an attractive inducement in that it is not so high as to unduly discourage placement programs from referring children in need of adoptive placement. During the last several years, significant increases in the age and severity of handicaps of the children being placed by Spaulding have expanded actual placement and maintenance costs to nearly $3000 per child. Nevertheless, the agency has always tried to be sensitive to what "the market would bear" so that its fee would not be seen as a deterrent to referral.

Spaulding's ability to charge and receive purchase of service fees from all referring agencies and courts was made much easier in early 1969 when the Michigan Department of Social Services (MDSS) agreed to purchase Spaulding's services. Although Spaulding had previously placed several MDSS children, those fees had been waived to remove any existing or potential barriers to referral and to provide the new agency with opportunities to find families for the kinds of children its staff was seeking to place. Early in its history, the agency established a policy of occasionally waiving its initial purchase fee for a specific court or agency. This policy made it possible for other placement programs to determine, without taking a financial risk, if future referrals to Spaulding would actually lead to adoptive placements. In many instances, this was the only way in which the new agency could begin receiving the referrals needed to build a reputation for competence.

In early 1969, Spaulding approached the Michigan Department of Social Services regarding a group of state wards, children who were legally available for adoption but as yet unplaced. One child, a birth defect baby, had no arms. Another little boy was severely emotionally disturbed and had possible brain damage. All of the children faced a future of permanent foster or institutional care. After considerable candid discussion, the State finally conceded that these children were unlikely to be placed by MDSS staff and agreed to pay Spaulding, on an experimental basis, the equivalent of six months MDSS payment for foster parents (then $414) to find any of the children permanent adoptive families. No change in statute was necessary to permit the payment of purchase of service fees. What was necessary was a high level administrative decision to use budgeted dollars in an innovative and potentially cost-saving way.

After successfully finding families for several of these children, Spaulding again approached MDSS. Their intention was to develop a broader, more open agreement for access to the state wards listed on the state's adoption exchange as being in care for more than three years or otherwise considered eligible by MDSS for purchase of adoption service. The proposed agreement was readily accepted, for a recently completed study by MDSS of their own adoptive placement costs showed those costs to be more than four times higher than Spaulding's purchase of service fee. In addition, many more children were entering the public child care system as permanent wards than were being placed with permanent families, and MDSS knew that keeping them in temporary care was many times more costly than the cost of adoption. This study and Spaulding's placement record helped to make MDSS an early believer in the benefits of Spaulding's services to both children in need of adoption and the tax-paying public.

The purchase agreement between MDSS and Spaulding was instrumental, in turn, in convincing other placement programs to purchase Spaulding's services. Up to that time, many county judges were either hesitant or unwilling to pay Spaulding's fee. Part of this was due to unfamiliarity and initial resistance to paying an agency for adoption services. Another major obstacle was that money for those payments would have to come from each respective county's Child Care Fund, a fund traditionally used to provide only foster care payments. Judges were understandably concerned about the MDSS attitude toward purchase of adoption service, for it was MDSS which audited the Child Care Funds and reimbursed only those services which it approved.

When MDSS agreed to purchase service from Spaulding, many county judges felt that they, too, could legitimately use child care funds to purchase similar services. Agencies often followed suit once they were convinced that the purchase of adoption services for the state's wards was "respectable" and reimbursable. The use of Child Care Fund money for purchasing adoption services became even more widely accepted after Spaulding requested and received a rule change and written confirmation from MDSS that the Child Care Fund could, in fact, be legitimately used for the purchase of such services. Meanwhile, Spaulding had simplified its tremendously variable fee-charging policy, a policy which was still based directly upon equally variable foster parent payments. Instead of charging a variable fee, Spaulding began to charge every referring court and agency a flat $400 fee which was, at that time, the state-wide average of six months payments to foster parents. In January 1971, Spaulding increased its fee to $500 and in July, 1974, to $750. In all cases where a child had been referred before the fee was increased, but where the placement had not been completed until after that increase, referring agencies and courts were charged the lesser fee.

THE NEW PURCHASE OF SERVICE FORMULA

Throughout Spaulding's history, its purchase of service fee has existed more as a symbol of payment than as an actual reimbursement for adoptive costs. This situation was created partly by the emergence of unexpectedly high levels of required post-placement services and partly by continuing market resistance to paying the full cost of placement. As early as 1973, Spaulding's Board passed a resolution to increase its fee to more closely reflect actual costs. Although it has taken several years to implement this plan, the agency is now working to develop a full-cost, flexible reimbursement formula. Once completed, Spaulding's use of a case-specific purchase fee will provide each referring program with a documented record of all costs incurred during the placement and maintenance of the child for whom they purchased Spaulding's services. The reimbursement formula will consist of the sum of:

1. the average cost of general family recruitment efforts,
2. the actual cost of bringing the specific child and family together,
3. the actual cost of post-placement service to the specific family, and
4. the average cost of post-confirmation service provided to adoptive families to support their placements.

The first two parts of the total purchase of service fee would be payable after placement; the last two payable after the adoption is legally confirmed. Spaulding will be able to detail the cost of each placement with greater accuracy and increase their purchase of service income to a realistic level through the implementation of this formula. By this means, the staff hope to fulfill the original intent of the agency's founders that it place the burden of permanent family costs on the agency or court having custody of the child and depend upon purchase of service as a major source of operating funds.

On a broader range, Spaulding anticipates that public and professional understanding of actual adoption costs will lead to increased public awareness of specialized adoption service and to further improvements in the adoption field. Although the agency believes that the time has come when it is not unrealistic to ask referring agencies and courts to pay for the full cost of the service the child is receiving, it remains to be seen how quickly Spaulding will be able to convince other adoption professionals and governmental leaders of the appropriateness of the position.

PROBLEMS IN PURCHASE OF SERVICE

Despite the advantages which the use of Spaulding's services offer the child, the tax-paying public, and the referring agency or court, many placement programs have had great difficulty accepting any attempts by Spaulding to increase its purchase fee. Historically, there has been a tendency on the part of some courts and agencies to balk at paying Spaulding any fee whatsoever.

By 1977, the average cost of initiating and maintaining the adoption of a Spaulding child has risen to more than $3000, while the purchase of service fee remains $750. A purchase of service fee increase seems necessary. Yet each time the agency has raised its fee, it has had to move with caution and significantly limit that increase so not to charge agencies and courts more than they would be willing or able to spend on the purchase of adoption service. Failure to take these philosophical and financial realities into account would have totally defeated the agency's primary goal of benefiting children and jeopardized the establishment of the principle of purchase of service.

Despite Spaulding's careful considerations, some agencies choose not to refer children because they either do not have sufficient flexibility in budgeting or enough money specifically earmarked for purchase of adoption services. These budgeting problems exist because purchase of service is not yet a widespread practice among adoption and foster care programs, and many individuals and organizations are not aware of its availability or appropriateness.

These problems also exist because of a budgeting practice known as "line-item budgeting" in which money is specifically budgeted only for precisely defined purposes. In some instances where available funds have been depleted, it is possible to transfer money from other budget categories into the depleted category. However, procedures for transferring already budgeted funds vary greatly in complexity and, in many cases, transfers become a practical or political impossibility. It is the resulting rigidity of budget categories which frequently prevents the flexibility required to meet a child's need for permanence at the moment when a chance to achieve it arises.

Despite the financial realities of placement program budgets, Spaulding has never refused the referral of a child because a referring court or agency could not afford to purchase its service. If a placement program is unable to locate the funds necessary to pay Spaulding's fee, the agency's staff first tries to help them find ways to finance the purchase of service. If no ways exist, staff then determine whether or not that program will be able to place the child within a reasonable period of time (usually defined by Spaulding as six months) by any alternative means.

In order not to limit such a child's chances for adoption, the Spaulding Board and staff decided they would waive their purchase fee in cases where the child would probably otherwise remain unplaced and reimbursement could not be negotiated. It was the agency's conviction that the finding of capable families was too important a need to jeopardize the future of a child because money wasn't available from the most desirable source. As a result, they felt that serious efforts to raise funds elsewhere should be undertaken for the infrequent cases in which lack of payment by a court or agency was the primary obstacle to providing a permanent placement.

Another problem Spaulding encounters is that many placement programs have unrealistic policy limits concerning the amount of money which can be spent to purchase adoptive services. Inadequate attention to long-range planning for children and a lack of financial incentive to place children with adoptive families has meant that agencies and courts are frequently unwilling to spend money to purchase adoption services, even though that amount is far less than keeping the child in on-going foster or institutional care. Few placement programs are making provisions to move in the direction of more realism. One exception is the Michigan Department of Social Services. Since December 1, 1976, MDSS guidelines permit full-cost reimbursement for specifically identified hard-to-place children as computed by the formula discussed earlier. As of May, 1977, the maximum allowable reimbursement is the equivalent of two years payment to foster parents (or $2,912.70 for a child under age six, $3,628.10 for a child between the ages of seven and fourteen, and $4,343.50 for a child thirteen to eighteen).

CHANGES IN SERVICE AND PURCHASE OF SERVICE FUNDING

When Spaulding was established, the expectation was that virtually all operating costs would be covered by purchase of service income once the agency began accepting referrals on a regular basis. Shortly thereafter, it became clear that higher costs and professional resistance to paying actual costs meant that a more reasonable goal was for one-third of its budget to be financed by purchase of service. However, as early as 1970, it became obvious that even this estimate was unrealistically high. Because increasingly older and more handicapped children were being referred, the Spaulding staff were placing fewer children than had been originally predicted, and placement and maintenance costs were rising. As a result of the greater time and money needed to successfully place children, purchase of service income remained lower than anticipated.

The Spaulding Board and staff had originally anticipated a steady growth in the proportion of income derived from purchase fees as the evolution of the agency's reputation led to an increase in the number of children referred for placement. This latter assumption held valid for Spaulding's first two calendar years of operation when the agency found permanent adoptive families for 33 children (1969) and 37 children (1970), but this trend did not continue.

Between 1971 and 1973, the placement activities of Spaulding steadily decreased, (1971 — 28; 1972 — 22; and 1973 — 16) for reasons described further in "The Children Spaulding Places," p. 63. From 1974 to 1976, the agency averaged 18 placements per year. In brief, the decrease occurred because the agency began placing progressively older and more severely handicapped children who required more extensive post-placement services. As the cost of placing each child grew, it became increasingly clear that the agency's purchase of service fee was gradually covering less of the child's actual placement cost and that the highly variable amount of effort spent on different kinds of children made flat-fee purchase rates totally unworkable.

As Spaulding struggled with these problems and the shifting focus of service which these problems necessitated, the staff began to realize that many of the difficulties they were experiencing would eventually create obstacles for other placement programs. As a result, the staff felt they could most benefit all children needing permanent families by using the insights and expertise they had gained to help other programs seeking to place similar kinds of children. These realizations gradually led Spaulding to begin spending more staff time training and consulting with other adoption professionals. As these activities increased, less time remained to devote to the preparation of new children and families for adoption.

It should be noted that increased difficulty in finding adoptive families for progressively older and more handicapped children (as well as the greater placement effort, skill, and cost involved) was anticipated by Spaulding as an inevitable result of a desired pattern of growth which it sought to stimulate in the field of adoption. Although this was the primary reason for which the agency was established, the rate at which these events occurred was not fully expected. It was this speed, plus the comparatively slower acceptance of the philosophy of purchase of service and the increase in training and consultation, which helped to stretch Spaulding's placement staff beyond the point where they could continue to place increasing numbers of children each year.

The year 1977 will see the implementation of the full-cost, case-related, flexible reimbursement formula. Gradual acceptance of the financial realities of adoption service are expected to enable purchase of service income to eventually become the agency's primary source of operating funds. This optimism exists, to a large extent, because the Federal government has recently begun to provide major incentives for placement programs to increase the quality and extent of their services. In October of 1975, amendments to the Federal Social Security Act went into effect which allow full Federal matching funds under Title XX for adoption-related services, including purchase of service. Further regulations in early 1976 formalized earlier interpretations that adoption, as a service for children, could be based on a definition of the child without parents as a "family of one." Under this definition, a child can receive federal assistance for his adoption (75% federal, 25% local participation) if his annual income falls within federal eligibility limits. This provision makes virtually all parentless children eligible for assistance. As a result, it is expected that this amendment will eventually make possible a full-cost reimbursement for Spaulding and other placement programs with purchase of service policies.

OTHER SOURCES OF FUNDING

With the exception of purchase of services fees from courts and agencies, Spaulding depended, until 1974, upon the donations of individuals and groups for the financial assistance required to continue providing its services. Until that time, the agency had no private endowments and received no large private donations except for the several thousand dollars in "seed money" received during its first two years of operation. Donations from a relatively small group of committed supporters had managed to keep alive a dream that started on a shoestring.

Originally, Spaulding had been interested in pursuing some of the more traditional financial sources available to adoption programs. For instance, early in its history, it applied for admission to the Michigan United Fund. Spaulding was denied regular membership because of United Fund concern regarding possible duplication of services with other adoption agencies, but was encouraged to reapply the following year.

Following much Board discussion, however, Spaulding chose not to pursue United Fund membership. First, it was decided that if the agency was going to be an alternative to current placement practices, it would have to refrain from seeking money from sources that would put Spaulding into direct financial competition with other placement programs who were going to be asked to purchase Spaulding's services. Furthermore, in order for the agency to effectively provide services to the children not being served by other placement programs, the Board and staff reasoned that they must be able to respond quickly and decisively as new information or circumstances were encountered. To be as responsive as was considered necessary, the agency had to retain the freedom to act without having to wait for an outside financial source to give approval of money to be spent or of any non-tradional action which might have to be swiftly taken. In addition, effective responsiveness could not be maintained if, in order to continué to receive funding, the agency was forced to expend extensive staff effort to fight annual philosophic battles over its innovative practices. More generally, the agency concluded that it should never put itself in a position of having to compromise its alternative and innovative philosophies because it was receiving money from any potentially restrictive or traditional funding source.

The final reason why Spaulding did not choose to seek United Fund membership was that it believed a placement program is only as strong as the financial base upon which it depends. As a result, the agency did not want to lock itself to any single funding source whose available assistance might significantly diminish and force the agency to curtail its services.

Although Spaulding never again sought United Fund membership, it has, from time to time, accepted small unrestricted grants from various local United Funds within Michigan which were interested in supporting the services of the agency on a special non-membership basis. The choice to pursue independent funding has allowed the agency total freedom to provide its services without fear that funding sources will limit or cut off financial assistance as a result of conflicts over philosophy, policy, or implementation of service.

Because Spaulding receives only limited public funding (through purchase of service fees from public welfare agencies and county courts), its attempts to increase financial support and expand the geographic area from which it draws that support consist primarily of appeals to private individuals and community service organizations. The agency's method of appeal consists of efforts to expand the public's awareness of the services it provides children, parents, and the field of adoption together with efforts to keep their supporters informed regarding the activities and progress their support has made possible.

The agency actively carries out an annual written and word-of-mouth campaign to solicit memberships and donations to help cover general operating costs. It uses two approaches to interest potential donors in its services, for there are both humanitarian and economic benefits to the work which Spaulding performs. For people who are primarily interested in the children being placed, Spaulding provides concrete examples of the human benefits which adoption gives to children who have previously been shuffled through the foster care, group home, and institutional care system. For people who are concerned with the efficient use of funds provided by the tax-paying, donation-giving public, Spaulding highlights the tremendous financial savings produced by helping waiting children find permanent families through adoption rather than through continuing foster or institutional care and services.

In addition to its public appeal for funding, Spaulding's sources of support include monthly donations from members of its Child-of-the Month Club, Spaulding "memberships," sponsorships of individual adoptions, special projects by volunteers or community service groups, individual bequests and gifts, and grants from private foundations.

The Child-of-the-Month Club

The Child-of-the-Month Club was established in August, 1969. Originally called "Child-A-Month Club," its purpose was to permit individual contributors to combine modest regular donations ($10 per month) to help meet the cost of placing one child a month. In time, the name of the Club was changed to "Child-of-the-Month" to highlight the fact that the placement described in the monthly bulletin distributed to club members was but one of the placements the combined membership had helped make possible.

For Spaulding, the Child-of-the-Month Club serves several purposes. It provides an additional source of income for the agency, it helps to publicize that Spaulding exists specifically to find families for those children other agencies and courts have not been able to place, it helps to publicize the existence of children who are in need of adoptive families, and it educates the community about the characteristics of the children who are waiting to be adopted.

The Club's membership currently consists of 120 regular contributors. There are also a number of complimentary members who receive the Club's bulletin in honor of their previous donations of time or money. The Club holds great promise as a vital and personalized way for individual donors to benefit children. Since 1969, more than $100,000 in Child-of-the-Month Club funds have been made available to support the placement activities of the agency. However, Spaulding has yet to find the organizational means to expand this idea into its full potential as a major funding source.

Spaulding "Memberships"

Spaulding also offers "memberships" in the agency in return for general donations of various amounts. Several different kinds of memberships exist. "Life" memberships are available to individuals or groups who make contributions of $1,000 or more. Annual donors of $5, $10, $25, and $100 receive "regular," "contributing," "sustaining," and "supporting" memberships respectively. All memberships entitle the contributor to vote for Board members and thus, join the public group ultimately in control of the agency. However, few contributors exercise this right, prefering to leave actual control in the hands of those in closer contact with the agency. The membership principle does preserve, nevertheless, the legal openness and potential of citizen control that its founders felt vital in permitting the agency to move beyond the traditional pattern of sole agency control by Boards of Directors.

Sponsorships of Individual Adoptions and Special Projects

Church groups, service clubs, informal groups, and individuals also occasionally choose to sponsor part or all of the placement costs of a specific child. Spaulding has recognized that many groups prefer projects that are "theirs" and, as with all donors, need and deserve to be kept informed concerning what their contributions are accomplishing. For example, as part of a special interest in children with Down's Syndrome, one service club sponsored the placement of a girl with this handicap, thereby contributing to the philosophy that these children are adoptable. The club funded efforts by placement workers to review appropriate medical and educational research, to identify and interview the families of several Down's Syndrome children and adults, and to evaluate several Down's Syndrome children. As a result of these efforts, the Spaulding staff learned a great deal about Down's Syndrome children which they have used to place subsequent children with this handicap and to encourage other placement programs to find families for similar children. The service club has had the satisfaction of knowing their involvement made possible the placement of several children and expanded the definition of adoptability for many other agencies and courts. The following year, another service club provided funds for the Spaulding staff to write the handbook, "Older and Handicapped Children are Adoptable: The Spaulding Approach," which has been available since August 1974 and has received national attention.

Individual Bequests and Gifts

Spaulding has also received bequests and gifts from Board members, other individuals, and personal estates. In addition, the agency has received small amounts of income from bank interest, dividends from donated stocks and bonds, gain on the sale of gifts of stocks and bonds, and farm income in the form of rent paid by a neighboring farmer for leasing the land surrounding the farmhouse in which the agency is located.

The Clark Project

In July, 1974, the pattern of funding at Spaulding was significantly changed by the receipt of a two year grant from The Edna McConnell Clark Foundation of New York City. This grant allowed the agency to provide technical assistance and education in a project designed to establish a national network of referral agencies sharing Spaulding's general philosophy and focusing solely on the placement of children considered hard-to-place. In addition to Spaulding for Children in Michigan, initial membership in the network included Spaulding agencies from New Jersey, New York City, and Ohio. The network, eventually called "Family Builders," now includes a group of nine agencies across the nation (see p. 300).

The Clark Project also included unified planning efforts to develop a flexible, case-related purchase of service formula, to expand Child-of-the-Month Club membership, and to form a close working relationship with the North American Center on Adoption which is located in New York City.

The final segment of the grant provided for Spaulding's participation in a program of wide-ranging consultation, information-giving, and training efforts with other child placement programs and community groups throughout the country who wished to learn more about the agency's approach to the adoption of older and handicapped children.

The decision to accept the initial Clark Foundation grant was not undertaken lightly. The stakes were clear to the agency's Board and placement staff. To embark on the Clark Project would require a further commitment of agency time and energy to a more national strategy (see "The Clark Project: The National Strategy," p.299) and confirm Spaulding's role as a training and consultation agency, but it would also divert agency attention away from efforts to overcome the enormous obstacles which continue to hinder the placement of older and handicapped children in Michigan. There was strong division of opinion on the preferred course of action. Eventually, the pressure of combined forces (the opportunity to expand the agency's influence through the consultant's role, the absence of a cohesive strategy among interested programs, parents' groups, and individuals within Michigan for dealing with adoption issues and problems, and the agency's pressing financial limitations) decided the course of action and the agency Board accepted the Clark grant. Impressive though the results have been, many Spaulding people yet feel a sense of having left large tasks undone in their own backyard. A viable strategy to work with that group of identified children in Michigan who should be the subject of permanent planning remains Spaulding's most incomplete challenge.

THE EFFECT OF SPAULDING'S SMALL BUDGET

Even with the receipt of its grant from the Clark Foundation, Spaulding's budget is still quite small by national standards. Although the agency has a number of financial resources, the pattern of income from these sources is far too uneven to create the financial security enjoyed by placement programs having regular, interest, or endowment incomes large enough to solve the problems of meeting high placement and post-placement costs. The difficulty of operating an agency on a very tight budget, without the benefit of generous endowments, has not discouraged Spaulding. In fact, because limited financial resources demand efficient use of time and materials, these realities may well be partially responsible for the agency's success. Spaulding's small budget serves to prompt staff to keep close watch on the overall activity of the agency and motivate them to consistently seek ways of improving philosophy, techniques, and organization.

Lack of "money to burn" has also helped Spaulding better understand the financial situation of many of its adoptive families. The agency has realized that good money management, rather than how much money one has, is the important factor in being able to do a job well, be it support an agency or a family.

The Spaulding staff are honest with families about the reality that funds are frequently hard to find and that it is sometimes difficult to publicize a continuing need for money without jeopardizing the public's faith in the agency's stability. Freely sharing these problems generally produces a significant and positive impact on families. They often become beneficially cost-conscious, more helpful, and more understanding. They see Spaulding as an organization comprised of people like themselves who have financial concerns but who are trying to do the best job they can with the time, money, and talent they have available. The families are responsive to this similarity, and many admit to a sense of kinship and a feeling of lasting commitment to the agency.

Spaulding has always had to work hard to obtain its operating costs, yet organization growth, large budgets, and financial comfort have never been major agency goals. Although greater financial stability would be welcome, the agency's financial resources have not yet been a factor in Spaulding's ability to find families for children in need of adoption.

SUMMARY

It is contrary to Spaulding's philosophy to charge fees to parents as a means of obtaining financial support for the agency. The Board and staff are opposed to such fees because they feel parents are already providing an expensive and beneficial service to the community by adopting older and handicapped children. In addition, many misunderstandings, such as parents' beliefs that they are "buying a child" or "buying service" for themselves, are created by the existence of fees.

Instead of charging fees to parents, the agency has instituted a policy of purchase of service fees in which referring agencies and courts are expected to pay adoption costs for the child they refer for placement. Difficulties remain in the establishment of this policy, however, for it is a new concept in funding to which many referring programs have not yet become accustomed. Problems in budgeting for purchase of service also exist for other programs interested in Spaulding's services but whose operating funds are allocated only for other precisely defined purposes, such as foster care or institutional placement.

The Spaulding Board and staff had originally intended that purchase of service fees would provide most, if not all, of the agency's income. However, this has not been the case. The increasing time and cost of finding adoptive families for progressively older and more severely handicapped children, as well as the agency's growing focus on training and consultation, have decreased their yearly number of placements and greatly diminished their purchase of service income. To help alleviate this difficulty, a more relevant purchase of service billing system is being implemented in an effort to point out *actual* costs to referring programs.

This full-cost billing capability is an effective first step toward negotiating more realistic purchase of service fees. Clearly, federal and state participation in purchasing adoption services is one of Spaulding's primary interests. Their belief is that permanency should be as adequately funded as foster care, protective services, day care, and other temporary care programs.

The agency's purchase of service income is supplemented by several other sources of funding. These include: The Child-of-the-Month Club, Spaulding memberships, special sponsorships, and bequests or grants. Although greater financial stability would be welcome, the agency's small budget has not yet had a detrimental effect on its functioning. Rather, families are sympathetic to an agency which has financial difficulties similar to those problems families may experience.

3

Sources of Funding in Adoption

For Children: Subsidy and Other Sources

Adoption programs can offer a valuable service to those older, handicapped, and minority race children considered hard-to-place or "unadoptable" by being alert to the various forms of financial assistance available to help such children. The most important source of assistance is adoption subsidy. Available in most states to certain children needing adoption, it may begin at the placement of the child or upon confirmation of the adoption, depending upon law and practice. Where commencing at confirmation, foster care payments are sometimes available to help families meet their additional expenses until a subsidy order is issued.

TYPES OF SUBSIDY

There are three basic kinds of subsidy payments. These are medical subsidy, support (or maintenance) subsidy, and special services subsidy. The scope and intent of medical subsidy varies from state to state but is usually intended to cover some or all of the costs related to specific medical conditions as well as subsequent therapy, rehabilitation, and special schooling associated with those conditions. Medical subsidies are generally intended to cover medical conditions which existed prior to adoption and which will eventually create expenses not covered by an adoptive family's medical insurance.

Support or maintenance subsidy is usually intended to supplement the cost of the on-going care and maintenance of the child. It may be of fixed duration for special short-term costs or last until the child becomes an adult. It is frequently but not solely used for children who would benefit by being adopted by their foster families. It is also used to enable families to adopt specific hard-to-place children who otherwise are not likely to be adopted.

Special services subsidy usually consists of one-time payments for emergency services or payments for repeated services not covered by medical or support subsidy. Special services subsidy may cover the legal and court costs of the adoption, other costs incidental to the adoptive placement (such as pre-placement visits), and the costs of medical and related treatment not covered or only partially covered by insurance and by other community services. This form of subsidy may also cover the costs of certain other special services such as physiotherapy, psychotherapy, occupational therapy, remedial education, rehabilitation training, extraordinary corrective dental treatment, speech and hearing therapy, wheel chairs, braces, crutches, prostheses, day care, transportation, and any other expenses related to the special medical care and treatment of the child.

RATIONALE FOR SUBSIDY

The availability and use of adoption subsidy has played an important role in increasing the number of older, handicapped, and minority race children placed for adoption. Proponents of this form of assistance are convinced that appropriate adoptive placements cannot be made for many of the children currently available for adoption unless supplemental financial provisions are continued after the adoption. Without subsidy, moderately and severely handicapped children who need extensive physical, psychological, psychiatric, educational, or occupational services can be adopted only by higher income families willing to assume the total costs of such care or by families whose income is low enough to qualify them for Medicaid coverage. Even where such services would be covered by community or insurance programs for children born into the family, families are generally not covered for the pre-existing conditions of adopted children. Proponents also see subsidy as a valuable aid in recruiting prospective parents for children with these and other special needs. Without the financial protection of subsidy agreements, good parents with limited incomes would either find it impossible to adopt or would face financial risks unfair to parents willing to assume such special responsibilities.

Subsidy also makes it possible for agencies and courts to avoid delays in finding willing and appropriate families for children who have as yet undiagnosed medical problems. Such placements, however, depend upon both program and personal philosophy as well as the availability of subsidy. Before medical subsidy was available, agencies and courts willing to find adoptive families for children with potentially severe medical needs often postponed placement until medical problems were identified, stabilized, or cured. Although many professionals still prefer to postpone such placements until the child's medical status is known and treatment has begun, such delays add unnecessary millions of dollars to annual child care costs and deny children the security of permanent families at a time when they need that security most.

Finally, individuals who favor adoption subsidy point to the numerous children whose foster parents consider them to be valued and vital members of the family but who cannot afford to adopt them if it means the loss of foster payments for the child's support. Since the presence of other children often makes such support essential, the availability of adoption subsidy could mean the difference between a need for the child's sudden removal by a social worker and the creation of a permanent, secure placement.

Many of the older and handicapped children Spaulding has placed have been adopted only because the agency's staff was able to assure parents that help was available to assist in paying for the cost of medical needs and daily care. Subsidy has enabled the agency to place children in many capable families with marginal incomes. It has also enabled the staff to place children in other families with more adequate incomes, but where family funds were needed to meet the needs of other children in the family. These families would probably not add children through adoption if it meant lowering their family's style of living, abandoning plans for higher education for their children, otherwise exposing themselves to an uncertain financial future, or assuming known medical risks against which they cannot be financially protected.

Spaulding workers feel that the assumption of a permanent responsibility for providing the day-to-day care and emotional support for a child with extraordinary needs is an enormous commitment to ask of most adoptive parents. Families who adopt should not have to bear the high risk of financial insecurity because they have adopted. To ask this will unnecessarily reduce the number of potential parents available and leave additional children in more costly and often less secure substitute care arrangements.

The Spaulding staff also support the use of adoption subsidy for philosophical as well as practical reasons. They believe the community which intervened in the original parental relationship of the child should be responsible for the child's future, even if this means providing financial support after the adoption, in order to assure the degree of permanence and family stability the child should have. If an adoptive family is willing to offer the child a permanent family relationship and assume the responsibility for his rearing, they are taking on a major obligation. Nothing in social philosophy or good social welfare practice justifies requiring that community interest stop when adoption occurs.

THE MODEL STATE SUBSIDIZED ADOPTION ACT

The Spaulding staff believe that good thinking concerning adoption subsidy is reflected in the Model State Subsidized Adoption Act distributed by the Office of Child Development, Department of Health, Education, and Welfare. It describes as eligible for subsidy those children who will probably not be adopted unless financial assistance is provided. Thus, eligibility is determined even before it is known which family may be adopting the child. The act also recognizes that subsidy increases the possibility of a continuing community commitment when lack of commitment would predictably deny a permanent family to a child.

Under this model law, any child under the legal jurisdiction of a public or voluntary licensed placement program and legally free for adoption is eligible for subsidy if he is to be adopted by a foster family with whom he has been living and has, based upon professional opinion, "established significant emotional ties." Any child with a mental or physical disability, emotional disturbance, a recorded high risk of physical or mental disease, or who is older, a member of a sibling relationship, an ethnic or racial minority, or any combination of these, is eligible for adoption subsidy if it is determined that without such subsidy it is unlikely that the child will be adopted.

Types of subsidy under this model law would include special services subsidy (usually a one-time payment to cover legal or court costs, preplacement visits, special medical costs, therapy, or prostheses, etc.), time-limited subsidy (usually a periodic payment for a specific length of time), and long-term subsidy (usually periodic payments designed to meet the child's long-term financial needs which, "in the absence of other appropriate resources provided by law and in accordance with state regulations," can continue to or even beyond the age of majority). Both time-limited and long-term subsidy would be periodically adjusted so as not to exceed the then current appropriate foster care rate for similar children.

Subsidy would begin with a written agreement between the family and the State Department of Social Services (or its equivalent) and could be signed at any time before the confirmation of the adoption. Subsidy could continue beyond one year if the family completes an annual sworn certification declaring that the child is still in their care and the condition still exists which precipitated the need for subsidy. It can continue as long as the child remains a legal dependent and the condition persists, regardless of the place of residence of the adopting parents at the time of application for adoption placement or legal confirmation. This annual sworn certificate helps protect subsidy programs against potential abuse, but above all provides predictable support with little administrative expense to assure maximum savings over other alternative forms of care. It also assures the existence of future support — a condition which must be known in order for many potential adoptive parents to make a reasonable decision concerning their ability to adequately assume responsibility for a child.

Finally, records regarding subsidized adoption would be considered confidential and an appeal procedure for adoptive children denied subsidy would be established according to state administrative procedures.

Despite its many positive aspects, it is Spaulding's contention that a large conceptual loophole remains in the Model State Subsidized Adoption Act as of this writing. Some adoptive children exhibit a high risk of physical or mental disease. However, under the Model Act as it is now written, subsidy is available only if that risk is recognized at the point of placement. Subsidy would not be granted for children whose pre-existing condition was undiagnosed at the time of placement, when the child's condition was not revealed to the placement program by the biological parents, or when the child's condition is not revealed to the adoptive family by the adoption program. Although the number of children who may be denied subsidy for these reasons is not extensive, the Spaulding staff believe that subsidy should be made available to all children with pre-existing physical or mental conditions, no matter when those conditions are discovered.

ADOPTION SUBSIDY IN MICHIGAN

Although many states have subsidy laws, few provide comprehensive adoption subsidy programs with the potential for enabling all children available for adoption and needing subsidy to be placed with the parent(s) who can best care for their physical and emotional needs. Michigan is one state where such a program currently exists. In its repeated amendments and consistent efforts to develop such a program, Michigan has overcome many of the difficulties which can result when legislated subsidy efforts are vaguely formulated or are burdened with inappropriate, costly, and anxiety-producing investigations of a family's financial needs.

The primary intent of Michigan's subsidy program, since its inception, has been to furnish a means of providing a permanent family for a child who otherwise might not have one. Proponents of the state's first subsidy bill were primarily interested in increasing the number of adoptions of parentless children by people interested in adopting them, providing that could be done without extreme financial risk. More specifically, supporters of this legislation recognized that non-subsidized adoption of these children was unwise and financially unfeasible for many parents otherwise capable of appropriately caring for such children on a permanent basis. In addition, many judges and legislators defended the bill because of the tremendous savings to the public compared with leaving children in substitute care (See Table 1 for the latest available Michigan figures). Those

TABLE 1

Annual Child Care Costs in Michigan per Child

Summer 1976*

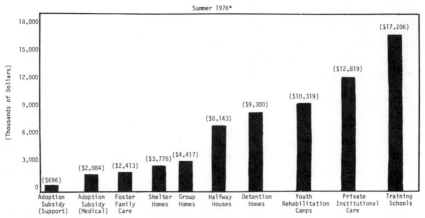

*Statistics courtesy of the Michigan Department of Social Services
Figures shown here for all forms of child care, except adoption subsidy and foster family care, are computed on the basis of operating costs and do not include all service, supervision, and administrative costs associated with state, county, or community support and service workers or programs.

who lobbied for or voted for the first bill reasoned that any plan which simultaneously improved the quality of life for a large number of people and provided an overall saving of tax dollars certainly deserved the support of legislators.

Legislation providing for both medical and support subsidy was first passed in 1969, first implemented in 1970, but not granted by more than one or two courts until 1972. Under this law, a family was eligible to receive subsidy if the adopted child had been in foster care four or more months prior to his adoption, and if the agency or court responsible for the child had made reasonable efforts to place him but had been unable to find anyone who, without the aid of subsidy, was willing and qualified to adopt the child.

Problems with Subsidy Legislation

Although many hard-to-place children were subsequently adopted, the 1969 law created two basic problems. First, the law clearly stated that subsidies were to be tied to county funding. As a result, when the child resided in one county and the family in another, the judge representing each county often tried to convince the other that subsidy payments were the other's responsibility. In addition, frequent and extended delays in the adoption process were created by these disputes between judges. If families moved into a different county during their adoption, further confusion resulted. The elimination of such disputes and delays was possible only after the law was amended and funding became a 100 percent state responsibility.

Secondly, difficulties concerning subsidy still existed for many Michigan families who wished to adopt children from outside the state. Individual laws governing the use and availability of adoption subsidy continue to remain highly variable. As of April, 1977, 42 jurisdictions (41 states and the District of Columbia) have adoption subsidy laws.[1] Thirty jurisdictions specifically provide support or maintenance subsidy, 24 specifically provide medical and surgical subsidy, and 15 specifically provide for special services subsidy.

Many states from whom Spaulding accepts referrals offer only medical subsidies. To further complicate matters, medical or support subsidy programs are so widely divergent that a child or family easily eligible in one state may not come close to being eligible in another. Further, subsidy procedures between states with such programs are often poorly coordinated because of the varying policies and long distances involved. Because the extraordinary commitment and effort needed to overcome these obstacles was often not forthcoming, many children who needed

[1]Those still without adoption subsidy laws include Alabama, Arkansas, Guam, Hawaii, Louisiana, Mississippi, New Hampshire, Oklahoma, Puerto Rico, Virgin Islands, West Virginia, and Wyoming.

subsidies were going without this service if they were part of an inter-state adoption.

Although the 1972 amendment giving the state 100 percent funding responsibility solved many problems, it failed to eliminate other major difficulties which had plagued Michigan since the implementation of its subsidy program. For example, it did not alter the requirement that subsidy could be granted only if the placement program had ". . . no notice of any other persons who are presently willing and qualified to adopt the child without subsidies." According to the interpretation of many judges, this requirement meant that placement professionals were required to prove with certainty that they could not find an adoptive family who did not need subsidy. They could not merely demonstrate appropriate good-faith efforts and techniques before a subsidy could be granted. The law also allowed, but did not mandate, that an appropriate but financially needy foster care family be given preference in adopting the child over strangers who did not need subsidy. As a result, restrictive interpretations of this provision frequently increased the difficulty of placing children with the available parents who were most appropriate for them.

In addition, the 1972 law did not address itself to the problems of the foster family who could not afford to adopt because to do so would mean having to replace their higher foster care payment with what was then a much lower subsidy payment. Michigan corrected these remaining problems in its total revision of the state adoption law which became effective January 1, 1975. Under this revision, support subsidy could be awarded in any amount up to, but not more than, the foster care payment which would have been received from the Michigan Department of Social Services for that child. The total result of these changes in the law has been an increased use of subsidy as a valuable and appropriate tool in effecting sound adoptions for many more children.

Nevertheless, some concerns remain for Spaulding and other Michigan adoption programs. Despite the progress made by the 1975 law, the interpretation and administration of that law continues to vary widely from one county to another. The statute also continues to be ambiguous enough to provide all of the individual probate judges in Michigan's 83 counties with a great deal of latitude in their interpretations of the law. Thus, workers must know not only the law itself, but the procedures and peculiarities of its interpretation and administration by each judge they encounter. Such information is available only through individual worker experience.

A second concern is that some judges and child welfare professionals continue to philosophically oppose adoption subsidy for a variety of reasons. As a result, some children remain without parents, while other children do not receive the subsidy to which they are entitled because many placement workers neglect or refuse to inform adoptive applicants of its availability. Workers who do not give adoptive families the option to accept the financial assistance provided by adoption subsidy run the risk of forcing those families to undertake the total financial obligation of the child they adopt. Consequently, children who need supplementary services may not be adopted or may not receive the necessary services available.

A third concern is created by procedural difficulties in filing for support and medical subsidies. While support subsidy under Michigan law must be requested when petitions to adopt are filed, petitions for medical subsidy for pre-existing conditions may be filed at any time. Many of the state's courts, however, continue to have difficulty accepting the desirability of such flexibility in medical subsidy cases. On occasion, these difficulties have resulted in opposition to medical subsidy requests filed after the placement of the child.

A fourth concern is that *some* judges contribute to continued frustration for parentless children by insisting upon employing "tests" of eligibility not required by the law when requests for adoption subsidy are made. They either refuse to comply with the law or they avoid the issue by insisting they are not able to fix the sum to be paid (as the statute indicates they must do) without examining the family's financial status. A few judges refuse to grant subsidy in any form!

Because of these attitudes and conditions, workers interested in placing children needing adoption with appropriate parents must pursue the availability of subsidy during their initial work with the child. They must determine, in every case, whether or not subsidy is available from the jurisdiction in which the child resides, which funding source will provide the payment, and under what conditions that payment will be forthcoming. It is also necessary for the worker to know precisely what the subsidy will cover, how much will be paid, and what difficulties or uncertainties may be encountered in the future within the agency or court having custody of the child.

Spaulding's Use of Subsidy

Since Michigan's subsidy law became effective, the agency has used subsidy extensively (see Table 2). Even before adoption subsidy became available, however, Spaulding was able to find families who wanted to adopt children whose care was extraordinarily costly. Nevertheless, Spaulding workers readily agree that the availability and use of subsidy has aided greatly in finding families for additional older, handicapped, and minority race children. Subsidy has enabled the agency to continue to place children whose special needs require treatment, rehabilitation, or special educational services not available through the public schools:

services too expensive to be paid for by most parents without the aid of adoption subsidy. Subsidies have been particularly valuable in paying for the costs of services for emotionally handicapped children whose needs were not physically defined and who, therefore, were not eligible for financial assistance from organizations offering aid only for physical disabilities.

Spaulding workers ordinarily do not decide for the adoptive parents whether they need or should receive subsidy. However, they do make certain that every adoptive family knows of the availability of subsidy. When the risk of placement without subsidy is too severe, the family may be urged to accept subsidy in order to protect the child's future. Since 1972, more than half (54.7%) of the children for whom the agency has found permanent families have received medical and/or support subsidies. This proportion is significantly higher than the experience of most other Michigan adoption programs (see Table 2). It is the agency's

TABLE 2

Annual Subsidized Adoptive Placements
at Spaulding for Children (SFC) and Throughout Michigan
1972-1976*

	1972	1973	1974	1975	1976	Totals	Average
No. of SFC Placements	22	16	24	19	14	95	19
No. of Initial Subsidy Orders Written for SFC Placements	10	6	13	11	12	52	10.4
Percentage Subsidized SFC Placements	45%	38%	54%	58%	86%	--	54.7%
No. of Adoptive Placements Throughout Michigan (including "in-family" adoptions)	7645	8369	7177	6100	5221	34,512	6902.4
No. of Initial Subsidy Orders Written Throughout Michigan	17	77	98	269	126	587	117.4
Percentage Subsidized Adoptive Placements Throughout Michigan (including "in-family" adoptions)	0.2%	0.9%	1.4%	4.4%	2.4%	--	1.7%

*Statistics courtesy of Spaulding for Children and the Michigan Department of Social Services

judgment that of all Spaulding children placed, more than 90% should have received subsidy had the subsidy law been enacted for those children, had the child and family been eligible, and had the funds been available for such use.

Because they are intent upon matching children's needs with parents' abilities, the Spaulding staff have continued to place children with only those families potentially most capable of providing for those needs. Although the agency has encountered strong opposition from some judges and other child welfare professionals for its extensive use of adoption subsidy, the staff have continued to staunchly defend their position of requesting subsidy based solely upon the child's needs. In doing so, the staff use the language of Michigan's 1975 adoption law which declares that the amount of subsidy granted shall be clearly tied to that child's need for assistance, not the financial status of the family adopting him.

OTHER SOURCES OF FUNDING

Although most forms of private medical coverage offer protection against congenital problems afflicting a child born into a family, they only rarely provide benefits which cover serious pre-existing medical conditions of an adopted child. Where such conditions exist, adoption subsidy may provide all the assistance that is necessary. In those cases where it does not, however, other resources are available to help cover medical, support, and emergency expenses.

Title XX
The most far-reaching financial resource potentially available for children who are adopted is Public Law 93-647, which includes the recent social services amendments to the Social Security Act known as Title XX. The goal of Title XX is to provide federal funds (to states who apply to receive them) to promote services and administrative activities needed to assure permanence for children.

According to the 1975 Child Welfare League of America report entitled "How to Use Title XX to Promote Permanence for Children,"[1] the goal of permanence involves both the freeing for adoption of those children in foster care who have little chance of returning to their previous home and the creation of a permanent family placement. It is the goal of Title XX to make it possible for children separated from their family to be reunited with that family under conditions which promise stability and continuity, and to keep a child united with his or her legal parent(s) by preventing family breakdown or other conditions leading to neglect or abuse. It is the belief of the Spaulding staff that such services for children can be legitimately argued as applicable to either biological or adoptive families and can, therefore, be used to help provide post-placement services and prevent adoptive disruption.

However, the availability of Title XX funds for any purpose depends completely upon the lobbying efforts of workers, citizen organizations,

[1]This report may be obtained from the Child Welfare League of America, 67 Irving Place, N.Y., N.Y.

and activist advocates who understand the necessity for including these services in their state's plan for the use of Title XX funds. While it appears to the Spaulding staff that services for children in danger of losing their families comes squarely within the boundary of what should be and could be covered by Title XX, the staff's assumption that these funds are potentially available for post-placement services to adoptive families to help prevent family break-up or disruption is still highly speculative at this point. Although some state plans for the use of Title XX funds do use broad enough language regarding post-placement services to potentially incorporate services to help prevent disruption, the Spaulding staff know of no state now using Title XX funds for this specific purpose.

In many states, other resources to help handicapped adopted children also exist in the form of Supplemental Security Income, Medicare, Medicaid, Crippled Children's programs, Early Periodic Screening, Diagnosis, and Treatment (EPDST) programs, and Chore Care programs.

Supplemental Security Income

If a family adopts a handicapped child, that family may be eligible for Supplemental Security Income (SSI Disability payments from the Social Security Administration) provided the child is considered totally disabled and the parents' income level is low enough for eligibility (in Michigan, at this writing, approximately $9,800 for a family of four). For the latest eligibility standards, contact the nearest office of the Social Security Administration.

In order to be considered totally disabled by the Social Security Administration, the child must have no better than 20/200 vision, have a visual field limited to 20 degrees or less, or be prevented from doing any substantial gainful work by a physical or mental impairment which is expected to last for at least 12 months or is expected to result in death. Payment levels are determined by the age of the dependent, whether or not he is in school, his ability to pay rent, and the level of his parents' income if he is under age 18.

Medicare and Medicaid

A person determined to be totally disabled by the Social Security Administration is eligible for both Medicare medical and hospital insurance after he has been entitled to SSI Disability payments for 24 consecutive months. All SSI recipients in Michigan are also eligible for Group I Medicaid which usually pays for expenses not covered by

Medicare, including all medical and hospital costs during the first two years of SSI Disability payments when a person is not yet eligible for Medicare.

In Michigan, children become permanent court wards at the time their parents' rights are terminated. These children are considered to be a "family of one" by the Social Security Administration until their adoption has been legally confirmed, and are, thus, eligible for Medicaid if they do not have more income and property than eligibility requirements allow. This means that most adopted children in states electing this definition and procedure are eligible for Medicaid until their final adoption order has been written.

After confirmation, the child is no longer considered to be a "family of one" and the income and property of the entire family must fall below Medicaid eligibility requirements in order for any member of that family to be eligible for Medicaid. This limitation shifts the entire burden of post-confirmation medical subsidy from federal government participation to state and local funds for those cases in which parents are unable to secure private medical coverage. This shift further complicates placement procedures and appears inconsistent with the official position of the federal government to meet the medical expenses of children. For more information on this program, including coverage limits and exclusions and the client's share of payment for certain services, contact the nearest office of the Social Security Administration.

Crippled Children's Programs

In some states, including Michigan, SSI Disability recipients under age 21 are also eligible for their state's Crippled Children's program or its equivalent, which is often administered by the State Department of Public Health. Such programs are usually able to provide financial assistance in the form of payments directly to the provider of medical, surgical, laboratory, diagnostic, consultation, and therapy services. Michigan and some other states also offer SSI Disability recipients under age 21 eligibility in their Early Periodic Screening, Diagnosis and Treatment (EPDST) programs. These programs provide comprehensive health care services in the form of regularly scheduled appointments at designated screening centers.

Chore Care Programs

In Michigan, as well as some other states, parents with totally disabled children over 18 are also eligible for partial reimbursement from their state's Chore Care or Chore Service Program simply for providing care for their child at home. This program, administered by their Department of Social Services or its equivalent, is only available if their child's income does not exceed approximately $180 per month. For the most recent information on this program, contact your State Department of Social Services or its equivalent.

Additional forms of assistance, not tied to either the income level of the child or his parent(s), may also be available to adopted children in their new families. These services are provided by Departments of Vocational Rehabilitation, Veteran's Administrations, the Social Security Administration, and special interest organizations. To be eligible for some of these programs, the child's adoptive family must meet certain eligibility requirements.

Vocational Rehabilitation

The Department of Vocational Rehabilitation, or its equivalent in each state, is usually able to provide vocational evaluations, vocational guidance and counseling, job placement, training for finding jobs, corrective surgery, appliances, and medical supplies to individuals of employable age who have a mental or physical disability which is a handicap to their employment. Work tools, equipment, licenses, and initial stock and supplies may also be available. Individuals are considered to be mentally disabled if they are mildly or severely retarded or if they have a mental, psychoneurotic, or personality disorder which has been diagnosed by a certified psychologist or psychiatrist. Disabling physical conditions can include visual and hearing impairments, orthopedic impairments, and amputations. Eligibility is determined by a vocational counselor who makes a determination based upon psychological, vocational, and medical evaluations. The local Department of Vocational Rehabilitation or its equivalent should be contacted for further information.

Veteran's Administration

The Veteran's Administration offers two programs which can provide financial assistance to families who adopt. These are Service Connected Disability Compensation and Non-Service Disability Pension. In the first (which is not tied to family income), the payment amount depends upon the veteran's degree of disability (determined by the Veteran's Administration), and the number of dependents in the family including adopted children. However, greater numbers of dependents do not entitle the veteran to higher payments unless his degree of service-connected disability is at least 50%.

To be eligible for the second program in which family income is a factor, a veteran with a non-service related disability must be totally disabled (or over 65 years of age) and have at least one day of wartime service. Payment levels increase with the number of dependents in the family including adopted children. Since both programs are quite complex, consult the nearest Veteran's Administration regional office for more information.

Social Security

The Social Security Administration provides Survivor's benefits to both adopted and biological children. Children whose adoption has been legally confirmed prior to the death of a parent who is eligible to receive Social Security benefits must meet the same requirements as biological children in order to obtain these benefits. If a biological or adopted child is eligible to receive more than one parent's Survivor's benefits, he is entitled to receive only the single benefit package which pays the greatest amount. For more information, contact the nearest office of the Social Security Administration.

Special Interest Organizations

Many special interest organizations and parent advocacy groups are not only able to provide families with money to help pay for medical expenses, summer camp, and other activities, but can also furnish resource information to parents and placement workers concerning the kind and extent of services available to children with specific handicaps. Parents of other children with similar mental, physical, and emotional problems, who know where and how resources for their children can be obtained, are also a valuable aid to "newer" parents and concerned placement workers. Service organizations such as Lions, Elks, Moose, Rotary, Kiwanis, Civitan, and others may also provide glasses, hearing aids, or other assistance for handicapped children. The names and addresses of representative special interest organizations and other available resources are included in Appendix D, "Resources for Adoption Workers and Parents," (p. 363). Further information concerning the names, addresses, and telephone numbers of local service organizations may be obtained from any local Chamber of Commerce.

SUMMARY

A variety of increasingly available adoption subsidies exist to offer valuable forms of financial assistance to families who adopt older, handicapped, and minority race children. Without the availability of subsidy, many children in need of expensive medical, emotional, educational, or occupational assistance could not be adopted. Most families simply do not have the financial resources to provide for these children's special needs. In addition, many foster parents would not be able to adopt unless adequate subsidy were available to help meet those costs of child care formerly covered by foster care payments.

Legislation of high potential benefit to the adoption of children is provided by the Model State Subsidized Adoption Act, a far-reaching plan to furnish many children with the assurance of receiving needed services. Such legislation is badly needed, for few states now have totally comprehensive subsidy programs, and some have no subsidy programs at all. One state which does have a comprehensive subsidy program is Michigan. Over time, difficulties in this legislation have been eliminated by progressive amendments introduced by concerned individuals. However, the rate of implementation of this subsidy program continues to be slow.

While subsidy provides the major potential source of funding for adopted children, other financial resources are also available. Title XX federal funds, Supplemental Security Income, Medicare, Medicaid, Crippled Children's Programs, Early Periodic Screening, Diagnosis, and Treatment Programs, and Chore Care Programs provide financial resources to adoptive families and their children. The Department of Vocational Rehabilitation, the Veteran's Administration, the Social Security Administration, and local special interest or service organizations are also able to provide assistance to some adopting families.

Teamwork and Collegial Supervision

4

More than any other factors, the development and practical application of the concepts of teamwork and collegial supervision have been primarily responsible for Spaulding's organizational and placement success. Once their evolution began, these concepts helped to create the innovative working relationships and problem-solving techniques which have produced the policies, practices, and attitudes known as the Spaulding approach to adoption.

Teamwork is defined by the agency as the method by which all members of placement staff work together to share problems, provide mutual support, resolve disputes, and share responsibility for all major placement decisions. Collegial supervision is a means of placement staff supervision in which all placement workers are expected to share equally in decision-making responsibility. The staff believe that a continually effective teamwork approach cannot be achieved. unless collegial supervision is utilized as the exclusive means for managing the team's actions.

As with all aspects of Spaulding's approach to adoption, the agency's decision to practice teamwork and collegial supervision was not established by memoranda on given days. As the agency developed, these concepts have been continuously shaped and refined as the most common sense responses to the events, problems, and crises encountered by the Spaulding staff in the course of seeking permanent families for older and handicapped children.

The approach was developed slowly and painfully; partly from those portions of traditional social work and adoption practice appropriate for working with all children, and partly out of the practical child-centered philosophy gradually developed by the Director, the

Board of Directors, and each newly hired worker. Each policy, practice, and attitude taken from the social work profession, child welfare practice, and traditional adoption knowledge and technique had to be re-examined to determine its applicability to the successful placement of children considered hard-to-place or "unadoptable." Under these circumstances, Spaulding's small staff deliberately rejected many long-standing practices, including the traditional supervisor-supervisee relationship. In its place, they gradually improved the concepts of teamwork and collegial supervision into a natural and practical approach to serving children in need of adoption.

COLLEGIAL SUPERVISION

Early in its history, Spaulding's process of making placement decisions and solving problems differed little from the process still used by most placement programs. Each worker was supervised by the Director, who also served as the case supervisor. Any issues or difficulties related to the worker's job were discussed and acted upon inside that well-defined hierarchical relationship. For most of the first year, the Director and one worker comprised the agency's entire placement staff. During that time, they labored together, one teaching the other about social work and adoption, and both analyzing problems and working out solutions.

As the agency hired more workers, increased the types of services its staff provided to adoptive children and families, and placed greater numbers of children, the Director no longer had enough time to meet individually with workers to discuss all of the children, family, and system-related problems which were a major part of preparing and maintaining each adoption. It was also no longer possible to separately discuss with each worker more comprehensive, but equally important, issues such as the effect of gradual changes in workers' viewpoints or the impact of legislative actions on agency policy and practice.

In addition, it became increasingly inappropriate to require the workers being hired by Spaulding to participate in the traditional pattern of regular, individual supervision. Workers hired were those who would aggressively search for and use new and better ways of placing children, who would argue against and challenge adoption myths and outdated attitudes, and who did not have to rely upon a supervisor for advice or approval in every new situation.

Furthermore, as each staff member grew increasingly capable of discovering and using new and better ways of sucessfully placing older and handicapped children with adoptive families, there was a greater challenge of ideas among staff and less reliance upon the Director for guidance, supervision, and the best solution to difficult problems. When the need arose, workers continued to seek assistance, but they were just as likely to consult another worker as go to the Director.

The most essential factor in the final acceptance and actual success of collegial supervision among staff was the ability of the agency's Director to willingly move from a position of traditional authority and control to a position of one voice in a group of equals. If collegial supervision is to succeed, supervisors, too, must function as peers, rather than as superior members of the team. As a result, it was imperative that Spaulding's Director maintain some caseload responsibilities. By participating as a team member, the Director was able to significantly increase her own job satisfaction. By experiencing on-going placement problems first-hand, she was able to eliminate many of the difficulties encountered by traditional supervisors who operate one step removed from actual practice.

The Director's ability to face problems and challenges head-on allowed her to gradually replace initial anxieties and misgivings concerning collegial supervision with healthy flexibility and trust in the increasingly capable and independent staff. Under the circumstances, the willing abandonment of traditional supervisor-supervisee relationships in favor of shared responsibility for decision-making and supervision was a sensible step forward. The staff recognized that maximizing an older or handicapped child's opportunities for adoption required frequent and complex decisions. They also realized that the process of continually making those decisions was too much responsibility for any one person (be they worker or supervisor) to successfully assume.

In Spaulding's earliest phases of collegial supervision, attempts were made to implement a total sharing of all agency responsibilities. . However, the staff found, through experience, that the relaxed, informal, and democratic atmosphere of collegial supervision is not the most effective method for administering all agency functions. Administrative responsibilities, such as coordinating fund-raising activities, working with the Board of Directors, over-seeing office operations, and managing the agency's property proved too unwieldy when shared by the entire staff. Because it was the most practical solution, these responsibilities were returned to the Director, and other staff continued to offer advice and suggestions when requested. Thus, all placement issues are handled within the team. All other issues are handled by the Director in her role as agency administrator.

The Spaulding staff also recognized that professional relationships with other agencies and courts, as well as acceptance by the general public, were more easily created and maintained if Spaulding's Director conducted the agency's affairs as if she were supervisor of all placement workers. Lines of responsibility within the agency, including acceptance of final responsibility, were much more clearly understood by other child welfare professionals and the community at large if one member of staff was regarded as the agency's primary administrator. As a result, although Spaulding has had no traditional supervisor-supervisee relationship since early 1972, non-professionals as well as professionals outside of the agency are often unaware of the precise nature of staff relationships and the process by which the placement staff makes decisions.

TEAMWORK

The development of Spaulding's teamwork approach to adoption began to evolve during the early 1970's as a way to help workers through their pain, frustration, and anger when a placement did not work out. The few "broken" adoptions (or "disruptions," as they are called at Spaulding), which occured during the earliest years of the agency's existence were poorly understood. As the rate of these unpredicatable experiences increased, they began to have a seriously demoralizing effect upon the placement staff. In order to continue placing children, workers had to find a way to survive the emotionally devastating experience of seeing a carefully planned placement fall apart after the child had entered the family.

As frequently occurs, workers who felt responsible for a placement also felt responsible for a disruption. They felt they had failed to adequately prepare the child or the family, and had not paid close enough attention to existing or potential problems. Each worker considered herself deeply committed to making the most appropriate possible placement for each child and prided herself on doing the job well. Yet, no worker was prepared to encounter parents who requested the removal of their adopted child, or to place children who later suggested that ending their adoption was the best solution to the problems they faced within the family. Workers became tremendously depressed when they learned that all their hard work would not last and that much of what had already been accomplished had to be repeated in order to fulfill their commitment to the child.

Teamwork offers staff the opportunity to provide group support for each other and more successfully overcome the nearly inevitable feelings of pain, anger, guilt, and frustration which occur during and after a disruption. However, this approach has done more than just help Spaulding workers cope with the demoralizing effects of disruption. It has also provided a way for workers to share the responsibility for all decisions, difficulties, and feelings of failure which exist in finding permanent families for older and handicapped children. Because of the overwhelmingly positive results of working together during crises, teamwork has gradually become the sole method of placement operation within the agency.

Ground Rules for the Team Approach

As the sharing of responsibility for decision-making emerged as the most appropriate response to the conditions Spaulding workers encountered, the agency's staff began to recognize that implicit acceptance of certain "ground rules" for sharing decisions must exist if the system were to function effectively. The ground rules which were formulated represented the combined effort of all placement staff to share responsibility in such a way that children and families would always benefit from the best possible decisions, but never be forced to wait through delays caused by inefficient bureaucratic machinery. These were not formal guidelines or policies but an unwritten, mutually developed philosophy meant to serve as a shared basis for the flexible group discussion, problem-solving approach the placement staff had already begun to evolve.

The following ground rules were eventually clearly articulated and agreed upon by the total team:

1. Decisions regarding affirmative action to be taken on behalf of a child or family, (except decisions about what family a child should be placed with), might be made by an individual worker without consulting the team. Any specific negative placement decision, such as the decision that a child or family is not ready for adoption, must be considered by the team before any action can be taken.
2. .The final decision that a specific child and family "fit" together and will benefit most by placement together should only be made after the team determines that all other realistic possibilities are less appropriate.
3. No individuals can make changes in the agency's basic philosophy, make commitments for another worker, or rearrange another worker's schedule without first obtaining the agreement of the team.
4. Each worker must assume personal responsibility for their individual caseload and share responsibility for the total work of the agency.
5. Guidelines, methods, and procedures are never considered unalterable. All should be improved to appropriately reflect chang-

ing times and conditions. None should be maintained solely because they are traditional.

Teamwork at Spaulding does not presuppose that workers must share every decision and action with others, or always consult with others before they take action. All workers are expected to make independent decisions and learn from their own experiences as well as the experiences of their co-workers. Each worker is encouraged to make decisions regarding their caseload and is responsible for these decisions. Individual assignments are completed, and caseload responsibilities met, at the worker's discretion and with minimal amounts of team involvement unless such intervention is requested or proves necessary.

Staff members are not expected to make specific placement decisions involving children and families without consulting the team, for it is the agency's intent to minimize the conflict among families and staff which occurs when two workers make commitments to place the same child with two different families. Nevertheless, Spaulding workers have sometimes made such decisions when no other alternative seemed practical, when a worker wished to avoid a substantial delay, or when experience or expertise led a worker to independently conclude which child might be most appropriately fitted with a specific family. Under these conditions, workers have sometimes discussed the possibilities for a specific placement with the child or family before discussing it with the team. It is also the agency's intent that final decisions concerning "fit" between child and family be made by the team, and the individual worker is always reminded that any other procedure is outside the agreement of the team.

In no case has an individual staff member ever decided that a child or family should not be placed together. Staff recognize that negative decisions often occur as result of individual worker conflicts with children or families. In an effort to avoid inappropriate decisions or individual errors in judgment, the staff always seeks total team discussion in such cases.

Achieving Worker Cooperation

Since an effective and functional team approach requires that placement staff work closely together, Spaulding seeks to hire workers who are able to work cooperatively with the agency's current staff. Team members believe that cooperation among workers offers a child and family greater probability for a successful adoption because it provides greater opportunity for clarification, verification, and review of all information and opinions regarding the placement combination.

By knowing well the beliefs and opinions of co-workers, a worker can frequently predict the decisions others would make under similar circumstances. This knowledge helps an individual worker feel more confident in making decisions, minimizes the possibility that judgments will be arbitrary, and increases the likelihood that future individual decisions will reflect the team's increasing experience.

The existence and maintenance of the cooperative spirit underlying all aspects of the Spaulding approach to adoption is dependent upon the desire and ability of every staff member to be a trusting, sharing member of a closely-knit group. This cooperative spirit depends upon the ability of workers to respect each other's styles and values as being of equal merit and quality. Despite personal differences and occasional conflicts, workers are willing to go out of their way to extend themselves to help each other on behalf of their children and families. There is a common mission, for the workers know that in order to place older and handicapped children with permanent families, they must be able to work closely and effectively together and provide each other with the continuous emotional support the job requires.

The achievement of a cooperative staff relationship is neither a passive nor an easy process. Workers cannot simply depend upon time or the good will of other workers for that goal to be reached. The establishment of cooperative team functioning and the resultant ability to more effectively and appropriately place children is achieved only when workers problems, and proposed solutions, as well as each other's strengths, weaknesses, and mistakes, is the most effective way to build emotionally supportive staff relationships.

At Spaulding, working together became possible as workers learned to know each other better. They found, by experience, that a willingness to seek help and information from other workers was a valued and respected skill, and that the admission of mistakes would not be used against them by vengeful co-workers. It took time for such openness to develop, for most individuals tend to make sure they will not be repeatedly hurt before they begin revealing their weaknesses to others. Yet, despite the time and risk required, the results of a cooperative staff relationship have been worth the effort. In fact, the Spaulding staff is so convinced of the benefits of teamwork that they recommend similar staff relationships be created in all other programs working to find permanent families for older and handicapped children.

Worker Competition

Although the Spaulding approach to adoption characteristically offers a constant and mutual challenge to each worker to defend her ideas and suggestions, the success of the agency's team approach is based upon the understanding that personal competition among workers is not expected or tolerated. The agency believes that child welfare programs which encourage a placement "quota system" provide an environment which is detrimental to effective team functioning. Programs in which workers are expected to place a specific number of children each year tend to foster a competitive spirit by forcing workers to compete with each other for the "best" or easiest-to-place children or families.

If job security depends upon a worker's ability to meet such standards of success, the welfare of the child is sacrificed for the apparently higher ideal of increasing the number of placement attempts made by individual workers. Since short-term and long-term placement successes count equally in the filling of placement quotas, the continuation of quality placement work becomes impossible. Also sacrificed during such competition is the thoughtful planning and preparation which constitutes the key difference between a good placement risk and a poor one.

Productivity requirements exist in programs where the visible proof that placements have occurred (or have occurred at a specific rate) is considered more important than the quality of child and family preparation for adoption. The dilemma between the need to show others such placements are possible (or are being accomplished as fast or faster than any other placement program in the area) and the need to take the time to adequately prepare children and families for adoption can be a very real problem.

The struggle to find a workable solution is especially difficult when public or personal demands for immediate or substantial placement success exist. Despite the prevalence of such conditions in child placement programs, it is Spaulding's experience that forced solutions in the placement of older and handicapped children are usually brief solutions. The agency has found that the best strategy for achieving successful adoptions, and by far the surest method of achieving long-term worker and agency credibility, is to take the time necessary to develop the kind of partnership between worker and child, and worker and family, that will ensure the continual joint solution of problems.

At Spaulding, there is no quota system to distract from quality placement efforts. The staff recognize that counting child placements is not a valid way to measure worker expertise or assess the quality of child placement work. They believe that the necessity for meeting placement quotas discourages workers from spending time to adequately plan the adoption, prepare the child and family, and work with the family once the child has been placed. With no pressure to place specific numbers of children, workers can focus on working cooperatively, thus ensuring that the widest placement choices are available.

At Spaulding, all children placed are regarded as agency placements, never as "belonging" to an individual worker. The staff believe that it is too easy for a worker who assumes personal responsibility for specific children and families to lose sight of the positive characteristics of potential adoptive families prepared by other workers. Such short-sightedness cannot help but narrow an individual child's opportunities for a permanent family.

Rivalry for individual praise and recognition for a "successful" placement seldom occurs at the agency. Workers know that no adoption can be considered successful just because the child is placed with a family. There is no way to unerringly predict where, when, or to whom a disruption will occur. There is no guarantee that a new or unforeseen problem will not lead to a disruption.

Finally, competition for promotion within the agency is both inappropriate and irrelevant. Not only does the staff believe that seniority within a child placement program by no means guarantees a higher level of ability, but they realize that on any occasion, the talents and perspectives of another worker may be required to create or maintain a placement. At Spaulding, there are differences in worker speed, size of caseload, and tasks assigned. These differences are accepted by the staff, for workers are primarily concerned with helping each other to resolve problems and ensuring the permanence of all the children placed.

Conflict and Resolution

Although the placement staff generally operates as a smoothly working team, no staff, including that at Spaulding, always works together in an ideal way. Despite their similar backgrounds and compatible attitudes, occasional periods of stress do occur which temporarily weaken the agency's team cohesiveness. However, staff members work hard to overcome these difficulties which, for two reasons, are not usually long-lasting. First, even with all their experience, the agency's workers realize they still have much to learn about the placement of older and handicapped children for adoption. As a result, the need for all to help each other with the complex tasks required of them is far stronger than their need to compete. Second, each worker feels strongly that stress among the team members creates additional problems in a job that is already difficult enough.

The conflicts which sometimes do occur at Spaulding usually involve disagreements over the placement readiness of children and families, which applicants appear most appropriate for specific children, or what strategies should be used in working with another agency or court. The team approach to adoption does not eliminate anger or frustration. It does, however, provide increased opportunities for common commitment, extraordinarily close professional relationships, and friendship which make it possible for workers to survive and move beyond their conflicts.

The team approach also provides specific techniques for resolving those conflicts. In some cases, attempts at solution may be delayed for a few days or weeks to allow tempers to cool to the point where the problem can be resolved under more objective circumstances. More frequently, however, in an effort to avoid smouldering problems, workers are strongly encouraged to freely ventilate their feelings so disagreements can be resolved and the workers can get back to the business of placing children and maintaining placements.

On occasion, the team has reprimanded a member for not accomplishing an assigned or necessary task, or for making a serious mistake in individual judgment. However, even under these circumstances, the group's process of resolving a problem is a balanced system of credit and criticism which allows workers to defend their actions. It is their intention that solutions to conflicts among staff not be arbitrary or authoritarian. Instead, it is intended that the knowledge of human relationships and problems which workers use to help children and families should also be used to improve relationships among staff.

Although most discussions among workers can be characterized as direct and to the point, there are certain times when personal feelings get out of hand. The team makes concerted efforts to treat each other with compassion and respect, and to remain aware of each other's "soft spots." Each member realizes that their willingness to treat a child and family with compassion and respect is often determined by their need to be treated that way themselves by their co-workers. Yet despite these efforts, there are times when these highly sensitive and vulnerable areas are uncovered or even pummeled. Such situations usually occur unintentionally, but are occasionally created out of anger or retaliation. The team has found that the only effective solution to this problem is to provide collegial "first aid" for the resulting pain, for as long as it is needed, and to reprimand the person responsible.

THE TEAM MEETING

Team meetings provide the Spaulding staff with opportunities to meet regularly as a group to make placement decisions, seek each other's advice and support, and evaluate child, family, personal, or agency problems and needs. These meetings also serve as the arena for discussion of adoption philosophy as it applies to the agency's placement of children and provide an opportunity for workers to determine how the agency can better serve other placement programs and promote broader and more effective community education.

The agency also holds "staff meetings" and "clerical meetings." Staff meetings, held as frequently as the situation demands, include both placement workers and clerical staff and are specifically scheduled to discuss agency-wide operations (such as worker schedules, division of labor, and coordination of placement-clerical responsibilities, philosophy, and future). Clerical meetings include only the clerical staff and are held to discuss specific clerical problems and assignments, such as bookkeeping tasks and the receiving and routing of information.

Team meetings usually occur weekly at the agency or at the home of a worker and usually last approximately half a day. There is no regularly scheduled meeting time, for the process of arriving at a suitable time involves fitting the meeting into the existing schedules of all workers. If team meetings conflict with long-distance travel (or worker's vacations) and cannot be rescheduled, the meeting for that week is omitted.

Although much discussion occurs during the formally organized team meetings among all members of the placement staff, problems which require group or individual consultation frequently cannot wait for a regularly scheduled meeting. As a result, discussions among workers must frequently be sandwiched between other activities (i.e., meetings or telephone contacts with children, families, workers, supervisors and administrators from other adoption programs, special interest groups, local, state, and national committees, reading or updating files on children or families, traveling, answering correspondence, or attending seminars, conferences, or workshops).

Team meetings are used to make all major case-related decisions and assignments, and individual workers use them to seek help in solving the problems they have encountered. Because of the emotional demands of placing older and handicapped children, frequent discussion among workers is necessary to provide mutual support or to help workers think through issues, talk things out, or regain a sense of perspective.

Workers describe team meetings as "grappling sessions." These sessions constitute the regularly scheduled portion of Spaulding's process of sharing what each worker is doing, why they are doing it, how each is reacting to what is being done, and what suggestions for improvements might exist. For these reasons, team meetings form the foundation of the valuable and continuous process of informally evaluating and improving individual and program performance, obligations, strengths, weaknesses, and relationships with others. It is a process of information-sharing and problem-solving which serves to repeatedly remind the placement staff just how much harder the same process is for children and families.

Format of the Team Meeting

The first part of each team meeting is usually devoted to discussions of relevant pending legislation, correspondence, speaking engagements, conferences, and, on rare occasions, fund-raising projects. Workers may share announcements of importance to others, as well as schedules and commitments for the coming week. The second portion of team meetings is generally focused on pre-placement and post-placement progress, problems, and solutions concerning referred children and adoptive families.

There is no firm rule about who begins the session or in what order topics are discussed, but the group's leadership and responsibility for recording the contents of the meeting usually rotate among the entire placement staff. Although the most important items invariably receive attention first, the sequence of discussions is usually determined by whomever manages to command the floor once the previous discussion has been completed. Despite a lack of formal agenda, an earnest attempt is made to continue each team meeting until all workers have had an opportunity to discuss all they need to discuss with the group.

Assigning Child and Family Cases

Team meetings also provide the organized means of assigning children and families to the worker who will be responsible for the overall coordination of their prospective placement. This shared decision is reached by determining which worker is best able to work with each specific child or family needing assignment. Since there are no placement quotas, children and families are not assigned with the idea of maintaining a certain average or competitively sized caseload. However, every assignment is made with the intent that no member of the placement staff will be expected to assume an unreasonably heavy amount of work.

Each worker has different skills, interests, areas of expertise, and personal styles. Differences also exist in how workers organize the work to be done. As a result, the team tries to distribute primary responsibility for cases according to the existing skills, attitudes, interests, and previous commitments of the individual worker, and with the intent of balancing the worker's tasks between child, family, and post-placement cases.

The case may also be given to a worker who expresses a specific interest in the child or family, or to the worker who has already made contact with a family and begun to build a relationship with them. If a family requests a certain worker, that worker will be assigned whenever possible. A family who requests a specific kind of child will frequently be assigned to a worker who has a similar child on her caseload.

If a worker has used newspaper publicity on behalf of a child, families who respond to that publicity and who appear to be likely parents will usually be assigned that worker. The distribution of cases to ensure the best possible worker for each child and family is possible only if a manageable number of families respond to newspaper publicity on children. If there are more responses than can be handled in an orderly fashion, the responding families are assigned among all workers so that as few families as possible are "lost" because they do not receive an immediate response. Under these conditions, the team makes the ultimate decision as to which family is most appropriate for an available child. The worker who best knows the child usually has the most influence in that decision.

Worker assignments are occasionally made on the basis of geographic location of the child or family. Whenever possible, children and families within the same geographic area are assigned the same worker. In this way, worker time is used more efficiently because more than one child or family can be visited per trip, and more children and families can receive service with less delay.

Finally, assignments may be given workers who have the time available to take on a new case or who wish a new type of learning experience. The purpose of assigning cases is not to give the most difficult cases to the most competent workers, but to spread the work evenly so that each worker gains competence with different kinds of children and families.

Reassigning Child and Family Cases

The team meeting also provides the mechanism for reassigning primary responsibility for child and family cases whenever this becomes necessary. At Spaulding, worker turnover is conspicuously light. Yet despite these infrequent changes in staff, the process of reassigning all of a departing worker's cases to the remaining staff is well-planned. It begins as soon as the worker knows she will be leaving. Because of the extensive sharing of child and family information among workers, both in and out of team meetings, the primary responsibility for a child or family is reassigned to the worker who is identified as the most appropriate choice. Thus, each case is reassigned to the worker who has had the most extensive previous contact with the child or family, or the worker who knows the placement best. In the few instances where no other worker has had recent personal contact with a child or family, another worker must gain familiarity with the case by working directly with the departing worker before she leaves.

Although the Spaulding staff believe that adoption studies should ideally be written after the actual decision to "fit" a child and a family together has been made, worker turnover sometimes makes this impossible. Before workers leave the agency, they must complete written adoption studies. If their contacts with the family are too few to produce a useful study, they are asked to provide the worker to whom the family is reassigned with conscientious transcripts of those contacts. This ensures that the new worker will be familiar with all available information, that the stress associated with rearranging relationships will be minimized, and that the children and families involved will not feel abandoned when their worker leaves.

"Time-Out" Periods
Despite the seriousness of the tasks at hand, not all time at team meetings is devoted to business. Sometimes, seemingly irrelevant discussions and joking occurs. These "time-out" periods are, however, a vital part of placing older and handicapped children. They not only serve the purpose of helping workers feel more comfortable with each other, (which can eventually also enable each to work better with one another), but also provide the "breathing spaces" necessary in a demanding job which requires long, hard, and often inconvenient hours.

THE ADVANTAGES OF TEAMWORK

There are many advantages for children, families, and staff in the teamwork approach. As has been indicated, this approach provides workers with vital mutual support in coping with feelings of defeat and discouragement when confronting a disruption. The team approach also provides workers with a healthy outlet to ventilate their frustration and anger, and to receive the sympathetic understanding of others who know that these emotions are a very real and normal part of placing older and handicapped children for adoption.

Problem-solving in human relationships often produces personal stress for all involved, and it is during these times that workers especially need to be able to receive the support other workers can offer. When feelings and issues can be freely discussed, staff cannot only continue working together effectively, but there is a decreased likelihood that silent feelings will later erupt into a situation which might prove detrimental to children, families, or workers. When adequate support is available whenever needed, workers can re-charge depleted reservoirs of energy and commitment and more efficiently return to the difficult tasks which must be done.

Teamwork provides many more advantages for children, families, and staff. Since each worker develops a unique set of skills, approaches to problem-solving, and commitments to different kinds of children, no realationship between worker and child or worker and family is identical. Each worker functions better with different kinds of children and families or with different stages in the adoptive process. In a teamwork approach, this diversity of styles and skills can be ideally combined to offer the child his best possible opportunity to gain an appropriate adoptive family.

A combination of worker styles and skills also provides other benefits before and after placement. Since some children and families clearly prefer to be helped by one worker rather than another, exposure to a team provides them with the freedom to choose to work with whomever makes them feel most comfortable. In addition, if their relationship with a specific worker does not work out, both children and families have the additional security of knowing there are other workers, well acquainted with them and with whom they can freely talk, who can step in and assume supportive service responsibilities.

Because workers, too, may sometimes prefer not to work with a specific child or family, the teamwork approach furnishes members of staff with an ideal means for finding another worker who can offer the child or family a more positive relationship. The staff have found that such transfers of responsibility, which may be either temporary or permanent, are much more beneficial to child, family, and worker than continuing with a relationship that is not working well. These transfers among staff are actually exchanges, for the initial child or family worker must usually assume some of the second worker's previous responsibilities in order for her to begin working with a new case. Because the sole intent of transferring cases is to improve the possibility of a successful adoption, no decision is made to change a child's or a family's worker without that child's or family's consent.

When problems arise, families also find it easier to contact the agency when they can form a partnership with the entire placement staff instead of an individual worker. Being able to go to more than one worker for help allows both children and families to possess a more healthy independence and self-reliance throughout the adoptive process and provides them with the greatest possible opportunity for receiving and maintaining an appropriate placement. In addition, a team offers children and families greater knowledge and insight and a sharing of decision-making which helps to correct the biases one worker may develop. In this way, teamwork provides a more complete, objective, and accurate perspective of personal histories, family relationships, and areas of difficulty which must be well understood before a placement can be made with much hope for success. Families exposed to the different points of view which teamwork provides also more easily learn there are often several ways to approach the solution of a problem.

Another benefit of teamwork is that it eases the transition which occurs when cases must be reassigned because a worker leaves the agency. Children and families who have worked with a team do not feel deserted or poorly served when their primary worker leaves, for they already know one of the other workers will become their new primary worker. In this way, teamwork makes the transfer of responsibility and service far less traumatic for those involved.

Teamwork also creates opportunities for workers to discuss their doubts and concerns, and to verify perspectives when they are not certain their understanding of a situation is correct. When two or more workers simultaneously help a child or family, the opportunity for discussion with a trusted colleague during their travel is an invaluable aid to better and fuller communication and understanding among workers. Over time, staff working closely together come to know what each other means, not just what each other says, and this eliminates many potential problems.

Still another benefit of teamwork is that it provides a balance between too little worker commitment and the possibility of so great an emotional commitment that a worker becomes ineffective. When placement responsibilities are shared by a team, the negative effects of unwarranted emotional reactions which workers might have to a child or family can be modified with the help of other workers. Workers who become so emotionally involved with a placement that they become immobilized or ineffective may be helped to maintain a greater personal distance. Teamwork is also effective for a worker feeling a great deal of indecision or harboring a personal aversion or lack of commitment to a child or family. It is simply less possible for a worker to conceal these negative feelings. As a result, workers who are members of a team are much more apt to act in a forthright and cooperative manner with children and families.

The team approach also provides a built-in reward system, an essential ingredient in any program seeking to place older and handicapped children. The greatest reward for placement workers, other than successfully placing and maintaining a child in an adoptive family, is to receive adequate emotional support from co-workers and administrators.

At Spaulding, placement success and the easing of post-placement difficulties become rewards which are shared by all placement staff, including the Director. Aside from the esteem and support of one another, the staff also regularly enjoy more material forms of reward "for a job well-done." Currently, the agency assumes the cost of several "planned rewards" each year; usually the placement staff have dinner together at a favorite restaurant or attend a concert as a group. Originally, these occasions were paid for by the workers themselves. However, once the agency's Board of Directors became aware of the need for visible group rewards, they readily agreed that such recognition merited a legitimate agency expenditure. They recognized that it is clearly beneficial to children, families, and staff to develop a reward system which assures workers of regular acknowledgement and creates a rich feeling of group solidarity.

Finally, the team approach offers both new and seasoned workers increased opportunity for essential training. The agency has found that workers learn faster and work better when they are assigned as co-workers to observe experienced team members evaluate children, prepare families, and help families work out specific problems. In this way, new staff members acquire placement skills through practical experience, receive regular encouragement and advice, and learn to function as able and valued team members. This approach also provides continuous opportunities for in-service training as well as an efficient means for new workers to become sensitized to the adoption philosophy and working styles of the other workers in the agency. In addition, seasoned workers more easily keep their skills sharp, responses appropriate, and outlook up-to-date with the help of consistent team discussion and decision-making.

THE DISADVANTAGES OF TEAMWORK

Along with the many advantages of the team approach, there are some definite disadvantages. Certain problems occur in the creation and maintenance of teams which must be overcome if the team approach is to attain maximum effectiveness and include all staff members.

One major problem is that teamwork is not an appropriate working structure for all placement workers. Some workers may not be able to work well as a member of a group. Some workers may not be aggressive enough to be successful contributors to group discussions or may not feel comfortable requesting that other workers take time out of their schedules to help train them. Others may prefer to work in a more independent fashion while still others may find teaming a painful and threatening experience. The latter group may lack confidence in their skills, or fear that team contacts will expose their short-comings and bring on the disapproval of their co-workers. Some workers may also wish to avoid working in close tandem with other staff members because of personal conflict with them.

Another potential problem of teamwork is that its effectiveness depends upon the ability of each member of staff to assume their share of existing responsibilites. When this does not occur, there is a tremendous added strain on all members of the team. Such strain may result from worker frustration or personal problems and lead a worker to become detached from the team or lose interest in working together. Although detachment from other workers may not be disastrous to a worker's individual caseload, it does seriously decrease the efficiency of the team. While most of these problems can be eventually worked out, the most extreme examples of this difficulty — cases where a worker simply does not "fit in" with the rest of the team — can be a serious problem not easily resolved.

Teamwork presupposes that workers' attitudes and values will generally be compatible with those of other staff members. Workers who do not fit in are usually those whose views regarding "acceptable" family life-styles, parenting styles, or the adoptability of children, vary radically from other team members, and who are not able or willing to change their perspectives. Lack of fit may also occur if skill levels within the team are so variable that more highly skilled workers become so frustrated with co-workers that they are unwilling to offer support and training to the very workers who need them most. In such cases, the Spaulding staff have tried to increase the skills of the "out of phase" worker and, failing that, have had to wait for that person to change or leave the agency.

Small placement programs with low worker turnover will have fewer problems implementing the teamwork approach. Larger programs not only have more workers who must "fit" together well enough to function as a team, but will need more time to build trust, learn each other's skills, and be able to successfully balance worker schedules and caseloads. The team approach may also be more difficult to develop in large programs unless the administration is willing to be flexible enough to encourage the development of small groups or clusters or workers who could function as a team.

Another problem inherent in teamwork is the tremendous amount of time and energy which its existence requires. Critics of the team approach point out that it should be possible to "successfully" place older and handicapped children by a more efficient means at less cost. They maintain that teamwork requires too much time be spent in the establishment and maintenance of unnecessarily close working relationships between workers or between workers and supervisors. It cannot be denied that it may take a considerable amount of time for workers to get to know each other well enough to learn how each reacts to various situations and to develop the honesty and trust in each other necessary to enable the entire staff to work closely together. It also cannot be denied that it may take less time for a supervisor or administrator to make decisions which others implement than to feel comfortable allowing others to share responsibility and help make decisions. However, it is Spaulding's experience that the substantial benefits teamwork provides for children, families, and workers more than justifies the time needed to create an efficient team approach.

Much of the alleged inefficiency of teamwork stems from the repetitive nature of the teaming experience. Because all team members eventually require the same information, there is often a need to recount both history and rationale in order to inform someone who may not have been present for ealier discussions. Such reiteration, however, greatly increases the probability of creating a rich and readily available foundation of shared information and experience to be used in other problem situations or with other placements.

In addition, much of the "lost" time attributed to the team approach consists of efforts to keep up staff morale through discussions of work-related problems and the offering of reassurances to workers who need them. Even though a considerable portion of time is spent in this way and does diminish the time workers could spend in direct contact with children and families, the Spaulding staff do not regard their time-consuming responsibility for helping each other work out such problems as a waste of precious time. It is their conviction that if part of the team approach did not include the recognition of worker imperfection and the need for staff to offer support to each other, normal human frailty would seriously hinder the work of placing older and handicapped children for adoption.

SUMMARY

Spaulding's team approach to adoption reflects an attitude, a relationship between workers, and a problem-solving technique. It is a continuous and dynamic process shaped by workers who change and grow as they learn. It results from a willingness to work with others as equals and from putting this willingness into daily practice.

In implementing the teamwork approach, each staff member works to maintain a partnership of shared problem-solving, decision-making, and support-giving known at Spaulding as "collegial supervision." Each regards this partnership as a far more desirable alternative than worker competition or isolation, for each knows that the job of placing older and handicapped children for adoption is less emotionally draining and more rewarding if problems, decisions, responsibilities, and successes are shared.

The team approach also helps create a more efficient, productive, and successful adoption process. It provides a format which encourages a wider perspective and a broader range of experience than could be provided by an individual worker. It offers children, families, and work-

ers a better understanding of the readiness for and problems of placement. It also provides a continuous opportunity for training and a potent
means of increasing moral support among staff.

   Although the team approach at Spaulding originated and is most fully
developed among placement staff, workers have also sought to extend
the teamwork approach in their work with children, families, other child
welfare professionals, the agency's clerical staff, and the Board of Directors.

   The presence of the team approach will not automatically eliminate all
difficulties related to the placement of children. However, it is the agency's firm conviction that the perspectives gained and decisions made
through the combined efforts of all staff working closely together are
more beneficial for children, families, and workers than those reached
through any other type of working relationship.

Working With Children

5

The Children Spaulding Places

Who are the children for whom Spaulding finds families? They are children like Meg, born with no arms and no legs. Meg has formed a strong attachment to her adoptive family and they love her. Her whole family goes to the hospital for her special appointments, cheers her on when she struggles to use her new prosthetic devices, and does not permit her to get bogged down in self-pity. Meg has good days, and fights with her brothers on bad days, like any other child. Her brothers like her even though the fights are sometimes a bit unfair since an artificial arm can leave quite a mark.

They are children like Robbie, physically abused and brain damaged in early infancy, having more than a dozen seizures a day when the placement worker first met him at age three. He was not walking or talking, but was responsive, sought affection, and wanted to return it. Robbie was adopted by a single-parent mother. He now attends a special school for the multiply handicapped, is developing some language, and walks unaided (one of the strangest gaits in the world, but he walks!). His mother has since adopted two more children and he is now a loved and loving child with two older sisters and friends in the school and the neighborhood. He will be a dependent adult and eventually may have to be institutionalized, but his family has undertaken to give him the very best care they can and the best self-help skills he can muster to enrich his future.

There are also children like Barbara, a bright girl of 11, who lived in a psychiatric hospital for three years. She had known a great deal of rejection, but with the help of an understanding psychiatrist, felt ready to try family life again. She needed a patient but strong family who would not reject her and who would understand her need not to lose touch with her biological father. Barbara was placed with a family who had already adopted three older children. After several months of struggle, Barbara has made tremendous gains, has increased her self-confidence, and has found that people like her for her enthusiasm and warmth.

Meg, Robbie, Barbara, and other children Spaulding places share characteristics which have led most social workers to believe that families consider such children to be "unadoptable." Some of these children have moderate to severe birth defects or have experienced complications following birth trauma. Others are mildly to moderately retarded or are emotionally disturbed. Some have mental and physical problems which are not easily defined or well understood. These problems may be referred to as "slow development," "developmental lag," "minimal brain damage," or any similar term in current use. Still others are mildly to moderately handicapped by multiple problems such as brain damage, emotional difficulties, mental retardation, or learning disabilities. In many of these latter cases, it is difficult or impossible to determine which problems are responsible for the child's unusual behaviors.

Many of the children whom Spaulding places have a history which includes the partial or total disintegration of their biological families. Still other children had been considered "too old for adoption" by social workers who assumed that families wished to adopt only babies and toddlers. Some children are of minority heritage. Others have brothers and sisters and had been previously placed in one or more foster homes or institutions because a family "could not be found" to adopt the entire group.

The children Spaulding places have been referred to as "hard-to-place," "unadoptable," "waiting children," "parentless children," and "children with special needs." Some labels, such as "hard-to-place" and "unadoptable," are descriptive terms used by social workers. Other labels, such as "waiting," "parentless," and "special needs," have been coined by parent and professional groups who hope to increase public awareness of the children who are legally free for adoption, but who remain unplaced. These groups intend that the use of their terms will help to remove some of the stigma traditionally suffered by the unplaced child.

CHANGES IN THE KINDS OF CHILDREN PLACED

Spaulding has not always placed children with handicaps as severe as those of Meg, Robbie, and Barbara. Early in their history, the agency's staff placed some "unadoptable" children whom they would not now consider hard-to-place. The hard-to-place children for whom the staff were finding families when the agency was established in 1968 were defined as any white school-age child, any child of minority race, or any child possessing physical, mental, or emotional handicaps of any degree. In other words, "hard-to-place" children were those who were not in "perfect" health, not infants or toddlers, or not white.

Of course, the working definition of "older," "hard-to-place," and "unadoptable" varied from region to region and from one adoption program to another. Because of differences in individual program policy, the range of ages and even the kinds of children generally available for adoption varied within the geographic areas served by different adoption programs. Although an adequate supply of babies and toddlers continued to be available for adoption in many states through the end of the 1960's, some adoption workers could be found who occasionally placed a relatively easy hard-to-place child. These children were usually moderately physically handicapped rather than mentally or emotionally handicapped, and most often younger rather than older. Then, as now, the skill of the workers in placing these children largely determined which children found permanent families and which children did not.

The end of the "baby boom" arrived gradually in many states. In Michigan, the early 1970's marked the period when the kinds of children most adoption workers had been placing became almost totally unavailable. With healthy white babies and toddlers no longer available in the quantities necessary to keep all existing adoption programs in operation, some agencies focused their professional attention on other areas of service, some went out of business altogether, and others continued in the adoption field by placing the children who were available but who were viewed as "hard-to-place."

With other agencies and courts placing increasingly older and more handicapped children, Spaulding's philosophy necessitated that it place only those children who were not being placed elsewhere. As growing numbers of placement programs began finding permanent adoptive families for older white children, minority race infants, small sibling groups of young children, and mildly handicapped children, Spaulding began receiving referrals for children who were still older or even more severely mentally, physically, or emotionally handicapped than had previously been the case. In finding permanent families for all but a few of these children, Spaulding workers continued to demonstrate the adoptability of most children available for adoption.

The two programs which most influenced the kinds of children the Spaulding staff were placing were Homes for Black Children and the Special Project of the Michigan Department of Social Services. The success of Homes for Black Children, which was established in Detroit in 1969, greatly diminished the number of children of minority race referred to Spaulding. The Special Project, organized in 1971 and staffed by specially trained MDSS workers in several counties, greatly increased the number of hard-to-place children adopted through the efforts of Michigan's public agencies.

Because of the desire of the Spaulding staff to see other adoption programs place as many as possible of the children in need of adoption, the agency did not compete with Homes for Black Children and the Special Project (or any other programs) for referrals. Instead, Spaulding workers would offer information about Homes for Black Children to courts and agencies needing assistance in placing children of minority race. In addition, whenever a Michigan agency or court approached Spaulding with a child for placement, the Spaulding staff would refer them first to the Special Project or to Homes for Black Children. Spaulding accepted a referral only if those programs were unable to find a permanent family for a child or if the referring agency or court could not be persuaded to use the services of one of those alternative programs.

The number of black children referred to Spaulding has also been reduced in recent years because of the emergence of strong objections to trans-racial adoption by some black professionals who have become sensitive to the problems they feel are caused by cross-racial and cross-cultural placements. The Spaulding staff believe that when all factors are equal, it is better to place children with parents of the same race or culture in order to reduce the adjustment problems caused by trans-racial or trans-cultural barriers. In adoptive placements, however, all factors are seldom equal.

Although most placement programs in Southeastern Michigan no longer consider young children of minority race to be hard-to-place, they continue to find minority race children with handicaps more difficult to place than white children with similar handicaps. Nevertheless, the Spaulding staff believe that the disproportionately large number of minority race children waiting for adoption have the same need for permanence and a sense of attachment and belonging as other children. While the staff prefer to place minority children within minority family groups, racial and cultural considerations are never made paramount to the child's need for a permanent family. More specifically, the staff will not dismiss the possibility of a trans-racial or trans-cultural placement if appropriate adoptive parents from the child's racial or cultural background are not available.

By the early 1970's, Spaulding success in placing some of the children who had not been placed by other programs led the staff to revise their definition of "hard-to-place." The term presently refers to children older than eleven years, children with physical, educational, or emotional handicaps which are moderate to severe in nature, multiply handicapped children, or brothers and sisters who should be placed in the same family.

Table 3 contains an analysis of each of the kinds of children placed by the Spaulding staff each year from 1968 through 1976. No placement statistics from other programs are offered for comparison. Lack of publicly available verifiable information from other agencies and courts, as well as highly variable approaches to the recording of such information among programs, makes any attempt to derive accurate or representative comparative statistics impossible.

TABLE 3

Children Placed by Spaulding For Children: 1968-1976

	68[a]	69	70	71	72	73	74	75	76	Totals	Avg.
Children Placed	6	33	37	28	22	16	24	19	14	199	22
No. of Males	5	22	20	16	11	7	16	8	7	112	56%
No. of Females	1	11	17	12	11	9	8	11	7	87	44%
Percentage Caucasian	67%	67%	76%	75%	82%	82%	75%	53%	86%	146	73%
Number of Disruptions	0	2	3	3	4	4	4	1	0	21	10.6%
Type of Handicap											
Older	17%[b]	30%[b]	19%	32%	32%	56%	25%	53%	29%	63	32%
Educationally Handicapped[1]	33%	30%	41%	54%	64%	56%	38%	32%	79%	91	46%
Physically Handicapped	33%	30%	27%	25%	14%	38%	50%	26%	64%	64	32%
Emotionally Handicapped	50%	27%	46%	50%	32%	13%	50%	47%	57%	81	41%
Minority Race	33%	33%	24%	25%	18%	18%	25%	47%	14%	53	27%
Multiply Handicapped[2]	50%	48%	68%	79%	73%	88%	83%	75%	93%	147	74%

[1] Includes children who are retarded or brain damaged or who have learning disabilities which would normally qualify them for special educational programs.

[2] Two or more handicapping conditions. Includes educational, physical, and emotional handicaps. Also includes age, minority race, and siblingship as handicaps since these conditions continue to hamper the placement of many children.

[a] The agency began placing children in September, 1968.

[b] Older than age seven. Succeeding years defined as older than age eleven.

THE DECREASE IN PLACEMENTS

During 1970, the Spaulding staff realized the effects of five unanticipated factors were beginning to decrease the number of children they would be able to place for adoption each year. These factors were:

1. The impact of Spaulding's success on the placement activities of other agencies and courts.
2. A shift in referrals made to the agency of children of greater age or handicap.
3. The increasing need for post-placement services.
4. The increasing effort needed to find other adoptive families for those children whose adoption placements disrupted.
5. A shifting of agency resources to the training of, and consultation with, other agencies and courts.

With the spread of knowledge about Spaulding's placement successes, more and more agencies and courts decided there was no reason why they could not increase the range of the children they placed and begin to find permanent adoptive families for more of their available children. Their decision was based upon reasons which ranged from healthy competition and an inability or unwillingness to pay Spaulding's purchase fee to a new knowledge of techniques and a new willingness to try to place children in cases where they had previously assumed inevitable failure.

This increase in the placement of children traditionally considered hard-to-place or "unadoptable" was, and continues to be, one of Spaulding's major goals. Nevertheless, expanded definitions of adoptability in other agencies and courts have served to increase the age and severity of the handicaps of the children referred to Spaulding for placement. This evolution has increased the effort required to make each placement and diminished the total number of children placed.

The range of children placed by the Spaulding staff has expanded to the point where they are now finding adoptive families for multiply handicapped children, school-age children with Down's Syndrome, teen-agers with emotional disturbances, and children who are terminally ill. Many of these children require extensive post-placement services in order to maintain their adoptions. Post-confirmation services have become recognized as protective and preventative services which help avert the removal of the child from the home and help alleviate the extreme pressures which can occur when these children are adopted.

As the staff's experience with the placement of these children has grown, they have realized that even with greatly increased service efforts, the successful maintenance of adoptions of children with severe handicaps is threatened much more frequently than those of less handicapped children or healthy babies and toddlers. The staff must, therefore, not only provide increased service to minimize such threats, but must also immediately intensify work with the child and the adoptive family when threats arise. If a broken adoption (or "disruption," as it is known at Spaulding) does occur, post-placement services for that family are continued and work with the prospective replacement family for the child is begun to help all concerned understand what has taken place and to prepare them for what lies ahead. This increased post-placement service to adoptions which may disrupt, as well as to families adopting children who have disrupted from a previous family, significantly reduced the total numbers of children who could be effectively served by Spaulding.

The staff have also been serving fewer children in recent years because of their more intensified commitment to training of, and consultation with, other agencies and courts in an effort to help those programs place older and handicapped children into permanent adoptive families. More time and effort spent seeking to help the greatest number of these children by increasing the number of agencies and courts capable of placing them for adoption has reduced the amount of time available for Spaulding staff to work directly with children and families.

As a result of their training and consultation efforts, the Spaulding staff are placing children from an ever-widening geographic area and demonstrating that older and handicapped children can be successfully placed for adoption across seldom-crossed geographic boundaries. Although much effort has been required to overcome the obstacles which traditionally hinder such placements, important advances have been made. Through the end of 1972, only six of 126 children placed by the agency were referred by non-Michigan adoption programs. In contrast, approximately 50% of the 73 children placed between 1973 and 1976 have come from outside the State.

SUMMARY

The children Spaulding places are the children for whom other placement programs have not been able to find permanent families. When Spaulding was established in 1968, these children included any white school-age child, any child of minority race, or any child possessing physical, mental, or emotional handicaps of any degree. As a result of the placement successes of other adoption programs, especially Homes for Black Children in Detroit and the Special Project of the Michigan Department of Social Services, Spaulding is now finding permanent families for children with multiple handicaps, teen-agers with emotional disturbances, and children who are terminally ill.

During the last few years, the number of children the Spaulding staff have placed for adoption has declined. This has been due, in part, to the placement successes of other agencies and courts. However, it has also been due to the increasing need for post-placement services by the children now being referred to Spaulding, to the increasing effort required of staff to find other adoptive families for those children whose adoption placements disrupt, and to a shifting of agency resources to provide training and consultation for other adoption programs.

·The staff have realized that progress within other placement programs and changes in the characteristics of the children referred to Spaulding have meant the agency's workers can no longer continue to effectively serve large numbers of new children and families each year. However, the decline in the agency's annual number of adoptive placements in recent years has not decreased the staff's commitment to children. If anything, their commitment has become stronger and their mission more distinct as the children referred for placement have become increasingly older or more handicapped and have required more extensive post-placement and post-confirmation services.

6

The Evaluation of the Child

Spaulding's services to children begin with an initial evaluation of the child and include preparatory work and post-placement services which are designed to help the child adjust to and remain with his new family. The evaluation of the child will be discussed in this chapter. The preparation of the child and post-placement services will be discussed in subsequent chapters.

PURPOSES OF THE EVALUATION

The Spaulding staff believe that all children who are referred should be completely evaluated unless they are not hard-to-place by the agency's standards. The staff are convinced that many children are far more appealing in person than they appear from their written description. Further, they believe an in-person evaluation can often be responsible for triggering foster parent interest in adoption or creating opportunities for the workers from Spaulding and the referring agency or court to explore the appropriateness of other families already available to the referring worker.

The initial purpose of the evaluation is to determine whether the child can be successfully placed with a permanent family without Spaulding's services. The staff's decision to accept the referral is based upon a combination of factors which include their perception of the child's level of functioning, the availability of potentially appropriate and capable adoptive families, the placement skill and knowledge of the workers within the referring agency or court, and the possibility that an unreasonable number of problems will be created because the geographic distance between the child and the Spaulding staff is too great. (Distance becomes a factor in the decision to accept a referral only when the child is more than a one day drive by car from the agency.)

The staff do not accept or reject the referral of a child they consider to be hard-to-place until they have completed an evaluation and know the child well. The child's situation is always discussed by the workers as a group. A separate decision is made for each referral and no decision is based upon formula or precedent. Acceptance of the child's referral does not, of course, guarantee successful placement.

After a child's referral has been accepted, the information gained during an evaluation serves a number of additional purposes:

- it helps the Spaulding workers find an appropriate available family for the child
- it helps determine the areas which require pre-placement services
- it helps focus on anticipated problems during and beyond the period of initial adjustment to the placement
- it provides information which can be used to assist the child in gaining insight into himself now and as he grows older
- it helps Spaulding workers determine what degree of support and placement participation may be available from the referring worker(s) and program.

Finding an Appropriate Family

The evaluation of the child helps the Spaulding staff begin to know the child well enough to find an appropriate family for that child. (Family preparation will be more fully discussed in the chapter entitled, "Preparing Families for Adoption," p.131.) To find that family, the staff must acquire information about the child which can provide specific and thorough answers to such questions as:

What is this child's primary handicap?

What are this child's other handicaps?

At what level is this child functioning in terms of self-care, communication, and visual and motor skills, and how do these abilities affect his daily living?

What are the chances of this child becoming emotionally independent in adulthood?

Can this child respond best in a quiet, passive family or in one which is nosier and more assertive?

Is it better if this child is an only child or one of many?

What does this child do best?

What is most rewarding to this child?

What kinds of rewards and frustrations does this child bring to a family?

Will a family need special qualities, skills, or resources to parent this child?

Determining Pre-placement Activities

Accurate information about the child can help answer important questions regarding the form and direction of pre-placement activities. This information is best obtained through an in-person evaluation. Such an evaluation can help answer such questions as:

How much preparation of this child will be needed?

What form should this child's preparation for adoption take?

What additional resources will be needed (such as financial aid, therapy, medical or psychological evaluation)?

What resources are available for this child?

How long will it take before this child is emotionally ready for placement?

How long will it take before this child is emotionally ready for adoption?

Focusing on Adjustment Problems

The evaluation material also provides answers to questions about the adjustment problems which must inevitably be faced after the child is placed. These questions include:

What has been the quality of the relationship between this child and those who have cared for him?

Should any ties this child may have with a biological family, foster family, or institutional staff be maintained?

What is the quality of the relationship between this child and his peers, and between this child and his teachers?

What behavior in the foster home (or institution) was most rewarding to the foster family (or caretaking staff)? Which was most annoying?

Has the frequency of these behaviors increased or decreased?

Will these behaviors be repeated after this child is placed into an adoptive family?

How was this child handled when he was most upset?

How did he respond to the ways in which he was handled?

To whom did he go for support, assurance, or security?

Understanding the Child's Past

The information provided during the evaluative work-up, if carefully collected, can help the adoptive family and workers piece together existing clues to the child's past. These clues may exist in the recorded or recalled information of social workers who might have had contact with the child or those around him, in any photographs that can be unearthed, and in descriptions, names, nicknames, and birthdates of significant persons. If material about the child's past is incomplete despite persistent searching, guesses about important events might have to be made if they cannot be remembered by the child himself. When it is necessary for workers to resort to guessing, the child must understand that the information, though possibly correct, is actually only a "best estimate" of his past. However, even if it is somewhat incomplete, information about the child's past can help answer important questions:

How much does this child know about his past and the reasons he is available for adoption?

Does he talk about his past or about being adopted?

What does he talk about, and with whom?

Will this child be able to understand more of the information as he grows older?

Can the prospective adoptive family accept and deal appropriately with existing information?

Will the prospective adoptive family feel comfortable about answering this child's questions or volunteering information about him?

What important information is missing and needs to be filled in?

Where can the worker or family go for additional information?

Determining Degrees of Support

The child's work-up also provides an opportunity to gain information about the attitudes, skills, and commitment of the referring worker(s). The evaluation process also can have the additional benefits of building a stronger relationship between Spaulding staff and referring staff. During an evaluation, the child's referring worker often begins to share the Spaulding workers' deep involvement in finding appropriate families for all children waiting for adoption. Information obtained from the child's worker and the referring agency or court early in the placement process can help answer such questions as:

What is the referring worker's attitude toward, and understanding of, this child and his problems?

Who can best prepare this child and help him make the smoothest transition to adoption?

Will the foster family or institutional staff help this child make the move to adoption?

Will funds be available in the referring agency or court for the necessary visits between this child and the potential adoptive family?

Can the referring worker(s) approve of the family the Spaulding staff see as appropriate for this child?

What is the best strategy to convince the referring worker(s) to share the Spaulding staff's view that the family is appropriate?

COLLECTING INFORMATION ABOUT THE CHILD

From what sources do workers gather the information they need to prepare a child for adoption? Spaulding workers believe that looking at written records and talking with professional people is insufficient to insure the success of the child's placement. They believe that these sources must always be supplemented by personal contact with the child and other significant persons in his life. In fact, the Spaulding staff are firmly convinced that the most important source of information about the child is the child himself. In their experience, a personal understanding of the child is vital if the worker intends to convey an accurate and human impression of him to his prospective parents. Further, they believe it is impossible to adequately prepare a child for adoption or find him an appropriate family without knowing his developmental skills, needs, attitudes, expectations, and feelings. They believe that only seeing and talking with the child can provide this sense of who he is.

In collecting information about a child, workers try to see him under several different circumstances. If the child is of school age, the worker will try to visit him in school. Even if this proves impossible, the Spaulding workers feel it is imperative to talk with his teachers to get a comprehensive description of classroom behavior. It is their belief that the classroom and playground both offer good opportunities to learn more about the child. Each is a setting familiar to him, through which strange adults can pass without causing too much disturbance or obviously focusing attention on an individual child. If the child is not of school age, he can be observed with neighborhood playmates. When time permits, workers also like to observe children with their friends out of school, for children often behave differently in an informal group than they do at home or in the classroom. Geographic distance between worker and child does not always allow this amount of observation, however.

Meetings with the child are arranged either before or after observing him with others. The workers try to hold all meetings under conditions and in a place in which the child feels comfortable. These circumstances allow the child to talk privately about the matters that are important to him. Whenever possible, the staff believe it is best to see the child more than once, for it is easy to miss or misunderstand what may be important during an initial meeting.

In addition to gathering information directly from the child and his teachers (especially the teacher who knows him best), workers try to accumulate information and opinions from other significant people in the child's life. Important informational sources are the child's foster family or institutional caretaking staff, and his social worker(s). Other useful sources often include the child's biological family members, psychologists, psychiatrists, educational specialists, and physicians. The information the worker obtains from all of these individuals will help in balancing the positive and negative reports they uncover.

It is the experience of the Spaulding staff that a thorough and composite picture of a child in foster care is impossible without a talk with the child's foster mother, or better still, with his entire foster family. Spaulding workers have found that foster parents (or institutional staff, if the child is in such a setting) will more readily and openly talk about the child if they can see that the worker already knows the child and possesses a genuine interest in his future.

Although a series of meetings, rather than a single meeting, is often necessary to develop a personal and trusting relationship between child and worker or between worker and significant people in the child's life, extra meetings require extra staff time. Consequently, because of the great geographic distances which must be covered during some placements, Spaulding workers sometimes cut short the time spent personally gathering information about the child. This is done most often if no important information about the child appears to be missing and if there are no contradictions in the information in the child's written record or between the record and the observations of Spaulding workers. Under these conditions, information can usually be verified in one or two visits, or supplemented by the child's referring worker(s). The experience of the Spaulding staff has shown that saving time when such favorable circumstances exist will seldom endanger the placement. When contradictions do arise, however, it is essential to take the time to resolve them.

In order to adequately prepare themselves for meeting the child or the significant people in the child's life, the Spaulding staff usually study the child's written record before other informational sources are consulted. These records contain information about his placement history, his mental, physical, and emotional development, his biological family, and his foster family or institutional caretakers. Although there is no set order in which informational sources are explored, Spaulding workers most often choose to talk with individuals who know the child before talking with the child himself. This knowledge offers them the opportunity to check (through observation and asking questions) how their own perspective compares with the written description of the child. When contradictory historical information exists, however, the workers may elect to see the child first. In this way, they hope to avoid forming a prejudicial or incorrect view of the child that might be passed on to prospective adoptive parents.

Although records vary in completeness and validity, the Spaulding staff recognize that they should be read carefully. A written record can tell the discerning worker much about the way parents and workers feel about a child and thus about how he has been treated. A written record can also disclose revealing gaps in information. Knowing what is missing from a record is sometimes as important as knowing what is present. Accurate records and insightful perceptions can also provide invaluable early warnings of complex medical or psychological issues which must be dealt with during preparation of the child and family. Finally, a written record can divulge certain patterns in the child's behavior which need to be understood (for example, why he is repeatedly "bounced out" of foster families after approximately six months of care).

The Spaulding staff have also learned to "read between the lines" of casework histories because it is always possible that whoever recorded the child's history may have been biased in one way or another. For example, a report may have been written to provide the basis for termination of parental rights or carefully designed to avoid hurting the child's chances for adoption. A report might also have been negatively influenced by a foster parent who was having difficulty with the child. Because of such possibilities, Spaulding workers prefer to review the child's history with the child's current workers, not only to determine how well they know him and how they feel about him, but also to obtain any important information not available from the child's record.

Over the past few years, Spaulding workers have found that many adoption programs are beginning to keep good life records of children. Where incomplete information exists, workers often rebuild records as they get to know the child. It is the conviction of Spaulding staff that the records of any child in substitute family care should include photographs of the child's biological family, his foster family, and the child care staff important to him. Periodic photographs of the child and functional descriptions of his behavior should also be part of his record.

In addition to the belief that workers need to be aware of possible bias in a child's written history, it is the experience of the Spaulding staff that placement workers need to develop skill in interpreting medical and psychological reports if they are to obtain maximum information from these sources. These reports may be subject to the same kind of bias as are children's histories and can vary just as much in validity and completeness of information. Medical and psychological reports, however, are further complicated by technical vocabulary and writing styles which are often incomprehensible to the layman. The workers at Spaulding take advantage of each other's special training and the special training of volunteer consultants or Board members in interpreting these reports. Workers also frequently contact the authors of such reports and ask them to further explain their findings.

When even further consultation is necessary, the Spaulding staff contact other specialists including physicians, psychologists, or psychiatrists in private practice, in clinics, or at the University of Michigan Hospital in Ann Arbor. These individuals can help the workers, child, and family understand the meaning of the child's diagnosis. They also provide information about the validity of existing medical or psychological opinions relating to the child when the staff have doubts about these opinions.

COMPLETING THE EVALUATION

The final step in the evaluation of the child is completion of the agency's "Child for Placement" form which summarizes the staff's view of the child. This form contains as straightforward and realistic an appraisal of the child and his patterns of behavior as the Spaulding workers can obtain. It includes both positive and negative statements about the child and information about both his appealing characteristics and those characteristics which make him difficult to parent. Circulation of this form among Spaulding workers signals that the staff has decided to accept the child's referral. The evaluation is then written into the child's record by a Spaulding worker.

SUMMARY

The primary purpose of Spaulding's composite on-site evaluation of a child is to determine if he can be successfully placed with a permanent family without Spaulding's services. No referral is accepted or rejected until the evaluation is completed unless the child is not hard-to-place by Spaulding's standards. After a child's referral has been accepted, the information gained during an evaluation also helps the staff find the most appropriate available family, determine which pre-placement services need to be provided, focus on potential post-placement problems, help the child better understand himself and his past, and determine the degree of support and post-placement participation available from referring workers.

The Spaulding staff believe that the most important source of information about the child is the child himself. Other sources are the child's foster family or institutional caretaking staff, his social worker(s), his teachers, and his written record. Still other sources may include the child's biological family members, psychologists, psychiatrists, educational specialists, and physicians.

The Spaulding staff usually review the child's written record carefully before other informational sources are consulted. They are acutely aware, however, that such records vary in completeness and validity and often contain the biases of the writer(s). The final report on the child as compiled by the Spaulding staff is the most current and most accurate view of the child that is available.

7

Preparing Children For Adoption

THE NEED FOR PREPARATION

If the adoption of an older or handicapped child is to succeed, it is necessary to work closely with the child before he is placed into a family. The ultimate goal of preparing a child for adoption is to help him make a positive adjustment to an adoptive family. The Spaulding staff believe that if the opportunity for positive adjustment is to be maximized, the work of preparing the child cannot be left until he becomes legally available for adoption or is about to be placed.

Spaulding's objective in preparing children for adoption is to help them to understand the events of their lives and to cope with the problems and stresses they experience because of those events. The staff believe all children, especially adopted children, are more secure, have fewer problems, and more fully comprehend and accept their present situation if they understand their past and themselves in relation to it. Initially, this understanding is most readily achieved if events and their implications are explained to the child as they occur. However, too few children in substitute care are given such explanations. As a result, far too many are bewildered or frustrated by their lack of information or are left to defend fragmented or incorrect impressions of their past.

This confusion and, in many cases, the child's subsequent inability to adjust to normal family life frequently jeopardizes an otherwise well-planned adoptive placement. The child's confusion and the anxiety which may accompany it can be exhibited in any number of problematic behaviors including hyperactivity, poor school performance, psychosomatic illness, runaway behavior or truancy, inability to make friendships, withdrawal, or aggression. The presence of some or all of these behaviors can create tremendous pressures for the adoptive family and may make it difficult or even impossible for them to love the child, to accept him, or to feel adequate as his parents. Although adoption workers cannot totally remove a child's doubts or eliminate his adjustment problems, skillful work with the child before adoption can diminish their impact.

THE WORKER-CHILD RELATIONSHIP

A comfortable relationship between worker and child is the key to successfully preparing a child for adoptive placement. Building the necessary relationship need not take additional time during the pre-placement period if the child is prepared for adoption by a person who has worked effectively with him while he has been in temporary care.

If, however, someone other than the child's regular worker is doing the preparation (as is the case when Spaulding workers prepare children for adoption), or if no one has worked effectively with the child in temporary care, building a working relationship will take considerable extra time. Nevertheless, the Spaulding staff believe that additional time taken early in the preparation process is well spent.

To prepare a child for adoption, workers need to discuss a number of important issues with the child and, as far as possible, help resolve them. First, workers must deal as realistically and candidly as possible with the separation of the child from his biological and foster families and with his placement into a new family. As much as possible, the child must be helped to distinguish past and present fantasies and realities. Success here, however, often requires patient workers who are able to provide frequent explanations and reassurance. It is the experience of the Spaulding staff that an adoption has a much better chance for success when the issues involved in separation are explained in terms the child can understand, when a worker is able to offer support to the child while honestly discussing matters which may upset the child, and when worker and child are able to grieve together over the wounds of both the past and the present.

The move itself, whether one of several or the only one within memory, is sure to raise doubts about whether a new family will keep him if his old family did not. Doubts about the permanence of the arrangement will make him hesitate to commit himself to a new family.

For a child who has loyalties toward previous families, changing families is quite upsetting. The presence of such loyalties is natural, and the child need not give them up in order to be adopted successfully. Nevertheless, it may seem to the child, and indeed to many workers and families, that faithfulness to a previous family implies unfaithfulness to the current family. Under these circumstances, the child may become involved in a conflict of loyalties which will create anger, guilt, and frustrations within him as well as within many of those around him, and which may result in his rejection of (or rejection by) one or more families.

At this time, placement workers can help the child by being sensitive to his fears, hopes, and conflicts about his placement. They can help resolve his conflicts by explaining to him, in language he can understand, what it is like for most children to leave one family and to be placed in another. The Spaulding staff often talk about how most children feel somewhat scared when they enter a new home because they do not know what the people are like, how they are expected to behave, or exactly what the differences are between foster care and adoption. They also try to help the child talk about his other anxieties and fears — how he may want to join the family and still not want to go, or how he hopes his new family works out, but fears it will not.

Of course, when talking with a child concerning his feelings about his prospective placement, workers must also be sure they offer a clear explanation of the problems which may occur. Despite their initial anxieties prior to such explanations, the Spaulding staff have found that most children not only understand that all families and children have their good times and bad times, but most are willing to stick with their decision to be placed for adoption once it is explained that a worker will always be there to talk to if anything goes wrong.

It is the experience of the Spaulding staff that discussing important information about the family, such as similarities and differences in the expectations of his new and previous parents, will reassure the child and help make the adjustment to his new family easier. It is especially important for him to know which of his actions will be praised or punished, and what punishments he is likely to receive if he misbehaves.

Communication Aids

During their preparation for adoption, many children are able to discuss important issues and provide answers to questions which help workers locate an appropriate available family for each child. Some children, however, especially those who are very young or who have been badly hurt emotionally, may not be able to express their feelings directly or to respond to expressions of feelings. In working with these children, the Spaulding staff have learned to use "concrete," rather than "abstract," methods of communication. These simple, visual communication aids are invaluable resources for the worker who is committed to helping the child adjust to himself and his new placement situation.

The shared creation of scrapbooks and lifebooks by worker and child is an aid which Spaulding workers have found to be particularly helpful in promoting communication with young, non-verbal, or troubled children. Such scrapbooks may also be used effectively with teen-age children. Scrapbooks and lifebooks can include the child's complete history up to the present time, stories about important periods or adventures in his life, photographs of the child in his biological, foster, or institutional family, and descriptions or pictures of the child's likes and dislikes (foods, songs, places, games, etc.) which help make him the person he is. Scrapbooks not only help the worker and prospective family know the child better (often with the child acting as "tour guide" through his book), but also provide the child with some continuity and understanding of his own often disturbing and fragmented past. In particular, they can be used to help him understand a past which should not be ignored.

Scrapbooks and lifebooks are two of the most helpful aids available to the placement worker. They are especially well-suited to the building of a good relationship between worker and child. These aids not only involve a specific task which is a natural and easy bridge from one visit to the next, but also provide the child with a much-needed sense of control over his experiences by offering him the opportunity to guide others through the significant and cherished memories of his life. Through lifebooks and scrapbooks, a child sees that he is the product of all his experiences, positive as well as negative, and that there is no one incident or experience that is solely responsible for who or where he is. Of equal importance is that these books can serve to remind a child that he can survive and grow even during periods of rapid or frequent change.

Play is the young child's most natural means of self-expression and, for this reason, is another useful communication technique. Through leisurely play using puppets, dolls, pictures, or other toys, a child can freely act out fears and other emotions which he may be experiencing but cannot express directly. The enterprising placement worker will also find other means to help communicate with a child. These may include maps to show the location of old and new families, drawing equipment, simple puzzles, or skill toys. Using such aids, the placement worker can begin to help the child focus on known as well as previously unexplained events in his life and help him take his past more comfortably and openly into his new living situation.

The Child's Participation

The Spaulding staff believe it is necessary for the child to feel he is actively participating in the planning of his placement. It is important for the worker to make sure that the child sees himself, as well as his foster and adoptive families, as instrumental in making decisions regarding the adoption. The child's role, if he is young, will probably be indirect, but it will still be important. To feel that he participates in the decisions which are made, the child must be confident that what he says to the worker will influence the choice of his prospective placement. The child's recognition that his feelings and wishes are known and taken into account gives him a sense of control over his life. This feeling of having helped to make decisions can make the difference between his acceptance or rejection of adoption or of a specific family.

Children cannot be coerced into adoption. In every case, their objections become apparent by one means or another, and the placement will be a difficult one for the child, family, and worker. To minimize the possibility of inappropriate placements, Spaulding workers use personal judgment, as well as the group decision-making process, to understand and interpret the child's feelings about families in general or about any one family in particular.

PREPARING ADOLESCENTS FOR ADOPTION

Adolescents have at least as great a need for adoption preparation as do younger children. Not only has the teen-ager had a longer period of time in which poorly understood events, problems, or stresses could occur, but he has had more time to develop and defend incorrect impressions of his past. It is not until their misperceptions are corrected and their past is understood that most older children are able to create and maintain realistic expectations of adoption and a permanent family.

Extensive preparation for adoption is necessary for adolescents who have spent most of their lives in institutions or who have lived in a succession of foster homes. Without adequate preparation, many of these young people will have great difficulty adjusting to or accepting a family relationship because they will know very little about family roles, tasks, and expectations. Some institutionalized children will never fully recover from the degree of deprivation they have experienced. However, it is the experience of the Spaulding staff that although such problems increase the need for preparation, they do not necessarily make these children unadoptable. Whatever the circumstance, the adoption of an adolescent should be considered a possibility until it becomes clear, after careful study, that it is not.

In addition to the problems created by the older child's more extensive experiences with foster care or institutionalization, the preparation of adolescents for adoption is a particularly challenging task because most adolescents react to the worker's initial suggestion of adoption with either outright rejection or marked uncertainty about its feasibility. They often describe themselves as too old or too attached elsewhere to make a commitment to the development of relationships with an adoptive family. They may resist adoption because they feel they cannot trust others who want to love them as their own or because they are clinging to the hope that they may someday rejoin their biological family.

Many potential adoptions are never realized because a teenager's initial response of uncertainty or refusal misleads well-meaning staff into leaving him in his "temporary" setting. Awareness by placement workers that initial responses of this kind are normal is essential for appropriate preparation. With their knowledge of adolescents' pride and desire for independence, Spaulding workers initially accept an older child's refusal or uncertainty and do not argue with him. They encourage the young person to keep the possibility of adoption open — to "decide later " — and to find out more about adoption before he totally rejects it as a choice for his future. They suggest that although he may not feel a strong need for family ties now since he is approaching the age where he is becoming independent, he may later enjoy being remembered on birthdays, coming back home for Christmas, or being a part of other important family gatherings. It is the staff's intention to help young people avoid making decisions against adoption. Such actions may later force them to "save face" by continuing to react negatively to alternatives which have since become appealing to them.

For this reason, an important part of Spaulding's preparation process involves making it possible for an adolescent to see adoption as a reality by introducing him to a family who could consider adopting him or to an adopted adolescent his own age. In this way, adoption is offered as a viable and understandable option. With this first-hand information, the adolescent is in a better position to make an informed decision. If he still decides to reject adoption, he will now at least know what he is turning down.

Obviously, however, not all older children will want to be adopted. Some older teen-agers may enjoy their independence too much to want to enter into what they view as a submissive relationship. For other young people, ties with their biological parents, even if existing only in fantasy, may be too exclusive and primary or too strong to permit close ties with any other parental figures. Some children may also be part of a sibling group in which an older child is a parent figure. These groups may form their own self-contained family with no need, as they see it, for adoption.

SPAULDING'S RESPONSIBILITY FOR PREPARATION

Over the past several years, the Spaulding staff have sought to shift responsibility for the pre-placement preparation of children away from themselves and onto each child's worker(s) from the referring court or agency. The decision to modify their original approach was made not only to help meet growing requests for training from workers in other placement programs, but to meet the need to reduce the ever-increasing workload of the Spaulding staff.

As greater numbers of children from other states and Canada have been referred to the agency for placement, the practical difficulties created by the great geographic distances involved have made many of these children inaccessible to Spaulding workers for the bulk of their necessary pre-placement preparation. At the same time, the increasing skill of workers from referring agencies and courts in preparing these older and handicapped children has made it less necessary, in many cases, for the Spaulding staff to assume this responsibility. In the few cases in which they feel the child's worker needs assistance, Spaulding workers will suggest strategies and methods by which the child's worker(s), foster parent(s), or institutional caretaking staff can prepare the child adequately for his adoption and help him make a smooth transition to his new family.

Despite their efforts to minimize problems and to improve children's understanding and acceptance of adoption, cases exist beyond the staff's control in which crucial areas of concern to the child are not always adequately handled. Cases of inadequate preparation, though infrequent, most often occur when great geographic distance between programs makes it difficult for Spaulding workers to consult regularly with the referring worker(s), or when the referring worker(s) cannot or will not take the steps necessary to ensure adequate pre-placement preparation.

SUMMARY

Children who are to be placed into adoptive families need to be prepared for their adoption. Children are more secure, have fewer problems, and more fully comprehend and accept their present situation if they understand their past and themselves in relation to it.

The key to successfully preparing a child for adoptive placement is a comfortable relationship between worker and child. When such a relationship exists, children can be helped to discuss their feelings and concerns about such matters as previous parents, separation, conflicting loyalties, and expectations for the future.

Adequate preparation requires that workers take the time to get to know the child well. Scrapbooks, lifebooks, and leisurely play using puppets, dolls, pictures, or other toys can be used to aid workers in discussing emotionally significant issues with children who are young or otherwise unable to express their feelings directly.

Children need to feel they have actively participated in the planning of their placement. The feeling of having helped to make the important decisions may make the difference between a child's acceptance or rejection of adoption in general or of a specific family in particular.

Adolescents have just as great a need for adoption preparation as do younger children. However, the preparation of adolescents is often an exceptionally challenging task. Not only has the older child awaiting adoption had more extensive experience with foster care or institutionalization, but his growing desire for independence may seriously conflict with his desire to belong to a family of his own. As a result, all older children should be encouraged to find out as much as possible about adoption before rejecting it as a choice for their future.

8

Spaulding's Use of "Foster Care"

Spaulding does not have a foster care program like that found in most child placement agencies. Since the agency's beginning, the Board and staff have been opposed to a series of temporary placements for children, arguing that such placements do not provide a child with the sense of stability, confidence, and well-being that comes from knowing his placement is intended to be permanent.

Early in their history, the staff's philosophical commitment to permanent placement resulted in an absolute refusal to maintain any type of "foster" or temporary care program. In the minds of both founders and staff, worker attention directed to temporary care (and away from adoption placement activity) could not help but subvert the original purpose of the agency.

THE NEED FOR TEMPORARY CARE

Throughout its history, the agency's original purpose has remained unchanged, and the staff have continued to focus their efforts on finding adoptive families for older and handicapped children. Over time, however, the staff have recognized that temporary care, if used appropriately, could significantly improve the adoption prospects of some of the children referred to them for permanent placement.

Few of the children referred to the agency are in need of extensive temporary care. All children referred are legally free for adoption and already within the child welfare temporary care system. All are already housed in a foster home, group care home, or an institutional setting, and all usually remain in that setting until an adoptive family has been located and prepared to parent them.

Temporary care, as used by Spaulding, is not "foster care" in the traditional meaning of the term, for it exists, in every case, only to facilitate adoption. The staff remain opposed to all forms of care which do not include clear goals or plans to limit its duration. As a result, their use of temporary care always takes the form of a specifically defined, short-term plan intended to be a firm step toward a permanent placement. That is, the children are always placed in temporary care with the intention that they will move toward a permanent living situation as soon as possible.

Temporary care at the agency is normally provided by experienced adoptive families who function as "bridge families" between the child's previous parents and his prospective adoptive family. Occasionally, temporary care is furnished by adoptive applicant families who have completed the agency's preparation process and demonstrate the capability to parent an older or handicapped child. No matter who provides the care, the progress of the children is closely monitored in a team effort between the temporary care family and the Spaulding staff. (For related information, see "Bridge Families," p. 222.)

THE THREE FUNCTIONS OF TEMPORARY CARE

At Spaulding, temporary care may serve three distinct functions. It may be "emergency," "diagnostic," or "facilitative" in nature. Emergency temporary care is used for the child who, for whatever reason, needs to be quickly removed from his most recent placement. Emergency temporary care is usually necessary because a child has to be removed before an adoptive family can be prepared to parent that child on a permanent basis. Such a move may be the result of a disrupting adoption in which another family (sometimes a family of the referring agency, sometimes a Spaulding family) is both unable to continue with the placement and unable to care for the child until an appropriate replacement family is found.[1] Removal may also occur from a rapidly deteriorating foster or group care placement. The opportunity to place a child with a competent and caring temporary family offers the staff valuable additional time to find and prepare a replacement family able to provide the child with permanent care.

The second use of temporary care at the agency is for "diagnostic" purposes. Such care, prior to adoptive placement, helps secure additional information about the child in those circumstances where the staff feel they must obtain a greater degree of understanding before they can

[1]For more information on disrupted adoptions, see "Coping With Disruption," p. 195.

hope to achieve an appropriate permanent placement. It is the experience of Spaulding workers that this form of temporary care often provides an indispensable opportunity for determining the child's true range of functioning within family, school, and neighborhood, and for gaining a clearer and more objective diagnostic picture of his mental, physical, or emotional problems.

Although both the "emergency" and "diagnostic" functions of temporary care facilitate adoption by improving the child's chances of being placed with a permanent family able to meet his specific needs, the Spaulding staff more specifically refer to their third use of temporary care as "facilitative." This term applies to those situations in which the purpose of the placement is not to fulfill emergency or diagnostic needs, but to help support and sustain the proposed adoption in other direct ways.

Facilitative temporary care is often undertaken in those cases where visits between child and family have progressed to the point where placement is the next logical step, but remaining legal problems or technical complications (such as working out an adoption subsidy) inhibit timely placement. To help maintain the momentum and the growing commitment between child and parent(s), the potential adoptive family may be licensed by the agency as a foster family to permit the child to be placed without unnecessary delay.

Similar arrangements may also be used in those cases where great geographic distance between the child and his prospective adoptive family makes the cost of a series of extended visits prohibitive. While this obstacle may be overcome by using a single visit spanning a weekend or several weekdays, such acceleration of placement preparation eliminates the process of gradual adjustment and invariably introduces a much greater risk of poor "fit" between child and family into the prospective adoption. To increase the placement's chances of success where distance is a factor, children and families who desire to do so are moved by the Spaulding staff directly from their initial visit into "foster care leading to adoption." In this way, none of the natural momentum of the developing relationship is lost, and the child and family are given the time they need, in a live-in 24-hour-a-day situation, to determine if they can become committed to living together on a permanent basis.

Such "foster care leading to adoption" has also been used for teenagers with complex mental or physical problems, or children whose life situations have been such that it is uncertain whether they are able to form adequate personal attachments. For these children, a living experience of considerably longer duration than traditional "visits" is often necessary to determine if they are willing or able to join an adoptive family. In these cases, facilitative temporary care serves as a means for determining if a family relationship can be achieved.

COMBINING THE FUNCTIONS OF TEMPORARY CARE

Although temporary care at Spaulding may be used for any of the three distinct purposes mentioned above, a temporary placement may be made for more than one purpose. In its most complete form, a temporary placement may begin as an emergency measure, and be continued, first, for diagnostic purposes, and then to facilitate an intended adoption. A child referred to the agency may, for example, need to be quickly removed from a previous placement and require initial emergency temporary care. The placement may be continued to answer specific questions about the child's functioning which arise during the emergency care.

Once answers are available or problems resolved, and a diagnosis made, the placement will most often continue uninterrupted until an appropriate family is found. The appropriateness of the family, as well as the choice of the most feasible type of living situation for that child, is determined by the information obtained during the "diagnostic" phase of the temporary placement.

In actuality, of course, there is no visible change in the family arrangement when a shift in the purpose of the temporary placement occurs. The change is primarily in the thinking of the placement staff: when the original purpose of the placement is fulfilled, the goal of the placement may change if other reasons exist for it to continue.

An example of the full use of temporary care at the agency is the case of 13 year old Marshall, who was referred to Spaulding soon after his first adoptive placement disrupted. Because Marshall was described by the adoptive family as "seriously emotionally disturbed" and the Spaulding worker who evaluated him felt his behavior was often inappropriate, the staff concluded they should not begin the process of placing him with another adoptive family until it could be determined if the previous family's observations were valid. Although the child needed to be moved into temporary care because of the family's inability to continue the placement, it was necessary to determine if he was as disturbed as reported, or if the family, instead, might have become worn out and angry in response to the intense, unresolved difficulties they were experiencing.

Marshall was placed with a temporary care family. After several months, family and staff decided that although he did have some deep emotional disturbances, he was still likely to benefit more from family living than from institutional placement. Once the answers to the staff's questions about Marshall were known, that placement began serving a facilitative function while an adoptive family was sought who could live with a child in need of professional counseling and whose day-to-day behavior was unpredictable. As often happens, it appears that the temporary care family may become his new adoptive family. This is not yet certain, however, for although the family has made an initial commitment to adoption, Marshall has not yet been able to do so.

The use here of Marshall's successful placement as an example is not meant to imply that "foster care leading to adoption" is an easy solution to the many problems of placing all older or handicapped children for adoption. As many problems may develop in this form of temporary placement as in adoptive placements, and workers must be prepared to provide full service to these placements whenever the need arises.

A significant number of these placements do not work out even after extensive efforts to provide complex post-placement service. One teenager, for example, was unable to become part of another family because she so desperately wanted to be with her biological mother. This desire existed even though it had been impossible for Becky's mother to give her the consistent care she needed when Becky was a young child. After an unsuccessful attempt to adjust to an adoptive placement, Becky, her social worker from the referring agency, and her Spaulding worker determined that she had developed enough self-sufficiency to enter a group care placement.

The lesson learned from the "foster care leading to adoption" placement was that Becky had such strong ties to her biological mother that adoption would not resolve her difficulties or be successful for her. As of this writing, Becky is doing well in her group care placement and has begun to re-establish contact with her mother after several years of separation.

MAKING TEMPORARY CARE WORK

Whether the purpose of temporary care within an adoption program is to meet an emergency, clarify a child's level of functioning, facilitate an adoptive placement, or any combination of these, temporary placements must be carefully planned, continuously controlled, and specifically goal-oriented if they are to be successful. If this is not done, significant problems will develop. Neither child, family, nor worker will know in which direction the child is moving, to what degree movement is occurring, or even if the child is ready to move on to adoption.

A major part of planning a temporary placement of any kind, and remaining aware of its progress, is forming a working partnership with the child and family. (The creation of a partnership with the family is described in more detail in "Preparing Families for Adoption," p.131.)

Forming a partnership with the child requires the establishment of mutual trust, yet in those cases where the child's history makes trust difficult or impossible to develop, the worker must still clearly explain to him why he is being placed in this type of setting. The child should understand how the "bridge" family can help his worker(s) know him better and assist him toward the next step in his life, whatever that may be. The attempt must always be made to help the child understand what is happening to him, how he feels about where he is, where he has been, and where he might be going. It is the experience of the Spaulding staff that a child will feel more positive toward a prospective "bridge" placement if he understands that none of his placement workers will ever try to dissuade him from maintaining ties with that family, even if he is adopted by someone else.

Spaulding's temporary care placements usually last no longer than six months, but it is the individual circumstances of each placement which determine the specific length of the temporary care. In some cases, placements have extended for more than six months while an active search continued for an appropriate replacement family. In other cases, when the child is ready for permanent placement in less than six months, he may be placed as soon as he is ready and the family is available. The agency does not maintain an extensive temporary care network. As of this writing, eight children are in temporary care status under Spaulding's auspices. Of those eight, seven are moving toward adoption.

Despite careful planning and continuous monitoring of placement progress, the determination of a child's readiness to leave temporary care is sometimes a very difficult decision. The "right" time for the child's move varies with the complexity of the child, the individual characteristics of the placement, and the worker's experience. It is the conviction of the Spaulding staff that the chances of an appropriate and timely decision being made (either to move the child or to continue to maintain him in temporary care) are greatly increased if the child and the "bridge" family help make that determination.

For such involvement to be possible, child and family must first agree upon, and work toward the achievement of, specific temporary placement goals. These goals most frequently involve extending the duration of the placement (from two weeks, to two months, to six months, for example) or gradually modifying the child's behavior by helping him meet first one and then another series of specific and mutually agreed-upon objectives.

Once placement goals are defined and plans for achievement set, the child and family must be allowed to determine the outcome of their temporary placement. In some cases, the child and family decide the child should be moved from the "bridge" family into a permanent placement. In other cases, where both agree, the temporary care family becomes the child's adoptive family. In neither case at Spaulding is there prolonged dispute between the family and the worker over the family's decision, for the agency's primary purpose is to place children into stable, permanent families. The Spaulding staff place high priority on helping children and families maintain already established relationships if they wish to do so. The existence of a mutual psychological attachment between child and family always takes priority over judgmental decisions workers may make concerning the appropriateness of a placement.

In some cases, the child and family will disagree over whether the placement should remain temporary or become permanent. However, it is the experience of the Spaulding staff that unresolved expectations between children and parents usually do not become extended disagreements. The staff have learned that these difficulties occur infrequently when all parties agree at the beginning of placement with what the purpose of the placement will be. Consequently, Spaulding workers go to great lengths to make sure temporary care families understand that their obligation to the child includes assisting him into another permanent placement whenever that is possible.

Occasionally, some children and families are not able to state clearly whether they desire to remain together as a permanent family. Often they are able to show their commitment only through subtle verbal communication and their behavior. As a result, workers may need to discuss the apparent meaning of these subtleties or behaviors with all members of the family in order to help parent(s) and child resolve the issue. If a child and family cannot decide whether the child should move on or remain where he is, it is the worker's responsibility to clarify the issues and help make the final decision (with team assistance when necessary) on behalf of the child's future. Frequently, it is the worker's knowledge of the participants and the nature of their placement which makes it possible for the child and family to move toward the type of placement which is actually desired.

Although the worker who places the child may hope the "bridge" family becomes the child's permanent family, those hopes must always be held in realistic restraint in case the parent(s) and/or child decide against adoption. The child or family who agrees to temporary care cannot be faulted for fulfilling their original agreement, and each, for the sake of all involved, should receive the worker's full support.

Although temporary care leading to adoption is not always successful, high-level commitment and hard work by the placement staff can result in eventual permanency for some children who would not achieve that goal unless this form of service had been made available to them. As a result of such planning, some of these children have entered into more secure and confident adoptive placements because both the child and family have been given the opportunity to communicate to each other, through either words or behavior, that "this is my family" or "this is my place."

SUMMARY

Despite their opposition to the use of traditional forms of foster care for children who are legally free for adoption, the Spaulding staff have found that temporary care, if used appropriately, can significantly improve the adoption prospects of some of the children referred to them for permanent placement.

At Spaulding, temporary care always takes the form of a specifically defined, short-term plan intended to be a firm step toward a permanent placement. It may be used for children in need of emergency placement or to help the staff arrive at a better diagnostic understanding of the child. Temporary care may also be used to facilitate a permanent placement in other ways, especially as a form of "foster care leading to adoption" in cases where great geographic distance between child and family makes the cost of a series of pre-placement visits prohibitive or where children have complex mental, physical, or emotional problems.

Whether the purpose of temporary care is to meet an emergency, clarify a child's level of functioning, facilitate a permanent placement, or any combination of these, temporary placements must be carefully planned, continuously controlled, and specifically goal-oriented if they are to be successful.

The Children Spaulding Does Not Place

9

Although the Spaulding staff find permanent families for most of the children other programs seek to refer to them for placement, some exceptions do occur. The children Spaulding does not place fall into three categories. There are, first of all, those children whose referrals are refused even before an in-person evaluation is made because they are not the kinds of children Spaulding was established to place. A second category of referrals is not accepted because of information obtained about the children during their evaluation. The final category includes those few children whose referrals are accepted, but for whom no adoptive family is found.

CHILDREN NOT ACCEPTED FOR EVALUATION

There are certain kinds of children for whom the agency will not accept referrals. These are the children who the Spaulding staff believe can be successfully placed for adoption without their services. They include those who are young and healthy and for whom families are already available on waiting lists within other placement programs as well as those who have mild physical, mental, or emotional handicaps and for whom the staff believe the referring programs have or could possibly develop appropriate adoptive placement possibilities. Spaulding workers encourage all other programs to place these children themselves. When this is not possible, they may also suggest that the child be referred to another program that has been able to place similar children.

Although the agency does not accept these referrals, the staff view it as advantageous for other workers to make such referrals. The initiation of the referral process not only provides workers in other programs with repeated opportunities to learn of the relative ease of the placement in question, but to take advantage of frequent suggestions to begin considering the possibility that they may already have applicants capable of parenting many of their available children.

CHILDREN NOT ACCEPTED AFTER EVALUATION

Every referral that is accepted for evaluation is assigned by the Spaulding staff to one of their workers for an evaluation work-up.[1] These choices are team decisions and are based upon worker expertise, current caseload responsibilities and diversity, geographic location of the child, and, with out-of-state placements, worker knowledge of the adoption and child welfare system of that state or province.

Usually the worker assigned to the child feels confident as the evaluation proceeds that the child is an appropriate referral. In these cases, the worker who completes the work-up can make the decision to accept the child for referral. However, if the worker has substantial reservations about a referral or believes the referral is clearly inappropriate, acceptance or refusal must be a team decision. In other words, an individual worker can accept, but cannot reject, a referral. This is in keeping with Spaulding's desire to provide every consideration to the children who have the most difficulty being adopted.

A number of factors, considered together, are used by the Spaulding staff in determining if a child will be accepted for referral responsibility. This decision depends, first, on the staff's assessment of the child's ability to benefit from placement. The child who is so severely damaged that he lacks a sense of awareness of himself and his surroundings will probably not benefit from a change of placement and, therefore, will not usually be accepted for placement.

Likewise, the referral of the child who already appears to be in his best possible placement will not usually be accepted. Although a few of these children live in an institutional setting, they are more typi-

---

[1]An on-site visit to evaluate the child is negotiated between Spaulding and the referring program, with the cost borne by the referring program. Under the agency's purchase of service fee system, this is the only cost "risked" by the referring program (For further information on Purchase of Service, see p. 9). The cost of most on-site visits varies between $50 and $200, which includes round-trip transportation, food, and lodging for the Spaulding worker. Many referring agencies and courts use the worker's time to provide informal in-service training in addition to completing the evaluation of the child, a process which Spaulding for Children encourages.

cally children in long-term family foster care who appear to have adjusted well and to have developed strong ties to their foster home.

Some children who have complex or severe emotional or physical handicaps may have made a tenuous but positive adjustment in their present placement and may be too vulnerable to move. Uprooting such children often produces emotional trauma too severe to merit even a move to the best possible adoptive family. However, if the foster family cannot or will not adopt, and if the Spaulding staff determine that the child can survive the move and make an attachment to an adoptive family, the referral will often be accepted. Under such circumstances, adoption is viewed as a more desirable placement because the staff believe foster relationships are more likely to disrupt under stress.

The decision to accept a referral also depends upon the workers' shared perception of whether the child is likely to be placed by the referring agency or court within a reasonable period of time. The time period considered reasonable differs for each child, but is viewed by the Spaulding staff as the time after which the child seems unwilling or unable (for whatever reason, including attachment to his temporary family) to form new parental attachments. The estimate of this time period is based upon information gathered from the child, his caretakers, and his teachers. Workers compare this information with what they already know about the child's fears, concerns, and feelings toward his current placement and toward adoption.

In addition, the decision to accept a referral depends, in large measure, upon the team's knowledge of the immediate availability of prospective adoptive families for the child. This decision is based upon the staff's experience in finding families for older and handicapped children. If the possibility appears extremely limited that a family can be found and prepared to adopt that child within a reasonable time, the agency may not accept the referral, at that time but instead place that child on a waiting list for possible placement in the future. This decision is not usually made, however, without an evaluation of the individual child and his situation.

The staff's decision to accept a referral may partially depend, too, upon the location of the child being referred to them for placement. If the distance is so great that the Spaulding worker cannot be sure that the child will be provided with necessary pre-placement services, or if his distance from a prospective family would prevent the vital series of visits that both the child and family require, the agency may consider rejecting the referral. However, geography is never the sole factor in the rejection of a referral. It is only in the extraordinary case that extreme distance, the complexity of the child's problems, and the potential difficulty of family recruitment combine to make placement appear impossible and acceptance of the referral unrealistic.

The ability of the Spaulding staff to find appropriate, capable adoptive parents for specific kinds of children and, therefore, the decision to accept the referrals of those children, depends to a limited extent upon the attitudes of the communities in which families are sought. Although the staff is sensitive to the readiness of the community to accept the child they would seek to place there, community acceptance and support are never the most important factors in the decision not to place a child.

Finally, on rare occasions, Spaulding workers may be so heavily scheduled that it is impractical for them to immediately accept the referral of a child whose placement is anticipated to be especially time-consuming. As a result, it has sometimes been necessary to delay a child's evaluation. Despite the staff's small size and the extensive demands of post-placement services, such delays are infrequent and short-lived.

Although the Spaulding workers consider only a few children to be absolutely unadoptable, they realize that even putting into practice the belief that almost all children are adoptable if enough staff time is available is an unrealistic goal. Some children will not benefit sufficiently from adoptive placement to warrant the unusual effort that placement would require. In addition, such extraordinarily time-consuming efforts would severely limit the service a worker could provide to other children. Without objective decisions concerning effects on overall service, an entire adoption program could hypothetically dedicate itself to placing one or two children with no assurance that it could find appropriate families or maintain the children in those families. With this in mind, the Spaulding staff try to find the middle ground of working with children who have no other options for placement while simultaneously challenging other welfare programs to place children with lesser handicaps.

If, after lengthy debate, the workers decide not to accept a referral, they tailor a response to fit the referring agency or court. This response explains the reasons for the agency's decision, describes the major problems seen in the child's future which must be dealt with, and offers assistance in making the most appropriate plan for the child's future. This response is presented in both written and verbal form, for the staff recognize that verbal messages alone often get distorted despite best efforts to the contrary.

OTHER CHILDREN NOT PLACED

In addition to the children who are not placed because their referrals are considered inappropriate, there are some children who are not placed because the staff are unable to find adoptive families for them. Some of the children in this latter category are those whose referrals have been conditionally accepted without an on-site evaluation, usually because the child's distance from the agency has made an on-site evaluation impossible or impractical. These children are, in fact, children who would have been considered too seriously damaged to benefit from adoptive placement had they been evaluated by a Spaulding worker prior to referral. However, since the staff have begun to refuse referrals in those cases where an on-site evaluation cannot be made, the number of children accepted for placement but not placed has diminished greatly.

The rest of the children who have been accepted for referral but who have remained unplaced tend to be those who workers have grown to believe either would not benefit from adoptive placement or could not be placed. Without question, failure to place these children has been due to lack of worker commitment and the team's failure to detect and remedy this deficiency. Realizing this, the staff are now more keenly aware that they must help each other build and maintain high levels of commitment to all children accepted for placement.

While most handicapped children are appealing to at least some families, several children with severe multiple handicaps have not been placed because families could not be found who were willing to adopt them. An example of such a child is a 14 year old boy referred to the agency in 1971. He was a trainably retarded child (functioning on a first grade level), poorly coordinated, and small for his age. He blinked frequently, had a head twitch, speech defect, and an explosive temper. Spaulding was never able to find him a family.

AN OVERVIEW

Accurate records of the three categories of children Spaulding does not place are not available. No records have been kept of the children who have not been accepted for placement because their referrals were considered inappropriate. The most recent (1976) total caseload information available does offer, however, an interesting picture of those children whose referrals have been accepted by the agency staff. During the past several years, approximately 50 percent of the children referred have been placed or are in the process of being placed. Another 25 percent have been placed by workers in other agencies and courts. The remaining 25 percent have not been placed within six months of their referral. There is no way to predict how, when, or even if the Spaulding staff will be able to find appropriate adoptive families for the children in this last group. The effort, however, continues.

SUMMARY

The Spaulding staff do not find adoptive families for all of the children other programs seek to refer to them for placement. Some referrals are not accepted because the staff believe these children can be placed for adoption without their services. Those in this category include young and healthy children as well as those who have mild physical, mental, or emotional handicaps. Other referrals are found to be inappropriate, and are rejected only after the child's evaluation has been completed. The factors which, when considered together, could lead to the refusal of a referral in these cases include decisions that the child will not benefit from a change in placement, that the possibility of finding and preparing a family to adopt that child within a reasonable period of time is extremely limited, and that the child is too far from the agency to receive adequate pre-placement preparation. Finally, some children are not placed because the staff are unable to find them adoptive families. These have included children whose referrals have been conditionally accepted without an on-site evaluation and those who have remained unplaced due to lack of worker commitment.

Of all the children accepted for referral, 50 percent are placed by the Spaulding staff and 25 percent are placed by workers in other agencies and courts. The remaining 25 percent are not placed within six months of their referral. While it is obvious that Spaulding's approach to adoption will never guarantee that all of the children referred will be placed, the agency's approach does offer many older and handicapped children their greatest opportunity for adoption.

Working With Families

10

Finding Families for Children

Spaulding for Children's work with families consists of four primary activities. These are finding families for adoptable children, preparing them for adoptive placement, maintaining children in these families after placement, and working to replace the child with another adoptive family should the adoption disrupt. Each activity will be discussed in the following four chapters. A review of the agency's two major approaches for finding families will be discussed in this chapter.

The Spaulding staff use two distinctively different approaches to finding families for children. The first consists of an on-going program of community education aimed at providing general adoption information to the public. While these efforts do reach some families who plan to adopt, this technique is not the agency's most efficient means of locating families for children in need of adoptive placement. The second approach consists of carefully planned publicity efforts designed to interest families in specific children. This approach is referred to by the agency's workers as "individual family finding."

Both "community education" and "individual family finding" have been used by the agency since it began operation, and both remain in use today. Each approach can inform the public about adoption, attract applicants for adoption, and promote the agency's philosophy. As will be described in greater detail, each approach is now used to achieve different but supplementary goals in the overall process of finding families for children.

COMMUNITY EDUCATION

Part of the agency's effort in community education is directed toward informing the public of current adoption trends. The public needs to know which children are currently available and what expectations, procedures, and requirements are to be found in each adoption program. The community must be helped to accept new adoptive families and to change the prevailing concept of adoption, i.e., that it is an activity which occurs only when infertile couples decide to parent a healthy, young "orphan."

Early Attempts to Find Families for Children

The agency did not always differentiate between "community education" and "individual family finding" as clearly as it does now. When Spaulding first began its operation, its contacts with the public were aimed at meeting two separate needs. First, the staff were convinced that many families were interested in adopting children traditionally seen as hard-to-place or unadoptable. In an effort to prove this, the staff needed a means to locate and attract these families. Second, they needed to develop a broader reputation and make the public aware of their existence. Early in the agency's history, community education and individual family finding were used to achieve both of these goals.

The earliest Spaulding recruitment effort occurred in September, 1968, only several months after the agency was established. A general newspaper article describing the agency was circulated in *The Detroit News.* An inquiry meeting open to the general public followed. The article contained a description of Spaulding's non-traditional methods and premises and was supplemented by a "Child is Waiting" column about a Spaulding child which described an attractive little girl needing adoption. Over four-hundred calls from potential applicants were received. Spaulding volunteers called or corresponded with each family and offered transportation and baby-sitting arrangements prior to the actual meeting held on a Sunday afternoon in *The Detroit News* — WWJ auditorium.

However, the agency's naive use of publicity also created several serious problems. The unexpectedly large number of applications received was initially extremely gratifying (110 applications following this one meeting). Although serious community interest on a large scale had been anticipated, it could now be validated. Large numbers of people existed who would immediately respond to the efforts of an agency described as not having traditional rules, but able to humanize its appeal for parents.

Despite the amount of work ahead of them, the Spaulding staff set out to respond to all applicants as quickly as possible. Applications were handled in chronological order and assigned a "proceed" or "no proceed" designation. Explanatory letters were sent to those families who expressed interest in the kind of children the agency would not have available, thus reducing the applicants by about half.

The Spaulding staff then began the task of working with the remaining applicants. However, despite their best intentions, they could not adequately handle the response, for the staff consisted at that time of the Director and one part-time social worker. The resulting delays in processing the applications produced frustration and resentment on the part of families.

The staff noted, too, that applicants who were genuinely interested in adopting hard-to-place children frequently focused their interest immediately upon a specific child or a narrow group of children. Many of these applicants could successfully adopt other children, but their early focus prevented many of them from ever becomeing interested in a wide variety of children.

The experience of the Detroit meeting taught the staff several valuable lessons. First, they recognized the need to retain manageable control over the flow of applicant families. It was clear that the agency could not continue to respond to well over 100 applicants each time they sought families. However, the lesson was not that newspaper publicity should never be tried again, or that the agency should wait until it had the ability to handle almost unlimited responses. Instead, the Spaulding staff concluded that they needed to refine their use of this method for finding families. They needed to learn which children needed to be publicized and which did not, what information needed to be conveyed in articles about children available for adoption, what newspapers to use, and which circulation areas were most productive. The staff also needed to learn when to seek families and how to develop a response system which could efficiently handle the inquiries of all interested applicants.

Second, the experience of the 1968 Detroit meeting taught the staff the early lesson that people do not always accurately perceive the information they are given. Numerous inquiries concerning applicant status arrived at the agency for many months from families who had been interested in the kinds of children the agency would not have available; from families to whom the staff had sent clearly written "no proceed" letters of explanation. Consequently, the staff realized that even careful consideration to clarity in such letters sometimes does not produce the intended result. They learned to repeat important points of information as well as to check frequently to determine with what understanding that information was being received.

Finally, on the basis of the 1968 experience, the Spaulding staff recognized the necessity of speed in responding to potential applicants. In spite of the rapid response with which the workers had tried to reply, even a delay of only several weeks had been long enough, in some cases, to seriously dampen the enthusiasm of some families. While delaying tactics may be considered by some agencies or courts to be an effective method of controlling caseloads or testing applicant interest, adoption programs attempting to offer older and handicapped children their greatest chance at adoption will do only harm by arbitrarily eliminating or discouraging the interest and enthusiasm of any potentially appropriate applicants.

As a result of these experiences, the Spaulding staff gradually modified their recruitment program and learned to appropriately limit their use of community education in finding families. After almost two years of improving their techniques of presenting adoption information to the public, the staff, then consisting of three full-time and part-time social workers, were able to begin attracting an ever-increasing percentage of applicants seriously interested in adopting older and handicapped children. Between one-quarter and one-third of the families who attend Spaulding's information meetings are appropriate applicants. Approximately one quarter of these appropriate applicants (or one in 12 to 16 of those who originally express an interest in adoption to the Spaulding staff) actually adopt a Spaulding child.

Educating Families Seeking Young Healthy Children

During the early 1970's, the Spaulding staff also began to receive requests for information from an entirely different kind of applicant. Early in their history, the staff had been primarily seeing applicant families who were interested in the older or handicapped child in which the agency specialized. Within a few years, however, a new influx of families, discouraged by long waiting lists in other agencies but still desperately searching for healthy young children to adopt, began contacting Spaulding.

Although the staff was not placing the healthy young children many of these applicants were seeking, the agency was receiving enough inquiries about these children that by 1971 the staff decided to expand their informational services for all interested prospective families. The decision to make this commitment evolved, first, out of the belief that the public had a right to know what was actually happening in the field of adoption, and second, out of the conviction that adoptive applicants require a degree of sophistication and assertiveness in order to pass through the adoption process successfully. The problem facing the Spaulding staff was compounded because other adoption programs in Michigan had not yet developed an adequate means of responding to the growing numbers of potential applicants and vast numbers of prospective parents who were searching for adoptable children. At that time, most other adoption programs were not yet willing to talk frankly with these frustrated but still waiting applicants.

Most adoption programs were focusing on decreasing the size of their applicant groups rather than increasing the number of potential adopters. Instead of more clearly informing the public about how adoption was evolving and what kinds of children were available, many programs developed self-defeating policies which offered little information to potential adopters and which increased the public's rage at the programs themselves. The public saw these agencies delivering the double messages of "children need families" and "our intake is closed." In response to this problem, the Spaulding staff were determined to provide opportunities for honest information about existing alternatives in adoption; to offer families enough information so they could informatively choose between older and handicapped children, long waiting lists, or giving up the idea of adoption.

The staff also realized that many families who had finished Spaulding's general preparation process for adopting older and handicapped children had been waiting for a child for over a year. Some were still waiting for younger and less handicapped children to be referred to the agency. The Spaulding staff gradually became aware, for the first time, that some of these families were actually resisting the opportunity to adopt the kinds of children in whom they said they were seriously interested. In contrast to outwardly expressed (and sometimes sincere) interest, these families were actually still hoping to adopt younger or less handicapped children. In looking for a solution to these problems, the Spaulding staff considered three alternatives. They could recruit children from other adoption programs (the kinds of children these families were actually seeking), they could suggest that families wait until the kind of children they were seeking were referred to Spaulding, or they could stop working with families interested only in relatively younger and less handicapped children.

The staff concluded that it was not reasonable to attempt to recruit the kinds of children other agencies were already placing, since agencies could not be expected to pay Spaulding's purchase of service fee to do something they could do themselves. As a result of their considerations, the staff decided that their primary responsibility was to the children who had been referred to them and who would not otherwise be placed. The staff reaffirmed an earlier belief, which had now been put to the test, that it was not their responsibility to find children for families, no matter how fine the families were or how willing they were to wait.

The implications of this decision on Spaulding's approach to finding families were enormous. Families were to be sought only for those children considered hard-to-place by Spaulding's standards who were actually or potentially available to the agency. No longer would the needs of any family applying to adopt be given priority over the needs of any child referred to them for placement. From then on, applicants would be told they could not expect the staff to meet their requests for young or mildly handicapped children. They would also be told not to expect to adopt from Spaulding unless they were willing to adopt the children who were available.

Adoption Inquiry Meetings

As a result of their decision to find families for children, the staff were faced with the need to find a method to expand their informational services to all families interested in adoption while simultaneously attracting adequate numbers of families who could be appropriate parents for the children who were referred to the agency. These children were those who were older at the time of referral than children previously referred, and those with more severe handicaps.

This situation led the Spaulding staff to significantly modify their adoption inquiry meetings to meet these needs. At that time, the agency's staff had also recognized that information offered at their inquiry meetings was being presented in an inconsistent way. As a result of worker oversight or boredom at presenting the same information time after time, some content would be forgotten at each meeting. Spaulding's solution to this problem was to develop written materials in the form of an outline to be used by workers. The staff also decided they should share responsibility for information given by assigning a team of two workers to each meeting. Each was to compliment the presentation of the other in the hope that all necessary and appropriate information concerning what people needed to know to make the right kind of decisions about adoption would be delivered.

Plans to improve inquiry meetings also called for the development of a means to more adequately answer the kinds of adoption questions Spaulding workers were now frequently receiving. In an effort to also find a way to present introductory adoption information to families in the most economical way, and to ensure that families interested in adopting older and handicapped children received further information, the staff developed a series of two distinctly different adoption information meetings.

The first of Spaulding's two adoption information meetings was a Public Adoption Meeting (PAM) which was usually held on the first Sunday afternoon of each month. The purpose of the PAM was to share general information regarding the legal and social aspects of adoption, the existing myths about adoption practice, the kinds of children currently available, and the kinds of services provided by Spaulding. Those attending were also told about the Spaulding Adoption Meeting (SAM), usually held ten days later on a Wednesday evening. This meeting was provided for people interested in learning more specific information about the agency's philosophy, its methods of working with other placement programs, and the kinds of children placed by its staff.

Wishing to make adoption information as accessible as possible, the Spaulding staff initially held their meetings in the geographic area most convenient to those people who had inquired. Gradually, however, the repeated use of newspaper publicity in *The Detroit News* narrowed the area from which they drew most of their inquiries to Southeastern Michigan, the most populated area of the state. Eventually, as the placement and training commitments of the staff continued to increase, one worker again began to handle the content of each inquiry meeting.

At first the agency separated PAM and SAM sessions. In time, however, the workers leading these meetings began to complain of the awkwardness of this format. Three problems existed. First, it had become increasingly difficult to contain the information discussed to the appropriate meeting. In many cases, families attending Public Adoption Meetings were asking questions which related specifically to Spaulding. Likewise, many attending Spaulding Adoption Meetings were asking for clarification of basic adoption information and issues. Second, although most families who inquired about adoption information were usually directed to a PAM and SAM, a steadily decreasing number actually attended the Spaulding Adoption Meeting. This occurred as the public became more knowledgeable about the kinds of children Spaulding placed, and fewer families interested in younger or less handicapped children attended SAM's. Third, the staff found themselves in the middle of a poorly designed intake process. Families entered Spaulding's information-giving preparation approach to adoption following a judgment by either the case-aide secretary or a placement worker as to how much basic adoption information they knew and understood. With more than one set of standards being used to define the degree of adoption information possessed by inquiring families, there often was an inappropriately wide range of knowledge present at both PAMs and SAMs. As a result, it was frequently discovered during a family's subsequent individual preparation for adoption that there were major gaps in the information that family needed in order to decide if they were capable of parenting an older or handicapped child. When this occurred, the intended efficiency of inquiry meetings was lost, for a worker had to spend additional time providing the missing information.

By early 1972, Spaulding workers had identified that the difficulty of separating Public Adoption Meeting and Spaulding Adoption Meeting material created a major obstacle to their ability to adequately prepare applicants for adoption. Due to these difficulties, the staff decided to combine the meetings into SPAM, (the Spaulding Public Adoption Meeting). The outline used for conducting SPAM was devised by combining the outlines of the two separate meetings.[1] Although the content of the Spaulding Public Adoption Meeting has since been informally revised, changes in Michigan's adoption law and the increasing level of the public's awareness of adoption problems and methods have underscored the agency's need to make periodic formal revisions.

At the Spaulding Public Adoption Meetings, the presentations are informal and questions and discussions are encouraged. The worker shares general information regarding the legal and social aspects of adoption, the kinds of children currently available, and the services offered by the agency. The worker also provides specific information about Spaulding's philosophy, specific methods of working with parents and other placement programs, and children being placed by the agency. Responsibility for conducting these meetings rotates among the placement staff.

Workers no longer provide descriptions of children actually available for adoption to those who attend inquiry meetings. Instead, the staff discuss the children they have most recently placed. In this way, the problem of families focusing too early on specific children and becoming disappointed because these children are not still available when the family finishes their general preparation process is eliminated.

Another reason for combining PAM and SAM was the agency's growing commitment to help establish a system of general public adoption education with other local placement programs. Throughout its history, Spaulding has sought to work closely with other placement programs to find permanent families for children by providing adoption information to the public. The Spaulding staff hoped that initial agency interactions would eventually evolve to broaden each available child's opportunities for adoption by enabling each program to "pool" its resources and share staff, families, and children. Such a relationship has never materialized, however, because of basic differences in the kinds of children placed and in the philosophy and methods used by each program in its work with children.

Other Current Methods in Community Education

In addition to their regularly scheduled inquiry meetings, the Spaulding staff use a variety of other media efforts to promote adoption and find families. These have included television, radio, magazines, newspapers, and pamphlets. Panel discussions, interviews, and question-and-answer sessions with questions submitted by viewers or listeners have been presented on television and radio. Participants have included staff,

---

[1]Comprehensive topical outlines for workers to use when presenting adoption information can be found in Appendix C, pp. 349-362.

Board members, adoptive parents, and children either available for adoption or already adopted. Information about the agency, its specific approach to adoption, and its reaction to adoption-related issues has appeared in magazines, books, and newspapers. The staff also fill speaking engagements for community clubs or groups as a way to promote adoption, for they know such discussions significantly improve the probability that children will be adopted and will enter a community that is prepared to understand the unique situation they bring with them.

The agency at one time also presented adoption information to the public through the activities of a Speaker's Bureau. This group, which was organized in 1971 and remained active for two years, consisted of a small number of community volunteers who would show a prepared slide-talk describing the agency and its operation. The essential purpose of this activity was to raise funds to support the agency, but community education was chosen as the means to achieve this goal because information presented would also do much to help prepare communities for these new kinds of adoptive families.

Finally, large amounts of important information have been steadily spread by word-of-mouth. As more and more parents adopted from Spaulding, increasing quantities of both general and specific information about adoption, the agency, the children available, and the way Spaulding worked with families found its way into the community. General newspaper articles, continuous parent group support, and a great deal of discussion between agency staff, parents, and professionals have also helped the agency attract many appropriate families.

INDIVIDUAL FAMILY FINDING

Adoption programs actively committed to placing older and handicapped children must sometimes recruit parents for individual children. Although inquiry meetings provide a valuable public service to those who contact the agency for adoption information, Spaulding's experience has shown that these general information meetings are not the most effective technique for finding appropriate families to adopt specific waiting children.

On the basis of their early recruitment and community education efforts, the staff have learned that persuading capable families to respond to older and handicapped children is not a major problem. The problem has been, rather, to keep from becoming deluged by responses to publicity about available children. Methods of community education do attract many appropriate families, but they also result in many inquiries (and applications) from people who are not truly interested in or capable of parenting children who are placed by Spaulding.

All adoption programs need a means of attracting applicants which offers broad information but limits applicants to those people seeking the kinds of children who are available. Without such means, adoption programs must be willing to spend time working with applicants who desire the kinds of children who are seldom, if ever, available.

Because of Spaulding's small size and specialized focus on older and handicapped children, its placement workers have tried to gain control of the level of public response by refining their publicity efforts so that the number of families who respond, and who eventually adopt one of the children referred to the agency, is sufficient without becoming unmanageably large. The staff have recognized that successful control of applicant response is essential if their placement program is to be effective.

As the agency's staff learned to distinguish factors which raised the percentage of appropriate applicants and to use the mass media effectively, individualized publicity became the most efficient means of attracting appropriate families when more applicants were needed. As a result, individual publicity efforts are now used more extensively than more general community education approaches.

This does not imply that individualized publicity efforts always provide the Spaulding staff with as many appropriate families as are needed for all available chilalen. No approach to finding families is that effective. It has been their experience, however, that individualized publicity has been the most effective means found to date of attracting sufficient potential adoptive families, and of reducing the number of applicants looking for the kinds of children who are either not placed by the agency or not currently available for adoption.

Spaulding workers have also been able to control applicant response by honestly publicizing and personally explaining to potential adoptive families the responsibilities, problems, stresses, and rewards which accompany such adoptions. In this way, staff do all they can to help applicant families decide, in an informed manner, whether adoption in general, and a Spaulding adoption in particular, is right for them.

Although public adoption meetings are still used on a regular basis, this generalized intake process has so far contributed comparatively few adoptive families to the number who eventually choose to parent a Spaulding child. As individual family finding (often also called "publicizing") has become more effective for finding appropriate families, the use of community education techniques has continued, but more as a community service than as a direct recruitment device.

Newspaper Publicity

Finding families means actively seeking parents for children. It does not mean sitting and waiting for parents to "walk through the door."

Regularly scheduled radio or television shows, each focusing on an individual child, a group of brothers and sisters, or even several unrelated available children, have been used effectively for individual family finding by other agencies. However, the Spaulding staff have found that their most effective technique in finding families for children is to use newspaper publicity that gives the public accurate and specific information about individual children available for adoption.

Since its establishment, the agency has used the columns of three Michigan papers. The most frequently used has been "A Child is Waiting," by Ruth Carlton, which appears each Sunday in the *The Detroit News* and is the only weekly adoption column in Michigan. The other two columns are "He's (She's) Adoptable," originally by Judy Hartzell and later by others in *The Ann Arbor News,* and a bi-weekly column by Arn Shackleford in *The Grand Rapids Press.*

The following are examples of actual newspaper descriptions of older and handicapped children subsequently placed for adoption by the Spaulding staff.

A child is waiting

Shirley needs loving parents

Shirley, a tiny 8-year-old with huge problems.

By RUTH CARLTON
Accent Metro Editor

Shirley is a tiny 8-year-old with cerebral palsy in both arms and legs.

Because it was thought she would be extremely retarded, she was put in a nursing home when she was 3 and stayed there until she was 7. Then someone discovered she was too bright to belong there, so she was moved to a foster home.

During her one year in the foster home she has made fabulous progress. It is now certain that she is educable.

This spring she was fitted with long leg braces and within a few weeks she was walking — with the help of a walker on rollers. She is tremendously excited about this. As a result her arms, knees and back are becoming much stronger.

The social worker says Shirley's biggest problem is not her physical handicap but her emotional problems.

"You have to realize she wasted half her life in a nursing home. There she was waited on rather than taught to do everything possible for herself."

IN THE ONE YEAR in a foster home she has learned to dress herself except for shoes, to make her bed while lying in it. She can pull herself onto the bed, go to the bathroom alone. She has learned how to fall so she doesn't hurt herself, and she can get back up alone.

Her biggest problems come from being deprived of a mother, the social worker says. In the nursing home there were so many adults taking care of her that Shirley responds with equal affection to everyone. She has never learned any special relationship to one person, never realized what a mother is.

She is also a stubborn child. The therapist who works with Shirley on exercises says she usually works very hard. But on a stubborn day she will do nothing.

Shirley needs to be adopted by parents who are emotionally very strong, yet very loving and warm. Shirley will qualify for medical subsidy, to pay all medical expenses, and probably for child support subsidy as well.

THE MOST IMPORTANT thing she needs is parents strong enough that they will not be manipulated, and patient enough to give a stunted personality time to recover.

If you think you qualify, and would enjoy nourishing this little girl so she can develop to her full potential, whatever that may be, call Sue Schrocn at Spaulding for Children, 1-475-2500, or write her at Spaulding for Children, 3660 Waltrous Road, Chelsea, Mich., 48118.

A Child Is Waiting appears every week in the Accent on Living section of The Sunday News and every Monday on News-4, WWJ-TV, at 12:30 p.m.

30 want to adopt Sharon, who is 9

Thirty calls came in to Lutheran Social Services last week asking to adopt Sharon, the pretty 9-year-old girl featured in A Child Is Waiting last Sunday.

The agency is setting up a series of group meetings for the applicants in the near future.

Lutheran Social Services is one of nine agencies in the metropolitan area which banded together two months ago to study adoptive homes for any child anywhere in Michigan who is waiting for adoption.

An Upper Peninsula agency, for instance, might have a 12-year-old boy for whom they are unable to find a home. At their request The Sunday News would feature him in A Child Is Waiting.

Then one of the nine agencies would accept the applications, carry through the adoption study, place the boy in his new home and continue to help the family through the long adjustment period, just as long as the family wants help.

Anyone wishing to refer a child for a home search may call Maureen Shea, chairman of the nine-agency pool, at 313 TU 3-2100, or write her at Catholic Social Services, 9851 Hamilton, Detroit 48202.

Reprinted From The Detroit News

At 4, personable Suzy enjoys being a helper

A child is waiting

Suzy is a well behaved little girl who enjoys being a helper.

By RUTH CARLTON
Accent Metro Editor

Suzy is the princess of the hospital ward — a gay, flirtatious 4 year old who has something to say to everyone and enjoys making people laugh.

She's also the big helper. In a children's convalescent ward where everyone else comes for a short stay and returns home, Suzy is the old settler.

She gets drinks of water for other kids, helps them with puzzles, ties their shoes and calls the nurse for them.

THE HOSPITAL is Suzy's home; she's lived here all her four years.

She was born with abnormalities that made it necessary to remove her bladder and rectum and create two artificial openings in her abdomen for elimination. She wears two bags attached to her skin.

Soon she can be taught to change these bags herself; this will make it possible for her to attend regular school. Now she attends a school for crippled children.

Suzy also was born with club feet and wears special shoes during the day and sleeps in a brace to make her feet turn in.

Spaulding for Children is looking for a home for Suzy.

"UNTIL I met Suzy I was terribly depressed about her," the social worker says. "But she has so much personality, you can't see her as handicapped.

"Also I met the mother of a child who has this same medical condition. This woman said, 'Once you get used to the idea of the collection bags, and changing them, you find it is not that bad. It's just getting used to the idea.'"

Spaulding, which has found adoptive homes for children without legs, or blind, or deaf, or brain damaged, can understand this mother who adds:

"My daughter is now 10 years old and she doesn't feel handicapped at all."

THE SOCIAL worker thinks Suzy's biggest problem in adjusting will be not having 40 people around at all times. She has never been in a normal home. And the idea of a special relationship to parents is totally foreign. Dozens of adults have cared for Suzy and accepted her affection.

Spaulding for Children, a specialized adoption agency serving only handicapped or older children, is looking for parents for Suzy. Call Sue Schroen at 1-475-2500 or write her at 3660 Waltrous Road, Chelsea, Mich. 48118.

Crippled Children's Commission can pay the full cost of Suzy's medical care when she is adopted.

A Child Is Waiting started in The Sunday News Aug. 18, 1968 and for seven years has appeared regularly in the Accent on Living Section and on News-4, WWJ-TV, at 12:30 p.m. every Monday.

2 homes ask for little, blond Pam

Catholic Social Services had two homes ask to adopt 7-year-old Pam, the beautiful little blond pictured here last Sunday. Pam has cerebral palsy and is totally dependent.

Both of the applicants have a realistic view of the work and patience involved in such an adoption. A single woman who applied has worked with handicapped persons including cerebral palsy victims. The couple who asked to adopt this little girl have a 5-year-old handicapped child and feel what they have learned in these five years could also help Pam.

Maureen Shea is head of adoption for Catholic Social Services.

Reprinted From The Detroit News

'For right family, a great kid'

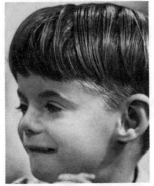

WHEN HE MEETS a stranger, Martin picks up very clearly the message of whether he's acceptable.

By RUTH CARLTON
Accent Metro Editor

Martin is 8 years old but about the size of a 5 year old.

"His looks really put some people off," the social worker says. Yet he has no real physical deformities . . . just an unusual face. He has had eye surgery and has only partial vision in one eye. Otherwise he is physically healthy.

A broken adoption left Martin with a lot of unhappiness, and as a result he is not trusting of either adults or peers.

"He is very stiff, rigid," the social worker says. "When you touch him, you have the feeling of touching a board rather than a child."

Martin is behind in school and the teachers find him a very wearing child.

MANY ADULTS try not to look at him because it makes them uncomfortable. Martin is very aware of this. When he knows people are uncomfortable, he aggravates the situation with facial contortions, ticks and squints.

Spaulding for Children is now looking for adoptive parents for Martin.

"Maybe because Spaulding has placed children with all kinds of physical handicaps, I was not put off by his looks," the social worker says. "I liked him and found him very spontaneous, very verbal. From what I saw that day you would not guess he was slow. But he is. We just don't know how slow."

He can add and subtract and count up to 50. He can recognize many written words. He likes to draw pictures, swim, climb on monkey bars and hang upside down. He recently learned to ride a two-wheeler and is very proud of this.

What kind of parents might adopt Martin?

"IT WOULD be best if they had no preconceived idea of what a child should be like, or should be interested in or able to do," the social worker says.

Parents who adopt an emotionally disturbed child must be prepared that the child may not be able to give back to them affection and warmth.

"Because the condition is evasive and vague, it's hard on families," the social worker says. "When you know a child is retarded or has cerebral palsy, it is explainable.

"Also, emotionally disturbed children present a different kind of pressure: Parents expect them to change. It's very dangerous to believe, 'We will love him and he will love us and everything will get better.' It may not get better. You have to be willing to live with it."

Still, she believes there are families strong enough to adopt Martin. "For the right family, this will be a great kid," she says.

IF YOU would like to adopt Martin, write Mrs. Marty McClatchey at Spaulding for Children, 3660 Waltrous Road, Chelsea, Mich. 48118 or call her at 1-475-2500.

10 families ask for Mary

Ten families have asked to adopt Mary, the 8-year-old girl featured here last Sunday.

The Children's Aid Society reports that all 10 responses came from the Detroit area, and all but one were from married couples. One letter, written by a foster mother, came from a couple whose own daughter had convinced them to ask to adopt Mary.

Mrs. Suzann Ray at the Children's Aid Society is looking for a home for Mary. You can call her at TE 1-3300 or write her at 71 West Warren, Detroit, 48201.

Reprinted From The Detroit News

Much of the success achieved from Spaulding's use of newspaper publicity has been due to the advantages of wide circulation and easy accessibility inherent in that form of communication. However, much of the staff's success has also been due to their use of the following guidelines when describing specific children available for adoption.

First, columns should always include an accurate description of the child's abilities as well as information about his handicap, if he has one. They should avoid descriptions of children that attempt to sum up too much in a few words, any words or phrases that tend to be interpreted negatively by the general public, or descriptions that fail to give a clear picture of the extent and variety of the child's abilities and problems. The reporters who write these columns should believe that descriptions should be written in understandable terms and should contain an honest and realistic estimate of the child's potential.

The child also should be described in terms of his level of functioning, avoiding potentially misleading or negatively viewed labels. The child's first name and specific descriptions of his behavior should be used. Readers should be told "Jimmy is functioning on a first grade level at age 10" rather than "the child is retarded." They should be told he "has considerable difficulty getting along with people and is afraid to form close relationships" rather than "the child is emotionally disturbed."

Third, although the child's problems or difficulties should be indicated as clearly as possible, his more positive side should always be emphasized. Such information may consist of his interests, skills, and desire to be adopted, or anecdotes which help give a clearer or more understandable picture of a real child who does not have a family of his own.

In addition, if the child is physically or mentally handicapped, a realistic estimate of his ability to become independent in the future should be included. Emotional, heartrending stories tend to attract families whose response is purely emotional, rather than realistic. The potential adoption has a greater chance for success if the child's needs are made known in a positive, optimistic, and realistic way.

It has been Spaulding's experience that a written description of a child will not satisfy everyone. Conservative social workers often feel that descriptions which are too specific will frighten away prospective applicants. Medical professionals, on the other hand, frequently believe that too little information about the child's health is included to provide an accurate picture.

The view of the Spaulding staff is that descriptions of children must be written for potential adoptive parents; that is, the information should enable parents to decide if they would be interested in adopting the child. To obtain the most appropriate level of description, Spaulding workers help reporters answer the questions the reporters themselves would have if they were interested in adoption. Current foster parents and experienced adoptive parents also assist workers in suggesting appropriate information.

The staff also believe that newspaper columns should always include a clear facial view of the child described. Some courts and agencies have published sketches of children, pictures of the backs of children, side views, or pictures that were hazy, with the intention of concealing the identity of the child. Pictures such as these, however, contain little emotional appeal and the well-intentioned, yet misguided protection they offer may delay the adoption of the child by failing to elicit responses from potential applicants. Instead, Spaulding workers suggest that a relatively large, candid picture of the child be used. Larger pictures more clearly show the child and candid pictures reveal how he typically appears to others.

Finally, a description of the specific kind of family sought should not be included unless this is absolutely imperative. Narrowing the range of applicants cannot help but dissuade other appropriate prospects from responding. If any qualifiers are necessary because certain unusual circumstances exist, the reader should be told, for example, that "workers are interested in talking with any family, although a family with no other children close in age would be ideal."

In order for the Spaulding staff to find appropriate parents through newspaper publicity, newspapers had to be found which were aware, or could be made aware, of problems in the field of adoption. To be effective, these newspapers had to be willing to commit considerable resources to publicizing available children, for publicity poorly done could have been ultimately more harmful to a child's chances for adoption than no publicity at all.

It is also imperative that the assigned reporter know about adoption. Like anyone else, a reporter may lack information, have acquired incorrect information, or may believe in certain adoption myths. The agency's staff assist reporters in acquiring the information they need by inviting them to the agency's in-service training sessions, Spaulding staff meetings, conferences, workshops, and state level adoption committee meetings.

The purpose of this preparation is to help the reporters communicate current problems and developments in adoption as accurately as possible. In addition, the reporters must understand the necessity for describing the child as humanly and understandably as possible, for using a clear photograph of the child, and for talking with the child's worker to make sure that all appropriate information is included. Sometimes, a contract or free-lance journalist can be found who already has special skill, knowledge, or commitment to adoption.

Resistance to Newspaper Publicity

Although the Spaulding staff feel that the use of newspaper recruitment is their most successful technique for finding families, they have occasionally encountered resistance from adoption professionals and others to the use of this technique for publicizing available children. Those who are opposed to newspaper publicity generally offer one or more of the following three reasons for their attitude:

1. It is not right to "sell" children or put children on the market by "advertising" them.
2. The biological family may see the child's picture and their interest in the child may be renewed. This renewed interest may create problems for the child and sometimes even more problems for the adoption program.
3. The publicity may cause embarrassment to the child, either because he may not want his picture in the newspaper or because friends or neighbors may make fun of him.

All three reasons are serious concerns and merit thoughtful responses.

Is it right to publicize the availability of children?

Part of the criticism of adoption publicity has occurred because many people equate publicity efforts with advertising or selling. This is understandable, for both publicity and advertising are methods of attracting public interest. It is true, too, that advertising is closely associated with selling. In adoption, this association is especially felt by some adoption programs that charge fees to applicants.

All of these negative perspectives too frequently overshadow the important fact that publicity can greatly facilitate adoption by bringing to the public's attention the positive characteristics of the children who are available for adoption. They also overshadow the tremendous increase in reader interest in adoption which can occur as a result of such publicity. This is especially true when, as in the case of "A Child is Waiting," a short news item is also included to tell of the families who responded to the child in the previous week's column. In this way, readers learn that all sorts of children with all sorts or problems do find families who will adopt them. As a result, readers who suspect they could parent such children may become less hesitant as they see that other normal adults come forward with similar interests.

Another advantage of newspaper publicity is that an appropriate family for an adoptable child can usually be found promptly. Without such attempts, children may wait endlessly, relying solely on the possibility that the "right" family might apply. No child should ever be made to wait for placement if that wait is potentially damaging to that child. Despite the arguments which exist against publicizing individual children in need of adoption, the Spaulding staff believe it is best to continue using a proven method, especially if failure to use it may leave children unplaced.

In the past, lack of public awareness and interest have been largely responsible for many children remaining unadopted. Making the community aware of waiting children and their need for permanence is exactly what is necessary to offer a child his greatest chance for adoption.

Will the child's previous families object to adoption publicity?

Some agencies and courts (including many who have primarily served unwed mothers) have questioned whether previous parents' rights to privacy and peace of mind might be disturbed by the publication of a child's picture. In almost all cases, this is an honest and thoughtful consideration. However, determining on the basis of these concerns alone whether or not publicity efforts should be made presupposes that the parent's rights are more important than the child's rights. While the Spaulding staff take the family's attitudes into consideration, they firmly believe that when it is necessary to make a choice, the child's need for adoptive placement must come first.

Some courts and agencies dealing with children whose parental rights have been terminated by court intervention still fear that publication of a child's availability for adoption will renew the interest of former parents and create "problems" for the child. It is true that it may be more comfortable for former parents to not see pictures or descriptions of the child if, for example, they did not adequately care for him and did not seek his removal. The Spaulding staff have found, however, that the professional anxiety over this possibility is far greater than the real problem. The agency's staff have helped prepare scores of columns for publication, but have had only one experience of contact with relatives who have responded to that publicity. In that case, the biological aunt and uncle who recognized and responded to a newspaper picture and description of their two nieces became serious applicants for those children.

The Spaulding staff have found that most parents who voluntarily surrender the custody of their children cooperate with an adoption program's efforts to place the child. These parents are usually more alarmed by the prospect of the child going unplaced or being placed in a succession of temporary situations than they are by the choice of methods used to find an appropriate adoptive family. Those families who have involuntarily lost custody of their children may, in many cases, also cooperate with an adoption program's efforts to find adoptive families once they have worked through their feelings about their separation from the child and have focused on the child's need for a permanent substitute family.

Some families whose parental rights have been terminated are never able to focus on the need of their children for a permanent family. For this reason, adoption workers must always remain clearly aware of the child's possibilities for such a placement. If those possibilities are expected to be significantly delayed or decreased without the use of newspaper publicity, the responsible adoption program must place the child's need for permanence above the family's desire for no publicity.

Conflicts with former parents sometimes can be minimized by using a newspaper column which circulates in a geographic area other than the one in which the child's former parents live. However, it may still be necessary in some cases, to alienate the family opposed to publicity in order to adequately serve the child.

Is publicity harmful to the child?

The Spaulding staff recognize that children have rights to confidentiality and privacy. However, they have found that children sometimes feel very differently about the methods used to find families for them than do many adoption workers. Many children are, in.fact, delighted to have their picture and story published. Some children find it reassuring that someone cares enough to want to help children like them find an adoptive family. As a result, workers should never assume that a child does not want to appear in a newspaper. Workers should also be very aware that it is often their own projected feelings which result in refusal to use such means to help a child.

If the child is able to understand that it is his picture and description which will be used, Spaulding workers try to have him help make the decision to use newspaper publicity. Worker and child discuss why the agency wants to use his picture and what having his picture in the paper will mean to him. It comes as no surprise to most children who have been in foster homes or institutional settings that special efforts must be made to find an adoptive family for children like them. Of course, some children choose not to have their need for adoption publicized. That is their right, and workers allow the decision to be theirs. In such cases, the Spaulding staff would search out other ways to find potential parents, such as utilizing another child of similar age and description for the newspaper effort.

Even if the child is not considered old enough, or is otherwise unable to make an informed decision concerning publication of his picture in a newspaper, his feelings must be taken into account. Although he may not be able to give permission, he may be able to feel the repercussions of other people's comments about the publicity. No matter what reaction might occur, the adoption worker makes the decision for or against the likelihood of finding an adoptive family for the child without using that publicity.

To date, the Spaulding staff do not believe that any of the children they have publicized have experienced ridicule or other negative feelings as a result of that publicity. However, in anticipation of this possibility, the workers prepare each child for this experience by explaining to him why newspaper articles are written and how families are found for children.

Since no family finding technique can guarantee successful recruitment in every case, Spaulding workers are cautious not to pin all of the child's hopes for placement on the use of individual publicity. It is more appropriate to help the child understand that newspaper publicity serves *two* important purposes: to help find families for all children in need of adoption and to help find a family for him.

Many of the problems which accompany individual family finding, including the child's feelings of rejection if no family is found immediately, can be reduced if workers believe in, and communicate to the child, the wider potential that publicity offers to all available children. The sensitivity that most children have to others in situations similar to their own is a valuable resource in convincing them of the value of newspaper publicity. Once they understand that the Spaulding staff are trying to find families for many children, most children cooperate enthusiastically with individual family finding efforts.

The Worker's Role in Newspaper Publicity

Adoption programs contemplating the use of individualized newspaper publicity must not expect this technique to eliminate effort for adoption workers. Rather, widespread publicity techniques bring with them the added work of follow-up and decision-making in order to make them productive. Successful publicity efforts are only an early stage in the process of placing older and handicapped children with informed and committed adoptive families. They only bring prospective adoptive parents and workers together.

Spaulding's early experience with unmanageably large numbers of applicants taught the staff the importance of timing in responding to potential adoptive parents. In spite of the rapid speed with which the staff had tried to reply, a delay of only several weeks had been long enough to frustrate and discourage some families. The origin of the families' feelings was their assumption that the agency's use of newspaper publicity implied a great degree of urgency in placing that child. Many of the families who responded to this urgency felt their response represented a golden opportunity for some waiting child. In return, they expected prompt recognition and response from the agency. From their perspective, adoption professionals not exhibiting the same degree of immediacy appeared callous or unfeeling, to say the least.

The staff's eventual understanding of these feelings has helped lead to the evolution of the agency's present response system. Workers do nothing to lessen the interest and enthusiasm of potential applicants. Single-parent families or couples who call or write in for information about the agency and the kinds of children available receive immediate replies. Family and worker negotiate their future contacts in terms of the degree of the family's interest. For some, this means referral to other agencies; for yet others an agreement that the family needs more basic information at a SPAM meeting and additional time to think things through before making a decision.

If committed to the placement of the child, the child's worker is, by far, the most qualified person available to respond to interested applicants. Newspaper articles about children should include the name of the child's worker, the name of the adoption program, and the program's telephone number so that respondents can directly contact that worker. Providing the worker's name permits prospective parents to make contact quickly and easily and personalizes the process into which they are entering. The staff have learned that most responses come within the first twenty-four hours after publicity appears. Therefore, the most efficient use of worker time requires that the child's worker assumes telephone responsibilities during the first day following the appearance of publicity and identifies all appropriate prospects who call.

There is, of course, no way to know when a worker fails to identify a potentially appropriate family . There is no doubt that some are missed, especially when workers feel they have "enough" applicants to work with, when families do not accurately represent themselves, or when worker prejudices are activated by something the family says. At Spaulding, awareness of the potential for such error and the employment of experienced workers who are trusted to have a good grasp of what it is they are looking for in applicants helps to decrease the incidence of these unfortunate mistakes.

Since absolute answers regarding the appropriateness of a family are not possible, the Spaulding staff realize that intuition, (i.e., instinctual response or "gut reaction"), tempered by experience and the team's ability to challenge individual decisions, must be both accepted and encouraged. The staff also realize that such intuition is based upon the sum total of a worker's experience. At Spaulding, it is a combination of staff trust and worker commitment which permits the luxury of listening to, talking about, and making use of worker intuition.

During the early days of Spaulding's teamwork approach, workers usually sought out other staff members to help with all phases of initial applicant preparation and determination of appropriate potential adoptive parents. Today, Spaulding workers have acquired enough skill and self-confidence to make many of these choices on their own. They use the team members as consultants when they are pressed for time and/or puzzled by information being received. This skill and self-confidence has helped the agency's response system reach its present level of effectiveness. Its efficiency has also increased because of the use of the most informed worker (the child's worker) as the primary contact person with potential applicants, and because of the agency's efforts to focus on appropriate families as quickly as possible.

About fifty percent of those people who respond by telephone calls or letters are initially considered to be appropriate prospects for placement. This determination is usually made during the family's first telephone contact with the child's worker and is based upon the family's understanding and forethought. Some calls are very short. However, others are very long, lasting more than half an hour, for it is at this time that the worker begins to explore the individual's or couple's understanding of the child. Do they understand the physical and mental characteristics of the child as described in the article? Can any misunderstanding be corrected? Will they provide a realistic placement possibility for this child? Might placement with them be an improvement over the child's current placement? Are they interested only in this child or might they become interested in another older or handicapped child?

Those who are realistic in their thinking, who have correctly perceived both the intent of the publicity and the characteristics and needs of the child, are placed into one of two groups by the child's worker. One group consists of the respondents interested only in the specific child publicized; the second consists of those who are or might be interested in other children as well. Where there is a need for clarification or where the individual or couple had delayed their decision, workers recontact the potential parent(s) so that no initial mistakes are made regarding the interests of the applicants.

Once these interests are known, appropriate applicants for either the child publicized or other available children must be assigned to workers.[2] The child's worker always tries to work with all applicants specifically interested in the publicized child. Those interested in other available children, or those who the child's worker does not have time to work with, are assigned to other workers. At Spaulding, these other workers are willing to change their schedules to make the time needed to share various responsibilities for children and families, for they know they, too, will be asking for similar kinds of assistance in the near future.

Since the staff wish to respond rapidly to all interested families, the

[2]In some areas of the country, applicants have been first referred to adoptive parent groups who, in cooperation with adoption programs, provide initial application and screening of adoptive applicants. This technique affords applicants good information and frees placement staff to work with only the most appropriate applicants. No such parent groups with the capacity to informatively determine the appropriateness of applicants for older and handicapped children have yet been developed by, or are otherwise available to, the staff at Spaulding.

assignment of a worker to families who may be appropriate for other children is made by common agreement among staff and depends upon worker availability and the geographic area covered during the worker's upcoming travel schedule. If a family who has responded to individualized publicity appears interested in and appropriate for some other child, that child's worker will usually contact that family.

Using all possible tools and techniques, workers try to quickly complete all initial contacts with all potential applicants so that within two weeks, part of a team meeting can be used to discuss information which must be obtained before the team can begin focusing on a specific family for a given child. This decision is influenced by the family's attitudes (level of interest in children, in adoption, toward problems and their solution, toward discipline, toward themselves, etc.), and the characteristics of their family life style (active or passive, dependent or independent, the presence or absence of children and pets, experiences with children, degree of warmth in relationships, etc.). If, for some reason, all families originally interested in the publicized child lose interest or prove inappropriate, it may be necessary for the staff to return to the group of applicants with wider interests in an effort to find a family for that child.

Families tend to feel satisfied with Spaulding's handling of responses to publicity and their speed in meeting with families. By using the most informed worker as the first person to talk with the families who initially appear to be the best suited to parent a specific child, the staff demonstrate that they wish to pursue families' interests intelligently and to offer them as much information as possible from the beginning of their contact.

When No One Responds to Newspaper Publicity

On the basis of their work with children, the Spaulding staff have found that newspaper publicity is the most successful technique for finding families for specific children. Even with years of experience, however, the staff are not yet able to consistently predict when a publicity effort will result in the adoptive placement of the child publicized. For some children, there may be instances in which newspaper publicity will not be effective. After preparing a child for adoption, deciding which newspaper will be most effective, providing information about the child to reporters, and publicizing the child, workers occasionally find that no applicants respond.

The experience of the Spaulding staff has been that workers become discouraged when newspaper publicity brings no response. To avoid discouragement, workers need to be convinced that newspaper publicity is not concerned only with the placement of an individual child. Time and effort spent in preparing publicity is not wasted even if no one responds to he child being described. All published information concerning the kinds of children available and the problems which exist within the field of adoption contributes to the understanding of both the process of adoption and the placement programs who offer their services to the community. With every article and column which appears, the public (including the physicians, lawyers, and ministers to whom the public looks for advice) has more accurate information upon which to base their decision to eventually adopt or to more accurately understand, accept, and assist those who do.

Reporters and editors, too, become discouraged if there is no immediate response to newspaper publicity efforts. Under these circumstances, they must be able to receive commitment and support from adoption workers to be convinced to continue an adoption feature. They must be persuaded that an occasional lack of response does not mean the column is a failure and helped to understand that regular columns provide a valuable service to the community and to the children needing placement.

The Spaulding staff do not drop attempts to find the child a family when a newspaper column brings no response, for they believe that the worker's first concern in such situations must be for the child. In some cases, they will repeat publicity in the same newspaper. This is done because some potential parents need more than one reminder of the availability of a child before they are ready to move toward adoption. In other cases, the staff will repeat publicity in a different newspaper in order to reach different families. In addition, workers will also present the child at all inquiry meetings and to all applicants as a primary example of the waiting child who needs a family.

The staff believe that available children must be kept visible to the adopting public. It is their conviction that if children are to be given the permanent placement opportunities they deserve, adoption professionals must repeatedly try every publicity technique to which they have access before saying that they have tried to place a child for adoption and have failed.

SUMMARY

Spaulding uses two distinctly different approaches to finding families for children. These are "community education" and "individual family finding." Community education is an on-going program through which the agency helps the public understand issues and problems in the field of adoption. While a wide variety of media (television, radio, magazines, newspapers, and pamphlets) are used to disseminate this information, worker-led inquiry meetings are most frequently used to convey both general and Spaulding-specific information to interested individuals.

Although community education efforts produce interest among many families, the agency has found that individual family finding in the form of newspaper recruitment is its most effective technique for finding families for specific children. This form of publicity has been criticized because of its apparently close association with selling and advertising, because of concern that it might be harmful to children, and because of the possibility that it may cause a child's previous family to show re-newed, but inappropriate, interest in the child. However, the Spaulding staff feel these objections represent unsubstantiated fears and believe the use of newspaper publicity should be determined solely by the child's chances of finding a permanent family if this technique is not used.

For newspaper recruitment to be most effective, accurate and specific information about individual children available for adoption must be made available to the public. Workers must be prepared for frequent high levels of response as well as occasional instances of no response at all. Although lack of response tends to be discouraging, both children and workers must be helped to remember that adoption columns which do not find a family for the publicized child frequently find families for other children and always add to the public's knowledge of the needs of children who are older, handicapped, and of minority race.

If no one responds to newspaper publicity, workers must not drop their attempts to find a family for that child. If children are to be given the permanent placement opportunities they deserve, adoption profession-als must repeatedly try every publicity technique to which they have access before saying that they have tried to place a child for adoption and have failed.

Preparing Families for Adoption

11

Spaulding's approach to preparing families for adoption is based on their fundamental premises regarding the family's role in the adoption process. The staff have high respect for applicants. Throughout the adoption process, they strive to create a relationship in which worker and family credit each other with significant personal value, rather than one in which status and power are attributed only to the worker. They believe that families, and not the agency, provide the greatest service to children in need of permanence.

The staff also have a realistic view of families. They do not believe that they are in the business of finding "perfect parents." Workers do not expect applicants to have an unblemished family history, to have totally consistent patterns of discipline, or to be completely free of interpersonal problems.

As a result of these beliefs and expectations, the staff will place children with families who have problems, doubts, and anxieties as long as those families can cope with their own difficulties and the additional difficulties presented by a child. The workers assure applicants, potential applicants, and adoptive parents that it is normal and acceptable to have problems and to admit that problems exist. The agency is primarily concerned that parents are able to offer children the care and security they need; not that the families be problem-free. This philosophy enables the staff to place children with many capable parents who would probably be eliminated as applicants by some adoption programs.

Similarly, the staff do not expect to find families who are totally prepared to adopt an older or handicapped child when they first come to the agency. Rather, they expect to find that many applicants have serious misconceptions about the adoption process, the children actually available, and their own capacity to parent those children. The staff believe they have a responsibility to discuss these concerns with all potential adoptive families and to correct any misinformation they may have. They also believe they have a responsibility to do this in a way which is not degrading or humiliating to any applicants.

It is Spaulding's experience that individuals who select themselves to be adoptive parents on the basis of thorough and accurate information not only consider themselves to be serious candidates for adoption, but have a greater chance of successfully maintaining their adoption. Applicants who have a clear understanding of the probable demands of the children they adopt are in a good position to determine whether they can actually provide for the child's needs and make him a part of the family. The staff are convinced that applicants who carefully think through the positive and negative aspects of adopting a specific child and honestly appraise their ability to nurture that child are highly likely to be adequate parents.

Because information about specific children is readily provided and informed applicants are encouraged to assess their own capabilities, the staff do not spend long hours trying to untangle what are almost always complex motivations to adopt. Instead, they provide applicants with as complete information as is available and work closely with them to help them achieve the clearest possible understanding of that information and of their own reactions to it.

ESTABLISHING A WORKER – FAMILY PARTNERSHIP

It is the staff's belief that if the adoption of an older or handicapped child is to succeed, the worker(s) and the family must strive for complete confidence in each other. The development of trust requires that placement workers begin working closely with the potential adoptive family long before the child is actually placed.

In working with families, workers make every effort to avoid the creation of barriers that will later have to be broken down before the solutions to placement problems can be found. Beginning with the family's introduction to the agency, workers try to establish both an atmosphere which responds to applicants' concerns, interests, capabilities, and sense of urgency, and a pace that maintains the natural momentum of the placement process.

The staff also try to make applicants feel comfortable by consciously working to minimize those aspects of the adoption process which frequently threaten prospective parents.[1] The intent at Spaulding is to make each relationship as ordinary and relaxed as possible and to diminish the distance which is often felt between family and worker in other programs. As a result, professional titles and credentials are not displayed, "jargon" language is not used by workers, and first-name relationships with families are common. Workers also dress casually. The typical dress for staff, all of whom are female, is sportswear such as slacks or jeans.

The staff also try to make families more comfortable by assigning the most appropriate worker to each family. This may be the child's worker if the family is responding to publicity about a specific child, or a worker who has had prior contact with the family and has proven her ability to work successfully with them. However, prime consideration is also frequently given to the match between worker skill, style, current caseload size and composition, and the applicants' needs and style. The assignment of a particular worker can also depend upon the applicant's geographic location, the availability of the worker, or the applicant's request for a specific worker. (For more information on how cases are assigned, see "Teamwork and Collegial Supervision," p. 41.)

As applicant families become convinced by workers and experienced adoptive families that the agency will place a child with them even if they are not perfect, the family will usually risk trusting the worker enough to begin discussing some of their problems, doubts, and anxieties. At first, they typically choose topics that involve little risk, but with continued reassurance, most gradually become comfortable enough to risk discussing concerns which are at the heart of parenting older and handicapped children. Only after the staff have continually shown applicants that they can and will listen, answer questions, offer advice, and even accept and deal with anger and frustration directed at workers, can real work begin.

It is the goal of the Spaulding staff to develop a relationship in which worker and applicant feel comfortable sharing their thoughts and concerns about adoption, family relationships and experiences, and the developing partnership between the agency and the family. If this interdependent relationship develops according to plan, a true partnership is formed between worker and family, with each contributing as they can. The degree of this alliance (often termed "intimacy" by Spaulding workers) is the only known predictor of the success of a placement.

---

[1] The workers at Spaulding realize that it may well take a considerable amount of time and effort to make families feel comfortable and to convince them of the staff's sincerity. The workers know that many of the families who have had previous negative experiences while attempting to adopt elsewhere are so much on their guard that it is often difficult, and sometimes impossible, to successfully rebuild their trust. However, families who are able to maintain or rebuild their trust in adoption workers will have increased confidence in the information they receive and in the workers' ability to be of help in times of need. They will also show an increased willingness to come to the worker with questions and problems both before and after placement.

The creation of a partnership built upon trust enables the worker to be sensitive to the family's current and previous problems as well as to the adequacy of their solutions. It also gives workers the information they need to make the earliest possible identification of problems, usually before those problems threaten to disrupt the adoption. The closer the worker and family come to achieving this partnership of giving and gaining, the more comfortable each will be working with the other when need arises, be that before, during, or after placement.

Partnership Risks

A close partnership between workers and families has certain disadvantages, however. The development of trust and open communication means there are no illusions. Each knows the other's abilities and liabilities; their best and their worst. Families know what workers, the children, and they can and cannot do. It also means that workers, in knowing the family well, know the family's weaknesses well. Often, this knowledge leaves the worker more concerned about the family's ability to parent a child or weather the future than they would have been had they not known the family so thoroughly.

Spaulding workers feel they must guard against letting their extensive knowledge of a family's problems and weaknesses jeopardize the family's chances to adopt. All families have problems, but those who do admit to problems can run the risk of a worker's undue assumption that their problems are far more extensive than they concede. A worker with this fear could fail to place a child in the home or avoid working further with the family.

In a close partnership, it is also tempting to ignore a family's problems and weakness and concentrate on their strengths. However, the staff believe that it is always far better for the child if the worker is aware of all the positive and negative aspects of the family the child will be entering. Not only does this awareness allow him to help the family cope with their difficulties, but it enables him to work more effectively to maintain the adoption.

The Spaulding staff are convinced that the traditional investigative relationship between an agency or court and a prospective adoptive family frequently results in far greater placement risks than those which are created by the trusting partnership they strive to develop. They believe their straightforward approach is more effective than refining evaluation techniques in an effort to better detect any parental efforts to cover up imperfection. They prefer to seek a partnership that allows parents to be open with workers and allows workers to trust the parents' judgment. The Spaulding staff believe a placement cannot be successful unless parents look honestly at their own tolerance levels and capabilities and still conclude they can parent a specific child who has been thoroughly described to them and who they have met and talked with. The problem with the traditional worker-family relationship is that it is both counter-productive and unrealistic. While the traditional placement program attempts to find the most appropriate or "best " parents, the families constantly fear that any discovered problem or imperfection may be viewed by the placement staff as reason enough to deny them a child or to take their child from them after placement. This situation often produces predictable, intended, and devastating results: parents who can convince adoption workers that they have no problems receive children; those who honestly admit even common imperfections, no matter how good their parenting ability, are typically denied a child.

Applicants to Spaulding often arrive at the agency expecting the traditional relationship to exist. They assume it is impossible to be honest and still receive a child. To counter this expectation, workers discuss with parents, during the preparation process, their conviction that all families and all adoptions have problems, and that the agency will not remove the child because problems exist but rather will help work to solve the problems so that the family will be able to offer an even better adoptive experience to the child.

Establishing Parental Rights

The Spaulding staff have found that fears of the child's removal are substantially eliminated if the family can be made aware of, and accept, the agency's conviction that the family is ultimately responsible for the child as soon as the child is placed. Spaulding's premise that placement (rather than the end of a supervisory period) signals the establishment of the parental role and the implementation of the parent's custodial rights was unique among all adoption programs examined by the authors. Other adoption programs tend to view the period between placement and confirmation (which in Michigan and many other states is usually a year) as the time in which an adoption worker determines if the parents should complete the adoption of the child. Spaulding workers believe the decision that families should and will adopt is made as they are passing through the agency's process of preparation. That is, the placement of the child should signal the commitment of both agency and family to the adoption of the child.

Although the prevalent attitude in adoption programs is that custodial rights of agencies and courts take precedence over those of the adoptive parents during the year of supervision, Spaulding's belief in the early establishment of parental rights to the child seems in keeping with existing Michigan law. Once the child is placed with the family, his presence is treated by statute in the same way as the presence of a biological child. The Spaulding staff maintain that anyone seeking to remove a child from his placement must obtain the voluntary coopera-tion and consent of the adoptive parents or must prove clear examples of neglect or abuse on the part of those parents. The rights of the adoption program to move the child prior to confirmation should not take prece-dence over the parents' legal rights to the physical custody of their child. Imperfection in parents, in the view of the Spaulding staff, is not a legal basis for removing the adopted child once he has been placed.

The staff believe it is necessary that parents feel a sense of reassurance that their children will not be removed from their homes if they en-counter child-rearing difficulties. Families who feel comfortable in this regard are able to develop healthier attitudes toward adoption and more comfortable relationships with the agency. This is especially apparent when a problem arises after placement. Parents who are fighting to keep their child will insist that problems are insignificant, if they admit that problems exist at all. They will spend their time and energy warding off workers instead of working to overcome problems. When families are frightened and defensive, even highly competent and experienced workers have great difficulty working with them.

Just as importantly, Spaulding workers have learned that the early establishment of the parent's custodial rights is what most adoptive applicants really desire. It is the staff's belief that the implementation of this philosophy is primarily responsible for their ability to create a trusting partnership between family and agency.

The Volunteer Family's Role

The staff have also learned that many of the difficulties applicants have in developing a trusting partnership with an adoption program can be overcome by offering them opportunities to meet with families who have already adopted from the agency and know its adoption process. (At Spaulding, these families are called "volunteer families.") Such occa-sions not only give applicant families the opportunity to talk about the agency with another family but to talk with someone they will probably trust more readily than an agency-loyal worker.

By talking with volunteer families about their relationships with Spaulding workers and their experiences with their adopted child(ren), families new to Spaulding are reassured that the agency follows the approach to adoption which has been discussed with them. Applicants can also observe the kinds of partnerships which exist between adoptive families and the agency's staff and see for themselves that families can speak openly with their worker without risking lack of understanding, degradation, or loss of their opportunity to adopt.

In addition, meeting adoptive families gives applicants the opportunity to view the problems and responsibilities that go along with adopting the kinds of children they are seeking to adopt. The Spaulding staff recognizes, however, that such contacts do not work well with all applicants. Some are not ready to face the reality of adoption and may be overwhelmed by seeing older and handicapped children in a family setting. These applicants are not, of course, ready for adoptive placement.

Other families project too great a sense of total assurance to agree to meet with volunteer families. In such cases, workers must be sure that their attitude is justified and that pride does not inhibit the family's real understanding of what they face. Still other families feel they do not need to use Spaulding volunteer families because they already have access to other adoptive families who can provide the same kind of help. While these families may be able to accurately tell them about adopting children, they are not able to offer information about relationships with Spaulding workers; information which could have served as a foundation upon which to begin building family-worker trust.

PHASES OF PREPARATION

During their preparation for adoption, families must make two decisions. First, they must decide whether they should adopt through Spaulding. Second, they must decide what kind of child they will find rewarding. To help them make these decisions, workers talk with them about the agency, the kinds of children Spaulding places, and the attitudes and capabilities needed to successfully adopt an older or handicapped child. The staff tell the families about the problems they can expect in such adoptions and about the possibility of disruption. The decisions which need to be made require applicants to thoroughly examine their parenting abilities and their personal preferences. After the applicants have made the initial decision to adopt through Spaulding and have reviewed their parenting skills carefully, workers begin to consider them as potential parents for the children on their caseloads.

First Phase: Decisions

The information upon which parents base their decision to adopt a child from Spaulding is given to parents during one of the agency's public adoption meetings (SPAM's) or during the introductory visits between worker and family. (For more information on Spaulding's public adoption meetings, see "Finding Families for Children," p. 105.)

During these meetings, both single-parent families and couples are given information about adoption and the attitudes and skills needed to successfully adopt an older or handicapped child. They are also given the opportunity to discuss what they may know about parenting. After exploring how these attitudes and capacities are important to adoption, applicants are better able to make an informed decision about their interest in, and capability of, parenting the kinds of children placed by the Spaulding staff.

If applicants are still interested in working toward the placement of a Spaulding child, a written application is made available. If the worker anticipates that the applicant might have difficulty in reading, understanding, or filling out the application, the worker and family complete the form together. The form itself asks for a minimal amount of personal information and for directions to the family's home. It omits questions concerning the kinds of children "acceptable" to the family. Omitting these questions helps avoid the family's tendancy to focus on a narrow range of possible children. Completing the form together helps establish and strengthen the concept of "partnership" as a basis for the family-worker relationship.

Many of the questions to which answers are needed are not asked directly by Spaulding workers. Much of the information is gained through general conversation about children, parents, and family interactions. If a question must be asked directly, workers try to explain why it is asked and what specific information is sought. This allows the family a greater opportunity to talk freely without having to "second-guess" the worker's actual intent.

Adoptive Family Characteristics.

In helping applicants decide what kind of a relationship a family would expect from an adopted child and what kind of a child would best fit into the family, Spaulding workers talk with them about a variety of important issues. Since strong emotional support is needed to parent any child successfully, the staff discuss the family's sources of emotional support and the strength of that support. With couples, they determine the strength of their marriage and their level of emotional support to each other. Since older and manipulative children frequently play one parent against another, it is necessary to alert adoptive parents to the possibility of succumbing to these tactics. Workers do not assume that peace and quiet in the home is necessarily indicative of marital strength or family support, for it may be a facade covering underlying and unresolved tension. With single parents, the staff review the availability of relatives (especially grandparents) and friends to help with the child's care.

Workers explore the relationship between parents and children already in the family. When the adopted child arrives, the children will have to share their parents even further and form relationships with at least one new brother or sister. Consequently, the staff talk about the way the parents and children relate to each other and speculate about how they will function after the arrival of one or more adopted children.

Since adopting often produces additional areas of tension for the family, workers also consider the family's reactions to stress. How much stress can they tolerate? At what point does stress become disruptive? Families differ greatly in what they can accept or tolerate. Some find it very stressful if a child wets his bed or does not have proper table manners; other families consider these to be relatively minor matters and become upset only if the child sets fires or runs away. Obviously, children who produce intolerable tension in a family should not be placed with that family. Although perfect matches are impossible, the staff attempt to find a family with a good chance of tolerating most of the child's identified and typical behaviors. Workers discuss various kinds of child-rearing problems so the family can clarify what kinds of behavior they consider tolerable or intolerable and what kinds of problems they can tolerate best.

Because the ability of the child to gain entry into the family is also essential for successful placement, the staff seek to discover whether it is easy or difficult for a stranger to become one of the family, how different the child can be and still be accepted, whether the adopted child has to conform exactly to the family's expectations, or in what ways he can deviate and still be accepted.

Because the eventual behavior or ultimate intellectual potential of children cannot be accurately predicted, workers talk with the family about their ability to deal with the unknown or to take risks. Can they risk the uncertainty of living with a child whose future does not look significantly more positive than his past? Can they take the risk of seeing a child's physical condition deteriorate or of seeing a retarded child grow older and even further behind children his own age? How would they cope with the possibility of losing their own health, patience, or energy, or of not having adequate financial, medical, or social resources to help meet their needs in times of crisis? The family who can adjust to changing conditions will be a better possibility for placement than the family who cannot tolerate uncertainties.

The staff explore the family's degree of optimism, their expectation that things will turn out well, and their ability to see some good in all situations. These characteristics are important ones for adoptive parents. Individuals who are pessimistic about a child will have little motivation to encourage him and help him to develop to the greatest extent possible. Workers search for a family committed to working out the child's long-range problems, instead of giving up. They look for a family's understanding of both the positive and the negative realities of parenting children.

Workers discuss the family's capacity for patience and the importance of a sense of humor during the more difficult times of parenting older and handicapped children. A healthy sense of humor, which is direct enough for the child to understand, is very helpful. It would be painful for any handicapped child to grow up in a family that found it fun to constantly tease him, and he would be unprepared to distinguish between fun and taunting. Children who are not used to teasing often have a difficult time getting used to this in a family. However, if light-hearted teasing is directed at everyone in the family, and is a sign of affection, the child will get used to it and usually learn to tease back.

The staff also consider the parents' health, for it is necessary to determine whether they have medical problems which would seriously interfere with their ability to care for the child. A handicapping condition in an applicant is not necessarily a reason for that applicant's rejection. A father in a wheelchair might, for example, make a good parent for an active child. The parent in a wheelchair might be quite self-sufficient, more available, and able to spend more time with his child. In addition, a handicapped parent who has learned to live with and adjust to a disability may very well serve as an excellent model to a child who must learn the same things for himself. A parent's health or medical condition is only important to the adoption in terms of the physical and emotional demands imposed by an adopted child, for parental resources should not be seriously overloaded. These facts must be known and weighed carefully in terms of both the child's and the family's needs.

In addition, workers talk with families about their financial ability to adopt. The staff are not particularly concerned with the specific amount of income a family has, but rather with parents' ability to manage what they have in order to adequately provide for the needs of another family member. Very early, families are told about the availability of adoption subsidies and are encouraged to use them if they adopt a child who is eligible. (For more information on adoption subsidy, see "Subsidy and Other Sources of Funding," p. 25.)

Finally, starting at this time and continuing throughout the entire preparation process, workers frankly discuss both the kinds of problems which accompany the adoption of older and handicapped children and the possibility of adoption disruption. The increased ability of staff to talk calmly and comfortably among themselves about disruptions has allowed them to discuss these issues more freely with families preparing for adoption. Spaulding workers previously discussed disruption potential with applicants only at the end of the preparation process, and then only out of an effort to be candid. They now discuss it with applicants earlier in the process and with less difficulty.

Honest discussions of potential problems usually dissipate the aura of secrecy traditionally surrounding adoption disruption. By discussing these matters prior to placement, the family can better understand some of the problems their adoption may have and may become more willing to talk about problems as they occur. Through their discussions of disruption, workers convince many families that help is available from the agency for the problems which might arise. They also convince many families that some disruptions can be averted if the families request help with their problems as early as possible.

The expectation throughout the preparation process is for the staff and the family to move toward placement together unless obstacles prohibit that placement. Where obstacles exist, workers and families work out problems so they may begin once again to move toward placement.

"Stretching" Families

Not all families who begin Spaulding's adoption process with their focus on a specific kind of child will continue to be interested in that kind of child or handicapping condition throughout the preparation process. As families gain knowledge of currently available children, they frequently respond positively to specific children whom they had not previously considered. This widening of the parents' horizon may be spontaneous or it may be actively encouraged by the staff. If the staff have a child for whom they believe a specific family would be most appropriate, they will suggest that the family consider that child.

The process of stretching families' interests (or "stretching" families, as it is more commonly called at Spaulding) is a regular part of the agency's approach to adoption with all applicants. It is not, however, a means of placing a kind of child the family never really wanted. When the staff suggest that a family consider adopting a child they had not previously thought themselves capable of parenting, the suggestion is always based upon intimate knowledge of the family's parenting skills. Moreover, the final decision to adopt a specific child always belongs to the family. Workers are convinced that families should not feel obligated to a placement in which they are not interested or confident.

Talking with a family about a child who does not exactly match their initial interests is only done when the worker is sure that family could comfortably say "no" to this possibility and understand they would not be penalized for doing so. To help ensure honest responses, the staff repeatedly stress to applicants that is is always acceptable to make a decision to not adopt a specific child.

With experience, Spaulding workers have become wary of feeling so pleased at finding an interested family that they omit adequate preparation of the family. They have also learned to guard against falsely bolstering parents' confidence in their abilities or "stretching" them too far so that they begin to believe they can parent a child who, in fact, they cannot handle. These mistakes could inflate a parent's expectations and confidence so greatly that they could become hopelessly depressed when problems arose. This might lead to rejection of the child as well as parental feelings of guilt and anger.

Second Phase: Fitting the Child and the Family

If the family decides they want to adopt a child from Spaulding and the staff see no major problems which must be worked out, the family moves on to the second phase of Spaulding's preparation process. To help families determine which kinds of children they are most interested in and capable of parenting, workers begin focusing on the specific children the applicant might adopt. As volunteer family contacts and contacts with the placement worker continue, the family's general interest in adoption usually begins to narrow to specific characteristics which seem most appropriate to the family and the worker. Eventually, an individual child or several children will be described to the family as available.

Unless the family has responded to a specific child in newspaper publicity, workers usually make the decision as to which children are offered for a family's consideration. Some families are capable of parenting, and are considered appropriate parents for, several available children. If they decide not to work toward the adoption of one of these children, another will be presented to them. In other cases, there may be only one child available who seems appropriate for that family. The determination that a specific family is most appropriate for an available child may occur during their first contacts with the agency, during the preparatory process, or often even after the process has been completed. As the agency's steadily improving family-finding practices have gradually brought in an increasingly higher percentage of appropriate applicant families, earlier placement decisions have resulted.

The Spaulding staff generally consider the appropriateness of waiting families (those who have completed the preparation process) or families in preparation before they use newspaper publicity for a child. Usually about a dozen such families are waiting at any given time for an appropriate child to be matched with them. Occasionally, workers may recognize that a family who has previously adopted from the agency might be interested in a waiting child. As of this writing, approximately 30 children have been placed with families who have previously adopted from the agency.

At Spaulding, the actual process of placing a child with a family involves describing the child and family to each other (called a "presentation"), making it possible for them to see each other (called a "showing"), and scheduling one or more "visits" between child and family, lasting several days or weeks, in order to provide them with a final opportunity to decide whether to go ahead with the adoption.

Presentation of the Child

When the family begins to focus on a specific child, the process leading to eventual placement follows a regular pattern. The first step, "presentation," consists of making information about the child available to the family. The presentation usually begins with a verbal description of the child and his present level of functioning, past history, and projected future. (Workers advise parents not to include other family members in such meetings. The decision not to consider a specific child can be an emotionally sensitive issue, and the inclusion of other children at this point can complicate the problem.)

In order to provide a shared basis for continuing discussion and to assure the parents that they have been given all available information concerning the child they are considering, workers frequently provide the parents with copies of those parts of the child's written record which would be most helpful in understanding him. Following a successful presentation and the family's expressed willingness to see the child and proceed further toward placement, the worker may provide the parents with the child's total record so they can consider all written information, better understand the varied opinions and observations which are part of that history, and be assured no information is being withheld.

Although this is still controversial, the Spaulding staff believe that sharing the child's written record with his prospective parents benefits the child by benefitting his adoptive parents. Not only does sharing all available information make the child more real to the family, but it also demonstrates the staff's willingness to participate in an open and candid partnership with the family by removing any hint of mystery or feelings of concealment from the placement process. In addition, providing all available information to the child's prospective parents helps alert the staff to the problems the parents may have in dealing with any portion of the child's known history or level of functioning.

During the presentation, the potential problems involved in the placement are also discussed with the family. The worker shares past experiences with similar children and discusses with the family their experiences with people who have children with characteristics similar to the child they are considering. In addition, the worker explains the educational and medical resources the child will need. This may result in a visit to a local special education classroom for the family interested in a retarded child or a child with educational handicaps, or the verification of the availability of medical treatment and funding programs for a family considering a physically handicapped child.

"Showing" the Child

When the family expresses serious interest in a specific child, a "showing" is arranged. Showings can be either "blind" or "known." In "blind" showings, the child is not told that a prospective family is observing him to help them decide if they want to adopt him. In "known" showings, the child knows the family who has been described to him is interested in his adoption.

In a "blind" showing, the child's worker may take him to a shopping center, park, or zoo where the interested family can inconspicuously wander by the child and his companions or casually "run into" the group he is with in a public setting. In this type of showing, prospective parents may also sometimes observe the child in a room through a one-way glass.

At Spaulding, blind showings are used when a child's physical appearance or behavioral characteristics have resulted in his unplaced status, or when the family's worker is not certain how that family will react to the child. A blind showing may be chosen if the worker is concerned that the family may show a visible negative reaction to the child's pronounced handicapping condition. Such showings are also useful in cases in which the worker wishes to avoid building up the child's hopes for adoption or in instances where the worker expects that the prospective parents will decide not to proceed any further with the adoption process.

The disadvantages to this approach are that the prospective parents may not learn as much about the child as they would like. They may not be able to observe more than the child's physical appearance and a limited range of his behavior. Also, if the child "catches on" to the purpose of the meeting, his faith in the worker may be greatly decreased.

"Known" showings are used when workers are reasonably certain of a family's solid intentions to adopt; i.e., that the family's reaction to all information about the child indicates there is reasonable certainty that no physical or behavioral problems exist in the child which will keep those parents from wanting to go further with the placement process. Known showings can have highly detrimental emotional consequences if a child is convinced he will be adopted by the family but they decide not to adopt.

The staff believe this approach is particularly useful with most older children who are alert or experienced enough to know exactly what is happening if their worker does something out of the ordinary such as taking them to a shopping center, park, or zoo. Workers believe known showings must be used with these children if they expect to maintain the child's trust. Workers need to carefully prepare these children for the experience by explaining that there is no way to absolutely predict whether a specific family is going to eventually become the child's family, and that the only realistic approach is to move forward one step at a time.

This approach is successful with nearly all older children. To date, only one older child for whom a known showing has been arranged by Spaulding workers has not been able to accept this honest approach and has felt rejected when a specific prospective family decided not to adopt him.

Spaulding workers believe that decisions regarding showings, like all other decisions involving finding and maintaining permanent families for children, must support the premise that the child remain as protected from emotional and physical damage or abuse during that process as possible. The method of showing that will offer the child his best chance for adoption with the least risk of hurting him is used. The decision concerning the actual approach used is usually made by the team and is based upon what the child and family need to know in order to move on to the next phase in the adoption process — the actual meeting.

No matter what kind of showing is used, Spaulding workers have learned that prospective adoptive families must be given ample time after seeing the child to proceed with an adoption decision. Although the family's worker can usually judge the family's initial response to the child quite accurately by talking with them soon after the showing, initial reactions must not be considered to be final decisions. Families must be given opportunities to talk among themselves and with the worker to resolve all areas of concern.

Introducing the Child

Before the child and the family are introduced, they must either be prepared to meet with one another for the first time or, if the showing was known, given further information which will enable each to know the other more thoroughly. Although the family will be given all available information about the child, they will still need assistance in planning their meetings with the child. The family must decide, with the worker's assistance, where, when, with whom, for how long, and in what form their meetings with the child will occur.

The decision is determined, to a large extent, by the practical problems of the distances involved and convenience to the child and family. When the geographic distance between child and family is great, more than one step in the adoption process may be combined or intervals between steps may be shortened so the family can remain in the area for several days. The referring worker and the Spaulding worker negotiate an appropriate plan after agreeing that a faster pace will not hurt the child or hinder his ability to move into an adoptive family. Beyond the practical necessities, consideration is given to the child's interests, the parents' comfort in various situations, the child's tolerance for novel or public situations, and the length of time it takes the family and child to become comfortable with each other.

If the prospective parents have been adequately prepared to meet a child, the timing and pace of this part of the adoption process is also determined by the child's readiness to meet the family. The Spaulding worker and the referring worker(s) are responsible for determining the best manner in which to prepare the child and for deciding when he is ready to meet the family. The child must be given information about the family that he understands, considering his age and capabilities. The information should include photographs, stories, and anecdotes. All information should demonstrate what he can expect to find in his new family. The information given to the child and the method in which it is presented depend upon the workers' knowledge of the child, how well he understands and accepts his separation from his previous parents, and how much information he has already been given about his future. Further placement plans cannot be made until this initial preparation is completed.

accompanied by significant problems. The majority of children are prepared for this meeting by their referring worker(s), who may well lack experience in placing older and handicapped children. Although Spaulding workers often assist with this preparation, great geographic distance between them and the referring court or agency may make such assistance difficult or even impossible. If there is substantial distance between the residence of the family and the child, it will take considerable travel time and intricate coordinating efforts to plan the meetings and to reschedule them if necessary. The availability of the Spaulding worker is never an issue. The staff feel that it is important that they take whatever time necessary, whenever necessary, to meet with the child, family, and referring worker(s) in order to maximize the child's opportunities for adoption.

Visits Between Child and Family

If family and worker decide to continue toward placement, a series of visits with the child is planned. The number and duration of visits is determined by the child's age, his readiness, his location, and the family's specific circumstances. Some visits extend over a few days. Others go on for several weeks. If visits are too few or too short, the future will seem insecure to both the child and his family. Longer visits provide the child and the family with an opportunity to see each other twenty-four hours a day, day after day. This experience helps each determine if they are capable of establishing and maintaining the continuous relationship they are contemplating.

Spaulding workers are careful not to schedule too many visits for younger children, for they will become easily confused by numerous visits and the seemingly constant moves from one family to another. The speed at which this portion of the adoption process occurs is very important. Young children perceive time differently than adults; delays which seem short to adults appear endless to children. As a result, care must be taken to minimize delays once placement becomes a reality for the child.

When the child and family initially meet, the meeting should be informal, usually centering on a family activity such as a picnic, a trip to the park or zoo, or a few hours walking, playing, or eating. It should be a meeting between child and family, not between family and adoption workers. If one or more workers must participate in order to make the early part of the meeting more comfortable, that participation should be minimized or eliminated as soon as possible.

Spaulding workers often help transport the child to visits with the family in order to keep in close touch with the developing relationship and to be on hand to answer any questions the child or family may have. Workers can often prevent later difficulties if they are alert to the questions and problems that arise as the initial period of best behavior on the part of the child and family gradually gives way to their more normal behavior. Families are frequently too excited during the early stages of the adoption process to hear or fully understand the implications of the information provided by the worker. As a result, workers repeatedly review developments between parents and children immediately after each visit to provide information, explain behavior, and further prepare the child and parents to make the legal commitment to become a family.

THE FAMILY'S ADOPTION STUDY

Initially, Spaulding workers completed their written summary of a family's interests and capabilities at the end of the preparation process. This "adoption study" was written whether a specific child was available at the time or not. Eventually, the staff concluded that this step was a poor use of valuable time. If the family had to wait long for placement, the study information became out-dated. In addition, information prepared in this way could rarely speak to the issue of how the family studied would respond to a specific child.

As a result, the staff concluded that the most efficient use of time would be to complete the written material only after a child had been identified for a specific family. Thus, the adoption study is now used to describe how parents can become the most appropriate family for a specific child. When there is some assurance that a placement will occur, the family's worker combines all available information to create an up-to-date and relevant adoption study explaining the fit between a specific child and a specific family. This study is included in the information sent on request to the referring worker(s) and is ultimately provided to the court. Careful notes of all contacts, observations, and areas of concern must be kept by all workers involved with a family. If a worker leaves the agency, the written material must first be assembled in a final form.

Another occasion for the completion of an adoption study occurs if family and worker agree that Spaulding is not the appropriate adoption program for that family. In these cases, available information about the family is made available to whatever other programs the family contacts. Although this may be a futile effort because some programs insist upon completing their own study, the Spaulding staff believe that the family is entitled to this service as a matter of course.

DO ALL APPLICANTS ADOPT?

As can be seen in Table 4, not all families who begin the agency's adoption process actually adopt a child from Spaulding.

Table 4

Outcomes of Spaulding's Applications
September 1968 to December 1976

Applications Resulting in Placements	176	39.0%
Applications Withdrawn (to seek adoption elsewhere)	159	35.3%
Applications Withdrawn (for other reasons)	95	21.0%
Inactive or Terminated Cases	21	4.7%
Total Applications	451	100.0%

Approximately two out of every five families who make application to Spaulding for Children adopt a child from the agency. The remaining three-fifths who do not, however, either voluntarily withdraw their application, are placed on inactive status, or have their adoption application terminated by the agency.

Withdrawn cases generally involve clear communication that the applicant is no longer interested in the kinds of children the Spaulding staff are placing, or that the agency cannot place the younger or less handicapped children that family is primarily interested in adopting. Since the agency was established, the most common reason for withdrawal has been families' recognition that Spaulding did not place the kinds of children they really wanted. The staff try to help these families (and families on inactive status), by suggesting parents' groups and adoption programs who might know where to find the children sought by the family.

In addition, should Spaulding workers become aware of an appropriate available child in another adoption program, they will refer the family to that agency or court, offering to provide the family's completed adoption study directly to that program upon the family's request. Rarely does the contacted program decide to refer the child to Spaulding for placement planning. Such negotiations are delicate and, although the Spaulding staff are committed to the future of all children who are or should be available for adoption, they are determined not to jeopardize their primary goal of finding families for children by searching out children for families.

Of the 159 families who sought to adopt elsewhere, approximately half (76) are known to have succeeded. However, since not all families who withdrew reported back to the agency on their progress elsewhere, the staff do not have a totally accurate record of these families' rate of success.

Most of the remaining withdrawals occurred because the family moved, a pregnancy occurred which resulted in a family decision to postpone or abandon plans to adopt, or personal or family problems developed which interfered with any further placement planning. In some cases, families who initially withdrew have returned to the agency for post-placement services for children adopted from other placement programs. Some of these families also eventually adopt a Spaulding child.

ARE FAMILIES REJECTED?

In some cases, the attitudes and capabilities of families have evoked serious concern on the part of their worker even though they have proceeded through the general preparation process and believe they are ready to consider the adoption of a specific child. Workers may feel that the family either does not fully understand what is being discussed concerning the needs of the children, or does not demonstrate the capacity needed to parent these children. The family may disagree with this judgment, or there may be other conflict between applicant and worker. Whatever the problem, a worker may no longer be prepared to continue working toward placement with that family.

If the problem cannot be resolved between the worker and the family, the worker brings the problem to the Spaulding team. Very often the team's advice is to involve another worker. In this way, other workers are given the opportunity to help the family or assist the primary worker. The family must be informed early that an additional worker is needed. The family's primary worker tells them either indirectly, "You may prefer talking with another worker," or more directly, "You and I are not making headway and another worker may be able to help." In either case, the family usually sees the arrival of a second worker as a helpful effort to resolve the problems which are impeding placement.

The family and workers first concentrate on resolving the problems. If, however, the second worker shares the first worker's concerns about the family's capabilities, and the applicants are not able to make the adjustments needed, several alternatives which have been made known to the applicant since the beginning of the preparation process are available. Either the worker or the family can request a third worker or a combination of workers, or the original worker may review with the family the difficulties which exist. At no time is an individual worker empowered to require a family to withdraw their application. When differences continue to exist between workers and a family over the family's parenting capabilities and an impasse is reached, the family may temporarily assume an inactive status. (Workers may also suggest that families be placed on inactive status when parents wish to continue waiting for the kind of child workers do not believe will ever be referred. In addition, inactive status may occasionally occur because of unclear communications between a worker and a family who has actually withdrawn.)

If the family resists the suggestion that a less problematic child would be more appropriate for them, or that adoption may not be a realistic possibility for them, and if the staff agree that no further progress toward a Spaulding placement is possible, the staff as a team must decide that they cannot place a child with the family. Although Spaulding workers believe in a mutual education approach to adoption (and to social work in general), they reserve the right to eventually terminate those preplacement plans which continue to be impractical or unrealistic because of apparently unresolvable difficulties in the family. This apparent paradox is the result of the staff's ultimate commitment to children: that children with a troubled history do not need additional problems and that, as a result, all final decisions are made on behalf of the child.

Such absolute decisions, when a family is unable or unwilling to recognize or resolve significant problems, happen quite seldom (approximately a dozen times in the agency's entire history). Because such confrontations are uncomfortable and unpleasant for both the family and the staff, every effort is made to deal with families fairly and openly. The decision to discontinue working with a family is told them in a straightforward manner, even though it is very difficult to share this information. Workers feel it is advisable to directly inform the family that they cannot continue working with them because problems cannot be resolved. Manufacturing a fictional excuse or telling the family nothing, with hopes that they will become discouraged and withdraw their application, may be temporarily easier for the worker. However, the Spaulding staff believe this practice is not only unprofessional, but unfair to families.

SUMMARY

Spaulding's preparation of prospective adoptive parents is based upon the premises that families are worthy of high respect and are capable of determining, with the agency's assistance, whether or not they are capable of parenting an older or handicapped child.

It is the staff's belief that if the adoption of an older or handicapped child is to succeed, the worker and the family must strive for complete confidence in each other. The development of trust requires that placement workers begin working closely with the potential adoptive family long before the child is actually placed.

At Spaulding, trust and open communication develop in the worker-family partnership because the placement staff make every effort to put families at ease. Professional titles and credentials are not displayed, "jargon" language is not used by workers, and first-name relationships with families are common. Workers also dress casually. In addition, staff do whatever they can, including referring applicants to families who have already adopted from the agency, to convince applicants that Spaulding workers will place a child with a family who admits to not being "perfect," that they believe parental rights begin with the moment of placement, and that if post-placement problems develop, they will try to help the family work them out rather than automatically remove the child.

In keeping with these philosophies, workers take the time to prepare children and families for the process of adoption and the potential problems of living together. The staff help families learn about and extend their own parenting capacities and provide them with comprehensive and accurate information about the children available for adoption through the agency. This is done in an effort to increase the probability that the placement will succeed and to minimize the risk of disruption. Adequate adoption preparation enables parents and children to base their decision to adopt each other on practical appraisals of their individual capabilities and readiness as well as on realistic expectations of what their life together will be like.

During the preparation period, families are helped to decide whether to adopt a child from the agency and, if so, what type of child that should be. Worker and family determine if the family possesses characteristics necessary to parent an older or handicapped child. When these issues are resolved, an appropriate child is "presented," a "blind" or "known" showing takes place, and child and family are prepared for their pre-placement visits. Adoption studies are written only after a child has been identified as appropriate for a specific family and the family intends to adopt that child.

Not all families who begin the agency's preparation process adopt a Spaulding child. Many withdraw their application or adopt elsewhere. Those few families who are felt to be inappropriate parents for an older or handicapped child are honestly informed by the Spaulding staff that they cannot place a child with them.

Spaulding workers are convinced that families who are given the opportunity to play a significant role in the determination of their adoption develop a more positive outlook toward adoption, the adoption program, and their worker. These families, together with their worker, receive the mutual support of knowing each is helping the other toward a common goal. The staff are convinced that applicants who carefully think through the positive and negative aspects of adopting a specific child and honestly appraise their ability to nurture that child are highly likely to be adequate parents.

12

Maintaining the Adoption

Michigan adoption programs are required by law to provide supervision to adoptive families until confirmation — to observe the placement, make judgments about the family's rate of progress toward successful adjustment, and to report this information to the court. If a satisfactory relationship is in progress, the placement eventually becomes a legal adoption. In most states, a concurring recommendation of the placement agency is required by the Court before the adoption can be finalized or confirmed.

Many agencies and courts define these post-placement activities as "supervision." Since the Spaulding staff do not regard their role before or after placement to be that of a "supervisor," they use the term "post-placement service" to refer to assistance provided to a family between placement and confirmation, as well as after confirmation.[1] The goal of this service is to help the family remain together in an environment which is both physically and emotionally beneficial to the adopted child and to all other family members.

Spaulding workers are convinced that the placement of an older or handicapped child should not be regarded as a signal to end contact between the placement staff and the family. Because many, if not most, such adoptions will encounter major problems, their success after placement frequently requires the continued and active participation of staff in the family's adjustment process.

---

[1]Technically, services offered following confirmation constitute "post-confirmation service," but since these tend to be similar to services offered prior to confirmation, the Spaulding staff prefer to use one inclusive term.

The successful maintenance of an adoptive placement is seen as beginning with careful pre-placement preparation of the child and family who will be living together. Despite the staff's commitment to the need for such preparation, the workers have learned that it is often impossible to adequately prepare a child or family for all of the problems and difficulties they will encounter. Some adoptive families are able to solve their problems themselves; others are not. As a result, the agency has built into its approach to adoption the ability and readiness to provide substantial post-placement services to families in need of temporary or continuing assistance.

Much of this assistance is an extension of the work done with families before placement. The staff continue to assure families that most adoptions of older and handicapped children are problematic and that it is predictable, and even acceptable, for them to have problems. They also expect families to work toward the solution of their adjustment problems and to remain committed to the child in times of difficulty.

Early in Spaulding's history, workers regarded post-placement services as primarily supportive. These contacts with families gave workers repeated opportunities to let families know the staff trusted them and continued to believe they were good parents who could, with experience and the agency's occasional help, provide for the child's needs, offer him security, and have their own needs fulfilled as well. Workers still provide this reassurance, yet greater experience has taught that successful maintenance of placements often requires full use of the combined resources of staff and community. This has been especially true in recent years because of an increase in the age and severity of handicaps of the children referred to Spaulding. As a result of this evolution, there has been a corresponding increase in the difficulty of parenting these children. It is the complexity of these children, as well as the appearance of problems in many earlier placements as those children have grown older, which have steadily expanded the number of families who request the agency's assistance.

The Spaulding staff operate on the premise that families who adopt are entitled to assistance after confirmation as well as following placement, and that such services are essential to the success of many adoptions of older and handicapped children. These services sometimes continue for years following placement, and are often necessary until the child has reached the age of legal majority, and sometimes even beyond that point.

REASONS FOR POST-PLACEMENT SERVICE

Spaulding's experience has shown that no matter how well the child and family are prepared for their placement together, they will always encounter experiences for which they are not prepared. Workers will need to help parents and children cope with these events in their lives if the placement is to succeed.

Most families interviewed by the authors expressed the feeling that they would have preferred to have more completely or totally prepared for their adoption. They realized, however, that perfect preparation would always remain an impossible goal to achieve. Even under the best of conditions, discussion alone can never provide the experience necessary for the child and family to live together. This can occur only after the child has been actually placed into the family.

The experiences of the Spaulding staff with the adjustment problems of the older and handicapped children they have placed for adoption have increased their knowledge of the kinds of difficulties parents of such children should be prepared to encounter. As a result, the majority of problems which afflict new placements usually occur in areas which are familiar to the worker and which have been discussed, to at least some degree, by family and worker before placement. These include the initial problems encountered between the adoptive child and his family as well as the subsequent and often complex problems which develop after the child is placed.

Initial Adjustment Problems

Many adoptive problems represent experiences which commonly occur when at least one new person is added to a family. Frequently parents feel a need to discuss and explore reactions to the new family member(s). Although workers attempt to help families discuss the adjustments, stresses, and rewards of adoption in depth, the experience, when it finally arrives, is usually surprising and often unsettling. One family expressed the unexpectedness of the experience as follows:

> "The first or second week you're suddenly sitting there and you realize that its no longer just you and your husband. There are two children there and they have a part of your life you're not sure you want to let go of. That's sheer panic. It is tempting to pick up the phone and call to have them taken back."

Some parents expressed surprise at their own expectations and actions. One commented:

> "You learn so much about yourself. We didn't expect to react the way we did."

Anticipated adjustment problems often occur because a child's behavior is unpredictable or because there is a wide discrepancy between parental expectations and their child's subsequent behavior:

"One of the problems which is constantly on our mind is that we never know what to expect from the kids — never. They haven't been here that long."

"When we first got her, she couldn't talk. Even now when you're talking to her and she's staring at you, you don't know that she understands. Now I'm convinced that she's a bright kid, that there's not a thing wrong with her head, and that she deliberately stands there with her mouth open, staring at you, so she won't have to answer. But for two years, I didn't know that, and it upset me."

Sometimes, however, a discrepancy between expectation and actual behavior results in a positive experience for child and parent:

"I thought I'd have a pretty good idea of what he was like if I read the history and listened to what they told me, which was that he was pretty withdrawn and it would be hard to pull him out of this. I would say that within an hour's time we were just talking away and he hasn't stopped."

Other initial adjustment problems may result from parents' feelings of ambivalence following placement. Workers must frequently help parents understand that it is normal for them to sometimes love a child and want to be with him and at other times wish they were far apart. At times, parents may question if the adoption was what they really wanted, or if the experience was "worth it." Later, they may feel tremendously guilty that they had such thoughts or negative feelings.

Families may even come to doubt their parenting capabilities for these or other reasons:

"We felt stupid saying, 'Well, look, we've got the children; now we don't know what to do with them.' "

They may also begin to feel that the adoption is having a detrimental effect on their other children and is taking a toll on their family life. Such negative feelings, combined with considerable positive feelings for the child and the adoption, are a normal part of the "ups and downs" of a placement. Yet many parents fail to recognize this until they repeatedly hear from their worker, or see for themselves, that there are many other families who have survived similar feelings.

Much of the worker's time after placement, and often beginning soon after placement, is spent helping children and families distinguish between "growing up" problems and "adoption" problems. "Growing up" problems are those problems common to all children as they pass through childhood and adolescence on their way to adulthood. "Adoption" problems are those difficulties which result from children coming into new families and the children's and family's expectation that they eventually will be legally adopted. "Adoption" problems exist in addition to "growing up" problems.

Despite their preparation, some parents are unduly sensitive to their child's adoptive status. In extreme cases, they assume that every problem which arises with the child or in their family after placement is somehow directly connected to their child's adoption. Parents who tie most existing problems to the child's past often fail to see that his behavior may actually result from normal development, or his "testing" to determine which behaviors his parents will allow. Other parents are able to discuss and resolve this problem:

"At first, we thought it was because he was adopted . . . he'd been through a lot, you know . . . but then this guy at work kept telling me his kid was the same way, only worse, so we decided it was just because he's that age."

Spaulding workers have found that in many cases parents remain uncertain about what behaviors are normal for a certain age range or for children with a specific handicap. To complicate the problem, there is often a considerable discrepancy between the chronological age and the social or mental age of many of the children who traditionally have been considered "hard-to-place." Many are far more immature than children of the same age who have not experienced the same difficulties in life. As a result, it may be very difficult for parents to know what to expect as "typical" of these slower children:

"We have a four year old boy and a five year old boy, and Jenny (our adopted daughter), who'll be eleven. Sometimes I realize she's acting like a four year old and she's an eleven year old, and there's something in your mind that makes you uncomfortable when you see someone not behaving the way you expect them to behave. When she does things, I have to check whether I'm angry because she's wrong, or because she's not acting typically."

Although families are repeatedly told by the staff prior to placement that their children will experience certain difficulties, some must live with the child for an extended period of time before they clearly understand the accuracy of the workers' information. Until they reach that level of understanding, they frequently misperceive the source of the child's problems.

Complex Adjustment Problems

Despite the frequent occurrence of the initial adjustment problems described above, most adoptive problems are actually created by circumstances which are more extensive than the initial adjustment and reactions of parent and child to each other. These complex adoptive problems shape the content of most post-placement services offered to adoptive families. Such problems usually result from:

1. the child's reaction to his past or present circumstances
2. the family's reaction to the child
3. a breakdown in worker effectiveness
4. unpredictable circumstances which are detrimental to the adoption

These problems, then, may be related to the child, the biological or foster parents, the adoptive parents, the workers, or to the relationship between any or all of the participants in the adoption process. They may be directly related to the adoption or, though unrelated, may intensify the problems of adoption or be intensified by them. No matter what their source, post-placement problems are always specific mental or physical reactions to existing behaviors or feelings.

Because individual feelings and attitudes are involved, each problem is unique and requires clear understanding of complex situations before attempts at solution can hope to succeed. There are no easy, one-step, solutions. No specific characteristic, such as age or sex of the child, the marital status, income, number of children, age, religious affiliations of the parents, or lack of geographic accessibility to the adoption program, has yet been identified as contributing significantly more than any other characteristic to the occurrence of problems after adoptive placement.

The child's reaction to past or present circumstances.

Difficulties in the maintenance of the child within his adoptive placement may occur if the child has not been adequately prepared for adoption, if parents or workers do not understand the child's problems, or if workers misperceive the child's ability to function in an adoptive setting or in a specific adoptive family.

To help prevent these problems, the Spaulding staff spend considerable time clarifying the child's past history and evaluating its impact on the child's current behavior. If the preparation of the child and the family had been done adequately, either the referring worker or a Spaulding worker will have discussed these issues with the child and family before placement.

In spite of adequate preparation, adopted children may still nostalgically recall, or even express a desire to return to, a previous foster family or their biological family. As a result, adoptive families frequently feel they must successfully compete with previous parents for the child's loyalty and affection. Spaulding workers realize that such feelings are normal. However, they also recognize that parents may have a difficult time talking about these emotions and often feel more comfortable once they are helped to discuss their concerns.

Additional problems in the adoption may occur if the child cannot cope with his feelings regarding his past or his adoption. Such unresolved feelings are most frequently elicited by a history of unfulfilled expectations or rejection and often produce a subsequent distrust of adults. Such feelings may also result from one or more poorly understood or otherwise stressful separations from previous sets of parents or placements. Both kinds of feelings often result in an inability to form close personal relationships or to make an adequate commitment to adoption and serve, in many cases, to sabotage the child's placement with a new family.

Ideally, of course, all children should be given the opportunity to discuss and explore their past. Adoptive parents often need help with this, however. Although the great majority of adoptive parents consistently want to do what is best for their children, some do not have the confidence to confront the potential conflicts and problems which could develop as a result of opening the child's past up to him. Some families resist talking with the child about his past or try to ignore his need to do so. These families are usually unsure of their own feelings or those of the child and do not want to risk exposing, and having to cope with, what may be unpleasant facts or poorly understood emotions.

Then too, questions such as "Why didn't my mother want me?" or "How can I find out who my *real* parents are?" can be both emotionally and factually difficult for a family to answer by themselves. The Spaulding staff have learned that workers can help families respond to such questions by assisting them in explaining to the child what adoption is and what it means, by helping the child answer questions about where he came from and who he is, and by discussing with him his experiences in a world where most people are not adopted.[1]

Despite such efforts, these are problems which cannot usually be totally resolved at any one point in the child's life. Matters of such importance often reappear in a new context as "recycled" problems when the child enters each significant phase of his life; i.e., at school entry, adolescence, marriage, and parenthood. Workers' efforts to assist

---

[1]The Spaulding staff believe the terms "real" parents and "natural" parents, which are most frequently applied to biological parents, create problems because many families who adopt logically (but often incorrectly) assume the child considers them to be "unreal" or "unnatural" and, therefore, of less value. Many of these problems of assumed inferiority would be lessened if children and parents could be helped to understand that, from a realistic point of view, the child's "real" parents (be they biological, foster, or adoptive) are those with whom the strongest reciprocal emotional ties exist.

with these and other problems children present in an adoptive placement may be found in the chapter entitled, "Preparing Children For
Adoption," p. 81.

The family's (and other's) reaction to the child.

As has been discussed in the previous chapter, the Spaulding staff
make special efforts to prepare the family for their specific adoption.
While parent preparation efforts can never be so perfect as to eliminate all
post-placement problems, larger and more complex problems will exist if
parents do not get adequate preparation. Difficulties in maintaining the
placement will be encountered if, for example, the placement worker
misperceives a family's level of parenting ability, attitude toward the
child, or commitment to make the adoption work. Without adequate
preparation, there may well be a misunderstanding of the responsibilites
or effects of the adoption process.

Other post-placement difficulties may be caused if an adoptive parent
(particularly the one who is home during the day) is unable to adjust to
the needs of the child or has difficulty developing a satisfactory parent-
child relationship. In 24 hour-a-day actuality, the child may turn out to
be more of an emotional burden than expected for parents who intellec-
tually felt they could parent that child.

Maintenance problems may also develop if parents are not able to
accept the child as their own and, instead, treat him as a visitor or a guest.
Others may have unfulfilled expectations or be embarrassed by the
child's "inappropriate" behavior or inability to solve what they consider
to be "easy" problems. Serious difficulties for both parents and child
may also occur if parents attempt to force the child into the mold of their
own values and life style, especially if these differ radically from the
child's previous way of life.

To minimize such problems, the Spaulding staff try to arrive at an
appropriate fit between child and parents. If this does not occur, dependent and passive parents, for example, may discover that they have
adopted an active and independent child (or vice versa). After the child is
in the home, the parents may transfer their feelings about the child's
unacceptability to an apparent dissatisfaction with the child's age or
behavior, and sometimes open conflict may develop.

Finally, post-placement difficulties may occur because of other circumstances, such as marital conflict brought on by the presence of the
child. The child may also be rejected by people important to him (new-
found relatives, neighbors, or playmates), or he may not be able to
resolve competition or fighting with his brothers or sisters. Other problems may be caused by children already in the family "copying," with-
drawing from, or otherwise adversely reacting to a newly placed child.

Some post-placement problems which are a legacy of the child's past may be caused by biological or foster parents who cannot "let go" of the child; who either demand his return to them or attempt to seduce him away from his new family placement. Under most circumstances, these difficulties occur because the child's previous parents are either told or expect that their contact with the child must end completely. In addition, many of these parents do not feel their contributions to the child's development are adequately recognized by workers or the child's adoptive parents. In a few cases, the former foster family may exhibit signs of guilt or emotional disturbance. All such circumstances should be carefully discussed with the referring agency or court.

In fairness to parents, it is important to note that most parents survive the child-rearing stresses they encounter and that these difficulties do not create incapacitating problems for all families. Many parents learn quickly to prevent or solve problems as they experience them. However, because parents are not always able to solve all of their problems, postplacement services must consist, in part, of helping families develop their own resources for coping with problems and reassuring them that they are capable of employing those resources.

One parent expressed his family's greatest reward for achieving this success:.

"We thought we couldn't cope with a child who had some school difficulties — with reading difficulties — now we have three children with reading difficulties, and we cope."

Breakdown in worker effectiveness.

The worker's inability to anticipate or talk about circumstances that might produce difficulties is often related to many post-placement problems: In many cases, the difficulties could not have been predicted prior to placement, for it is impossible for workers to foresee and discuss all the possible combinations of issues or circumstances that might produce problems.

The process of giving and gaining information between worker and family may break down and seriously impair the worker's effectiveness and the success of the placement. Each may be at fault, for either the worker or family may misunderstand important information given by the other. In fact, communication barriers are frequently created because workers, families, and children are unwilling to discuss information which makes them feel uncomfortable or vulnerable. Children and families may also be hesitant to admit to problems for fear that the placement will be terminated if the worker gains knowledge of those problems.

Workers may develop their own motivation for their failure to communicate adequately with a family. Some workers are reluctant to discuss certain topics or fear they may jeopardize their effectiveness as workers by pursuing topics families may find distasteful or otherwise unpleasant. If parents are not able to talk about their own problems or the problems of their child, they may give workers both direct and indirect support for ignoring the child's past. They may also repeatedly frustrate the worker's efforts to discuss current difficulties within the placement. However, even more extensive problems may develop if the child and family are allowed to continue to ignore or fantasize their earlier life or present circumstances. As indicated in more detail in the following chapter, unresolved breakdown in problem-solving will almost always lead to the disruption of the placement.

Unpredictable circumstances detrimental to an adoption.

A variety of unpredictable problems may also occur after the placement of the child which create the need for post-placement services. Difficulties in maintaining the placement may be greatly increased if an unexpected illness strikes the child or any other family member of if there is a death in the family. Marital stress and financial difficulty may also represent unpredictable circumstances which could seriously threaten the adoption.

Such events may require the supportive intervention of the adoption worker in order for the family to survive the experience and remain together. Since the entrance of any new child into a family creates a significant amount of stress because that family must make certain necessary adjustments, the addition of subsequent unexpected circumstances may produce a traumatic emotional overload in even those families able to survive all other previous problems.

Obviously, families must be given assistance through these difficult times if the placement is to survive. Sadly, however, many families so fear what placement workers might do if they knew of existing problems (i.e., remove the child or report the difficulties to the Court) that they refuse to reach for the help available. At Spaulding, it is the workers' job to create a climate where sharing such information is a normal and natural part of the relationship between family and staff.

VARIETIES OF SERVICE DELIVERY

The services provided by the Spaulding staff to families following placement are of five varieties. These are:

1. Casework (individual worker contacts and team contacts)
2. Volunteer family contacts
3. Community resources
4. Social events
5. Parents' groups

Casework (individual worker contacts and team contacts)

The most commonly provided post-placement service is the ready help provided by the family's own worker. Since the child's pre-placement worker is usually a staff member from the referring court or agency and is frequently inaccessible and/or unable to help with post-placement problems, the Spaulding worker is the family's worker throughout the adoption. Usually, it is the same Spaulding worker who prepared the family for the placement.

As has been indicated in the chapter entitled, "Teamwork and Collegial Supervision," the task of maintaining a child in a family is not the sole responsibility of a single worker, but rather one which is shared by the entire placement staff at the agency. Spaulding's casework service, as well as all other services, derives its strength and support from continuous consultation, collegial supervision, and decision-making/problem-solving discussions involving the entire placement team.

When a family determines that they have a problem which requires agency support (that is, when the problem defies solution by the parents), they usually make direct contact with the worker who has been given primary responsibility for the maintenance of their placement. After that worker assesses the family's placement situation to determine what kind of help is required, that assessment, along with all relevant background material, is shared with the other members of the placement staff. That entire group discuss observations, conclusions, and recommendations with one another at regularly scheduled weekly team meetings.

Following discussion, the staff suggest alternatives for solution to the family's primary worker who conveys this information to the family. One or more of the other members of the staff is always available to assist that worker whenever their help is requested. The family, in turn, usually implements either the initial recommendation or an alternative triggered by that suggestion.

Both worker and family benefit from team contacts. In addition to offering a wider perspective and increasing the chances that a workable solution to a problem can be found, team contacts provide a family with additional information and support, a fresh outlook at their specific situation, and new insights into the potential solution of problems or difficulties.

As a further benefit, the presence of more than one worker can corroborate or correct the view of a worker not entirely sure of their understanding of a family situation. Since the problems of parenting an older or handicapped children are often complex, opportunities to discuss questions and explore options with other workers who have been directly involved with the same family are frequently indispensable resources for the successful maintenance of placements.

All staff members share the responsibility for providing this service and make themselves accessible should the need arise. The array of available skills plus the team's commitment to do whatever they can to help maintain the child in his adoptive family enables the agency's workers to work together cooperatively and successfully support a wide variety of families.

Continuing the Worker-Family Partnership.
It is the staff's intention that the partnership between workers and family developed during the family's preparation for adoption continue through the post-placement period. This partnership permits workers to share the important events in the lives of the child and the family and enables them to help families solve those problems which may significantly affect the child and his future with the family. Workers feel that problems which negatively affect the successful maintenance of an adoption are better controlled when families and workers are well-informed, able to discuss information and feelings openly, and capable of sharing efforts to solve the crucial problems which arise.

In order for workers to provide the services needed to maintain placements in which significant problems exist, families must be willing to accept assistance. Although such willingness is essential for service delivery, and willingness obviously produces far more positive consequences than does refusal, the Spaulding staff do not consider a successful partnership to exist if it is the worker who must initiate service. At Spaulding, the key ingredient in a successful partnership is the family's ability to ask for aid whenever it is needed. However, the staff must also recognize and accept that the family may see diminishing contact with their worker(s) as evidence of a successful placement.

The development of the kind of partnership sought by the staff depends upon their ability to convince families that problems and subsequent worker involvement are often a routine part of the adoption of older and handicapped children. If families are to ask for assistance and not simply show a willingness to receive it, they must be convinced that the staff will not only continue to be supportive when problems occur and believe that families should discuss those problems and seek help for them, but will continue to guarantee that the child will not be removed just because problems exist.

The staff must take great care when conveying these messages to families. For example, although workers may say that problems are a normal part of adoption, the worker who is inexperienced, insecure, or tired can still give the message "but of course, if you are good parents, you won't need our help." Such conflicting messages, no matter how infrequent, inevitably rekindle a family's doubts and insecurity and make more difficult the task of building trust.

With all adoptive families, the worker's job is to help resolve problems in their early stages so they do not progress so far that the family loses their commitment to, or capacity for, continuing with the adoption. To minimize the occurrence and severity of problems, the content of presentation materials must be repeatedly reviewed with the child and family, both before and after placement. (For more information, see "Preparing Families for Adoption,"pp. 131.) Despite families' best efforts to listen to and understand information, most are so excited about the prospects of the approaching adoption that they do not hear all that is being said. In addition, they tend to "play down" the seriousness of potential problems in adoption, or do not believe such problems will ever exist for them. For these reasons, the staff's post-placement services include the creation of continuing opportunities for families to compare their experiences with those of other families, to ask questions, and to seek advice.

Workers show families how to help themselves by reviewing and interpreting what has happened before, during, and after placement, and by working to help keep communication open between child, family, and staff. Whenever the services of a worker are sought, Spaulding families usually offer descriptions of their successes and problems as well as their attempts at solution, and the worker assists in reviewing alternatives or in searching for other resources.

The services provided by Spaulding workers are not final solutions but a series of explicit suggestions for working out the unique problems encountered by a specific family. To be able to offer appropriate suggestions, workers sift and discuss the family's problems, incorporate the non-verbal information family members are providing, and rely on their recollections of which suggestions produced positive results in previous circumstances.

Both before and after confirmation, a Spaulding family can choose to accept or reject a worker's advice or suggestion. Families, not workers, are expected to make the final decision about what they can and cannot comfortably accomplish within their adoption. Although workers do try to persuade families to accept what they consider to be their most appropriate suggestion, a family is rarely required to implement a recommendation. Only if the child's presence in the family becomes demonstrably harmful to him prior to confirmation would the staff intercede with the court to set aside the parental rights of the adopting family. This action would only occur after the staff have negotiated with the family to determine the most appropriate solution. When problems exist which do not, in the workers' opinion, endanger the child, the staff will do whatever they can to help the family maintain their right to parent the child.

It is not always easy to define the boundaries of staff responsibility. The worker who offers post-placement services must walk a fine line between protecting the child and upholding parents' rights and decisions; between encouraging the family to do what is best and pushing them so far or fast that they become alienated from the placement program and its workers. There is no simple formula for minimizing major difficulties once the child has been placed. No action or solution is always adequate, true, or valid, because problems and perspectives vary with each child, family, and worker.

It should be emphasized that Spaulding's successful maintenance of older and handicapped children following adoptive placement is the result of clearly and repeatedly explaining to families that the workers not only desire to share responsibility for the child with the parents, but believe the family's custodial rights are primary. The family who has been adequately prepared for a Spaulding adoption knows the agency's philosophy as well as what the staff expect from parents. The workers have learned that the practical applicaton of their commonsense philosophy is what most adoptive applicants really desire. It is the staff's belief that the consistent practice of this philosophy is largely responsible for their ability to create and maintain a trusting partnership between family and worker.

Because post-placement services are given as needed, and problems may occur at any time, there is little difference between the kinds of services the staff provide to families before and after the adoption has been confirmed. There are, however, unavoidable differences before and after confirmation in the relationship between family and workers. Family anxiety is usually decreased following confirmation of the adoption. This anxiety results from the legal reality that the court shares custody of the child with the family prior to confirmation. In addition, Spaulding workers, as representatives of the placing agency, have the legal obligation to report periodically to the court on the progress of the child's adjustment. For these reasons, even those families who have developed a successful partnership with the agency tend to feel their adoption is more secure once Spaulding's obligation to the court is ended through confirmation.

Patterns of Contact
The pattern of future contact between the family and the Spaulding staff is usually formulated as the child nears placement. During the process of preparing, showing, and introducing a specific child to the family, the worker and family establish a tentative schedule for continuing assistance. Contacts can be initiated by the worker, the family, or someone outside of the agency or the home.

Worker-Initiated Contact — During the first several weeks of placement, workers usually initiate frequent contacts. Following this period of initial adjustment, most families make contact when they feel the need to do so. The workers supplement these calls by routine telephone contact and periodic, planned home visits. All unconfirmed adoptions are "active" cases, and these families receive on-going contact from workers. Families whose adoptions are confirmed remain "active" or resume that status as the pattern of service becomes more frequent. Workers expect most families to need at least sporadic assistance. However, workers initiate contact more frequently if the family is either unwilling, or finds it difficult, to call the agency.

Workers strive to make telephone contact with each of the "active" families at least once a month. The staff also try to maintain monthly telephone contact with families who have requested and received assistance with problems in the past. This routine contact often occurs less frequently than planned, however, for workers generally have other pressing demands upon their time (such as family crises, court hearings, or the preparation of other children or families for placement). As a result, the agency staff generally depend upon families to initiate contact whenever needed, unless they have reason to believe the family will not do so.

Workers call families for many reasons. For example, the worker may have made a previous commitment to call or may have concluded that the family would welcome a chance to talk. The worker may have found an article which is believed will be helpful to the family, or a community organization or newspaper may have asked the agency for some information which can be obtained only from certain families. The worker also may call to ask the family if they will serve as a volunteer family. At times, workers simply call to "chat" — to renew contact, remind the family of their availability, and keep abreast of adventures relating to the child, the school situation, and other members of the family.

Face-to-face contacts may also be used on a routine basis, but because of heavy worker schedules, they more frequently serve as a means of solving a problem which cannot be adequately handled on the phone. These visits customarily take place in the family home as a conveniece to the family. Workers prefer not to discuss problems in detail on the telephone if they feel families will speak more freely and comfortably in the presence of the worker about difficulties which defy simple solution. No worker at the agency would normally consider an unannounced visit if there was any chance it would create discomfort for the family.

Family-Initiated Contact — As placement approaches, some families clearly state their intentions to remain in regular contact with the Spaulding staff following placement. These families do not necessarily anticipate problems, but usually believe that regular worker contact will help prevent problems and, therefore, is the best available form of "adoption

insurance" they can get. Other families feel a greater sense of independence and have confidence in their capacity to handle problems that arise
or find their own resources in times of need. These parents may initiate
contact with the staff either at specific intervals or whenever they need
help. They may also rely upon the workers to make routine contact.

Worker's telephone calls to families may provide families with opportunities to request service. Given the opportunity, families may say, "I'm
glad you called. I've been meaning to talk to you about . . . " or simply
"When are we going to see you again?" Workers make time to see the
family whenever they are signalled, however indirectly, that a visit is in
order.

Agency staff know their families well enough to be able to clarify their
own general concerns with more specific questions relating to a placement's past or potential problem areas. Workers frequently review information given or received during their last conversation with the
family. They may ask "Are things better, worse, or the same?" or "Did
you try the ideas we discussed? Did they work? What else needs to be
done?"

The Spaulding workers have found, however, that they must be alert to
implied meanings behind simple positive answers to their inquiries.
Such follow-up is especially important because some families feel uncomfortable asking for help in spite of the staff's best efforts to encourage
them to do so. A worker who feels that a family may need the agency's
help will begin to approach this possibility indirectly, usually by reviewing typical problems related to the area of concern or by asking specific
informed questions which may make it easier for the family to seek and
accept help. The worker's ability to "draw out" a family depends upon
the strength of the worker-family relationship and the skill and style of
the worker.

Other Sources of Contact — On occasion, someone outside of the family or
agency identifies a problem and brings the need for service to the
attention of a worker. The most common of these outside referral sources
is the school. In most cases when school officials contact the agency, they
have already talked with the family. School personnel may feel the family
needs further assistance in understanding the child or his situation.
They may also want the agency's assistance in interpreting the school's
position on specific issues to the family.

Sometimes, referrals are made by social workers in other agencies or
the court. On rare occasions, the need for service is brought to the staff's
attention by a relative, a friend, or a neighbor expressing concern for a
child's behavior or a family's functioning. Many families call the worker

immediately when they have a problem which involves individuals outside the family. Their freedom in asking for the staff's assistance early indicates the extent to which the family views the agency's interests as coinciding with their own.

Lack of Worker/family Contact —— There are a number of reasons for no contacts between worker and family. Some families may not perceive a need to seek agency assistance. (The Spaulding staff believe they are entitled to that decision.) Other families may not have taken seriously the workers' offer to help whenever the need arose, or may find they are too embarrassed to request assistance because they once told their worker "Oh, sure, we can handle it." A family may believe that no social worker can solve their problem. They may also not contact the agency because they do not think their "old" worker is or could be still around, or they may not be aware that other workers are available to offer their assistance. This does not tend to be a frequent problem because of the staff's team approach.

Some families do not want others to know they have problems or else it is family policy, or part of their life style, to never discuss family concerns with others under any circumstances. Some families also believe that the characteristics of the children the Spaulding staff now place have changed so much since they adopted in the earlier days of the agency that their child is no longer considered problematic enough to merit the attention of the agency's staff. Others do not want to deal with the pain that working to solve problems may create. When workers recognize that difficulty, they work with the family to resolve the matter. In most instances, workers and families are able to establish a pattern of contact which provides an opportunity to focus on difficulties and discuss alternatives to reduce those concerns.

The pattern of contact often continues uninterrupted following confirmation. However, patterns may gradually alter with changes in the family's view of their need for services. Approximately 20% of all families who adopt a Spaulding child maintain a consistently high frequency of contact after confirmation. (The staff are usually very aware of the home and community situation of these families.) About 60% of all families sporadically contact the agency for post-confirmation services. The remaining 20% totally end contact once the adoption is confirmed. As there is no continuing legal reason or personal need to maintain contact, these families signal that no further contact is needed or desired. Since 80% of all Spaulding families continue some form of service contact with the staff, there exists abundant proof of the agency's claim that workers follow through with their offer of on-going assistance to children and families.

Volunteer Family Contacts

As has been indicated earlier, casework represents Spaulding's major method of service delivery to families. A supplementary source of assistance in the maintenance of an adoptive placement is provided through volunteer family contacts. As discussed in the chapter entitled "Preparing Families for Adoption," some families who have adopted a child through Spaulding offer to help other parents or children with the adoptive experience. These are Spaulding's "volunteer" families. The services they provide to other families are of two kinds: furnishing an informal introduction to "real" adoption; and supporting the adjustment efforts of other adopters.

In the first instance, the worker may suggest an applicant family visit a volunteer family to learn more about adoption, about specific handicaps, or about their own interest in children. The second role enables one adoptive family to provide another with the emotional support they need in order to solve their problems or to determine if the problems they are experiencing are typical. These contacts may be suggested by staff. However, families who need support or assistance beyond that available through their worker often seek out other families on their own initiative. Volunteer family contacts may occur once or for the purpose of solving a single problem. They may also evolve into a firm and long-standing friendship greatly beneficial to both families. Which volunteer family is contacted depends on the interests of the applicants, their location in the state, and the availability of families able to offer the kinds of services required.

Community Resources

At times, families require more specialized services than the Spaulding staff are capable of providing. Some situations demand that the family be served by community resources. For example, many of the children placed by Spaulding workers have such serious emotional problems that they require the help of a professional therapist who is also sensitive to the special adjustment problems of adopted children. These disturbed children, as well as those who are retarded or physically handicapped, also often require a range of services offered by educational specialists within the school system. For some families, effective support services may be obtained from clergymen or other counselors.

Since many Spaulding families now require the assistance of specialized resources, the agency's post-placement services frequently take the form of assisting families in contacting community resources. The decision to refer the family to one or more community resources usually follows a team judgment that the Spaulding staff cannot or should not provide the service the family requires. This decision is often a difficult one to make, for the choice is frequently between over-taxing a worker's time or ability and seeking an outside service that may be limited by long waiting lists or poor understanding of the needs and problems of older or handicapped adopted children. Too few professionals now providing counseling services to children and their families adequately understand the deprivational effects of a child's separation from his biological parents or the detrimental psychological effects of cyclical foster care.

Before suggesting alternative resources to a family, the staff explore their availablity and appropriateness, usually by making personal contact. Workers attempt to determine whether the community resource staff understands the adoptive experience and if they have the skills which the Spaulding team feel are important to the family. In addition, workers gather information concerning current intake policies, cost of services, potential sources of funding to cover these costs, and the potential obligations of the adoptive family and the referring agency. This information is then provided to the family.

If the family decides the services furnished by the community resource are not suitable, Spaulding workers will help look for other services. The cost of the community resource is rarely a factor in determining its suitability. Money is often available from community sources, special interest groups, or by virtue of an adoption subsidy through which parents may obtain psychological, psychiatric, or educational services outside the agency.

When families receive services outside of the agency, Spaulding workers continue to offer their support during the family's contact with those resources. For example, adoptive families may need help assessing the effectiveness of psychiatric or psychological treatment or the meaning of reports. They may also need assistance in negotiating with school personnel. Working class parents, new adoptive parents, or parents who have not previously had a child in school may feel quite uncomfortable talking to teachers, principals, or educational specialists about enrolling their child in school or making arrangements to have their child enter a special class or change his educational program.

Most school officials, teachers, and consultants realize that the placement worker's information and intervention can help them better serve the child, especially if he is entitled to special education programs. Thus, interpretations of the child's problems and needs to professionals in schools and other resources have become an increasingly large part of Spaulding's post-placement responsibility.

The staff's support during contacts with community resources is intended both to help the family directly and to demonstrate to them how to find services in the future. The staff believe that a family will probably not receive the services they require from available community resources unless social workers do more than "suggest" they need the service, advise them to make contact as soon as possible, and provide them with a name and address.

Whether or not community resources are involved, Spaulding workers view the post-placement experience as an exciting but difficult time shared by family and staff. They tend to regard the services they provide as the family's best opportunity to solve or cope with the problems they encounter. Nevertheless, they remain enthusiastic about coordinating their services with any community resources which work effectively with the kinds of children for whom they find adoptive families.

Social Events

A fourth important part of Spaulding's post-placement services program, and one greatly anticipated by adoptive families, is comprised of family-oriented social events. The large attendance at the two annual social events held at the Spaulding farmhouse attests to the success of the staff's partnership approach to adoption and the willingness and need of their families to maintain an active relationship with their workers.

One of these events, the Tree Trimming Party, is usually held on the Saturday before Christmas. Adoptive families are invited to gather to trim a freshly-cut tree, share holiday cookies and punch, encourage the children to break a candy-filled pinata, and await the arrival of Santa who has a gift for each child.

The second social event for Spaulding families and friends is the Ice-Cream Social, held each summer. As many as 200 people have attended these festivities which include a picnic lunch and all the free cake one can eat. There are a variety of games and prizes for the children and a craft table where items that have been made or provided by adoptive parents, staff, and volunteers may be bought.

Though not all families attend these events, all are invited. For those who do attend, the Tree Trimming Party and the Ice-Cream Social are felt to be a very important part of being a member of the entire Spaulding family (which includes adoptive children, parents, workers, board members, volunteers, and supporters). Both events give children and families an opportunity to visit with old friends and make new ones. They also give each person the feeling of belonging to a community of individuals who share common interests and experiences.

For many families, each is also a chance to visit with the various staff members they know. For staff, both provide an opportunity to see each family as a unit. Even the families who choose not to attend often feel a strong sense of satisfaction in being invited. Many of them express the feeling of belonging or of being remembered. Such experiences and

The Annual Tree Trimming Party at Spaulding each December gives Spaulding families an opportunity to get together during the Christmas season. There is plenty of ice-cream and cake and presents for the children brought by Santa himself.

The Ice Cream Social, held each mid-summer on the lawn of the Spaulding farm, is a good opportunity for children, families, staff members, and volunteers to share good times and renew acquanitances.

attitudes strengthen the relationship between family and staff and increase the likelihood of contacts in times of family crisis.

Parents' Groups

Parents' groups at Spaulding originated in 1970 in response to parents' requests for more support for their parenting skills than that which could be provided by casework and team contacts. One of the earliest and longest-lived parents groups consisted of two single parents and two married couples which met monthly over a two year period and only disbanded when the single parents transferred to a group formed exclusively for single parents by Spaulding and a nearby county public welfare department.

These families had asked for the opportunity to talk with other adoptive parents who could understand the difficulties of parenting an older or handicapped child. They felt other parents might offer alternative ways of handling the problems they were having. Some families simply wanted to meet with workers and other families on a regular basis to discuss mutual experiences.

Parents' groups had been expected to provide for the mutual sharing of parenting problems, but the reward of sharing parenting successes was not foreseen. The group's gave parents the opportunity to share positive experiences with those people who best understood how hard the job was and who could best appreciate their achievements. The groups were seen to be extremely supportive, for they provided reassurance that many of the behaviors which concerned adoptive parents were common to most children of a certain age or with a specific handicap. It was helpful, too, to have other parents point out progress made, for many parents could not easily see beyond the problems of the moment, and they tended to regard the social worker as an employed optimist.

Prospective adoptive parents occasionally visited existing parents' groups to gain a closer view of the potential problems the workers described. Such visits not only offered applicants a better picture of the needs and problems of the children, but provided group members with the opportunity to increase their own confidence by helping other parents.

Unfortunately, few of the Spaulding parents who might have benefited from participating in these groups have been able to do so. Since the agency serves families throughout Michigan as well as surrounding states and provinces, the greatest difficulty faced in forming parent groups is the long distances parents and workers must travel to meet together. Over time, the requirement of extensive travel also tends to decrease the motivation to sustain group efforts to find solutions to problems.

Serious obstacles to group participation also exist because individuals who do live near each other may not be at the same point in their placements, may not encounter similar problems, or may not encounter similar problems closely enough together in time so they can share them as a group. In addition, not all parents are willing or able to work well in a group, and this factor may further decrease potential group membership. Some parents are uncomfortable when talking about personal problems. Others resent open discussion in the presence of other parents.

For these reasons, parents' groups, though valued by staff as a significant means of family support, have never become a primary means of post-placement service at Spaulding. The staff feel that the geographic problems often faced by small agencies could be overcome if adoption workers were willing to form local groups by combining families from several placement programs. They have attempted a few such efforts, but the sacrifices of time and effort members needed to make in order to plan for and maintain the group have always outweighed the group's need to meet.

WHAT IS THE WORKER'S RESPONSIBILITY?

Workers at Spaulding have not always taken responsibility for the full range of services they now provide. Early in their history, the staff found that many families needed frequent reassurance and support from their workers as well as help in seeking the solutions to specific problems. In recent years, with an increase in the age and severity of the handicaps of the children placed, there has also been an increased demand for services to assist parents with the greater number of problems they faced in rearing these children.

The increasing demand for services, support, and reassurance has meant that the staff have frequently struggled to determine the optimal limits of worker involvement and responsibility. The desire to promote family self-sufficiency has evolved from a philosophical ideal to an increasingly practical achievement now that workers do not have the time to become involved with every major event that touches every child. To best serve their families, the staff must repeatedly decide what problems and difficulties they should become involved with, and which are best left to be handled by the family.

The problem of worker responsibility has been seriously compounded by unrealistically high parental expectations. Despite the staff's repeated warnings to the contrary, many parents feel that social workers can solve any and all problems they encounter. Such expectations were at least partially reinforced early in the agency's history when the staff's deep commitment to children and their comparatively small number of total placements led to attempts to solve every major post-placement problem encountered by their families. At that time, workers tended to feel they were not doing their job well unless they achieved this goal.

However, with more placements, the workers realized that they could no longer attempt to solve all of the major problems involving the children they placed. At present, the staff continue to encourage families to come to them for help with any problems they feel they cannot handle themselves. In cases where help is not solicited, the staff will intervene only in those problems which threaten the ultimate stability of the placement. They recognize that an oppressive caseload is more detrimental to quality of service than asking families to assume a greater portion of the responsibility for their placements.

Since making this decision, the workers have sometimes felt less effective than before, but they feel justified in encouraging parents to take more responsibility for meeting their own problem-solving needs than was previously the case. They have also begun to develop and make frequent use of a wide range of knowledgable community resources.

Despite the implementation of these more realistic goals, the staff have found that there is no easy method of determining how to make best use of limited worker time. With more experience, workers have increased their ability to organize their time and set priorities so they can help families with pressing problems and emergencies as well as leave some time for more routine work and other staff assignments. However, their challenging problems requires workers to consistently reorganize their schedules as new problems arise.

The team approach has been invaluable both in helping workers sort out their appropriate responsibilities and in reorganizing priorities so they are able to act in a timely and effective manner to help families. Since all members of staff are kept informed of events and problems in a large number of families, the team approach also allows informed workers to "substitute" for each other in emergency situations, thus further insuring that families receive the help they need even when the primary worker is unable to provide that assistance.

SUMMARY

The Spaulding staff are convinced that their services to older and handicapped children and their families must continue beyond the legally required "supervisory" period between placement and confirmation. Since the children placed by Spaulding workers almost always have physical, mental, and/or emotional handicaps, it is expected that families will encounter difficulties in raising them. As a result, the staff regard post-placement services as essential to the successful continuation of many of their placements.

There are many potential causes for the difficulties which families can encounter. While some stresses are expected during the initial adjustment period, serious additional problems will result if the family and child are not adequately prepared for the adoption. Even if careful preparation has occurred, events from the child's past may continue to haunt the placement or new and unpredicted problems may develop which can be detrimental to the adoption.

Spaulding workers depend upon the worker-family partnership, established in their earliest contacts together, to provide an array of opportunities for supportive service following placement. They depend most heavily upon casework services (both those which are offered by individual workers and those shaped by the team approach) to support placements. However, the addition of "volunteer" families, community resources, agency-sponsored social events, and where possible, parents' groups provide families with the kinds of valuable help and assistance which cannot be obtained from even the most skilled social worker.

Rocking Chair Acres

The past six years have brought a lot of love to Rocking Chair Acres. Single Moms Helen Cortright and Kathleen Ragen have adopted Katie, 6; Mike, 7; Kenny, 2; and Chris, 6. Each child was once considered handicapped in some way. Chris, a Spaulding child, born without lower arms or hands, has a smile for everyone. His exuberance and exhileration overshadow his handicap and all around him get caught up in the joy of life itself. At Rocking Chair Acres, variety is the spice of life and each individual adds his share to make up a unique family bound together by love. Add a five bedroom farm home, ponies, show rabbits, guinea pigs, dogs, cats, fish, and a pet monkey. Still, there's always room for one more!

The Hoffman Family

The Hoffmans adopted Todd, now nine, five years ago. The family's other children are Katy, Elly, and Joey. Along with their parents, they are regulars at the Spaulding annual Tree Trimming Party.

The McKinley Family

A single father, William McKinley, with a single son, 12 year old Dion (the best ever), and maybe more to come?

The Meagher Family

The Meaghers are a family of four children adopted from Spaulding (Larry, 18; Rex, 16; Floyd, 15; and Tina, 13) and three biological children (Jeanie, 14; Tim, 11; and Kevin, 6). Lots of families adopt children, but the Meagher's country home has more room than most. A family this size knows that time is a most appreciated gift, and they spend it together whenever they can — gardening, school plays and band concerts, and Sunday morning breakfasts. Adoptions, like marriage, involve a little luck and a lot of give and take. The old and the new Meaghers consider themselves lucky, but those smiles on their faces are the result of hard work at living and loving together. (Since this picture was taken, the Meaghers have adopted a family of four Mexican/American Indian children from Spaulding — Donna, 16; Ann, 14; Gilbert, 13; and Karen, 11.)

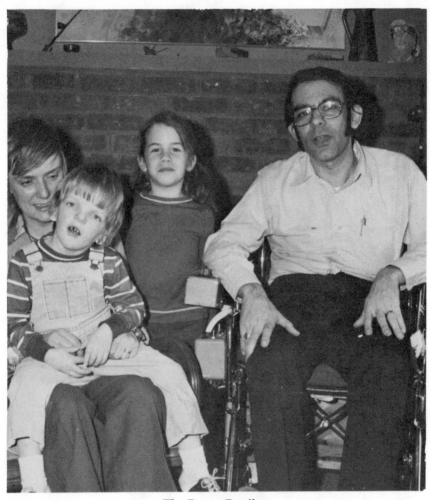

The Perros Family

Matthew, now five, was born with multiple borderline handicaps, including Median Cleft Syndrome. He was adopted at 2½ months of age, at a time when the range of both his physical and mental development were unpredictable. As a result of medical treatment and special educational programs, Matt is progressing well. The Perros' other child is Chris, age 7.

The Storr Family

Machelle was adopted in 1969 at the age of 7 months. Although a perfectly healthy young charmer, she waited for adoption because of her racially mixed heritage. Children like Machelle rarely wait for adoption now since more families, both black and white, are eager to parent such children. Mandy and Leroy Storr count themselves as lucky to have Machelle as one of their five children and feel that more families should experience the joys of adoption. Son Donnie, 18, is on the right.

The Wanger Family

Spaulding would not survive without the volunteer efforts of families such as the Wagners. Three of their children are adopted. Richard, 16, and David, 15, are in classes for the trainably retarded. Angela, 9, is in a regular class while Mary Beth, 6, attends Michigan School for the Blind. Six year old Beth Ann has emotional and learning problems.

The Yager Family

The Yagers, who all have motorcycles and love to go camping, just wanted a little girl. They adopted Laura, a Down's Syndrome child, now age 13, three years ago. Laura has learned to ride a bicycle, care for herself, and is a good swimmer. She is also starting to learn to read. Doing especially well in her special education classroom is very pleasing to Laura and her family, but being able to actually help others, especially Mom in the kitchen, is the best feeling of all.

13
Adoption Services to Working Class Families

In the judgment of the Spaulding staff, the traditional adoption agency policy of choosing adoptive parents who meet ideal white middle class standards as parents for hard-to-place children is a practice which is detrimental to the placement of such children.

Although Spaulding workers do place some children in middle class families, it is their conviction that most older and handicapped children are more readily assimilated into working class homes. They are also convinced that workers who wish to successfully place these kinds of children for adoption will need to feel comfortable working with these families. Unfortunately, however, social workers do not always understand or feel sympathetic to the values and life styles of working class families. A clarification of the dissimilarities between middle and working class families will assist social workers in their work with these families.

The Spaulding staff broadly categorize the families they work with as either middle class or working class. Workers view as middle class those families who receive a salaried income for professional or skilled-labor employment, have some college education, rely on the reactions of peers or the community to help define their success as a family, and expect that a child's social and educational performance will gain him access to improved social opportunity. The staff consider families to be representative of the working class if they work at unskilled or semi-skilled employment for an hourly wage, have a junior high school or high school education, do not heavily rely on social acceptance by peers or the community as a measure of family success, and are more relaxed about the child's social educational achievement. Most of the families who adopt children through Spaulding have more working class than middle class characteristics by these definitions.

The staff recognize that their definitions of these terms are not theoretically precise, and that most families do not fit neatly into either category. Large numbers of Spaulding's applicants have a family structure, methods of solving problems, or many values not typical of any one social class. The distinction clarifies many differences among families, however, and helps the Spauding staff find appropriate families for specific children. There are some children clearly more comfortable with one kind of family than another. Knowing the differences between a child's background and a family's background assists workers in understanding many of the discrepancies of "fit" which may exist between child and family.

MIDDLE CLASS/WORKING CLASS DIFFERENCES

It is the experience of the Spaulding staff that discrepancies between working class family attitudes and expectations and the more typically middle class background of workers can create tension or conflict between the adoption worker and the family. In addition, the worker's faulty understanding of these families can greatly hinder effective placement. It is clear that wholesale improvements in such relationships are essential. However, what is initially needed is clarification of the differences between the worker's experiences and those of the families they serve.

Values

Many working class families have personal values and a life style unlike that of adoption workers. Working class families, for example, may believe in sharply separating the behaviors and tasks designated for sons and daughters, while workers might favor less differentiated sex roles. Working class families tend to structure their family life around the parents rather than the child and to expect, and enforce, automatic obedience. Such a style might not be highly regarded by workers who favor a child-centered or democratic orientation. Many such parents view physical punishment as right and necessary for some or all children in the family. The adoption worker may be convinced that physical punishment is usually inappropriate for children and often a clear signal that the parents feel "out of control" of a given situation. Values and behaviors such as these, characteristic of many working class families, may be viewed so negatively that they may cause adoption workers to regard such families as unfit to adopt.

It is also characteristic of these families to have a very high (and sometimes unquestioning) regard for authority, both inside and outside the home. Such families may assume that persons whose educational background far surpasses their own have competence in many fields. This assumption can lead families to expect that a social worker can easily and quickly solve any problem which may arise with children after they are adopted.

Outside the home, working class families may appear passive and acquiescent in the presence of well-educated persons or persons of authority, including their adoption worker. They frequently feel they should defer to the authority of education or status, even if they do not agree with what is said. A family's disinclination to assert their ideas in the presence of the worker may be wrongly interpreted by the worker to reflect a negative motivation. The worker may label them "passive-aggressive individuals" and view them as resisting through inactivity or stubbornness. As a result, the worker may be uncomfortable during interviews with these families. Middle class oriented workers will need to build up a feeling of equality and trust with working class families before they can feel comfortable discussing specific attitudes or actions.

Many of these families also favor specific, clear-cut actions which lead to well-understood, immediate results. They may feel and show a decided impatience with an adoption process which is lengthy and complicated. Spaulding workers have found that this difficulty can be minimized if the worker consistently clarifies procedures and explains reasons for delays in the proceedings, even when not specifically asked to do so. In interviews, many families are most comfortable with an adoption worker who meets with their expectations by providing firm leadership, well-defined procedures, and clearly stated directions.

If adoption workers are to be most effective when serving working class families, they should deviate from the stereotype of social workers that the families are likely to have. They should be warm and informal in language and dress and in their attitudes toward themselves, the child to be placed, and the applicant families. Warmth and sensitivity on the part of the worker will usually reassure families and aid in the formation of working partnerships.

Communication

Problems in communication can arise because of differences in the nature and structure of the language used in working class and middle class families. Speech used in many working class families tends to be condensed and descriptive or action-oriented rather than analytical or abstract. Sentences used may be short and gramatically simple, with less than perfect syntax, and thoughts may be incompletely expressed.

From the middle class perspective, this type of speech hinders the extensive verbal expression of ideas, beliefs, and attitudes. The structure and function of working class language may also be viewed as tending to discourage the analysis or expression of intellectual concepts. These characteristics of the language development of children from working class families are often responsible for both their slower progress in learning to read or write and in acquiring advanced verbal skills.

Expressing concepts is not the main function of working class speech. Rather, it is a warm, emotionally rich means of communication used to increase mutual agreement among friends and relatives and to solidify individual's relationships with each other. By contrast, the language training of most social workers has prepared them to talk about concepts, feelings, and reasons for actions in a rather abstract manner. Middle class families are also usually better able to use language as a vehicle to express finely differentiated shades of meaning.

Despite these differences, working class families should not be viewed as non-communicative, for they can communicate quite effectively among themselves and their friends. They also should not be judged lacking in intellectual ability. Concepts are often formulated at a slower pace, however, or are not easily put into words. When concepts are expressed, they may appear as analogies or anecdotes. Middle class individuals not accustomed to a simple, abbreviated style of expression can easily miss the concepts that working class stories and analogies are intended to convey. As a result, the worker who expects these individuals to converse in his or her own verbally fluent, highly abstract manner is likely to have difficulty communicating with these families.

Workers must be aware that working class families may have difficulty understanding what is being communicated during interviews. Abstractions discussed by a worker may be comprehended slowly or with difficulty, and some families may nod and pretend to agree rather than admit their difficulty in understanding. Workers should be prepared to repeat ideas in different words, to give further explanations when necessary, and to give specific, practical, non-theoretical examples whenever possible. Concepts may be related to a family through example or analogy or by relating incidents which bear some relationship to a current problem.

To work with working class families, many workers will need to adjust their communication pattern so they can converse in a straightforward and easily understandable manner. A problem will arise if a worker feels and communicates a feeling of intellectual or verbal superiority, for families are sensitive to, and rightly resent, the feeling someone is "talking down" to them.

Education

Adoptive applicants from classes other than the worker's own may not have the same educational goals for their biological or adopted children as those held by their social worker. Working class families may welcome a certain measure of education for the benefits received in increased job opportunities and skills, but they may be uncomfortable with education for its own sake or with obtaining educational goals which are higher than those of friends or relatives. Families who place a low value on education are likely to expect, or be satisfied with, lower academic achievement of their children than are most middle class individuals.

Some parents may have less than a high school education. They may read poorly or haphazardly and may lack much general information known to the adoption worker. Parents who have done poorly in school often have difficulty in communicating with school personnel about their child's problems and in planning and carrying through parent-directed remedial programs. When Spaulding workers place school-age children with these families, they recognize the need to assist parents in working with the school or any other social agencies that prove difficult for the parents to approach alone.

Finances

The financial status of many families will be quite different from that of most adoption workers. Their income will usually be in the form of an hourly wage rather than a guaranteed salary. Their economic stability is vulnerable to unemployment, inflation, lay-offs, and strikes to a greater extent than middle class workers. Many of these families will be more concerned with "getting by" than "getting ahead" and may be able to live successfully on an income which the adoption worker would find hopelessly inadequate. Interviews or appointments scheduled at inopportune times may mean reduction in a week's pay and signal the staff's disregard for the hardship that may cause for the family.

Recognizing their relatively unstable economic position, some applicants may hesitate to assume what they believe to be the intolerable economic burdens of adoption. These applicants may make good adoptive parents in spite of economic difficulties. If adoption is to be encouraged among all families, financial support in the form of adoption subsidy and information about this support must be freely available. Help in obtaining subsidy may also be necessary.

APPROPRIATE WORKER VALUES

Differences will always exist between the life styles, patterns of communication, educational levels, and annual incomes of adoption workers and some of the families they serve. These differences, however, will not jeopardize placements unless workers reared by middle class standards misunderstand or disapprove of the values or ideals of these families. With this in mind, the Spaulding staff believe workers must be tolerant of other cultural traditions and values. They must recognize that different family situations demand flexible and varied approaches to both the preparation of children and families for adoption and the maintenance of placements once they have begun.

Social workers involved in the adoption of older and handicapped children should be individuals who are open and flexible; persons who can view styles of living other than their own as acceptable, even if those differences make them feel uncomfortable. At Spaulding, workers are hired who will not use their own family experiences and background as a major guide when working with families, for the staff realize that sensitivity toward individual and group circumstances, as well as respect and acceptance of differences, are essential characteristics for adoption workers committed to finding the most appropriate family for each child.

PLACING CHILDREN WITH WORKING CLASS FAMILIES

Spaulding workers believe that the children they place have fewest adjustment problems if they are placed with the applicants who are socially most like the parents the children have known. Every adoption brings with it more than enough difficult problems without requiring that the child overcome unnecessary barriers. Too great a difference in values or expectations can produce marked emotional stress and may well evolve into an intense struggle between child and parents or even a disruption of the placement. Because most of the children now placed by the Spaulding staff are from working class backgrounds, the agency seeks a large number of working class applicants.

Spaulding workers recognize that children with high intellectual potential may not always find their ability realized if they are placed with working class families. They also recognize, however, that these families tend to provide many positive experiences for children. For example, they are frequently able to provide adopted children with the rich emotional experience of becoming part of the large, extended, and closely-knit family structure often characteristic of the working class. Working class families also tend to be strongly person-centered, prizing informal, comfortable relationships which are based upon a warm, expressive, and humorous approach to life. In judging others and in rearing children, personal qualities and values are often considered superior to intellectual qualities. Personal troubles, problems, and difficulties are an expected and accepted part of life, and it is believed that one must cope with problems, rather than become overwhelmed by them. In the presence of such attitudes, children with mental and physical handicaps are accepted as they are. If they are seen as "different," it is usually in a matter of degree rather than kind.

Spaulding workers would prefer placing a child who is educationally handicapped in families such as these rather than in families which have middle class aspirations or expectations. Regardless of the parent's level of commitment or degree of parenting capacity, high parental hopes and aspirations could seriously conflict with the reality of the child's ability. At Spaulding, such a child would not be placed with any family until the parent's aspirations were thoroughly explored. It is the staff's belief that workers must be convinced, prior to placement, that the family under consideration has a clear understanding of the long-range experience of adopting such a child and can accept the child's limited potential to achieve.

Spaulding workers would prefer placing a child who is educationally handicapped in families such as these rather than in families which have middle class aspirations or expectations. Regardless of the parents' level of commitment or degree of parenting capacity, high parental hopes and aspirations could seriously conflict with the reality of the child's ability. At Spaulding, such a child would not be placed with any family until the aspirations of the prospective parents were thoroughly explored. It is the staff's belief that workers must be convinced, prior to placement, that the family under consideration has a clear understanding of the long-range experience of adopting such a child and can accept the child's limited potential to achieve.

SUMMARY

Spaulding workers have experienced considerable success in placing older and handicapped children with working class families. These successes have been possible because the staff feel comfortable working with these families.

In too many other placement programs, providing adoption services to working class families still creates insurmountable challenges because workers from a middle class background do not feel comfortable working with families whose life styles and values are different from their own. Communication difficulties frequently occur due to differences in the style of middle class and working class language. Educational and financial expectations may also differ considerably. However, it is the staff's belief that workers able to bridge these differences can be highly effective in placing children with working class families.

Working class families tend to provide many positive experiences for older and handicapped children. Family acceptance of these children is frequently high, and expectations for success do not tend to outdistance their children's potential achievement. Finally, the warm emotional climate and close extended family relationships which many working class families provide are highly beneficial to children greatly in need of these supports.

14

Coping With Disruption

At Spaulding, a disrupted adoption is regarded as the permanent, legal removal of any child from an adoptive family for any reason before the confirmation of his adoption. Under Michigan law, when this occurs, a judge sets aside the adoption order and either restores the child to his former legal custodian or assumes full responsibility for the future of the child by making him a ward of the court.

While the same circumstances may lead to removal of the child after his adoption has been confirmed, the staff do not describe the termination of a confirmed adoption as a disruption. The act of discontinuing a legally completed adoption requires a wholly different legal procedure which is identical to the process used in ending a biological parent-child relationship. This procedure, which in Michigan is called a "release," involves the voluntary termination of the parents' established rights to their child.

The staff use the different terminology to underscore this important shade of difference in the child's and parents' legal status and to make the terminology uniform for statistical purposes.[1] Although Spaulding workers believe parental rights and responsibilities begin at the point of placement, Michigan law requires "confirmation" (also known as "finalization" in some states) before the adoptive parents' legal rights are completely and solely their own.

Spaulding workers use the term "disrupted" adoption, rather than "broken" adoption, because they believe the term is a more accurate

---

[1]Early in their history, the Spaulding staff became convinced of the importance and inevitability of disruptions. Concerned about workers' general lack of experience with the phenomena, and with the hope of eventually being able to exchange or compare information with other agencies and courts, they developed careful terminology to describe the various stages or manifestations.

description of the experience which actually occurs. They see the adoption process — the continuous development of the relationships required for a child to become an integrated and permanent member of a new family — as being interrupted, not as having altogether broken down with the total and irretrievable loss of all that the child and family had managed to gain.

Even though a disruption is most definitely the failure of a specific placement to continue, the staff also regard a "broken" or "failed" adoption as an inaccurate description because it attaches a far too negative image to a situation which often does not warrant such a reaction. There is no evidence that disruption signals the end of either the child's capacity to form a relationship with another family or the family's capacity to form a relationship with another child. Instead, it affords a solid learning experience from which the child, family, and worker can salvage important positive pieces of information about themselves, others, and adoption in general with which to build a better future.

Unfortunately, many adoption workers doubt there is anything in a disruption that can be salvaged for the child, the family, or themselves. The evidence that workers are frequently unable to focus on the eventually positive effects of disruption is confirmed by what often happens to the child whose adoptive placement ends. He is usually moved to a foster care situation and left to recover — treated like a wound which, if left alone, will miraculously heal itself. The Spaulding staff believe it is these "cut and run" responses, in which the child is abandoned to time in order to be healed and in which the family is permanently branded as a failure, which cause disruptions to be irreversible and totally unnecessary failures.

Early focus on the positive outcomes of disruption aids workers in providing practical help to children and families whose adoptions are terminating. No matter how early or positive the worker's focus, however, providing effective support remains a difficult task. There are several reasons. First of all, the determination of the success or failure of an adoption has generally come to depend upon whether a child or family remain together. Though a gross and inappropriate determination, this view has become commonplace because it is such an easy measure to use. Second, most families and workers cannot initially look beyond the pain and trauma of the moment and their immediate feeling of having failed miserably in their attempt to achieve a permanent placement. Third, these feelings are often repeatedly reinforced by both direct and indirect messages from friends, relatives, and colleagues who have a simplistic view of a complex dynamic relationship and believe that every adoption is a "happy ever after" story.

ENCOUNTERING DISRUPTIONS

Early in their history, the staff at Spaulding did not realize that disruptions of older and handicapped children were a normal risk of the placement process. They felt that if children and parents were well prepared for adoption, and a trusting relationship between family and worker was maintained following placement, disruptions would be avoided. They did not yet realize that disruptions are not necessarily the result of staff failure except for those occasional difficulties directly resulting from workers' incompetence, laziness, or inexperience.

These realizations were slow in developing. When Spaulding was established in 1968, the initial two workers were too concerned about acquiring referrals of children from other agencies and courts and finding prospective adoptive parents to give much thought to the possibility of disruption. When their first disruptions did occur, in October and November of 1969, these events were regarded as unpredictable and were seemingly tied to marital problems which had nothing to do with the adopted children. This apparent unpredictability led the staff to further delay focusing on the phenomenon of disruption. By 1970, the staff (which now numbered four workers) began to realize that unanticipated crisis situations created by deteriorating parent-child relationships were occurring in a considerable number of placement families, and that a large proportion of these crises would eventually result in disruptions if not dealt with effectively.

This meant that disruptions might well require a significant proportion of the agency's service time in the future. Two trends in the agency's practice strengthened this belief. First, the children the staff were placing were becoming progressively older and more handicapped. Most children being placed had severe mental, physical, or emotional problems, and many were multiply handicapped. As a result, workers surmised that families would find it increasingly difficult to parent these children.

Second, in order to place these children, the staff had begun reaching out more frequently to families who were accustomed to dealing with problems and difficulties, but who also had fewer traditionally acceptable characteristics as potential adoptive parents. For example, Spaulding workers would risk placing a child with parents who had experienced several marriages, who were physically handicapped themselves, or who had been screened out or even rejected by other placement programs for a variety of reasons. (Workers estimate that at least 25 percent of Spaulding's families would probably be rejected by placement programs using traditional screening methods and requirements for accepting potential parents.)

Families accustomed to crisis were seen as good prospective parents for hard-to-place children because their patience and resourcefulness had been well-tested by past experiences. The staff felt these families were better able to manage crisis than the "untried" family who, having never survived a crisis, might succumb to the first serious threat to their equilibrium. There was some concern, however, that these experienced families might overload their capabilities if they had many additional stresses from a new child. As a result, it became necessary to consistently weigh the relative risks involved with both types of families.

The staff's worst fears that adoptions would begin to disrupt with uncontrollable regularity seemed borne out during a five month period in late 1972 when there were five disruptions. The emotional impact of these events made it seem as if every placement was in jeopardy. This period was made even more difficult because workers felt responsible for what had happened but could find no pattern of conditions or events to explain why these specific disruptions had occurred. Despite this dilemma (and perhaps, in part, because of it), they felt they had an obligation to help the children and families survive and move forward.

In an effort to prevent further disruptions, the bewildered staff began to slow down the "minimum delay" adoption process by which they had tried to reduce frustrating waiting periods for adoptive applicants. They also began to revert to more traditionally narrow ranges of acceptability of parents. They became more critical, more precise, and more cautious regarding each placement, seeking to recheck every step of the process in an effort to avoid similar mistakes.

As they tried to guarantee that placements would be permanent, workers grew more apprehensive and became immobilized. Even though they had become more cautious, they continued to feel a growing apprehension that the placements then in process were as susceptible to crisis and potential disruption as previous placements. By late 1972, the staff realized that the possible disruption of placements of older and handicapped children existed in such potentially enormous proportion that the absence of practical information about the causes and effects of disruption and a lack of worker skills to cope with the problem would seriously impair all placement efforts of the agency.

SPAULDING'S ANALYSIS OF DISRUPTION

The desire of the Spaulding staff to overcome their sense of helplessness and minimize disruptions led to an all-out effort to understand the disruptions they were witnessing. During late 1972, workers extensively analyzed the 12 disruptions which had occurred between 1968 and 1972 in an attempt to discover why certain children and families did not adjust to each other. It was the staff's hope that this information could help them make more appropriate decisions in the future. At that point, they felt that with the appropriate use of available information, they would be able to eliminate disruptions altogether.

On the basis of this review, however, the staff concluded there were no common experiences from disruption to disruption. Each seemed to have a noticeably different cause. In addition, no specific characteristics such as the age or sex of the child, the age, marital status, income, number of adopted or biological children, religious affiliation of the parents, or geographic accessability to the adoption program was identified as contributing significantly more than any other characteristic to the occurrence of adoption disruption.

Although the staff did find that there tended to be a biological child in the home who was the same chronological or mental age as the adopted child, they found no practical explanation for why many other families with such age similarities among their children did not disrupt. The only general trend found was that middle class families (particularly social workers and teachers) often had difficulty if they adopted children with atypical appearance and/or behavior.

The Spaulding staff believe this difficulty exists, first, because these parents are professionals with a high level of skill and a special capacity to work effectively with children's problems. As a result, many of these parents need to see measurable positive changes in the children they adopt in order to confirm their expertise for themselves and others. However, even if significant change for the better occurs, strong feelings of personal inadequacy often still exist for these parents as long as others still notice the child's atypical or less than average level of functioning.

A second reason for the increased likelihood of disruption for these parents occurs because placement workers also presume them to be skilled professionals who are capable of handling even the most difficult to parent children. Not only may provisions for supportive services be inadequate for the social worker or teacher who is assumed to possess all necessary knowledge and skills, but unusually challenging children may be placed with these families because it is also assumed that their training and experience allows them to easily overcome life-style or cultural differences between themselves and their child. As a result, the child may be "overplaced" in that undue expectations are imposed on the family (by themselves or others), when in reality they find the placed child too difficult to parent.

Despite the few concrete results of the 1972 study, the staff continued analyzing disruptions in an effort to find less complicated answers to the problems they faced. Their struggle with the problem and their review of disruption ultimately produced a number of significant outcomes. First,

the staff began to consider disruption as a normal possibility, an unavoidable risk of the placement process, rather than the result of mistakes
or inabilities they could accurately predict and eliminate. Having tried
and failed to find "quick and easy" rules for predicting potential disruptions, they began to operate under the assumption that no such rules
existed, and that the manner in which the unique characteristics of each
child and family intertwine must be reviewed separately in each case.
These realizations helped the staff cope with their own anxieties about
disruption and helped mobilize joint efforts in continuing to work with
children and families.

They realized it is impossible to adequately resolve or eliminate all
existing or latent problems in children or families prior to placement.
They concluded, instead, that the most practical approach to preparing
children and families for adoption is to create an intelligent balance
between taking the necessary time to resolve potentially disruption-
producing pre-placement problems and minimizing the duration of
placement delay. If the delay proves too great, no amount of worker skill
can save the placement. Significant delay, although different in duration
in each case, can so emotionally damage a child that he cannot be
successfully maintained in an adoptive family. It can also eliminate the
possibility of a firm, trusting, family-worker relationship by so effectively demoralizing a family that they will lose confidence in their
worker.

Their study also helped staff recognize that similar capabilities, circumstances, or characteristics among children or families can produce
totally different placement outcomes. As a result, single events or problems within placements now elicit less worker concern than broader,
more comprehensive difficulties. This wider perspective has also shifted
the workers' attention away from fragmented pre-placement analyses of
individual characteristics and toward a more realistically unified approach to the review of potential family difficulties. The staff now focus
on such issues as whether the child's history will interfere with his
ability to adjust to adoption, whether handicapping conditions have
been clearly identified and adequately explained to the adopting family,
and whether the critical role played by the child's remaining ties with
previous families is clearly understood by the adopting family.

In addition, the staff have gradually learned that the real need in
analyzing placements that disrupt is to provide verification that the child
was accurately viewed by the workers and accurately described to his
family. Such checks for errors are necessary if workers are to be sure they
are correctly representing the child to his future adoptive parents. Although the Spaulding staff still review the original placement decision,
lengthy analysis of individuals, motivations, and dynamics is no longer

their main focus during a disruption. Instead, the primary activity has become the constructive acts which lead to assisting the child and family through a painful time and to replacing the child with another adoptive family.

THE INEVITABILITY OF DISRUPTION

Although the Spaulding staff believe that the potential causes of a disruption can sometimes be identified in time to prevent the termination of a specific placement, their placement experience and their analysis of the phenomenon of disruption have led them to the conclusion that some disruptions are inevitable when placing children for adoption. As a result, they not only believe it is essential for adoption workers to be prepared for the reality and inevitability of disruption, but also that workers must realize that the percentage of placements which will disrupt significantly increases when the children being placed are older or otherwise handicapped by mental, physical, or emotional problems. When infants or toddlers are placed for adoption, it is usually only the inability of the parents to adjust to the presence or behavior of the child which leads to disruption. With children who are older or handicapped, disruption occurs not only because the parents are unable to adjust, but because child and family are unable to make the critical adjustments required of each other.

The acceptance by the Spaulding staff of the inevitability of disruption stems from their belief that workers can never learn enough about a child and a family to be able to defuse or eliminate all existing problems which are potentially disruptive. Even if they were convinced, prior to placement, that no major problems existed, they would still never be able to predict whether potentially disruptive problems would occur after placement. In addition, some pre-placement or post-placement problems cannot be identified as potential causes of disruptions early enough for workers to help families stay together. In some cases, the causes of disruptions can never be clearly identified.

Workers do not search for highly idealized parents or family situations in an effort to prevent disruptions. The staff believe that adoptions are similar to marriages: even with the best preparations and intentions, some thrive, some survive, and some break up. That is, they believe there is no absolute capacity within the social sciences to assure total success where Nature herself does not guarantee it. Instead of trying to create perfection and predict success, they feel it is more reasonable to predict that all children will encounter periods of crisis and stress as they grow and that, in some cases, these may be compounded by the dynamics of adoption. Since life consists of both mistakes and successes, there is no reason to expect the human experience of adoption to be much different. As a result, the staff consider their task as adoption workers to be that of helping individuals and relationships overcome major difficulties. Risk reduction, not elimination, is their aim.

WORKER CONCERN WITH DISRUPTION

No matter what their level of training, experience, or commitment, it is common for adoption workers to feel concern about the causes of disruption and their own role in preventing it. Many workers question if there are identifiable factors which, when isolated and examined early enough in specific cases, can offer opportunities to prevent a disruption. They may anxiously ask themselves such questions as "Can causes be identified before or after placement or before it is too late?" or "Once the causes are identified, can I offer the child and family practical suggestions for saving their placement?"

The Spaulding staff have found, both through their own experiences and those of other workers, that services to children and families may be significantly affected if workers are unable to resolve these concerns. If, for example, a worker is convinced all disruptions are avoidable, that worker may spend an inordinate amount of time attempting to identify and eliminate possible causes for disruption. Applicants may be intensely scrutinized and, in some cases, may even be rejected simply because they have a single characteristic in common with a family whose adoption disrupted. However, such devoted scrutiny will only increase worker anxiety, for despite the most profound effort, disruptions will continue to occur.

Workers can, of course, take certain positive steps to prevent some disruptions. Experience has convinced the Spaulding staff that a major key to minimizing disruptions is total sharing of all available information about the child with adoptive parents prior to placement. Another key is the implementation of the most thorough possible preparation of children and families so that all individuals can work together for the early recognition and appropriate solution of the many problems they are sure to encounter.[2] It is only by sharing information (including offering realistic expectations for the child's future to potential parents) in order to prepare the child and family for their placement, building trusting partnerships between families and workers, and providing

---

[2]To this end, the staff believe in providing the child's complete written record to the family. (For more information, see "Preparing Families for Adoption," p. 131.)

post-placement services whenever needed that workers can hope to prevent unnecessary disruptions.

Spaulding workers have learned, however, that even their best efforts to understand the causes and effects of problems within each placement, to obtain full information about the child and family, to help families explore their own parenting capabilities, and to provide intensive help after placement cannot provide an iron-clad guarantee of permanent success for families. In order to provide children with their best chance for permanence, it is necessary for workers to assume recognizable risks and to sometimes chance placement with families whose history or characteristics suggest there may be a greater than usual possibility that the adoption may not work.

To successfully place older and handicapped children for adoption, a worker's commitment to the child's adoptability, to the belief that permanent placement offers the child his best chance for a caring attachment, must outweigh all reservations about the child's possibility of placement. Workers must take risks, live with difficulties, and look for parents who can do the same. They must realize that unless they run the risks of an adoptive placement, the child's chances for permanence are zero.

THE CAUSES OF DISRUPTION

The experience of the Spaulding staff has shown that three kinds of problems tend to create circumstances which may lead to the disruption of an adoptive placement. These are:

1. unrecognized pre-existing problems
2. pre-existing problems that are known but left unexplored
3. unpredictable problems which occur after placement

The first group of problems leading to adoption disruption are those which exist prior to placement but which have totally escaped the awareness of child, family, and worker. No matter how carefully children and families are prepared for adoption, or how thoughtfully and truthfully workers, children, and families seek to recognize and discuss doubts, concerns, anxieties and unrealistic expectations, some will be missed.

In most cases, workers are unaware of the events or circumstances causing these problems, and the situations themselves are not yet recognized as problems by children or families. For these reasons, they are not brought to the worker's attention. In retrospect, however, it is clear that the worker's knowledge and understanding of such critical information could have helped them defuse or eliminate certain problems or, in some cases, conclude that the placement family was a clearly inappropriate choice for a specific child.

A second group of problems which may lead to disruption are those known by the child or family but not shared with the worker (or those known by the worker but ignored). Such circumstances usually occur because children or families are not aware of the significance of the problem. However, these situations may also exist because children, families, or workers purposely choose not to divulge and discuss the issues.

Some children or families do not trust the worker enough to "open up" for fear they would be embarassed by sharing intimate problems or self-styled solutions. As a result, they conclude that living with those problems and solutions is preferable to revealing them and risking the disapproval of the worker or lowered self-esteem. In addition, although workers emphasize that discussing problems helps create a more successful adoption, some children or families continue to believe that acknowledging problems will eliminate their chances for adoption.

In some instances, problems regarding the child and/or family are judged by a worker as capable of producing disastrous consequences for the placement being considered. While most workers seek to resolve such problems, sometimes they are purposely ignored. Workers may consider these problems too "delicate" or too "personal." Sometimes they do not want to begin a discussion which could produce immediate negative consequences because they consider the child or family not yet ready to acknowledge the existence of the problem. At other times, workers may avoid issues because they are afraid of the long-term effects the discussion will have on the child, family, or themselves, or they fear they do not have the skills to help resolve the problems they raise.

The third group of problems leading to disruption are those which are the result of unpredictable circumstances occurring after placement. Such problems can include financial stress, the illness or death of a family member, personal or marital stress, or the worsening of small problems which existed prior to placement. It is not that those events in themselves trigger a disruption, but under the additional stress of such circumstances, some families may not have the capability to parent a child with problems. As a result of this extra strain, they may find their normal coping skills have been stretched to the breaking point. Some parents continue to overestimate their abilities as they struggle to parent the child. Only when it is "too late" do they discover they have not realistically weighed the impact of a troubled child on their lives.

The recognition that unpredictable circumstances can cause a disruption has produced several significant changes in the thinking of the Spaulding staff. For example, they now more clearly realize that adoptive placement and the experience of family-living involve a dynamic process in which change sometimes occurs quickly but certainly occurs continuously. In addition, they are more aware that children are placed with families on the basis of *current* knowledge and understanding of the children and the families, that as time goes by, people and their relationships change, and that sometimes it becomes clear that parents and children are incompatible.

In recognizing that such change is normal, Spaulding workers no longer as readily blame disruptions on "worker error" or "incorrigible kids." Similarly, they are unwilling to label a family as "inadequate" because a specific placement did not work out. The staff now view disruption as a situation in which all of the individuals involved are under tremendous pressure and need all the support they can get in working out a solution that moves the child closer to his goal of a permanent family.

THE DECISION TO DISRUPT

No matter when or where it occurs, the decision to terminate an adoptive placement represents a very difficult time for both the family and their worker. It is, in almost all cases, a complex, slowly evolving, poorly understood, and painful situation. In addition to coping with uncomfortable emotions, workers and families must sort out the vast amount of information surrounding the decision to disrupt. Decisions must be made and solutions implemented quickly enough by both family and worker so that child and family will not suffer undue emotional damage.

In some cases, it is the family who decides that the placement is more negative than positive and that no improvement appears possible in the foreseeable future. In other instances, it is the child who signals his discomfort by misbehaving or "acting out" to the point of pushing the family to the breaking point. Sometimes, it is the worker who must make the decision because the family is unable or unwilling to do so. However, it is the experience of the Spaulding staff that in most placements which disrupt, the family has concluded that an end to the placement is inevitable long before that decision is arrived at by the worker. No matter how closely workers have kept in touch with a family, the family is always closer to, and almost always more aware of, their difficulties than are the workers. Yet, families often wait to contact workers in an effort to first work out their own problems or survive the crisis without involving "outsiders."

Whether it is the parent or child who requests a disruption or a worker who first senses such a move may be necessary, the worker must still decide if their efforts should be aimed at keeping the child in the family or removing him. The worker must decide whether the family situation can be sufficiently healthy for the child and family, or whether it will probably not improve.

When the family or worker is aware of the real possibility of disruption, both benefit from thorough analysis of the causes of the problems and the effects of potential solutions. It is for the purpose of ensuring a broad analysis that the prospect of a disruption is always brought before the entire Spaulding team for discussion. Although the worker may first discuss all possible alternatives with a family, the team's decision to move toward disruption or to further support the placement is crucial to the future of the family and the worker. The team's decision is based upon what they, as a group, have learned of the family's problems and their combined abilities to solve those problems. As a result, the family has a better chance of benefiting from the combined experience of the team, and no single worker assumes total responsibility or suffers the potential guilt associated with the momentous decisions ahead.

If the worker regards the disruption as necessary and the family does not agree, the worker must try to persuade the family that a disruption is actually in the best interests of the child. Helping the family understand the necessity for disruption is usually best accomplished by reviewing the history of the placement with the child and family and recapping "where things are and where they are going."

In some cases, the worker is able to assist the family who does not feel "ready," or who cannot talk about their problems by helping them list the positive and negative aspects of the placement. In other cases, the participation of the worker offers the family the opportunity to relieve guilt by sharing the responsiblity for the decision to disrupt. Together, the decision becomes more of a logical and mutual conclusion than an exercise in blame assignment or a decision made and delivered in anger.

REACTIONS TO DISRUPTION

It is the experience of the Spaulding staff that the decision to disrupt an adoption is always painful for everyone involved. The primary purpose of adoption is to offer parentless children a caring, beneficially nurturing attachment; a more permanent, secure, and consequently, more positive living arrangement than was previously available to them. When this goal is not achieved, children, family members, and placement workers have many painful emotions and feel they have failed.

The following are generalized descriptions of reactions to disruptions. Although a generalized approach is necessary in order to meet the practical considerations of space, time, and reader interest, these descriptions (which omit many of the feelings and events that contribute to the intricate and unique reality of actual disruptions) are oversimplifications of the actual complexity of experiences involved.

The Child's Reaction

The child who is in an adoptive placement that is disrupting will invariably begin to feel that something is "wrong" long before any direct mention is made to him of that possibility. Usually, the first sign that there is trouble takes the form of incomplete or conflicting messages about his being, or becoming, a permanent family member. Instead of hearing good messages that "things are going well," there may be a noticeable lack, or even total absence, of talk about "next summer," "next Christmas," or "doing things together" in the near future.

There may be frequent shifts in the messages parents give from "everything is all right" to "I don't think I can take any more." As these conflicting messages occur more frequently, the child may sense that his family is not committed to him, that they are still deciding whether he will stay, and that they are possibly concluding that the best way to eliminate family stress is to remove him.

A child's reaction to the possible or actual disruption of his adoption is determined to a significant extent by the degree to which he seeks attachment, or a feeling of "belonging," from the placement family. For the child who trusts the adults offering him a family and who arrives with the hope that he finally "belongs," the reality of a disruption is a bewildering and frightening experience which produces tremendous feelings of insecurity. His wish to trust in the goodness and fairness of the world of adults and his need to find a sensible reason for what is happening may lead him to conclude that the disruption must somehow be his fault.

For such a child, disruption becomes a self-fulfilling prophesy, a logical and deserved consequence of all the unacceptable and guilty thoughts he has. His worth deteriorates as a result of this self-blame. As his memories of earlier separation experiences are reawakened, he can assume blame for these as well and self-esteem deteriorates even further.

Most children will attempt to strike bargains by promising "to do *anything*" for "one more chance" or for the opportunity "to stay." As these impossible bargains fail or are eventually refused, and as fears of being "bad," "powerless," and "abandoned" persist, the child often experiences a period of genuine grieving. He may experience depression, anger, disbelief, a need to blame others, or a need to suppress his own feelings of hurt. He may insist that "I don't like it here anyway," or "It doesn't matter to me." In reality, however, he usually feels isolated, alienated, and miserable. He would probably rather be anywhere else, and he invariably trusts adults a little less than before.

The child who has already been hurt so badly that he has "given up" on the world — who is not seeking or cannot seek attachment and "belonging" from the family with whom he has been placed — often becomes impervious to the pain of the disruption. He is not mystified by the experience, for it is just one more example of the unfairness of the world. The child may feel anger toward himself for not being like "other kids." He may also feel worthless. Not only does he live with an active fantasy of what the lives of other children must be like, but he is the only person he knows who is consistently a "loser."

The child may also feel anger toward others; anger at this added piece of evidence that people do not care. Even though past experience prepared the child to expect "something like this all along," he is yet angry that "it didn't turn out." As his experiences with failure mount and his feelings of persecution grow, his hostility increases and the probability of dangerous behavioral problems, delinquency, and criminal behavior become steadily greater.

For the vast majority of children who experience a disruption, replacement into another adoptive family is "the treatment of choice," and the skills of the adults (parents and workers) involved with the child must help make this resolution possible. Despite past trauma, most children can make the adjustment from an unsuccessful adoptive placement to a new adoptive home if given enough assistance and support during this distressful period. One or more unsuccessful placements are rarely a reflection on a child's ability to succeed somewhere else, and workers must make further attempts to find another adoptive family should that be necessary.

The Family's Reaction

The distress which families experience during and following a disruption usually first takes the form of face-saving protest and anger directed at others for "what went wrong" or for not "preventing" what happened. Workers are most frequently blamed, for they are most readily seen as having either initial or primary "responsibility" for the placement. As a result, families often assault workers with hostile or accusative assertions such as "No one can live with this child . . .," "If we had really understood what we were getting into . . .," "If you had told us more . . .," or even "Why did you let us do this?" They tend to blame the child or worker for what went wrong because that is easier and less painful than blaming themselves. This can be a potentially damaging time for the child, for he is frequently scapegoated by parents seeking to minimize their own suffering.

In those cases where the family is able to move past their first reactions of protesting their distress by assigning blame to others, a period of self-blame frequently occurs. This is a time of bewilderment, despair, and tremendous guilt which follows the acknowledgment that they, too, were partly responsible. It is a time of sadness and grief, of "What have I done?" or "If only I had . . ." Some parents may detach themselves from the source of their pain through attitudes of futility and inevitability. Their apparent attitude of indifference seems to be "Since I could not have prevented it, why worry about it?"

The final stage, if it is achieved, is the acceptance of the disruption and survival of the feelings and experiences which accompany it. To achieve this stage, the family must realize that anger, guilt, and grief are normal reactions to a disruption; must be able to discuss their feelings with others; and must attain some degree of understanding of what happened, why it happened, and what the effects will be. It may take a considerable amount of time, however, for families to realize that they share responsibility for the disruption and that it is usually both inaccurate and unfair to try to blame any one specific person.

The Worker's Reaction

A disruption is also a personally painful experience for any placement worker. An adoptive placement begins with the expectation that the venture is worth the effort because of the positive experiences which will result. When a disruption occurs, a worker is likely to feel depressed and defeated, to conclude that time and effort have been wasted, and to believe their judgment has been faulty.

In part, disruptions are difficult to cope with because they are relatively new and unique experiences for most social workers. Infant adoptions do not often result in disruption, and when they do, there has usually been little support or helpful analysis from fellow workers. As a result, workers who place older and handicapped children frequently are faced with difficult experiences for which they have had little preparation.

Since they do not know what to expect or how they should react, many workers in charge of post-placement services to families begin to panic at the possibility of a disruption. Some begin to panic at the appearance of any problem within an adoption. Although they may continue to encourage families to be open in discussing problems, they become even more uncomfortable when families begin describing serious difficulties. Families are sensitive to this discomfort and become perplexed by the worker's inconsistency. In many cases, these workers become immobilized as difficulties increase, the complexity of the demands placed upon them to listen to and solve problems becomes greater, and disruption becomes a distinct possibility.

Worker anxiety may continue to grow in response to the fear that they have failed. The feeling that a major mistake has been made and that personal responsibility must be assumed further destroys the worker's sense of security. The anxiety which workers feel is not primarily for the child's predicament, but for their own vulnerable position. They may not know why events have occurred, what to do about them, or how other individuals will react. Not only may the worker feel inadequate, but there may be concerns about ultimately retaining one's job. Although there are usually many immediate and continuing demands made on the worker's time by other required tasks, the worker's own needs become of most immediate concern and are likely to take precedence over those of the child and family. As a result, the worker's main efforts are likely to be spent in moving beyond the stress the disruption has caused so more personally secure ground can be found.

When the placement of an older or handicapped child disrupts, it is frequently more comfortable for workers to ignore intense emotions than to confront the pain felt by all those involved, including themselves. Emotions can most easily be hidden by limiting contacts with disrupting families to a bare minimum, treating the child impersonally, and moving him as quickly as possible.

It is far more difficult to help the child and family work through the disappointment of disruption so that they can move toward another placement for the child, and help all who are involved understand that what they have learned can enable the child to make a positive move to a new family. Failure to move forward, out of fear or anger, only permits more damage to be done the child and family. A great deal of this damage can be prevented if the worker can offer appropriate help and support throughout the disruption process.

Workers willing to extend themselves to work intensively with children and families risk the resentment of some fellow workers who are unable or unwilling to do this. Efforts to replace a child may have to be made in spite of fellow workers' pessimism, lack of support, or attempts to undermine placement efforts. Such experiences may well discourage many workers from making difficult but potentially rewarding commitments to children and families.

Assigning Blame

Workers, like children and families, frequently believe that fault must be lodged with someone if a disruption occurs. Workers may seek to lessen their discomfort by absolving themselves of major responsibility for what has happened and blaming someone else. As with children's and parents' attempts to assign responsibility elsewhere, workers' efforts to shift blame away from themselves constitute a survival reaction offering at least temporary escape from the emotional trauma of the situation.

The effect disruption will have on individual workers depends upon a worker's expectations. The effect will be much different if workers feel they are, or should be, in control of all factors relating to the disruption, than if they view themselves as having only a partial, human level of influence, and feel they made the best decisions possible based on information available.

The need to blame someone else can be especially great if workers have a tendency toward perfection, feel undue levels of responsibility for placements, or pride themselves on making the best possible placements for "their" children. Under these circumstances, most workers initially blame others in order to create an efficient and necessary outlet for their anger that the adoption failed to continue.

Workers who felt that they had successfully made a permanent placement may initially blame someone else because they continue to believe that by the time the child was placed, they had done everything they could to secure a permanent placement. If problems subsequently occur, these workers must be convinced that it was the fault of others. Workers who are family oriented, and who perceive their job as finding children for "their" families, tend to blame the child or to feel that the child "just cannot be placed." Workers who find families for "their" children tend to feel that there is something "wrong" with the family.

Workers who are unsure, at the time of placement, if the placement was a "good" one usually blame themselves first when the placement disrupts. They tend to believe either that the disruption proves that the decision to proceed was a mistake, or that the disruption could have been prevented — if only they had done something they failed to do. These feelings of self-blame often take the form of "If only I had known the child or family better," or "If only I had seen them more frequently."

Like the children and their parents, workers may communicate hostile, but not necessarily accurate, messages about the "irresponsible" child and family. These messages may include assertions that the child "did things he had never done before," that the child or family "withheld necessary information," or that the parents "weren't sufficiently committed to the adoption." Families who blame the child may further contaminate the worker's perception of the child by calling him "disturbed" or indicating that ". . . nobody, but nobody, could parent that kid." Too often, workers are persuaded by such emotional statements that their earlier perceptions of the child were incorrect and that the child is truly disturbed. This is a convenient, but often mistaken, conclusion.

PREPARING WORKERS FOR DISRUPTION

In order to better prepare children and families, the Spaulding staff believe it is essential for adoption workers to be prepared for the reality and inevitability of disruption. As a first step, workers must know their own feelings and attitudes concerning disruption. Only by preparing to deal with their own reactions can placement staff hope to adequately help children and families understand their feelings and attitudes toward disruption before the child is placed, work toward the solution of post-placement and post-confirmation problems, and survive a disruption if it occurs.

It is helpful for a staff preparing to cope with their own reactions toward future disruptions to read all they can about the subject and to talk with other workers who have been through that experience. Gaining the knowledge that other workers with all ranges of placement skill and commitment to children have encountered disruptions and have survived is the most persuasive way for workers to become convinced that disruption is not an isolated phenomenon which is happening only to them.

The opportunity to discuss disruption with others is sometimes difficult to accomplish, however, for it requires placement staff to meet as a group to identify key issues and consider the emotional reactions common to the experience. The openness of the staff is crucial, and their ability to be supportive of each other, will largely be determined by their comfort in working out problems in the group. It is unfortunate that the administrators of some placement programs are reluctant to afford staff sufficient time together to forge these ties.

Experience has convinced Spaulding workers that frequent meetings among the total placement staff are essential if any practical preparation for disruption is to occur. Only through such meetings can the staff learn about each others' values and beliefs and begin to set the stage for working closely enough together to provide the emotional support imperative for workers experiencing disruption. Although an effective support system can be built only as a response to the actual stress of an ongoing disruption, knowing in advance that such a system will need to be built makes the task easier when a disruption finally occurs.

Aside from sharing the preparation for adoption, such group settings may eventually become the preferred means of making placement decisions. The Spaulding staff is convinced that *all* placement decisions must be shared, rather than individual, decisions. Sharing placement decisions makes it possible to share the impact of disruption.

A warm and supporting relationship among staff is especially important in helping workers overcome the overwhelming feelings of depression and guilt which frequently result when individuals feel that they have failed to maintain a placement. If workers feel emotional support from fellow workers, they can more easily maintain their view of themselves as competent persons. Teamwork, then, helps to provide the atmosphere of confidence and security in self and each other that is essential to the maintenance of high staff morale. The presence of the "team" and the support it provides also serve as a means of rewarding workers by providing *espirit de corps* in a difficult and demanding job that may otherwise supply few rewards.

The Spaulding staff realize that it is impossible to learn everything which must be known about disruptions from the experience of others. They also realize that discussing the phenomenon of disruption will not prevent a disruption from occurring. However, they believe that conscientious team preparation can provide workers with more realistic expectations of what is in store and a greater ability to react knowledgeably and effectively under conditions which are potentially damaging.

HELPING CHILDREN AND FAMILIES SURVIVE DISRUPTION

At Spaulding, workers consider disruption not as a catastrophe but as an additional challenge to be met. Their commitment to the child and his future — to finding him an adoptive family, to supporting that placement, and to replacing the child with another adoptive family if necessary — serves as the core of their motivation to continue to work in the face of discomfort and stress. They know they must take positive action, for there are children to be re-placed and families who need to be helped to overcome their distress.

The ability to continue with the task at hand during times of anger and frustration sometimes requires sheer grit and raw nerve. Yet, it is precisely the workers' capacity to remain functional and helpful which, in many cases, provides the child and family with the insight, skill, and support necessary to cope with problems, deal openly with changes in relationships, and survive the disruption. It is especially crucial, for the child's sake, that workers conquer those emotional difficulties which can easily lead to worker panic and immobility. Without the worker's help, many children cannot survive the trauma of disruption. They become incapable of forming the trusting relationships needed to make permanent placement possible.

If the risk of disruption is to be minimized, regular post-placement services to families adopting older and handicapped children are essential. Workers who lose contact with families after placement are likely to eventually find themselves confronted by distraught parents who demand the termination of the placement and the immediate removal of the child. Some of these families, feeling that their problems have not been recognized or responded to, may begin talking about disruption in a desperate effort to force their worker to react to existing problems.

Professionals entrusted with the responsibility for helping children and families must provide opportunities for regular contact and possess a willingness to resolve sensitive issues and points of disagreement. There is no excuse for workers to be surprised to learn that one of the families on their caseload has been experiencing conditions serious enough to cause a disruption, for it is not difficult for workers to maintain clear enough channels of communication so that a family's decision to disrupt does not come as a shock to them. In fact, the experience of the Spaulding staff has shown that it is impossible for workers to be unaware that potentially disruptive problems exist within the family if effective patterns of post-placement communication are developed with families who trust workers and feel they are partners with them in maintaining the placement.

There is a built-in expectation at Spaulding, established by the staff in their pre-placement work with families, that the family's primary worker will continue to help them through a disruption if this is at all possible. The continuation of the same worker-family relationship throughout the disruption process is not only part of the workers' job of helping families as much as they can for as long as they can, but is a commonsense decision which enables the family to benefit from the support and counseling offered by the very person who has worked with them most closely.

Unfortunately, some families will not allow their previous worker to continue to provide them services. For them, the worker serves as a reminder of an experience they would rather forget. Some workers, too, have developed such an accumulation of negative feelings that they cannot continue to work effectively with the family. For these reasons, it may sometimes be necessary to consider assigning the family a new primary worker.

The decision to change workers can present difficulties, however. In several instances where the Spaulding staff have brought in another worker to help a family, the new worker (no matter how closely they worked with the previous worker) was perceived by the family as comparatively ignorant about past and present family events or the specific characteristics of the child. A new worker was considered unable to continue offering the quality of information and reassurance which the family needed. Because of such complexities, the Spaulding staff have determined that a decision to assign a new primary worker must be made by the entire team.

At Spaulding, the worker has four obligations when helping children and families survive disruption. They are:

1. to help the family understand what has happened and why
2. to help the family interpret this to the child
3. to help the child and family cope with their reactions
4. to help the family assist the child in the move to another place-ment

There is no established order of events for a worker to follow in accomplishing these tasks, for the causes and circumstances in each disruption are unique. The order will depend upon what needs to be done first. Priorities may be determined by the degree of stress experienced by the child, the family, or the worker, with assistance extended, in turn, to the persons in greatest or most immediate need of support. Worker commitment to either the child or family may also dictate which obligation is met first. Priorities may also depend upon the length of time the family is willing to continue caring for the child and the ability of the worker and family to work together to find a replacement family. Other factors influencing the process are the availability of an appropriate replacement family, and the degree of awareness of what has happened, why it has happened, and what the effects on the future will be.

Ideally, the worker should work with the disrupting family to help them cope with their negative feelings while the child is still in the home. Depending upon the circumstances, the worker may also begin searching for a replacement family and gain the original family's cooperation in preparing the child for the necessary move. This is usually possible because most families are encouraged to fulfill their responsibility to the child by affording the worker the time to find and prepare an appropriate replacement family. In most cases, families are expected to be willing to keep the child in their home while the search for a new family is undertaken and the necessary preparation takes place. Most families see this as part of their responsibility to fulfill a commitment to improve the child's situation. Though they may not be able to live with the child permanently, they can usually assist the child toward a positive alternative. Most families feel they can work with an uncomfortable situation if they know the child will be leaving in the foreseeable future in a planned move.

It is the experience of the Spaulding staff that successful replacement of an older or handicapped child is a far greater possibility if the adoption worker is able to work with an informed and participating child and cooperative adoptive parents. If families are willing participants in planning for the child's future, their constructive actions will help alleviate the guilt they are most likely feeling over the disruption.

Although most families are able to keep the child for a short period of time after they decide a disruption is inevitable, some families and children may be in such intense distress, or the families may view the child's behavior as so intolerable, that the worker has no recourse but to remove the child from the home as soon as possible. Such situations, in which the child and family can be worked with only after the child is moved, often result in the highest level of anxiety for everyone involved, including the worker. The Spaulding staff are convinced that team functioning can be especially useful during these times to help workers sort out what they must do, to decide which tasks have the highest priority for child and family, and to get help with their own intense feelings.

One of the most difficult problems for families who are disrupting is the inability of the parents to tell the child he will be moving again. Although it is important for parents to be honest with the child, this is sometimes too painful for the parents to accomplish by themselves. They frequently find themselves caught between their own need to survive and their fear that the child may be seriously emotionally damaged by another move. If they cannot, in fact, tell the child what is happening, it is the worker's responsibility to force the issue, control the information communicated to the child, and make certain it is accurately related. In some cases, it may even become necessary for the worker to assume the responsibility for telling the child.

Parents and workers generally have difficulty breaking the news of the disruption to the child because they fear their explanation to him may be his first indication that the family is having serious problems. The Spaulding staff have found, however, that most children know long before they are told that something is wrong within their family. While it is often true that the child may not be able to describe the situation accurately, his responses frequently indicate a surprisingly accurate perception of the problems. Once the family understands that the child is at least partially aware of the growing problems within the placement, they may be much better able to discuss those problems in his presence as well as talk about the anger which has built up inside them toward the child, the worker, and themselves because the placement cannot continue. Even when such a point has been reached, however, the child may either agree with the interpretation of events or respond in an antagonistic manner. Spaulding workers have found that both the speed and direction of family progress in overcoming their disruption depend as much upon the child's responses as they do upon the responses of other members of the family.

Counseling sessions with the child and his family can be used to discuss relevant issues such as each family member's perception of problems and the effects of the disruption on each person. In particular, workers should help the child deal with his feelings of insecurity and hostility and help him sort out the feelings which have some basis in reality from those which exist because of fantasy or inaccurate perceptions.

The worker must help the child express his true feelings, even if it is initially necessary for the worker to guess what those feelings might be. By understanding and articulating these feelings, sharing plans for another placement, and refusing to be caught up in the child's game of "please say it isn't so and that I don't have to leave," the worker helps the child more realistically face the future. It is also helpful for the child if the worker is able to reassure him that most other children in the same situation would be just as confused, worried about the past, and afraid of the future.

Once the child begins to come to terms with the disruption and why it occurred, the worker can help the child by seeking out a family who can accept him, his history, and his problems. Eventually, the older child must strike a bargain. He must trade what he can offer for what he is being offered: "This is what I am willing to do in order to be a member of this family."

Although it is better for the child who must move to talk openly about the decision to disrupt, to express his anger and grief, and to see anger and grief expressed by others, he may choose to hide his real feelings in a desperate effort to overcome his position of powerlessness or to mask his hurt. He may, for example, deny his need to move, attempt to bargain, promise to change his behavior, plead for "one more chance," or offer impossible solutions to the problems which are preventing the placement from working out. Although workers should always take a child's feelings into consideration, it is essential that the worker not be seduced into trying to implement over-simplified, unrealistic, or inappropriate solutions, no matter how much they wish the child's placement could remain intact.

When counseling families, it is often wise for a worker to help the family discuss the reactions of other children in the family to recent and future events, especially their reactions to the projected absence of the new family member. Spaulding workers have found it helpful to describe how other families felt as they coped with disruption and to share written materials prepared by previously disrupted families. They have found that it is particularly reassuring for children and families to know others have encountered similar experiences.

During these discussions, parents and children usually begin to understand that disruption has a direct impact on all family members. Parents frequently become aware, for the first time, of the unintended message the removal of the child is conveying to other children: "If I misbehave I will be removed from the family, too." They often come to realize that their other children also may be feeling guilty because they wished their brother or sister would leave, and their wish has come true. Parents are usually greatly relieved to learn their other children are capable of understanding what has happened, but surprised to learn how often they must reassure those children that no one else will be leaving the family.

In helping families survive disruptions, workers should always seek to work as closely as possible with children and parents. However, there are always some cases in which families become alienated from their worker. When this occurs, workers should try to re-establish a working relationship or offer contact with another worker, for both children and parents are in great need of the services which an understanding and knowledgeable worker can provide.

Alienation most frequently occurs during times when the best interests of both the child and the parents connot be simultaneously served. The Spaulding staff are convinced that it is impossible for workers who are comfortable and secure only when they are pleasing parents to consistently make the decisions which are best for the child. As a result, it is vital that workers decide whether they, as professionals, exist primarily to serve the child or the family. At Spaulding, the worker's primary responsibility is always to serve the child. The staff believe that the worker must constantly remain the child's bastion of strength, for there may come a time when that worker seems to be his only ally. The worker must be able to offer him security, be clearly perceived by him as being "on his side," and be a person he can rely on to tell him the truth, even when that truth is painful for both of them.

RE-PLACING THE CHILD

Between 1968 and 1976, the Spaulding staff experienced 21 disruptions — a disruption rate of 10.6 percent. Of the 21 children whose adoptions have been terminated, 18 have been replaced in other adoptive families by Spaulding workers. Of the remaining three, one was replaced by another agency and one teen-age boy chose to live semi-independently with his grandmother. The third child was an 11 year old boy who apparently could not manage close family relationships. This judgment was made by the entire Spaulding staff (the "team") after evaluating his history of four adoption disruptions: two before his referral to the agency and two with Spaulding families. Although placed in a group care home, he has maintained contact with his most recent adoptive family.

Early discussion concerning the inevitable disruption of a percentage of placements involving older and handicapped children occurs as a regular part of the pre-placement preparation for adoption for all families. It is during this early phase of the adoption process that workers first begin to describe their commitment to finding permanent families for children, even when that means finding subsequent adoptive families for children whose adoptions disrupt.

Because of this commitment to permanence for the child, Spaulding workers will sometimes begin considering the appropriateness of potential replacement families even as they are placing a "high-risk" child with an initial adoptive family. This is not so much a conscious search for a next adoptive family in case one should be needed as it is an awareness by experienced workers that the child may have difficulty adjusting to a specific family or to adoption in general.

The point at which a worker begins to consider potential replacement families for a specific child depends upon the existence of combinations of factors which make a child and his placement "high risk." The seriousness of the child's handicap, the difficulty he is expected to have in adjusting to adoption, and the capabilities and tolerance the adoptive parents have in parenting such a child are all part of the assessed level of risk involved with the placement. The worker who has more experience with disruption can spot a potential disruption and begin to prepare for that possibility earlier than a worker without as much experience. Spaulding workers believe that no matter when they actually begin looking for a replacement family, it is inappropriate and, indeed, unwise, to share that information with the child or the adoptive family before they have decided that a disruption is unavoidable and while they are still learning to adjust to each other.

Although the staff keep no specific waiting list of replacement families, there is a strong preference for families who have previously adopted through Spaulding and who are well aware of what it means to parent a child who has experienced separations. It is also especially helpful if the family has adopted similar children so workers have a thorough understanding of their parenting ability.

As with any prospective family, replacement families must be thoroughly informed about the child in order to be able to make an adequate decision about their ability to parent him. The staff find that it is particularly important to discuss both the immediate and the long-term effects of disruption on the child. The worker must carefully explain the nature and extent of the difficulties which evolved during the placement with the disrupted family as well as the child's reaction to those conditions and to the disruption itself. If possible, the replacement family is put in touch with that previous family, for it is essential that they have the clearest possible understanding of the child's history and past patterns of behavior.

Because of the complexity of the child's past experience with disruption, replacement families must be even more skilled, more finely tuned to the meanings of separation and loss, and more sensitive to the complex reactions of the child than most "first-time" families. Although they do not necessarily need more commitment to the children, these families must remain keenly aware that the child will probably feel he was betrayed by people he expected to trust so it will take longer and be more difficult for him to make a positive adjustment and form a trusting, caring relationship with another family. In addition to having to rebuild their ability to trust others, many children who experience a disruption have to relearn that there are people who do care for them and what happens to them.

Finding a family who is able to meet these demands is truly a challenge. Parenting a child who has the additional problems created by a previous disruption is difficult to say the least. Many of these children regard material goods as the only true signs of affection, and are no longer able to feel that it is rewarding just to be with someone who can make you feel good about yourself.

Parents will find it is not enough to tell the child "I'm here because I care." A child who has been repeatedly hurt will often suspect that parents do not really care about him, but only about making themselves look or feel good. For families who seek to parent these children and workers who seek to find such families, rebuilding this trust seems to frequently consist of "one step forward and two steps backward."

Despite the slow pace, it is essential that placement workers and replacement families take the time and effort to help a child understand his feelings and his condition, and to help him slowly regain his confidence in others. If this is not done, the disruption experience (and the inappropriate reactions of the adults he subsequently comes into contact with) will only confirm his worst fears about himself and others. The worker will need to find a family who will not need to see immediate or tremendous changes in the child, and one which has the patience and fortitude to accomplish this task.

Because disruption is such a difficult experience for workers as well as children and families, workers will usually do all they can to select a replacement family they feel will not disrupt. As a result, all potential replacement families are carefully scrutinized in an effort to guarantee that they will be a doubly "safe" family. Despite their awareness that it is impossible to predict placement success, workers tend to choose those families most adept in their verbal assurances that they understand the child, that they will stick with him through difficult times, and that the child will experience a successful placement.

At Spaulding, the choice of the most appropriate replacement family is determined not only by the worker's and family's perceptions of the family's ability to successfully parent the child, but also by the child's suggestions for improvements in his next placement. The child is told that the process of looking for his replacement family is a shared search between the worker and himself. Although the child's answers to the worker's questions of "What do you want?", "What do you not want?", and "What do you think will work for you?" could be mostly fantasy, most children are able to offer insight into which family characteristics will best work for them. These may include the ages and types of parents or brothers or sisters the child prefers, the style of family living he prefers, or the location of the family home. His suggestions for these more visible aspects of his future placement may well offer the insightful worker valuable information which will increase the probability of a successful replacement. When the child is given repeated opportunities to express his likes and dislikes, the worker also has a clear sign that the child recognizes the reality of his proposed move.

When talking about likes and dislikes, the worker must be very careful not to promise anything to the child which cannot be delivered. Since the child who experiences disruption is especially vulnerable to losing trust in the world around him and the people in it, workers should be especially careful to guard against making impossible promises or offering false assurances of permanence which may not materialize in spite of everyone's best intentions. Rather than trying to guarantee success, it is more valid for workers to promise the child that they will do their best to find him an appropriate family, that they will tell him about the kinds of families who are available so he will be able to help make the decision, and that, in the meantime, they will "stick with him" until the future is resolved.

The opportunity to find an appropriate replacement family is improved if workers do not have to frantically search for a capable replacement family and the child can, instead, remain in his home until the new adoptive family is located. This also minimizes the degree to which the worker blames the family for the disruption while they are fulfilling their obligation to the child and frees the worker to concentrate more energy on the search for another adoptive family whose capabilities, attitudes, and expectations fit well with those of the child.

Despite their best intentions, however, it is sometimes impossible for the disrupting family to maintain the placement while the search for an appropriate replacement family is being conducted. If the child must be moved, an immediate alternative plan for the child's care must be formulated and put into action. All too often under these circumstances, workers will tend to work desperately to patch up a placement no longer beneficial to either child or family. The decision which should be made at this point is whether to place the child with an available replacement family (though possibly only partially prepared) or to place the child in a temporary setting.

If a potentially suitable replacement family is only partially prepared, the Spaulding worker may still elect to place the child with that family. Such a decision is most frequently made if the worker is concerned that any further delay would so add to the child's insecurity that emotional problems might result. Although the worker may sense that this is the "right" family for the child, the risk of another disruption is greater because many important issues relevant to the placement may not yet have been resolved. As a result, the worker proceeds with a significantly lesser degree of confidence than if the family were more fully prepared.

"BRIDGE" FAMILIES

If an appropriate replacement family is not yet available for the child, the Spaulding worker may choose to place him in a temporary "bridge" family. These are families who, in the staff's opinion, provide a more desirable solution to the need for short-term care than do more traditional foster families. They are families who have already adopted a Spaulding child, are well-known to the staff, and are willing to help prepare a child for replacement by providing licensed short-term "foster care." To be appropriate "bridge" families, the families must also have proven parenting skills and must be geographically accessible. In addition, the staff must believe the families are able to manage the problems of that specifically available child for the length of time required.

There are two instances in which Spaulding uses "bridge" families. The first occurs when a child must be removed immediately and a suitable replacement family is not yet prepared to take that child into their home. Under these circumstances, the child is able to live with a competent and caring family while waiting for his next adoptive family, and the workers are able to take the necessary time to find that family and adequately prepare them to parent that child. The second instance involves those children who the staff decide not to replace immediately, often because workers are not sure they accurately understand the child's mental, physical, and/or emotional problems and, consequently, do not yet feel that they can formulate the best plan for his future. In such cases, the "bridge" family and the worker form a partnership for the purpose of making a more accurate assessment of the child or for checking the accuracy of information gathered earlier about the child's behaviors, attitudes, or expectations.

This is necessary because the disrupting family often blame the child in an effort to explain to themselves and the world why their adoption ended. Their descriptions of him frequently become exaggerated, consisting of phrases such as "very disturbed," "really bizarre behavior," or "sick little kid." As a result, workers unfamiliar with the dynamics of disruption may become so "contaminated" by the parent's perceptions that they may react to those characterizations at face value. They may not know if they have inaccurately assessed the child unless they talk with the child or make appropriate use of "bridge" families. For this reason, Spaulding's "bridge" families work in close cooperation with workers to determine how the child is currently functioning in the family, in school, and in the neighborhood. Such insight is essential if a worker has any hope of correctly assessing the child's need and finding a suitable re-placement family.

"Bridge" families offer the child the security of a relationship he can take with him into his next adoptive placement. Such a family is often able to provide a calm haven for a child who has just gone through a troubled period in his life. Many children who experience disruption are not ready or willing to immediately begin forming ties of love and trust with a new family, but can manage being temporarily placed in a situation where such behavior is not expected or required. However, when a child is ready to leave his "bridge" family, he will usually have the added security of knowing he has an additional family who cares for him.

The most difficult problem in placing children with "bridge" families is that those families often become committed to the view that the child's disruption could not have been his fault. Despite extensive worker effort to the contrary, these families frequently feel they are rescuing the child from a previous family and seek to blame the previous adoptive parents for the child's disruption. Such inaccurate views of the earlier placement and unrealistic perceptions of the previous family usually result from a lack of access to, or selective perception of, information regarding the source of problems which existed in the previous placement. Some "bridge" families even take the extreme view that the child did nothing to cause his disruption: that the problems which led to the disruption would not have existed if the parents had been more understanding or had loved the child more. In some cases, "bridge" families are tempted to believe that love and understanding is all that is needed to prevent any recurrence of old problems, or that the child, by the time he leaves them, will be a "new person" who has solved all of his serious problems.

It is the experience of the Spaulding staff that many older children are manipulative enough to clearly understand these attitudes and to take advantage of them. They are experienced enough to know that if they play the role of a docile waif who needs love, they will get more than their share of rewards for doing so. In situations such as these, a worker must work hard to explain the real facts of the child's past (including a descrip-tion of his disruption) to the "bridge" family and describe how the child may be capable of manipulating families for his own ends.

Spaulding's temporary placements with "bridge" families usually last no longer than six months. However, it is the individual circumstances surrounding each placement, such as the length of time it takes to make an appropriate plan for the child or find a suitable family, which actually determine the length of temporary care. In some cases, the child has stayed with his "bridge" family longer than six months while the search continued for a replacement family. In other cases, the child has been ready for replacement earlier than six months because his assessment was resolved or a replacement family became available.

Often a "bridge" family will adopt a child they have "temporarily" cared for, although it is usually not the staff's expectation or intention that they do so. These adoptions usually come about because the "bridge" family has determined that "it is best if he stays here" or has recognized that "he has become part of our family." Such decisions sometimes cause amazement among the agency's workers because the child is not similar to the kinds of children that family had previously adopted or expressed an interest in adopting. The amazement is usually mild, however, because Spaulding families are committed to permanence for children and it is not unusual that they find it difficult to separate from a child needing a family.

Traditionally, only a few placement programs have encouraged foster parents to adopt the children placed with them for temporary care. Many adoption programs have, in fact, required that foster families give up their children either because the worker assigned to their case had initially labeled the placement as "temporary," or because there is a long list of adoptive applicants awaiting each available child. In contrast, the Spaulding staff believe that if close ties develop between children and the families caring for them, the child and all other members of such families may be seriously emotionally harmed if placement workers decide to end those attachments.

In those cases where a "bridge" family seeks to adopt, especially when the family expresses an interest in adopting a child unlike those who had previously held their interest, the Spaulding team assume responsibility for making certain the child and the family have carefully thought through their decision. In all such cases, however, the staff's attitudes concerning the child's future are greatly influenced by the existing feeling of "belongingness" between the child and the other members of his family, and are reinforced by their own clear understanding that the child would have never been placed with that family in the first place had the staff not regarded them as capable of adequately parenting the child.

PLACING ANOTHER CHILD WITH
THE DISRUPTED FAMILY

In theory, the Spaulding staff believe that no family who experiences a disruption should be considered automatically ineligible to adopt another child, provided the family is interested in doing so and the workers have confidence that the problems which existed in the family's earlier placement will not necessarily be repeated with another child. In reality, it is the staff's experience that the majority of families who survive a disruption decide they are not ready or willing to risk going through such a painful process again.

Of the 21 Spaulding families whose adoptions disrupted between 1968 and 1976, many remain so hurt by the experience that they do not believe any child (especially an older or handicapped child) would ever be able to fit successfully into their family. Included within this group, however, are a large number of families with whom workers would not be willing to place another Spaulding child. These are families who, by their own admission, were not able to gain adequate satisfaction from the child placed with them and who, for the most part, need the rewards achieved by nurturing a younger or less handicapped child. For many of these parents, the child's emotional response to his earlier life experiences made caring for him too difficult a task. Other parents apparently were not ready to believe some of the information about the child given them by workers prior to the placement, and discovered only after placement that workers' descriptions of the needs and behaviors which made the child difficult to parent were true. Still others were never able to fully comprehend that the kinds of children the staff place represent the most complex children available for adoption, and the most challenging to parent.

Among the families whose adoptions disrupted is a small, but significant minority who simply encountered a "bad fit" with their earlier placement and who workers believe could manage the adoption of another Spaulding child. Although the agency staff have negotiated the possibility of a subsequent adoption with several of these families, so far only two have overcome their negative feelings about disruption enough to adopt again. Both placements have been very successful.

Finally, this group includes some families who, for various reasons, are considered by workers to be poor prospects for future adoptions of any kind. These families may have serious marital problems, may not be able to successfully parent any child not born to them, may have promoted unhealthy competitive relationships between the adopted child and other children or one of the parents, or may have shown they no longer want the responsibilities of parenthood.

Although not an easily accomplished task, the Spaulding staff are convinced that workers and families can arrive at a clear understanding regarding future adoptions as long as they have established a satisfactory working relationship together. This is not to say that the family or the worker will not continue to be depressed or to have negative feelings about the child who disrupted or the placement experience itself. However, if workers are able to avoid or move beyond blaming the parents for the disruption, if families can be helped to be specific about what they need from a child, and if the workers and the family are able to discuss what has happened and what they have learned, there should be no significant disparity between the family's desires and workers' wishes for that family.

SUMMARY

A disrupted adoption is the permanent legal removal of any child from an adoptive family for any reason before the confirmation, or "finalization," of his adoption. Spaulding workers use the term "disrupted" adoption, rather than "broken" adoption, because they consider the adoption process — the continuous development of the relationships required for a child to become an integrated and permanent member of a new family — as being interrupted, not as having altogether broken down with the total and irretrievable loss of all that the child and family had managed to gain.

It is the experience of the Spaulding staff that some disruptions are inevitable when placing children for adoption. As a result, they not only believe it is essential for adoption workers to be prepared for the reality and inevitability of disruption, but also that workers must realize that the percentage of placements which will disrupt significantly increases when the children being placed are older or otherwise handicapped by mental, physical, or emotional problems.

The acceptance by the Spaulding staff of the inevitability of disruption stems from their belief that workers can never learn enough about a child and a family to be able to defuse or eliminate all existing problems which are potentially disruptive. Even if they were convinced, prior to placement, that no major problems existed, they would still never be able to predict whether potentially disruptive problems would occur after placement.

Although some disruptions are inevitable, workers can take certain positive steps to prevent some disruptions. However, it is only by sharing information (including offering realistic expectations for the child's future to potential parents) in order to prepare the child and family for their placement, building trusting partnerships between families and workers, and providing post-placement services whenever needed that workers can hope to prevent unnecessary disruptions.

Disruptions can be caused by unrecognized pre-existing problems, pre-existing problems that are known but left unexplored, and unpredictable problems which occur after placement. During late 1972, Spaulding workers extensively analyzed the 12 disruptions which had occurred at Spaulding between 1968 and 1972 in an attempt to discover why certain children and families did not adjust to each other. On the basis of this review, the staff concluded that each disruption seemed to have a noticeably different cause. For some, no specific cause could be determined. The study also revealed that no specific characteristics such as the age or sex of the child, the age, marital status, income, number of adopted or biological children, religious affiliation of the parents, or geographic accessability to the adoption program was identified as contributing significantly more than any other characteristic to the occurrence of adoption disruption.

No matter when or where it occurs, the decision to terminate an adoptive placement represents a very difficult time for both the family and their worker. The child's reaction to the disruption of his adoption is determined to a significant extent by the degree to which he seeks attachment, or a feeling of "belonging," from the placement family. The family will usually blame the child and worker, then feel guilt, before they are able to accept the disruption and realize it is usually both inaccurate and unfair to try to blame any one person for its occurrence. The worker is likely to feel depressed and defeated, to conclude that time and energy have been wasted, and to believe their judgment has been faulty. Like children and families, workers may also seek to lessen their discomfort and absolve themselves of major responsibility for what has happened by blaming someone else.

Workers who prepare ahead of time for the experience of disruption will feel less panic and be more effective in helping children and families understand their own feelings and attitudes. Although continuing with the task at hand frequently requires sheer grit and raw nerve, it is precisely the workers' ability to remain functional and helpful which, in many cases, provides the child and family with the insight, skill, and support necessary to cope with problems, deal openly with changes in relationships, and survive the disruption.

At Spaulding, the workers' obligations when helping children and families survive disruption are to help the family understand what has happened and why, to help the family interpret this to the child, to help the child and family cope with their reactions, and to help the family assist the child in the move to another placement. There is no established order of events for a worker to follow in accomplishing these tasks because the causes and circumstances in each disruption are unique. The order will depend upon what needs to be done first.

Between 1968 and 1976, the Spaulding staff experienced 21 disruptions — a disruption rate of 10.6 percent. Of the 21 children whose adoptions have been terminated, 18 have been replaced in other adoptive families by Spaulding workers. Of the remaining three, one was replaced by another agency and one teen-age boy chose to live semi-independently with his grandmother. The third child was an 11 year old boy who apparently could not manage close family relationships. Although placed in a group care home, he has maintained contact with his most recent adoptive family.

Although the staff keep no specific waiting list of replacement families, there is a strong preference for families who have previously adopted through Spaulding and who are well aware of what it means to parent a child who has experienced separations. As with any prospective family, replacement families must be thoroughly informed about the child in order to be able to make an adequate decision about their ability to parent him. If possible, the replacement family is put in touch with the child's previous family, for it is essential that they have the clearest possible understanding of the child's history and past patterns of behavior.

At Spaulding, the choice of the most appropriate replacement family is determined not only by the worker's and family's perceptions of the family's ability to successfully parent the child, but also by the child's suggestions for improvements in his next placement. It is the belief of the Spaulding staff that the child's suggestions offer the insightful worker valuable information which will significantly increase the probability of a successful replacement.

When talking with the child, the worker must be careful not to promise anything which cannot be delivered. Rather than trying to guarantee success, it is more valid for workers to promise the child that they will do their best to find him an appropriate family, that they will tell him about the kinds of families who are available so he will be able to help make the decision, and that, in the meantime, they will "stick with him" until the future is resolved.

The opportunity to find an appropriate replacement family is improved if workers do not have to frantically search for a capable replacement family and the child can, instead, remain in his home until the new adoptive family is located. Despite the best of intentions, however, it is sometimes impossible for the disrupting family to maintain the placement while the search for an appropriate replacement family is being conducted.

If an appropriate replacement family is not yet available for the child who cannot stay in his adoptive family, the Spaulding worker may choose to place him in a temporary "bridge" family. These are families who have already adopted a Spaulding child, are well-known to the staff, and are willing to help prepare a child for replacement by providing licensed short-term "foster care." To be appropriate "bridge" families, the families must also have proven parenting skills and must be geographically accessible. In addition, the staff must believe the families are able to manage the problems of that specific child for the length of time required.

Spaulding's temporary placements with "bridge" families usually last no longer than six months. However, it is the individual circumstances surrounding each placement which actually determine the length of temporary care. In some cases, the child has stayed longer than six months while the search continued for a replacement family. In other cases, the child has been ready for replacement earlier than six months because his assessment was resolved or a replacement family became available.

Often, a "bridge" family will adopt a child they have "temporarily" cared for, although it is usually not the staff's expectation or intention that they do so. In those cases where a "bridge" family seeks to adopt, especially when the family expresses an interest in adopting a child unlike those who had previously held their interest, the Spaulding team assume responsibility for making certain the child and the family have carefully thought through their decision. In all such cases, however, the workers realize that the child would never have been placed with that family in the first place had the staff not regarded them as capable of adequately parenting the child.

In theory, the Spaulding staff believe that no family who experiences a disruption should be considered automatically ineligible to adopt another child — provided the family is interested in doing so and the workers have confidence that the problems which existed in the family's earlier placement will not necessarily be repeated with another child. In reality, it is the staff's experience that the majority of families who survive a disruption decide they are not ready or willing to risk going through such a painful process again. Although the agency's workers have negotiated the possibility of a subsequent adoption with several of these families, so far only two have overcome their negative feelings about disruption enough to adopt again. Both placements have been very successful.

Working
With The
System

Children Who The System Fails: Reasons Children Are Not Adopted 15

The failure of this country's child welfare system to permanently place many of the thousands of children in need of adoption is, to a large extent, attributable to the kinds of attitudes and expectations which have formed the basis of traditional efforts to match healthy white babies and toddlers with "successful" applicant couples. Such attitudes and expectations, when applied to the placement of children who are older, handicapped, or of minority race, often result either in the professional decision that adoption is not an appropriate placement alternative for such children or that no families exist who are capable of parenting them on a permanent basis. But the problem is not just one of inappropriate attitudes. Other major factors hindering the placement of children traditionally considered hard-to-place or unadoptable exist within the organizational and structural charcteristics of both public and private sector agencies as well as the Juvenile Court system.

As a result of these conditions, repeated, long-term, and even unlimited delays in the permanent placement of older, handicapped, and minority race children remain common. Such delays tremendously increase the emotional problems which these children must try to overcome. The existence of these problems further damage many of the children and make them even less in demand for adoption. In many cases, their future is further jeopardized from exposure to the long-term effects of often impersonal, insecure, or unstable living situations.

Yet why does this continue to happen? How is it possible that children continue to be exposed to such abuses within the very system of agencies and courts given the legitimate responsibility for improving the welfare of children? It happens because despite widening public awareness and recent significant improvements, the system remains generally disorganized, uncoordinated, and inarticulate.

THE CHILDREN WHO NEED ADOPTION

On a large scale, the most visible evidence of the chaos within the system is the difficulty which exists in determining how many children in this country are in adoptive or foster care placements. Even more highly problematic is the matter of determining who these children are, where they are, how long they have been there, or describing the appropriateness of their present living situation or the plans which exist for meeting their individual needs.

Although the Department of Health, Education, and Welfare (HEW), in Washington, D.C., does attempt to determine the number of adoption and foster care placements each year by requesting placement figures from each state, they admit they have no reliable specific, or even general, information regarding the children in either of the two types of placement. The difficulty in determining even so basic a fact as the number of adoptions in the United States each year exists, first, because there is no requirement of any kind that placement figures must be reported by placement programs to any state, national information center, or overseeing organization. Not only do many placement programs fail to report adoptions to a central office within their own state, but some states do not report adoption figures to HEW. In addition, the collection of this information has been so poorly organized that many programs, and apparently even some states, have not clearly understood where or when to send their statistics.

Another reason for the difficulty is that no common approach for counting adoptive placements has yet been widely accepted. Therefore, individual programs and states continue to use different methods. An adoption that "disrupts" may be counted by one program and not another. Discrepancies can occur, too, when workers in one court or agency place children who are in the legal custody of another. One program, both, or neither may report the placement. Adoptions of more than one child at a time by the same family may also be reported as one or more adoptions.

In 1971, the last year for which national statistics are available, there were an estimated 169,000 adoptions. The latest attempt by HEW to update this figure, for the calendar year 1974, solicited reports from all states. The 43 states and jurisdiction that reported accounted for a total of approximately 107,000 adoptions.[1] No reports were received from Alaska, Arizona, Colorado, Guam, Idaho, Illinois, Mississippi, Montana, Rhode Islands, the Virgin Islands, and Wisconsin. Reports from Nebraska and South Carolina were so incomplete they were unuseable. Several states provided invalid data by reporting information for fiscal years 1974 or 1975. In some states, not all counties reported and, in several other states, only adoption petitions investigated or reported by the Department of Public Welfare (or its equivalent) were reported.

However, even with incomplete and overlapping information from all if not most states, the best estimates of the number of adoptions in this country are probably much more accurate than the best estimates of the number of children in foster care. Not only do variations of all the adoption recording and reporting problems also apply to foster care, but the average number of moves for each child in foster care demands more paperwork and greatly increases the difficulty of keeping accurate records.

Although many children removed from the custody of their biological parents remain in a series of foster homes or institutions until they reach legal majority, the need of most of these older and handicapped children for permanent placement has been so ignored in the past that no accurate count has ever been made. However, current national estimates of the children in temporary foster care who are in need of permanent families range from 100,000 to 350,000.[2]

These figures represent the best estimate of the number of children in foster care in need of permanent placement families at any given time. However, the actual number of these children is always changing, as some are being placed with permanent families while others are just being identified as needing another family. Because of a continuing increase in the rate of family separation and divorce, child welfare professionals generally agree that the number of foster care children needing permanency is increasing. In fact, they estimate that the number of children entering this category each year actually exceeds the number annually adopted.

Estimates of children in need of permanent families usually focus on those children in foster care whose parents' legal rights to them have

[1]*Adoptions in 1974*, Dept. of Health, Education and Welfare Publication No. (SRS) 76-03259; National Center for Social Statistics Report E-10 (1974).

[2]Unpublished information, Children's Bureau, Office of Child Development, Dept. HEW (personal communication, June 1977).

been legally terminated and who are perceived by local child welfare professionals as being "suitable" for adoption. Yet the number of children who could benefit from adoption is actually much larger. First of all, the figures commonly used to define the number of children in need of permanency do not include any of the more than 150,000 children who, whether in need of psychological/psychiatric help or not, are currently in institutions for the emotionally disturbed, mentally ill, or mentally retarded.[3] In addition, these figures also do not include any of the more than 100,000 dependent or neglected children, or the children declared ungovernable by their parents, school officials, or the courts, who have violated no criminal laws but who are, nevertheless, involuntarily confined in prisons throughout the United States.[4]

A considerable number of children in the categories mentioned above are not yet legally available for adoption, for their parents' legal rights to them have never been terminated in a court of law. This is not to say that all such ties should be severed in every case. It is reasonable to assume that some children from previously unstable or neglecting families who are now in foster homes or institutions could be returned to their biological parents if those families received effective counseling and were helped to provide care and security for their children.

However, in those cases where parents prove either unwilling or unable to provide that care and security on a continuing basis, parental rights should be severed. Unfortunately for many of these children, no one has yet chosen to assume the responsibility for ensuring them a permanent and secure future.

In some cases, courts are not always willing to remove children from parents even though the environment in the home is detrimental to the child. The decision to not remove a child is usually based upon the wide-spread public conviction that until abuse or neglect is proved, no one has the "right" to interfere with or intervene into the way in which parents rear their children. Achieving a child's availability for adoption would be made much easier if all parties (judges, attorneys, social workers, and families) were assured of clearly stated guidelines in the termination of parental rights.

---

[3]Complied from Richard C. Scheerenberger, PhD., *Public Residential Services for the Mentally Retarded, 1976*, National Assoc. of Superintendents of Public Residential Facilities for the Mentally Retarded, Morgantown, N.C. (personal communication); and unpublished information, Division of Biometry and Epidemiology, National Institutes of Mental Health, Bethesda, MD. (personal communication, March 1977).

[4]Wooden, Kenneth, *Weeping in the Playtime of Others*, McGraw-Hill Book Co., N.Y. 1976, p. 6. Used with permission of McGraw-Hill Book Co.

IDENTIFYING AVAILABLE CHILDREN

Any program determined to place older and handicapped children into adoptive families must first identify them within the system and publicize their availability. The children in need of permanent family placement are usually housed for long periods of time in quickly arranged placements originally intended to be temporary or short-term living situations. These children can usually be found in foster care homes, group care institutions, nursing homes, treatment centers for the retarded, or psychiatric hospitals. They are typically older, mentally or physically handicapped, emotionally disturbed, or of minority race. Many have been placed "where there is room" instead of where they will receive appropriate care.

Unfortunately, child care programs have traditionally afforded these children extremely low visibility. They have tended to become buried in impossibly large caseloads where social workers and other caretaking staff are regularly expected to be responsible for several times the number of children they can adequately serve and where employment survival depends upon the ability to "cover" as great a number of cases as possible in the shortest possible time.

With not enough time to care for all children in need, only the children who are in the most serious or obvious crisis situations will receive more than fleeting attention from those who are paid to care for them. Many adoption and foster care workers do not yet realize that every child in every placement may be in a kind of crisis — a continuing crisis of adjustment which requires constant understanding and support from parents and, when needed, from the worker. Those who do realize this situation frequently still do not have the time to patch more than the most demanding situations.

As a result, many of the older and handicapped children most in need of permanence have been placed in inexperienced or inadequately prepared foster homes, partly because such "temporary" placements typically demand less time and worker skill until a crisis occurs. When this happens, the most efficient use of time for an over-burdened staff is to quickly move the child to another foster home. In this way, lack of time, skill, and vision combine to create an insurmountable obstacle to the careful planning and support needed to assure placement continuity and permanence.

Children in institutions are particularly low in visibility, especially those who are moderately, severely, or multiply handicapped. Many of these children have been institutionalized by parents upon the advice of family physicians or medical specialists and "abandoned" with no conclusive plan for their future. Most often, they will never be made available for adoption.

Older and handicapped children who are not institutionalized have also tended to be categorized as next to impossible to place and held in endless abeyance while "psychologicals," "neurologicals," and other forms of evaluation are considered, scheduled, completed, filed, and maybe abandoned or forgotten, leaving the child with yet another label, but little else. Often these are delay and avoidance tactics which put off the day of assuming responsibility or making the more difficult decisions concerning planning, legal procedures, and placement. These activities have become so common, and now represent such respectable professional actions, that the procrastination which results is rarely criticized. Evaluations can be appropriately used if they serve the purpose of helping the placement staff find an appropriate family for the child. Objections are only made here to the prolonged or excessive use of measurement as a substitute for placement planning.

The existence of caseloads so large that adequate service is impossible for all cases also often produces the remarkably counter-productive result of workers willfully discouraging the adoptive efforts of prospective applicants. With workers already over-burdened, it is impossible for staff to find the time necessary to work with new applicants.

PROBLEMS INHERENT IN WORKERS' EDUCATION AND EXPERIENCE

Worker Training

The education provided in graduate schools of social work plays a significant role in the development of worker attitudes which may prove detrimental to adoptive placement. In the majority of these graduate programs, specific course content relating to placement activity is minimal. In most cases, students are expected to receive an adequate foundation for their future in adoption from a single field-work assignment.

What is often taught within the classroom is the ideal of providing a non-judgmental service which enables clients to resolve their own problems. Social workers, especially caseworkers, are taught that a correct professional attitude is that of assuming non-judgmental views of their clients. But when they leave school and enter the adoption field, they are immediately asked to make very fine distinctions, usually between those families who are or are not "appropriate." The workers are trapped between what they have been taught and the practical requirements of their role as placement professionals.

No matter how few requirements exist for applicants, or whether the worker finds children for families or families for children, such judgments continue to be necessary. Whatever the circumstances, the worker is charged with the responsibility of protecting the child who is to be placed. As such, the worker is put in the position of making judgments about applicants — determining if a person is honest and straight-forward, if he has drawn the right conclusions about himself and his abilities, and if he is capable of parenting a specific child in need of a permanent family.

Most adoption workers who enter the field graduate from schools of social work whose orientation reflect a problem-solving approach to social work practice. Such training leaves many placement workers focused on weaknesses, instead of strengths, and in possession of the unhealthy and often invalid belief that individuals and couples applying to adopt a child have problems which must be solved before they can become capable adoptive parents. As a result, workers trained in this model are frequently unprepared to work with potential adoptive families who do not view themselves as troubled "clients" seeking solutions to problems, but as human assets and resources able to provide long-range solutions to the plight of children in need of permanent families.

The conflict between these two perspectives tends to create an early and formidable barrier to the development of a good relationship between worker and applicant, and becomes yet another deterrent to a prospective adoption. Some families who apply to adopt will, of course, have problems serious enough to deter placement. However, many more older and handicapped children would be placed with capable adoptive families if workers and supervisors did not assume that all applicants who approach an adoption agency have social and psychological problems requiring solution. Such attitudes are a reflection of ideas prevalent in adoption practice at a time when the vast majority of people considering adoption were infertile couples seeking a substitute for biological reproduction — a time when both society and child welfare practice did not favor consideration of adoption by any applicant other than those without other alternatives for creating a family.

Other Worker Attitudes

Workers may also fail to place children with permanent families because they hold still other personal views regarding older and handicapped children or adoptive parents. Adoption workers' attitudes regarding handicapped children's "fitness" for adoption may often prove detrimental to the children's chances for permanent placement. For example, negative judgments concerning the appearance or condition of an obviously handicapped child frequently interfere with appropriate placement planning for children with problems. The test most often applied by workers to determine the child's opportunity for adoption is

"Would I want to adopt this child?" Too often the answer is "No." On the basis of such feelings, it is not difficult for these workers to quickly and conclusively decide that families do not exist for these children.

In addition, workers may fail to place children because their work experience is not sufficient to make them aware of the negative effects cyclical foster care has on children. Workers have traditionally reacted to apparently unsolvable difficulties between biological parents and children by removing the child from the home. Some social workers have an unfounded optimism about the continuity, stability, and healing power of substitute care arrangements. They believe that if children are placed into clean and otherwise "adequate" family living situations, time alone will solve the most troublesome problems and produce vast improvements in children's lives.

At the same time, these workers may be unaware of, or choose to ignore, the reality that many foster placements are likely to be unstable over time and may cause irreparable emotional damage to the child by subjecting him to multiple moves and repeated attachment/rejection experiences. These workers may fail to recognize that a child's separation from his previous parents, if not well understood and accepted by him, actually creates a profound fundamental problem for the child rather than a solution to his earlier problems.

Skill Development

There are many workers who have appropriate attitudes and expectations toward the adoption of children traditionally thought unplaceable, but who are not able to place them because they lack the necessary basic skills. Children who are handicapped mentally, physically, emotionally, or because of age or race often need assistance, special consideration, and special planning and follow-up. For these reasons, workers are not able to use the same methods or a similar pace to achieve the levels of success found in the traditional placement of healthy infants. Due to lack of training and relevant work experience, some workers do not have the expertise needed to confidently deal with the many difficulties which exist in finding a family for an older or handicapped child, preparing that child and a family for their adoption, and providing essential post-placement services.

Such workers may not be aware of the complexities created by the child's legal position. They may not know how to move a child out of the cyclical foster care system once he has become entrenched within it or how to make him legally available for adoption. They have not yet acquired specific insights into what they must do to make the system work for the children they are expected to serve. These problems are further intensified because placement programs often experience high rates of staff turn-over, resulting in a constant infusion of young and inexperienced workers who do not have adequate understanding of the system within which they work.

It is not an easy task for program administrators to admit that staff cannot place certain kinds of children because they do not know the children well, do not have their cases adequately organized, or do not have the placement skills the task requires. It is sometimes far easier for administrators to rationalize that responsibilities to children have been fulfilled by maintaining "high quality" foster care programs by hiring social work staff with graduate degrees. If permanence for children is to become a priority goal in child welfare, workers must be on-going students in acquiring skills they need. They must consciously seek to make the best possible use of their own life experiences as well as the shared experiences of their fellow workers and the adoptive families they serve. Mature human qualities must be developed, including an ability to coolly and correctly analyze complex situations, an enormous capacity for commitment, and large quantities of warmth and compassion which can be called upon to help the worker through frequently difficult and painful experiences.

Working with children who bring seriously damaging experiences with them into placement, helping families fulfill their own needs as well as those of the child, and discussing unpleasant issues which cannot be ignored is particularly strenuous and demanding work which demands more than the usual amount of time and persistance. As older and more troubled children are placed, their adoptions involve greater risk, disruptions occur more frequently, and workers more often have to contend with the sometimes bizarre, poorly understood, and upsetting events which occur in the lives of families. Although all workers are not able to cope with such circumstances, many can acquire the ability to do so given appropriate training and adequate administrative and group support.

PROBLEMS INHERENT IN PLACEMENT PROGRAMS

Program Characteristics

While the attitudes, expectations, and skills of placement workers largely determine why children grow up in less than stable family situations, other factors may prove to be equally difficult barriers to appropriate placement. The characteristics of placement programs and the manner in which they function can also be crucial factors. Programs which have complex, unwieldy, or arbitrary guidelines and procedures will certainly be responsible for adding to the difficulties which hinder placement. Staff may, in fact, become so lost in a morass of procedures that no long-range planning for the child's future is undertaken.

Agency organization also affects services. A totally integrated child welfare program with each worker offering adoptive, foster care, delinquency, day care, and protective services may well create "jack-of-all-trades" staff who cannot provide quality services for any specific client and who cannot be adequately supervised. At the other extreme, a totally specialized child welfare program may result in so successfully isolating intake, protective services, foster care, and adoption that a child and family can be passed from one worker to another with no continuity or overall strategy implemented to achieve a permanent placement. For example, the typical child who comes to the attention of a protective services unit may first have a protective services worker, then a foster care worker, then a foster care on-going supervision worker; all within the span of a few weeks. In most cases, no one individual has had the time to assume responsibility for knowing the child or for acquiring information beyond rudimentary identifying material concerning the foster family.

Such departmentalized treatment makes it difficult for workers to think of children or potential parents as anything more than warm bodies that are passing through a program assembly line. Workers whose program, caseload, or concern for "professionalism" prohibits them from personally getting to know the people they are serving have limited opportunity to see the children in care or the families who apply to adopt as people with real feelings. In many large placement programs, a wide-spread sense of impersonality, insecurity, rigidity, and a "follow-the-rules" mentality frequently discourage the new approaches and tactics needed to place hard-to-place children. Such a climate offers little encouragement for personal commitment and innovation, and rewards only maintenance of the status quo and "getting along with the right people."

In many programs, there is not a single reward for criticizing the present structure, for devising a new technique or trying a novel approach, or even for expending extra effort to provide higher quality or more appropriate service. Workers trying to place children under these conditions tend not to receive the recognition, support, and encouragement they need from their fellow workers and supervisors. Lack of reward frequently becomes its own punishment. Providing service becomes a chore or, even worse, a study in boredom, and workers lose their desire to do an adequate job of individualizing the process of preparation for, or maintenance of, an adoption.

Lack of administrative support comes in many forms; each is a devastating obstacle to workers' attempts to place children. Administrators sometimes do not listen to or respond to workers. Some will not resolve issues of conflict between workers or units, or will promise action but never act. Others have no interest in the programs they administer or no commitment to, or liking for, the children they ostensibly serve. Such conditions are found in too many programs. Even those workers who come to the job with a substantial degree of commitment are gradually depressed and demoralized by their own experiences and their frequent contacts with co-workers who have been depressed and demoralized in the same way. In a short time, there is very little commitment left.

Lack of Cooperation Among Programs

Further difficulties handicapping the placement of traditionally hard-to-place children stem from the failure of many large placement programs to work effectively together. Poor or non-existent lines of communication within and between local, state, and federal child care programs significantly add to program inefficiency. Unclear lines of responsibility within many of these same programs make it difficult for vital pre-placement, placement, and post-placement decisions to be made when they are needed.

The resulting lack of timely decision-making may well be the single most critical problem leading to the denial of stable family life for many children currently in the child care system. With little pressure for system-wide public accountability, children who enter the child welfare system continue to become lost within it, helping to perpetuate programs rather than receiving help from them. Mandatory, periodic, and quality court reviews of all children in care outside their own families would help to measure and, thus, highlight the problem of all children without permanent families. Several state and national standard setting groups are now supporting this concept.

Financial Disincentives

The costs associated with an adoptive placement also discourage the adoption of many children. Unfortunately, there are often financial disincentives for permanent planning. The short-term, seemingly high cost of an adoptive placement may hinder efforts to achieve permanence for even those children readily identified as needing services and having a legal status that would permit adoption (that is, those whose parental rights have been voluntarily or involuntarily terminated). It remains for adoption professionals to more effectively publicize the fact that traditionally long-term foster care or institutional placement and maintenance is far more costly to the public than the total cost of adoption. Not only is adoption a financially reasonable alternative to the mounting cost of foster and institutional care, but purchase of service systems for financing the adoptions of older and handicapped children have proven to be effective.

In addition, the way adoptive programs are funded often hinders adoptive placement. Combinations of federal, state, and local money are currently used to pay placement programs the administrative cost for keeping children in foster care or institutions. The annual budgets of many programs rely heavily upon such reimbursements of administrative costs to meet their expected operating costs. The loss of income which occurs when children are removed from such placements and placed with adoptive families could eventually create massive financial difficulties for child welfare programs; a point which is not lost on the cautious administrator. In this way, a massive portion of the child welfare system continues to accommodate to methods designed to temporarily care for children needing permanent placement. Once policies, procedures, and methods become established, it is often far easier to continue their use than to question their propriety or discontinue them in favor of more suitable alternatives.

Funding procedures for placement programs need to be redesigned to allow the needs of children to remain the most important concern of the child welfare system. One possible solution is a pro-rated "administrative" payment based upon an average length of stay in temporary care to be paid a program at the time of placement, with diminishing amounts available as the temporary placement continues. This plan would guarantee programs uninterrupted financial stability, and would create a monetary incentive for workers to move children who are or who should be available for adoption out of foster and other temporary care situations.

Over and above the ingrained need to retain the funds provided as administrative cost reimbursements, the maze of funding sources affecting placement programs plays a large and generally negative role in attempts to find and maintain permanent families for children. County and court budgets may be adversely affected by differing financial reimbursements or program priorities received from federal, state, local, or voluntary sources. Adoption service and subsidies, traditionally a local concern, have been particularly hard hit. In part, this occurs because the financial existence of the programs demands that administrators set aside valuable time to juggle the frequently changing guidelines of widely varying local, state, and federal reimbursement programs.

Significant responsibility for insufficient appropriations for adoption also falls upon the shoulders of local politicians who decide how local budgets are to be spent. Many of these public figures still think of adoption only in the most traditional sense: as a convenient solution to the problems of infertile couples. They do not view adoption as a necessary service for older, handicapped, or minority race children, or for those who otherwise have difficulty exiting from the substitute child care system. They often have just enough information to be vaguely aware that there is a diminishing supply of babies, and when budget cutbacks are required, they reason that infant placement programs sought out by families who cannot have children of their own should be among the first "non-imperative" services to have their funds cut.

But the problems of financing adoption are more extensive than seemingly high placement costs and the way in which programs are funded. It is incorrect to assume that governmental financial priorities are entirely to blame for the problem of over-burdened placement staff and administration. Many children are not permanently placed because this country does not yet ensure the well-being of all children whose futures are known to be in jeopardy. Although the public is willing to pay for the removal of children from their neglecting or abusing parents in the name of "protective services," they are not yet willing to pay for extensive services which may make it possible for these children to remain with or return to their biological families; a logical permanent solution for some of the children who enter the foster care system.

The major reason for this lack of concern appears to be a widespread view that families who have serious problems living together, even if they remain together, are no longer worthy of caring for children. This same attitude is also frequently shared by child welfare workers, supervisors, and administrators. Because of this similar opinion, it is generally much easier for child welfare organizations to ask for money for foster care than to seek financial support for services to maintain a child in, or return a child to, his problematic, and possibly marginal, biological family. It is also easier, especially for a worker who is not trained to help solve family problems, to remove the child rather than spend the necessary time to get involved deeply enough to help the family stay together or to reunite.

Many child welfare professionals are even less enthusiastic about placing other children with adoptive families who have disrupted. Not only are these children and families seldom given a second chance with each other, but the children are often labeled unadoptable and the parents seen as incapable of adopting or caring for any child.

If permanent family life for older and handicapped children is to be a realistic goal in child welfare, adoption workers and supervisors must be willing to challenge the traditional view that no one wants these children and work actively toward placing them. Similarly, that goal cannot be achieved unless child welfare administrators demonstrate their flexibility in the creative use of funds and the shifting of child care staff from foster or institutional care to services which exist to maximize opportunities for permanent placement. It is the task of all child welfare professionals who are committed to the well-being of children to work conscientiously toward overcoming the many difficulties now inherent in the child placement system. Their ability to do so will be a challenge to a profession which has traditionally claimed that children are this country's most important resource.

SUMMARY

Despite widening public interest and recent significant improvements, major problems continue to exist within this country's child welfare system which hinder the adoptive placement of children.

On a large scale, the most visible evidence of the chaos within the system is the difficulty which exists in determining how many children are in adoptive or foster care placements. There is currently no requirement that placement programs report placement figures. There is not even a widely accepted common approach for counting placements. As a result, no reliable information on either a specific or general level is available regarding the number of children involved, who they are, where they are, how long they have been there, or the appropriateness of their living situation. It is the authors' estimate that as many as 600,000 children are currently in temporary care and in need of permanent families.

Some of the obstacles to permanent placement exist because placement workers are frequently trained in traditional problem-solving approaches to social work services; approaches which are often counterproductive to the placement of a child with an appropriate adoptive family. Workers also fail to place children with permanent families because their own unwillingness to adopt the kinds of children most frequently available leads them to conclude that no others would want to adopt them either. In many cases, workers fail to place children because they lack the skill or insight needed to make the system work for the children they are expected to serve.

Other obstacles exist in the form of complex, unwieldy, or arbitrary program guidelines and procedures. Overworked staff, lack of placement planning or continuity of service, lack of administrative support, poor or non-existent lines of communication, and unclear lines of responsibility also hinder attempts at permanent placement.

Still other obstacles are created by the financial disincentives connected with placing children into adoptive families. The seemingly high cost of adoptive placement often leads to a decision to place children in temporary care, even though long-term foster care or institutional placement is far more costly than adoption. In addition, many placement programs have come to rely so heavily upon federal, state, and local administrative reimbursements for keeping children in temporary care that moving such children into permanent families could create massive financial difficulties for program administrators.

The largest obstacle to permanence for children, however, is the attitude of the public. Although the public is willing to pay for the removal of children from their neglecting and abusing parents in the name of "protective services," they are not yet willing to pay for services which make it possible for these children to remain with or return to their biological families.

16

Entering the System

SEEKING RESPONSIVENESS

No matter how good their intentions, how great their skills and commitment, or how widespread the actual need for their services, the Spaulding Board and staff knew a specialized adoption agency would not succeed unless they could establish legitimacy, demonstrate expertise, and obtain enough financial support to sustain agency operations. This depended upon ability to prove not only that there were children waiting to be placed, but that they could find families willing and able to adopt them. Agency survival also depended upon convincing other child welfare professionals that these older, handicapped, and minority race children could and should be placed with available families.

The Board and staff knew it would not be easy for other agencies and courts in the business of serving children to refer children to Spaulding because they would first have to admit they could not place some of the children in their custody. Some agencies and courts would argue they were placing their hard-to-place children and claim they did not need the services of a supplementary agency.

By the time the Spaulding staff were ready to begin placing children, they were convinced that establishing and maintaining older, handicapped, and minority race children in adoptive families required techniques greatly different from those typically used to place healthy white babies and toddlers. Confirmation that traditional methods were inappropriate came quickly with experience. However, although methods and techniques which Spaulding workers believed to be out-moded were being widely used by other placement professionals, the staff did not regard these practices to be the greatest obstacle to adoption of the kinds of children they were seeking to place. Instead, they considered the major obstacle to be the unwillingness of agencies and courts to place such children with the kinds of parents who were currently expressing an interest in adopting them.

As a result, early agency efforts to find (or help other placement programs find) appropriate families focused on convincing other professionals to seriously consider the parenting ability of the many individuals and couples who had already applied for adoption. The Spaulding staff argued that adoptive applicants did not have to be white, middle-class, professional people in order to be good parents. It was necessary, however, for workers to overcome their bias against traditionally "inappropriate" parents in order to give those children waiting to be placed their greatest chance to achieve permanency. Spaulding workers found that when such bias was removed, a single successful placement was usually an adequate incentive to change workers' attitudes toward the adoptability of a child traditionally hard-to-place or "unadoptable."

However, as the children referred to Spaulding for adoption gradually became older and more handicapped, the Spaulding staff learned that the average middle-class applicant family proved either unwilling or unable to care for these waiting children on a permanent basis. These experiences led the staff to redefine the "appropriateness" of parents and to begin to seek out the more "atypical" middle-class and "typical" working class families as potential parents. (For more information, see the chapter entitled, "Adoptive Services to Working Class Families," p. 187).

Throughout their history, the Spaulding staff also sought to convince other agencies and courts that a specialized placement program could more successfully find adoptive families for older and handicapped children than could other programs which required workers to provide a wide range of child-care services. It was their contention that it did not make any difference who placed a child so long as someone did and did so with an appropriate family. Further, they believed that if a traditional placement program had not been able to place a child with an adoptive family, a specialized program should be given the opportunity to try. Such efforts to obtain referrals clearly required the establishment of a cooperative relationship between the Spaulding staff and the referring staff, the elimination of competitive feelings, and the avoidance of any public suggestion that Spaulding's existence implied incompetence on the part of other child placement programs.

The Spaulding staff consistently sought to avoid the traditional competition which exists between the public and private sectors of the child welfare system. From the beginning, the staff refused to align themselves with either side, choosing instead to try to work equitably with both sectors. They refused to accept the private sector's assumption that public sector workers are, in general, inadequately trained. On the other hand, the Spaulding staff welcomed the participation of private agencies, rejecting the public sector's assumption that private agency staff are too removed from real-life problems because they are capable of "picking and choosing" clients at will.

Although Spaulding workers believe that the majority of children needing specialized services are, in fact, found within public sector agencies, they are convinced that private agencies have unique opportunities to provide innovative and appropriate placement solutions for such children. The private sector must be persuaded, however, that their efforts will be cooperatively received by public sector staff and that their involvement in the placement of older, handicapped, and minority race children will not prove financially disastrous to their agency budget.

Despite efforts to maximize their chances for acceptance, the Spaulding staff encountered serious obstacles. Early in the agency's history, there was widespread resistance from other child welfare programs to Spaulding's philosophy and goals, methods, and techniques, and especially the purchase of service system they promoted. In time, however, the agency's workers have come to understand these resistances and have learned to live with them, negotiating differences and aggressively pursuing permanent goals for children referred. Though some resistance remains, it is an indication of the agency's positive effect on the field of adoption that much of the early resistance has been replaced by respect and admiration.

During Spaulding's early years, the agency's determination to challenge the traditional foundations of adoption and change existing beliefs about the adoptability of hard-to-place or "unadoptable" children threatened most other child placement programs. Part of this threat stemmed from Spaulding's association with COAC, the Council on Adoptable Children, (see p. 323). A large number of Michigan's child welfare professionals perceived COAC as a volatile and ill-informed group of parents who organized in an effort to force the child welfare system to be more responsive to minority children. Although the agency's only actual tie with COAC was that some of those who had help found Spaulding were also COAC members, many professionals literally regarded Spaulding to be COAC's agency. Throughout their history, the Spaulding staff consciously avoided the hint of any complicity between the agency and the parents' group, limiting their contacts to speaking engagements or otherwise participating in special information programs at occasional COAC meetings. It was not until the agency's leadership role in the field was firmly established and the parent group organization began to significantly decline in numbers and impact that Spaulding sought a closer relationship with COAC in order to strengthen efforts within the state to place older and handicapped children. In 1975, an experiment in combining the mailing of Spaulding and COAC newsletters was undertaken and the agency's staff began to meet sporadically with COAC board members to discuss mutual goals.

Some of the early discomfort other agencies and courts experienced as a result of Spaulding's existence can also be traced to that agency's use of methods and techniques significantly different from those found in most other placement programs. Spaulding was new and, as was quickly apparent, not tied to a firm tradition of placement practices and attitudes. As a result, its staff were free to ignore widely accepted traditions and use innovative methods to achieve the successful placement of the children for whom, and with whom, they intended to work.

Other programs, committed to moving at a careful professional pace with time-tested and proven attitudes and methods, were made uncomfortable by the rashness of an agency which, by traditional standards, moved too quickly and was too eager to try the "untested." Many were angered, too, by Spaulding's aggressive intrusion into the traditionally private affairs of other placement programs. For example, early in their history, the agency staff undertook the unprecedented activity of contacting local agencies and courts concerning the progress of those programs in finding permanent families for all children in their custody who were legally free for adoption. Spaulding staff probed for descriptions of children yet unplaced, the period of time considered "reasonable" to pursue temporary goals for children, and what alternatives were being planned for a child if an appropriate family was not found within that reasonable period of time.

Finally, many child welfare professionals were upset at the frequency with which Spaulding workers took the position that many serious defects existed within traditional child placement philosophy and practice. Feelings of antagonism were also created by their frequently stated belief that the emotional problems created by the separation of a child from his previous family were too often inadequately resolved because few social workers knew how to help children with such experiences.

Under these circumstances, it is understandable that the Spaulding staff encountered negative reactions from other agencies and courts. In general, it was the administration and staff of programs who had not yet worked directly with the Spaulding staff who were most easily threatened by this persistent group of verbal, enthusiastic, and aggressive young women. As Spaulding became more successful, it became even more of a threat, for it became more widely known that workers from that agency were able to place children other programs with larger staffs and more funding had not been able to place. The problem was aggravated, however, because many administrators, supervisors, and workers in other placement programs also began to recognize that Spaulding's success existed because its workers were more committed, knowledgeable, and aggressive than most child welfare professionals.

The most enduring source of difficulty, however, in working with other adoption programs continued to be the agency's insistence that referring agencies and courts pay Spaulding a purchase of service fee to cover the costs of placing and maintaining a child within a permanent family. Early efforts to promote purchase of service as a logical and viable technique of meeting the cost of adoption both bewildered and angered many of the placement professionals who first heard about Spaulding.

In spite of the agency's excellent rationale for purchase of service fees, a placement program would typically hear about Spaulding's service, contact them, want them to place a child, and then retreat when they learned they were expected to pay a fee upon successful placement of the child. Their hesitation was not always related to financial difficulties within their program, however. Quite frequently, it was related to the general lack of awareness of the part of social workers concerning the realities of program funding; few supervisors or placement workers seemed to fully understand (or show an interest in) the origin and disbursement of operating funds. As a result, Spaulding workers often needed to patiently pursue such topics as the identification of available funding sources, the referring staff's previous experiences with purchase of service, and the amount of money needed — including travel costs — to place an older or handicapped child with an appropriate adoptive family.

Despite their policy of charging purchase of service fees to all referring programs following the successful placement of the referred child, the Spaulding staff waived fees whenever it was determined that a child could wait unnecessarily long for placement while money was being sought to pay for their services. They also waived fees in those instances where it was felt that the commitment of the referring program to the child was such that they might not find the purchase money and might choose, instead, to withdraw the referral of the child. In most cases, however, the Spaulding staff were able to persuade referral programs to pay the fee. In light of their successful efforts to convince other placement professionals of the validity of purchase of service, the staff remain convinced that it is important for concerned agency and court administrators to implement policies which would make it possible for placement programs to purchase specialized services for children with no other option for adoption. (For more information on the development of Spaulding's purchase of service system, see p. 9.)

Shortly thereafter, in early 1969, the Michigan Department of Social Services (MDSS) agreed to purchase Spaulding's services, on an experimental basis, to find permanent adoptive families for a group of state wards whom the state conceded their staff was unlikely to place. After successfully placing several of these children, Spaulding succeeded in developing a broader and more open purchase of service agreement with MDSS for the placement of state wards considered hard-to-place or "unadoptable."

As a result of growing awareness among child welfare professionals of these initial placements, the agency's early support from a local Department of Social Services and a single county court gradually grew to include other placement programs. Once the benefits of their services had been demonstrated, subsequent referrals and purchase of service agreements were more readily negotiated between the Spaulding staff and the staff of the referring agency or court. To facilitate the referral process, the Spaulding staff would suggest that programs with prospective referrals who were unfamiliar with their agency and its approach to adoption first obtain the recommendation or perspective of someone who had previously referred children to Spaulding.

CHANGING ATTITUDES

Creating professional responsiveness to the needs of older, handicapped, and minority race children who are or should be available for adoption has been a long and difficult task for the Spaulding staff. Yet the agency has achieved significant levels of responsiveness because many child welfare professionals and private citizens have gradually become convinced that adoptive families can be found for these children. Many have been persuaded that it is more appropriate for placement programs to contract for a specialized service on behalf of a child than it is to focus on charging fees to willing applicants.

At the heart of Spaulding's efforts to ensure system responsiveness is continuous, aggressive, persistent involvement in the activities of all levels of the child placement community. This requires strenuous efforts to open as many lines of communication as possible to the widest possible public and professional audience. Reaching the largest potential audience has meant participating in as many meetings, committees, advisory groups, and workshops as possible. It has meant taking advantage of all opportunities to achieve response — to work side by side with other agencies and courts — to endlessly nibble away at the edges of traditional philosophy and practice.

Achieving responsiveness has meant that Spaulding staff, Board, and volunteers have had to tolerate the risk of being scorned, as well as appreciated, for what they believe. It has meant that they have had to be willing to risk being rejected by many in the process of seeking out those people who would listen carefully and respond thoughfully to their convictions. It has meant that workers have had to be willing to face overwhelming odds on many occasions without succumbing to the pessimistic and discouraging conclusion that "it obviously cannot be done." As a result, they have developed a strong sense of purpose and perseverance and a willingness to exert constant effort in order to counter frequent rebuffs.

Although the staff's eventual success along these lines has been widespread, their earliest efforts to increase awareness and commitment in others met with little progress. This was due, in part, to an unwillingness among child welfare professionals to admit that placement problems existed concerning older, handicapped, and minority race children. They were not yet ready to recognize that the system needed to implement innovative methods and techniques in order to solve the problem upon which the Spaulding staff were focusing. The failure of the Spaulding staff to achieve immediate responsiveness was also due to the fact that Spaulding had not yet established credibility or a reputation. The agency's workers had not yet clearly demonstrated (and could point to no other existing program which demonstrated) that such children could be successfully placed for adoption.

Because the quality of responsiveness Spaulding workers sought was so slow in developing, the staff realized that to change what they believed to be inappropriate placement practices, they would have to begin focusing directly on the fundamental process of changing attitudes. Since then, the staff's chief task has been to convince administrators, supervisors, and placement workers from other agencies and courts that children considered hard-to-place and "unadoptable" can, indeed, be placed, but that traditional policies, practices, and attitudes need to be changed in order to do so. It has meant that they have had to convince other child welfare professionals of the necessity to review their current program policies in order to discover and change those attitudes and practices which discourage families from adopting (or from applying to adopt) such children.

Personal and program-wide attitudes are frequently solidly entrenched, however, and the Spaulding staff have discovered that attempting to convince others to change the often deeply held attitudes and beliefs which hinder the successful adoptive placement of certain kinds of children is usually both a slow and a frustrating experience. As a result, the agency's workers have learned that those who wish to change attitudes and practices must usually be content to work toward accumulating small gains over long periods of time. Fortunately, change can be accomplished by chipping away at existing values, for the Spaulding staff have found that most social workers, like most other individuals, can change if those around them are changing.

It is essential, however, for workers seeking to produce change to learn how to best gain entry to an agency or court. Change has a much better chance of occuring if it can be determined which individuals have the greatest impact on changing policy, and how those persons can be best persuaded to alter policies. Most people, if given a choice, will search out and work with the most congenial persons in any organization, although this is not necessarily the most effective way to facilitate change. The Spaulding staff have learned that to effect change, they must identify the people who determine policy and who can be worked with, even though working with these individuals may present considerable challenge.

Changing attitudes involves talking with other professionals, giving them repeated proof of workable and appropriate placement alternatives, answering questions, destroying myths, and helping to build commitment to individual children. During Spaulding's early history, the staff first felt themselves to be rather militantly radical, and many others also saw them in that role. With their intense sense of dedication to the placeability of all children, they became angry when they encountered resistance in any form. Although it temporarily made them feel better to release their anger and frustration in staff meetings, this did not resolve the problems they encountered. They realized that they had to become more knowledgeable, realistic, and sophisticated about their techniques before they could have an impact on the system, and that they had to learn to plan strategies for coping with the problems they faced.

Because Spaulding does not have legal custody of the children they seek to place, the staff have had to learn to change the attitudes of the referring programs who do have legal jurisdiction by being persuasive rather than coercive or demanding. The form this process usually takes is that of individual or small group persuasion. Professionals who are involved with actual child placement are usually more quickly responsive than those who are one step removed from the placement process. Usually individuals who become convinced these children can be placed will, in turn, attempt to persuade others. The exact content and approach of this persuasion depends upon the knowledge, skills, and personalities of both the Spaulding worker who is persuading and the individual the worker is seeking to convince. It also depends upon the kind and extent of the relationship which exists between them.

It is not the agency's intent to convince all other agencies and courts to be like themselves or like each other. Each program encountered will always have an individual history, different staff, and varying techniques. The intent is to change attitudes toward the needs of children and the definition of successful parenting so that more children in need of permanency can be placed with appropriate parents. To accomplish this, it is important to plant the seed of courage, individuality, and conviction; to convince others that change is both possible and beneficial.

The Spaulding staff's most successful means of persuasion has been to emphasize the costs stemming from the potential referral program's obligation to provide for children who remain unplaced. This appeal to conscience and professional commitment is supplemented by the agency's detailed and enthusiastic accounts of their own successful experiences with similar children.

Some agencies and courts are persuaded to refer a child by Spaulding's competence and expertise. Others become convinced by the agency's standing offers of open-ended help and assistance. Some agencies and courts are persuaded to refer children by the sense of empathy and support they receive from the agency's staff. In all cases, part of the goal of Spaulding workers in building a working relationship is that of creating comradery by convincing the staffs of other programs that they share problems and responsibilities and understand the task facing them is a difficult one. Often, other professionals are very responsive once they realize that Spaulding workers share the same interests, concerns, and difficulties as their own. In most cases, this means agreement with, negotiation of, or at least toleration of Spaulding's values and attitudes. It also means that other professionals often begin to see the Spaulding staff as offering a solution to their problems. At the same time, however, Spaulding workers encourage others to recognize that they could have probably placed the child they referred if they used more flexible criteria for finding families and altered some of the attitudes and techniques they use when working with children and families.

There may, of course, be factors in addition to the staff's powers of persuasion to motivate other agencies and courts and refer children to Spaulding. Some programs, who find themselves in financial difficulty because of the rising costs of foster care and institutionalization, have begun to refer older and handicapped children because there is administrative pressure to do so. Agencies and courts may also be convinced they should refer children to Spaulding after seeing others do so and achieve results. Other child welfare professionals may read about Spaulding's services in newspapers, magazines, or journals, or hear about them at conventions, workshops, or training sessions. Many programs want to learn to place such children themselves, for they have a real interest in older and handicapped children but do not know how to overcome the frequent placement obstacles they encounter. Still others are motivated to refer a child because they are curious about what Spaulding is doing and how it operates.

APPROACHES WHICH FACILITATE CHANGE

Cooperation

As a result of their experiences with difficult placement problems, the Spaulding staff have devised specific strategies to use when approaching other agencies and courts. Their primary strategy to persuade other programs to change their attitudes and practices is to demonstrate the placeability of children traditionally seen as "unadoptable." In most cases, other placement programs must refer a child to Spaulding or work closely with the agency on an individual placement before they are willing to attempt the placement of a similar child themselves. In either case, the Spaulding staff have learned that cooperation with other programs is the key to providing a child with his best opportunity for permanency.

In working with another agency or court, the ideal goal is to gain the cooperation of all program personnel. It is particularly vital to gain the support of administrators and supervisors, for without their cooperation, placement workers cannot gain the flexibility necessary to find appropriate families for children. With this support, workers not only have the necessary freedom, but are also given the assistance they need. Although the initial contact must set this tone, maintaining such a relationship requires frequent contact between each program's workers; usually by telephone and letter, but face-to-face as much as possible.

In working with individual agencies and courts, it is necessary to know the individual and collective views of workers on many issues. Their interpretations of children's needs and their attitudes toward children will vary. The strengths and weaknesses of specific workers also must be known. It is important to know which staff members are reliable, competent, and committed to the well-being of children. Some workers will know their children well; others will not. Some will have a great deal of commitment while others will have little. As a result, the Spaulding staff have learned that when a child is referred, they must never assume that the referring workers know or will get to know the child well or will automatically do what is necessary to help the child become a member of a permanent adoptive family. It is the Spaulding worker's role to stimulate the commitment of the referring agency or court worker. To facilitate this, they may provide specific practice techniques or work with the referring workers in a team relationship.

In working closely with other programs, the Spaulding staff sometimes find that their opinions and those of the referring agency or court staff are not compatible. Sometimes they persuade others to accept their opinions; at other times, they accept the suggestions of the referring program if that is the only way the child will be placed. In one major area, they work especially hard to persuade others to their point of view. Once an approprate family is selected as potential parents for a child referred to them, they will defend and support their decision to place with that family in the face of tremendous opposition.

To accept a referral, find a family, and then have the staff from the referring agency or court be unable or unwilling to complete the process because they do not think the family is appropriate is a potentially devastating blow, for that family may be the child's sole opportunity for adoptive placement. These rejections also result in a waste of valuable staff time. To minimize this problem, the Spaulding staff try to carefully negotiate the problems and complexities inherent in all proposed placements with referring agencies and courts and try to act both as advocate for the child and agent of the referring program.

Nevertheless, in some cases, workers from referring agencies or courts have an idealized family in mind for the child. At times, the differences between that fantasy family and the family actually interested in and capable of parenting that child are so great that the referring agency or court resists or refuses the family offered by Spaulding. The most common reason for such refusals is that the family regarded as appropriate by the Spaulding staff has resembled another family previously considered and rejected by the referring program.

Families prepared by the Spaulding staff may also face rejection if the referring program's expectations for parents are unrealistic, if the family does not meet the more traditional critieria applied by the referring agency or court, or if the referring agency or court staff feels the family has some characteristic which they believe unacceptable. If the referring workers disagree with the choice of a family, that decision is usually strongly challenged by the Spaulding staff.

Since a placement is never planned unless Spaulding workers feel they have a realistic and workable permanent plan for a child, they aggressively pursue these differences of opinion and often succeed in persuading the referring program to permit them to carry out the placement by the weight of their conviction and their past experience in the field. In most cases, their position is based upon their belief that the presence or absence of the characteristics creating the conflict do not play a significant role in determining the family's ability to parent the child in question, and that more ideal standards for parents will not necessarily ensure a "better" placement, even if such parents could be found.

Whenever possible, the Spaulding staff initiate the discussion of any reservations the referring agency or court may have about a family. It is better if both programs can accept the family selected and understand the unique placement risks involving that child and that family. Even more intensified problems can occur if the Spaulding staff ignore problems and concerns, falsely convince the staff from the referring program that the placement is a very stable and appropriate one, and are then forced to explain that the placement is disrupting. It is particularly difficult to recontact a referring agency or court and plan a replacement with another adoptive family when subterfuge has been employed in designing the placement in the first place.

To help minimize such problems, the Spaulding staff have learned that referring courts and agencies, much like children and families, must be prepared for the possibility of disruption before any placement occurs. At Spaulding, the process of preparing the staff from the referring program for that possibility is part of the original negotiation process for the child's referral. It consists, first of all, of a straight-forward discussion of the reasons why there is a higher risk of disruption in the placement of children who are mentally or physically handicapped, who have a past they can remember and have developed personalities of their own, or who, because of the emotionally damaging experiences they bring with them into placement, are more difficult to parent. Thereafter, it involves maintaining regular contact and making sure the referring workers continue to understand that the disruption of some placements is a normal part of finding permanent families for these kinds of children.

The ideal partnership is one in which the placement worker and the referring worker are colleagues who are both knowledgeable about, and committed to, an appropriate placement for the child. Under such circumstances, if a disruption becomes necessary, all decisions regarding the child can then be made solely with the objective of providing the child with a better family relationship.

Once they inform the staff of the referring program that disruption is an inevitability, Spaulding workers verify that there will be no charge for any of the work involved in replacing the child. The referring court or agency is asked only to participate in the costs of any other interim care, such as payments to foster parents or "bridge" families, and for reestablishment of medical coverage.

The process of overcoming obstacles to appropriate replacement also involves determining that the referring worker's superiors are willing to accept the replacement family chosen for the child. This negotiation is frequently difficult, for there can be frustration and anger on the part of both the referring worker and the placement worker during discussions following a disruption. This is especially true if a good working relationship between the workers has not been established. Although an entire inter-program relationship may have to be renegotiated between alarmed or concerned workers, it is essential to the future of the child that lines of communication be reestablished, expectations of each other be sorted out, and an understanding be reached about what can be done on behalf of the child.

As Spaulding's reputation has grown and their commitment to children has become more well-known, the agency's staff have learned that their anxiety over the reactions of referring workers to disrupting placements is largely unfounded. Over time, greater numbers of the self-selected agencies and courts which have referred children to Spaulding have gradually understood (and in many cases even come to share) Spaulding's philosophies, attitudes, and perceptions of adoption. In addition, they have become more sophisticated, more realistic, and therefore less critical about the problems and complexities of placing and parenting older and handicapped children.

In recent years, good relationships between Spaulding workers and the staff members of other placement programs have developed with increasing frequency. Spaulding workers have realized that frequent discussions about the possibility of disruption with referring courts and agencies throughout the entire range of the referral process prepares the way for fewer recriminations in their working relationships, and greatly increases the probability of an appropriate replacement should one become necessary.

Confrontation

Despite their best efforts to cooperate and persuade other placement programs to change attitudes and practice, the Spaulding staff have learned that social workers determined to change the child welfare system and convince the staffs of other agencies and courts to respond in new ways must be prepared to be rebuffed. Social workers, they feel, need to develop a measure of resiliency prior to encountering these situations. They have learned that it is sometimes necessary to fight long and hard to create the opportunities to place some children for adoption. It may even be necessary to become involved in head-to-head confrontations over those meaningful issues around which the lives of children revolve.

As a result, the secondary strategy used by the Spaulding staff to change attitudes and practice involves a process of "over-preparing" for any confrontations with other child placement professionals which may hinder a child's chances of adoptive placement. This strategy requires the early identification of problems and obstacles, and persistent persuasion (backed up by the reality of personal experience) that successful placement is possible. "Over-preparation" requires workers to rehearse, or "role play," the many possible arguments they may encounter (both from their point of view and from their opponent's point of view) as well as the alternatives which may logically emerge. This preparation helps them to identify and articulate concepts and points of difficulty, and prepares them to convincingly counter the arguments offered against placement. It is also a useful technique for enabling workers to logically defend their philosophies concerning children, families, parenting, and adoptability. As a result, the Spaulding staff are better able to face confrontations with a high degree of confidence and the flexibility necessary to continuously develop new strategies for improving a child's chances for permanency.

Although this approach encourages the agency's workers to formulate and express their ideas as well as defend their philosophies regarding critical issues, they are always aware that they must remain prepared for some defeats. They must not expect to win every struggle every time they try, for some struggles are never won and some are not won for many years.

Despite the steady gains made in expanding the definition of adoptability, an extensive amount of work is yet required to change the attitudes and practices that continue to hinder the permanent placement of older, handicapped, and minority race children. It is the contention of the Spaulding staff that the needs of such children will not be met on an adequate scale until administrators, supervisors, and placement workers learn to focus on the needs of all available children and to stand up to confrontation when a child's future is at stake.

The Spaulding staff feel that the major weakness in the field of child placement is that the education, training, social and economic background, and values of most social workers have not prepared them for such confrontations. As a result, they believe that most older and handicapped children remain unplaced because too many social workers still tend to seek the path of least resistance and work toward maintaining a policy of "going along," a highly congenial way of creating relationships with co-workers, other professionals, and private citizens which permits them to avoid problems. Since it is Spaulding's experience that difficult times are ahead for those placement workers who wish to begin finding appropriate families for children traditionally considered hard-to-place or "unadoptable," it is necessary for child welfare professionals to begin to accept challenge and confrontation as a routine part of their job. To achieve continuous success, it is equally necessary for them to be able to give as well as receive encouragement and support if they are to survive in the emotionally draining world of working to change tradition.

SUMMARY

Early efforts by the Spaulding Board and staff to gain credibility and persuade other agencies and courts to refer their hard-to-place and "unadoptable" children for placement were slow in developing. The new agency posed many threats to the established child welfare system because of their outspoken criticism of the methods and philosophies they felt to be ineffectual or detrimental to the adoptive placement of older and handicapped children. Further difficulties were created by the development of competitive feelings toward the agency and as a result of its association with the Council on Adoptable Children. In addition, Spaulding required referring programs to pay a purchase of service fee for children referred and subsequently placed; an unprecedented requirement which proved unsettling to many other agencies and courts.

Gradually, however, Spaulding achieved a positive response from other child welfare professionals as children were indeed placed and the fledgling agency offered its assistance to the staffs of other programs, frequently working side-by-side with them to place referred children. Although there is much more work to be done, detrimental yet deeply ingrained traditions and procedures are slowly being replaced by more practical, realistic, and appropriate attitudes. Purchase of service agreements are becoming more widely accepted, and the referral and placement of children traditionally considered hard-to-place or "unadoptable" is occurring with increasing frequency.

17

Training and Consultation

THE DEVELOPMENT OF TRAINING
AND CONSULTATION AT SPAULDING

Since the agency's creation in 1968, the Spaulding Board and staff have assumed an extensive mandate of convincing adoption professionals and private citizens that most older, handicapped, and minority race children can and should be placed into permanent adoptive families. Their ultimate strategy has been to serve as an example and a catalyst — first by placing children for whom other agencies and courts had not been able to find families and later by persuading other placement programs that they, too, could place similar children.

Although placement of children by the Spaulding staff began in 1968, the initial attempts at persuading others focused on obtaining referrals of older handicapped children for placement. The history of the agency's broader and more active attempts at persuasion, best described in terms of training and consultation efforts, is a history of increasing requests for information and explanations on the part of other agencies and courts who heard of Spaulding's activities. By 1971, the staff realized they could help many more older, handicapped, and minority race children find appropriate adoptive families by helping other programs place such children themselves.

It took the staff most of the first three years of the agency's life (1968-1970) before they felt confident enough about their placement methods to use that information to help workers in other agencies and courts place similar kinds of children. During these years of observing the wide range of attitudes and skills of other adoption workers who were just beginning to place "minimally" hard-to-place children, the staff gradually recognized that broad efforts to inform the public of the facts which formed the foundation of this new kind of adoption and to persuade other agencies and courts to change their attitudes and methods were essential.

Yet Spaulding workers actually became teachers by default. Although there were many other individuals in the area more schooled in the art of teaching, the Spaulding staff were the only child welfare professionals in the early 1970's in Michigan who were both experienced in placing older and handicapped children and willing to be open and honest about their own mistakes and successes. Within a few short months, they discovered they could do a highly credible job of helping other workers, supervisors, and administrators better understand the challenges of placing older and handicapped children. They could do this by clearly explaining their own attitudes and experiences to those who had not worked extensively with these children or with families interested in adopting them.

By 1973, the Spaulding staff had made a commitment to spend a significant portion of their time providing training and consultation to others. As they gained more experience, they realized they alone, as one small agency, could not provide adoptive families for the many children legally without parents and available for placement. The formal recognition that they could maximize their impact on the child welfare system and help increasing numbers of children by training the staffs of other agencies and courts to place similar children did not, however, lead them to stop placing children. Despite their increasing emphasis on training and consultation, they continued to demonstrate the placeability of children who have traditionally been considered extraordinarily hard-to-place or "unadoptable," both to retain their credibility and to keep learning.

The reputation of Spaulding as both a training and a placement agency has continued to grow as more placement professionals have become aware of the agency's successes. Requests for training and consultation have increased at a steady and rapid pace since a workshop given by Spaulding's Director concerning "Placement of the Hard-to-Place Child" at the Third Annual North American Conference on Adoptable Children in St. Louis, Missouri, during April 1972. So far had the agency's reputation preceded her that instead of the twenty to thirty social workers she had expected to attend, several times that number crowded into the room awaiting her. Following this experience, the Spaulding staff, sometimes as a group, but mostly on an individual basis to accommodate more requests, have averaged three trips each month to conduct workshops, conferences, or siminars throughout the United States. Members of the Spauling staff have also participated in workshops in Canada, Great Britain, and Australia.

In addition to the change produced in other programs as a result of the agency's commitment to training and consultation, this decision also produced significant changes for the Spaulding workers. Until responding to requests for training and consultation became a routine agency activity, the Spaulding staff had simply placed children the way they believed was best — by following a commonsense approach to working with children, families, and referring courts and agencies. However, formal requests for information and advice concerning specific practice issues, or the conflicting perspectives behind those issues, forced the staff to more carefully analyze their approach to adoption in order to be able to clearly explain what it was they did and why. This need to become more knowledgeable and articulate has also been instrumental in Spaulding's continuing success, for it has been responsible for creating not only a more consistent approach to adoption but a far better understanding among staff of how their logical and practical approach to adoption has combined with actual experience to make the placement of older and handicapped children a reality.

THE CONTENT OF SPAULDING'S TRAINING AND CONSULTATION

The term "training" traditionally refers to the art of preparing, instructing, or teaching, while "consulting" is generally used to describe the less formal practice of providing advice or an opinion. However, throughout the current field of child welfare, any intended distinction between the two forms of offering or sharing assistance tends to become quickly lost among professionals who feel that no matter what the content or purpose of a "work session," it is less humiliating to call in a consultant for "advice" than to admit to a lack of expertise and a need for training. Though it has been increasingly possible to interest social workers in various kinds of training, many continue to distinguish "consultation," which they regard as an acceptable exchange among equals, from "training," which for them retains its connotations of competition and superior-inferior relationships.

At Spaulding, "training" is the process of describing the specific methods and techniques of their approach to adoption and the attitudes which underlie those methods and techniques. It is also the process of influencing other child welfare professionals to place older and handicapped children using workable, if not similar, approaches to the problems which traditionally hinder the adoption of these children. It is, in fact, the practical application of theory and philosophy. Training is usually made available at workshops, conferences, or siminars in the form of discussions or simulations of the case-related problems which the Spaulding staff have experienced. However, training has also taken the form of working closely with the administrators, supervisors, and/or placement workers from a referring agency or court to demonstrate the actual placement of a specific child.

"Consultation" at Spaulding, on the other hand, is the process of more broadly focusing on the general planning and organizational aspects of actual adoption practice. The staff realize, however, that the process of consultation cannot be separated from what is occurring during training, and visa versa. No matter which method is used, the goal sought is successful adoptive placement, and successful maintenance of those placements, for children traditionally considered hard-to-place or "unadoptable."

Whether the method involved is considered by the participants to be training or consultation, the process is very similar to that used by the Spaulding staff to gain entry into and acceptance by the child welfare system in the agency's early years. As with all of the agency's efforts, the goal of training and consultation is to convince other professionals that older and handicapped children can be placed for adoption, but that traditional attitudes and practices must be changed in order to do so.

Despite these similarities, significant differences do exist between training and consultation sessions and the process used by the Spaulding staff during their early years to gain acceptance from other agencies and courts. Differences occur in the type of information presented, the quantity of information successfully presented, and the appropriate rate of presentation. Although increasing the enthusiasm of others and motivating the listener to seek further contact requires early and successful persuasion both when entering the system and when providing training and consultation, administrators, supervisors, and placement workers who participate in workshops, conferences, or seminars are more or less a captive audience. As a result, essential information, potential problems, and specific strategies to achieve success can be presented and discussed more quickly and often more directly than was generally possible when the new agency's very existence depended upon an ability to slowly, carefully, and convincingly persuade other professionals to refer a child for placement. During training sessions, for example, Spaulding workers purposely underscore the frequent complexities which accompany efforts to place older and handicapped children, and repeatedly stress that successful placement and maintenance of such children requires continuous extraordinary effort on the part of placement workers, supervisors, administrators, and clerical staff.

As the Spaulding staff have grown more knowledgeable about the children they place, less naive about the problems families who seek to adopt these children encounter, and more skilled in the approaches, methods, and techniques needed to help older and handicapped children achieve permanency, they have developed an increasingly more thorough understanding of the specific areas of expertise in which other placement professionals feel most inadequate.

Much of the inadequacy exists because most child placement professionals have not maintained contact with children and their families during the full range of years when "growing up" problems or adoption problems have occurred. Unaware of the realities of adoptive family life, lacking the valuable lessons gained by following an adoptive family through the complete cycle of child-rearing, and frequently hampered by their youth and lack of first-hand information on child-rearing, placement workers are often left with a gnawing sense of uncertainty and a driving desire to find someone who can help them acquire the skills in which they believe they are most deficient.

The various skills most often sought by child welfare professionals during Spaulding's training and consultation sessions include:

Working with Children

— working knowledge of physical, mental, and emotional handicaps and their implications
— helping a child understand his past, including the meaning and implications of his separation experiences, and preparing him for his adoption into a specific family

Working with Families

— finding interested families (including how to honestly describe an older or handicapped child in a positive enough fashion to interest prospective parents), establishing a working partnership, helping them to determine their parenting capabilities, and adequately preparing them to adopt a specific child
— helping others understand the meaning and implications of the separation experiences of a child placed in care apart from his family of origin (what happened, why it happened, and how it may change the child's ability to form close relationships in the future)
— helping families sort out, understand, learn from, and survive the special problems and difficulties of living with their adopted child as well as the routine "growing up" and family problems not related to adoption
— familiarization with community resources available to help the family in time of need

— offering services to children and families experiencing disruption

— replacing (into another adoptive family) children who have experienced disruption

Working with the System

— familiarization with the legal aspects of adoption
— locating children in need of adoption, overcoming the obstacles which traditionally hinder the placement of such children, and persuading the referring program staff that these children can and should be placed into adoptive families
— managing a caseload of older and handicapped children and maintaining a clear and up-to-date record of case-related information
— dealing with staff morale problems

SPAULDING'S APPROACH TO TRAINING AND CONSULTATION

The Spaulding staff have found that child welfare professionals frequently have mixed feelings about requesting the training services of another agency. While many professionals wish to improve their skills, they often feel that the need to request outside assistance implies incompetence, especially if they are concerned about protecting a well-established reputation in the field of child placement. As a result, the Spaulding staff have learned they must be sensitive to this problem and take considerable care in teaching others new skills without alienating them or making them feel inferior.

The type of approach used by the Spaulding staff may vary from an extremely informal contact to very formal and highly organized presentations of specific information tailored to a specific program. The format chosen depends, in all cases, upon the needs and wishes of the child placement professionals requesting information or assistance. However, whether formal or informal, the Spaulding staff believe it is essential to simultaneously approach placement workers, supervisors, administrators, and clerical workers. This belief comes not only from the knowledge that shared problem-solving sessions between all levels of program staff lead to the development of the most effective systems of mutual support and encouragement, but from the conviction that all professional levels within a placement program must be given the opportunity to learn together if they expect to create an open, trusting, and effective working relationship.

Placement workers need to be trained because it is their perception of which children are adoptable, which families are appropriate, and which children fit with which families that is at the core of child placement. After sharing knowledge and experience, workers can improve services to children, first, by considering adoption as a viable alternative for those children in care with no prospect of returning home, and second, by achieving more job satisfaction as a result of being better informed and more efficient.

Addressing administrators and supervisors helps them develop or reawaken an active interest in the welfare of children, increases competence, and improves confidence in their abilities. It is particularly vital to gain the cooperation of administrators and supervisors, for without their support, workers do not gain the assistance they need to make and maintain difficult placements.

Spaulding workers believe that effective administration requires constant knowledge of program operation and that administrators, especially those without recent case experience, must be helped to remain constantly aware of the problems faced by their workers and supervisors as well as the methods and techniques used to create and maintain permanent placements. The staff also believe that although it is not essential for administrators to know all the specific techniques used to provide services to children and families, knowledge of the practical application of current methods and techniques can only add to the effectiveness of services provided.

Finally, the Spaulding staff believe it is vital that the clerical staff of any placement program also be included in appropriate training activities. Though they may not be placement workers in the traditional sense, an informed clerical staff can greatly increase the efficiency and effectiveness of placement workers. Secretaries and other supportive staff are often involved with initial telephone or in-person contacts with potential adoptive families and, if well-informed, can detect important attitudes and provide helpful information to families. Since they are also frequently involved in the first contacts with adoptive parents in distress, their initial response may well make the difference between reassuring or alienating families, or even between supporting or disrupting a placement.

After many training and consultation experiences, the Spaulding staff have concluded that the most effective training occurs during shared problem-solving sessions focusing on the needs of older and handicapped children, not as a result of formal presentations or lectures. Such mutual involvement, plus the willingness of Spaulding workers to share their own problems and mistakes and to learn from those they "train," frequently helps minimize the threat, resentment, and distance often felt in a training situation and eventually leads both parties to share similar perceptions of the children, the families, the philosophies, and the practices which make permanent placements a reality.

From this common ground, Spaulding workers move on to the more difficult step of convincing those participating in training or consultation that they are going to have to find their own best solutions to their own unique problems. Replicating the methods and techniques of others does not ensure success, for success depends largely upon the quality of the people being trained, not the quality of the information being shared. To successfully analyze problems and implement potential solutions, child placement professionals must know the child and family, identify the specific problem which is causing difficulty, and understand the events surrounding that problem. They must have initiative, conviction, and confidence. They must be sensitive, objective, and nonjudgmental. Finally, because even the most careful adoption preparation cannot ensure placement success, workers must be willing to take all reasonable risks, even those which make them uncomfortable, to provide a child with his best possible chance for permanency.

Another highly successful method of training used by the Spaulding staff is to provide other child placement professionals from the referring court or agency with the opportunity to share in Spaulding's actual placement experiences. Although this direct method of teaching is feasible only when the number of trainees is small and the costs of such training can be negotiated with the referring program, sharing such immediate experiences in solving problems as they develop can produce invaluable lessons for those in a position to benefit from them.

It is the experience of the Spaulding staff, however, that no matter what phase of the adoption process is focused on during training, limits on available training time and the existence of an infinite number of potential difficulties surrounding a placement do not permit workers to receive more than a small amount of the information they might need to place the next child for whom they seek permanency. Although some experiences can be acquired through direct training, it is the staff's intent that child welfare professionals who benefit from the agency's training and consultation realize that much of the information and many of the skills they seek will have to be obtained through other sources, such as lectures, workshops, informal communication, or reading. To place older and handicapped children, they must learn for themselves where to get the information they need, how to get it, and how to use it once it is obtained.

SPECIFIC EXAMPLES OF TRAINING AND CONSULTATION

At Spaulding, sharing of experiences and information concerning the adoption of older and handicapped children has taken four basic forms. The first involves meeting with other child welfare professionals. Such contact includes:

- direct work with placement workers, supervisors, administrators, and clerical staff within public and private child placing agencies and courts
- formal training or consulting with other professionals at local, state, and national workshops, conferences, and seminars
- serving as members or advisors to local, state, and national adoption and foster care organizations, committees, and groups.

A second form of sharing experiences and information has been the development, preparation, and distribution of written training and educational materials. This has included the creation of two handbooks (one describing Spaulding in general and one focused entirely on adoption disruption), the creation and distribution of quarterly newsletters, and the distribution, upon request, of reprints of significant articles concerning purchase of service, adoption subsidy, and information on parenting children with specific mental or physical handicaps.

The third means of sharing experiences and information has been community education. This includes formal speaking engagements for service clubs or community groups as well as informal discussions of adoption and Spaulding's approach to adoption whenever and wherever possible, especially when media coverage is available (in the form of newspapers, magazines, books, television, or radio). The staff have also worked conscientiously with all prospective adoptive parents to let them know more about the children currently available for permanent placement, which obstacles hinder placements, and which procedures are generally being used by placement programs to overcome these obstacles.

A fourth means has been various special projects undertaken by the Spaulding staff. These include such efforts as the Grand Rapids Project, a two year project carried out in 1972-73 under the auspices of Spaulding for Children at the request of a Kent County Juvenile Court judge and funded by the Keeler Foundation and the Grand Rapids Foundation. The initial purpose of the project was to fulfill the Court's request for current information on the placement status of all children who had come within its jurisdiction. Many of these children, having experienced termination of parental rights and moved on to the supervision of various community agencies, remained in a variety of temporary care situations for several years. The Court wished to determine the appropriateness of the plans for permancence which had been made following the termination of parental rights, particularly in those cases where the children were older, handicapped, or of minority race. During the project's first year, a part-time Spaulding worker was attached to the Kent County Juvenile Court in Grand Rapids, Michigan, to help identify such children through a statistical review of all dependent and neglect cases within the Juvenile Court's jurisdiction between 1955 and 1972. In addition to gaining this information, the project worker also carried out a tactful, but aggressive campaign to convince area child welfare agencies to make greater efforts toward adoption for all legally available children.

The second year of the project consisted of a far more systematic review of each case in question to identify, more closely monitor, and where necessary create a long-range placement plan for each child. During the project's second year, the Court convinced the Kent County Board of Commissioners to establish a permanent position in the Court to continue the process of reviewing and monitoring long-range plans for both temporary and permanent wards. In July 1974, the project, by then fully identified as a project of the Kent County Juvenile Court, received the award of the National Council of Juvenille Court Judges for the outstanding educational program in a state.

The Grand Rapids Project was successful in combining the efforts of the Court and the Spaulding staff to identify a community problem: the existence and stagnation of hard-to-place children who were legally available for adoption but who had never achieved a permanent placement. The project succeeded because the judge and court staff who were involved were concerned enough about children to work toward improving services to them. They accomplished this by establishing an ongoing court responsibility in that Michigan community to monitor the activities of the child placing agencies, public and private, once they had custody of the children and the responsibility for providing a permanent placement.

As a result of these efforts, many people who thought that certain kinds of children should never be adopted began to see adoption as a positive and appropriate alternative for many older, handicapped, and minority race children. In addition, taxpayers in the effected county were delighted with the financial savings adoptive placement offered when compared with the costs of foster and institutional care.

Spaulding also received a grant in 1970 from a local service club to survey the literature on children with Down's Syndrome, contact parents and child welfare professionals who had cared for or worked with Down's Syndrome children, and evaluate the possibility of finding adoptive families for some of these children. As a result of this grant, the Spaulding staff were able to successfully place several Down's Syndrome children and prove to other placement professionals that adoption was an appropriate placement alternative for many children with this handicap.

Another special project, known as the Permanent Planning Project, began as a request for training and consultation from the Michigan Department of Social Services in 1972. The project's primary purpose was to provide a systematic review of children who were wards of the state, legally available for adoption, but not moving into adoptive families. Spaulding workers examined each of the nearly 600 cases to obtain a profile of the characteristics of every identified child to determine what was preventing them from being adopted. After identifying these problem areas, recommendations were made regarding ways in which better permanent planning could be developed and implemented.

This project's second phase, which began in June 1973, consisted of an agreement by the Spaulding staff to offer regional training sessions for Michigan Department of Social Services (MDSS) workers. These sessions were geared specifically toward the problems identified within each worker's region, but focused primarily upon methods of working with older and handicapped children in need of adoption and with families who wanted to adopt them. Periodic reviews of revised placement plans were also undertaken. Manpower for this project was provided by Spaulding staff and staff members of the MDSS on loan to Spaulding to be trained in the agency's approach to adoption.

The Spaulding staff provided this technical assistance because the Michigan Department of Social Services felt that the factors of "start up time," geographic distance, and extensive travel could most satisfactorily be met by a staff who had already proven their ability to work cooperatively with MDSS staff on the evaluation and placement of older and handicapped children and who were accustomed to traveling to distant counties on a regular basis. By placing responsibility for the project with the Spaulding staff, the MDSS felt they could eliminate a lengthy orientation on the special problems inherent in placing older and handicapped state wards and capitalize on the cooperative history between Spaulding workers and MDSS. The project not only offered the Spaulding staff a valuable opportunity to share information, but allowed them to expand their area of influence by making new contacts with many placement workers and helping them to place children traditionally considered hard-to-place or "unadoptable."

There have been many other training and consultation opportunities for Spaulding workers, mostly in the United States and Canada. In these instances, which have involved both child welfare professionals and parents' groups, the staff have most often explained Spaulding's efforts to achieve the successful placement of older and handicapped children or described specific aspects of the agency's adoption process, such as recruitment, preparation, maintenance, adoption disruption, and suggestions for successfully parenting older and handicapped children. By 1973, these requests were international in scope and reached as far as Great Britain and eventually to Australia. Since 1974, the Spaulding staff have also been working with the Edna McConnell Clark Foundation, headquartered in New York City, to develop a national network of adoption agencies (called "Family Builders") specializing in the placement of older and handicapped children. (For more information, see the chapter entitled, "The National Strategy: The Clark Project," p. 299.)

Finally, the Spaulding staff have worked to change the attitudes and practices of adoption professionals in Michigan and other states through membership on a variety of local, state, and national committees. These activities have included representation on the Advisory Board of the North American Center on Adoption, the Membership Committee of the "Family Builders" Network, the Placement Services Advisory Committee of the Michigan Department of Social Services, the Adoption Committee of the Michigan Association of Children's Agencies, and the Quint Agency Adoption Committee of Washtenaw County. Spaulding staff have also served on Michigan's Task Force on Unplaced Children and on various *ad hoc* sub committees developed in Michigan to initiate or improve services to children and to consider legislation affecting children.

THE RESULTS OF TRAINING AND CONSULTATION

Some children still became legally available for adoption in Michigan through "release," wherein parents voluntarily give up their parental rights and make the child someone else's responsibility. Yet an overwhelming majority of children, as high as 95% of those needing adoption, became available through neglect adjudication and the eventual termination of parental rights by a Juvenile Court judge who has determined that the family has neglected or abused the child. However, Spaulding's success in placing children traditionally considered hard-to-place or "unadoptable" and in simultaneously providing training and consultation to other agencies and courts has produced a significant increase in the number of placement programs interested in and capable of placing many of these children.

The Spaulding staff have, in fact, succeeded in making it unprofessional to talk about "unadoptable" children. What this has meant to children who are or who should be available for adoption is an ever-increasing chance of being adopted by a family willing and able to care for them. What this has meant to Spaulding is a gradual increase in the range of children available for adoption and, thus, an increase in the severity of handicaps among the children referred to the agency for placement.

In addition to their own success, the success of other placement programs and projects has led to changes in the kinds of children referred to Spaulding for placement. In January 1969, the United Community Services of Detroit approved a proposal to establish a program to find adoptive families for children of Black and racially mixed heritage. The creation of Homes for Black Children, in Detroit in May 1969, and their subsequent placement success (which has so far accounted for more than 600 placements) has clearly accelerated the movement away from the placement of healthy, young, black children at Spaulding. With a specialized agency of this type in the area, Spaulding staff felt that a child of minority race, with no physical, mental, or emotional handicaps, could no longer be considered hard-to-place in Michigan.

Another major change in the kinds of children referred to Spaulding occurred as a result of Project '72 of the Michigan Department of Social Services. The intent of this project (previously Michigan's "Homefinder" project and then "The 100 Most Wanted Families"), was for twelve experienced state workers, in eight counties, to use specialized recruitment techniques such as radio, television, newspapers, church bulletins, billboards, and public speaking engagements to place in adoptive families the 100 least requested "special needs" children then listed on the Michigan Adoption Resource Exchange.

Despite the fact that the Project's staff immediately focused on the most difficult children available to them and did not accurately estimate the extent of post-placement service requirements or the emotional impact of the task at hand, the Spaulding staff agreed that Project '72 should have the initial opportunity to place the children who were the responsibility of the Michigan Department of Social Services. Therefore, the Spaulding staff uniformly backed away from negotiating the referral of any Michigan child if the referral was appropriate to Project '72 and accepted for referral from the MDSS only those children whose placement had already been attempted by Project staff. As a result, many of the referrals to Spaulding from within Michigan involved children who were significantly harder to place than most of the children for whom the staff had previously found adoptive families.

During this same period, the agency's expanding schedule of training and consultation contacts produced an increasing number of appropriate out-of-state referrals. This has left the Spaulding staff with a dilemma which is not yet entirely resolved. That is, should they seek to place only the most severely handicapped children in Michigan (since other agencies in the state are now placing many moderately to severely handicapped children), or should they concentrate their efforts on helping child placement professionals in less progressive geographic areas learn to place children who may be much less severely handicapped than Spaulding's Michigan referrals? Their solution to date has been to combine these goals, accepting referrals on both groups of children. This dual response has so far been a most productive course of action, for the rising and falling fortunes of Project '72 and other Michigan-based adoption efforts have created a periodic need for the Spaulding staff to shift their focus from one group of children to the other.

Despite the uneven quality of placement effort throughout the state, however, the overall result of these labors has been positive. Significantly more older, handicapped, and minority race children are placed with adoptive families now than were placed a few years ago. As more placements have been made, Spaulding has found itself in the position of being a "back-up" agency to other programs within the field. Happily, this is the precise role the staff seek: conscientiously avoiding any competition with other child-placing professionals willing to find permanent families for children who are or who should be available for adoption, but offering assistance whenever those families cannot be found.

Differences in administrative, placement, and community education skills and capabilities among other agencies and courts have meant that the Spaulding staff receive requests to place children who represent wide variations in the degrees of difficulty their placement will require. To maintain their primary purpose of finding permanent families for only those children considered most difficult to place, the Spaulding staff do not accept the referrals of many of the children referred to them. In those instances when a program seeks to refer a child who Spaulding workers consider comparatively easy to place, the staff see themselves providing the most beneficial of possible services by helping those programs place those children themselves.

However, the need to make such decisions has sometimes created instances where the wrong decision has been made. That is, some of the children the Spaulding staff have not accepted for referral have later turned out to be appropriate referrals for the agency. In some cases, information about the child which the staff had determined to be accurate turned out to be inaccurate. In other cases, the family recruited by the prospective referral program has not been prepared well enough to successfully parent the child or the child's situation has turned out to be more complex than the Spaulding staff had initially believed.

For any of these reasons, the child may not be placed by the program who had tried to refer him to Spaulding. Under these circumstances, the child may be referred a second time. Such re-referrals signal to the Spaulding staff that they missed or misread crucial information regarding either the child or the referring program. Their second appraisal, therefore, is always carefully carried out with the knowledge that important information must exist which has not yet been discovered and that Spaulding may be the child's last opportunity to achieve a permanent placement.

One of the major reasons a child may not be placed by a prospective referral program is that he may simply not be considered appealing by the workers assigned to find him a family. This can also happen at Spaulding. The agency staff try to counter this possibility by looking for and highlighting the positive characteristics of all children referred to them. Failing this, they use their team approach to alert themselves to evidence of a low level of worker commitment to the child. The implementation of such countermeasures requires continuous and substantive effort, for there is always the chance that pronounced negative characteristics may draw attention away from a child's less immediately apparent positive attributes.

With more and more experience in placing older and handicapped children, the staff have discovered that talking with a child, his teachers, and his foster parents or caretakers as part of the evaluation will reveal ways in which the child is appealing in behavior or appearance. Because they are able to discover positive information about the children they seek to place, Spaulding workers can then offer a more realistically balanced view of that child and are in a better position to recruit families and prepare prospective parents to adopt the specific child. In those cases where workers cannot present a child in a positive manner because they find little appealing in the child, the placement team usually assigns the child to another worker better able to respond constructively to him in order to provide him with a greater opportunity for adoption.

Although the training and consultation efforts of the Spaulding staff have significantly changed the philosophy and practice of placing older and handicapped children, the job is never done. First of all, it is impossible for the agency's workers to expend as much time and effort providing training and consultation as is needed and also maintain vital placement skills by actually placing children in need of adoption and providing necessary post-placement services. Second, it is much more difficult to raise money to provide training and consultation to other placement programs than it is to find funds to place specific children. In addition, it is difficult to maintain the higher levels of responsiveness and enthusiasm created during a training or consultation session when such efforts involve "one-shot" appearances instead of a series of follow-up contacts. Furthermore, the rapid turnover of workers in most placement programs means that there is always a flood of inexperienced workers who need information on the specialized job they face in placing hard-to-place children.

Another problem associated with training and consultation is that all too frequently there has been attributed to Spaulding and its staff a magical power — a power to do what is far beyond human means. Workers, supervisors, and administrators from other agencies and courts often expect the agency's staff to be able to provide a painless solution to every difficult problem or to successfully place, without delay, every child referred to them.

In spite of these difficulties, the Spaulding staff have discovered that training and consultation produces significant personal rewards. Their realization that they are functioning as an integral part of a successful and innovative program is tremendously gratifying. In particular, they are able to gain substantial satisfaction and a deep sense of accomplishment in knowing that a single agency can, with concerted individual and team effort, make a difference. The ultimate satisfaction, however, is achieved in knowing that their efforts have helped to stimulate placement professionals in other agencies and courts to find permanent families for children traditionally considered hard-to-place or "unadoptable."

SUMMARY

The attitudes and skills required to place older, handicapped, and minority race children are far different from those required to place healthy young children. As a result, it is the belief of the Spaulding staff that training placement workers, supervisors, administrators, and clerical staff is necessary if children traditionally considered hard-to-place or "unadoptable" are to be placed with appropriate adoptive families.

Not only do informed professionals increase the probability that more available children will find permanent families, but administrators, supervisors, and workers who have thought through the issues central to the problem of placing older and handicapped children for adoption and who are confident of their skills will feel more secure in their efforts to meet the needs of children and families, gain insight into the obstacles which prevent placement, and develop practical approaches for over-coming those obstacles. Training helps child placement professionals develop a commitment to the welfare of each older and handicapped child prior to placement, and to the welfare of the adoptive family as a unit after placement. It also helps them prepare for the disruptions they will inevitably encounter as well as develop a willingness to take reasonable risks in making the placement decisions.

At Spaulding, "training" is the process of describing the specific methods and techniques of the agency's approach to adoption and the attitudes which underlie those methods and techniques. It is the practical application of theory and philosophy. "Consultation," on the other hand, is the process of more broadly focusing on the general planning and organizational aspects of actual adoption practice. Training and consultation are usually made available at workshops, conferences, or seminars in the form of discussions or simulations of the case-related problems which the Spaulding staff have experienced. However, training and consultation have also taken the form of working closely with the administrators, supervisors, and/or placement workers from a referring agency or court to demonstrate the actual placement of a specific child.

The type of approach used by the Spaulding staff may vary from an extremely informal contact to very formal and highly organized presentations of specific information tailored to a specific program. The format chosen depends, in all cases, upon the needs and wishes of the child placement professionals (or parents) requesting information or assistance.

It is the experience of the Spaulding staff, however, that limits on available training time and the existence of an infinite number of potential difficulties surrounding a placement do not permit workers to receive more than a small amount of the information they might need to place the next child for whom they seek permanency. Not only must many of the skills which are sought be obtained through other means, but placement professionals must learn for themselves where to get the information they need, how to get it, and how to use it once it is obtained.

The Spaulding staff have also shared experiences and information through the development, preparation, and distribution of written training and educational materials, through formal speaking engagements for service clubs or community groups, and through informal discussions of the agency's approach to adoption held whenever and wherever possible. In addition, members of the Spaulding staff have served as members or advisors to local, state, and national adoption and foster care organizations, committees, and groups.

Finally, Spaulding workers have been involved in numerous special projects. These have included the Grand Rapids Project, a request by the Juvenile Court in that Michigan city for help in determining the appropriateness of the permanent plans which had been made for all of the children who had come within its jurisdiction; the Permanent Planning Project, a request from the Michigan Department of Social Services for help in conducting a systematic review of children who were wards of the state, legally available for adoption, but not moving into adoptive families; and a project designed to place several Down's Syndrome children in order to prove that adoption is an appropriate placement alternative for many children with this handicap.

The results of Spaulding's demonstrations of adoptability and of the staff's training and consultation efforts have been gratifying. Significantly more older, handicapped, and minority race children are placed with adoptive families now than were placed a few years ago. As more placements have been made, Spaulding has found itself in the position of being a "back-up" agency to other programs within the field. Happily, this is the precise role the staff seek: conscientiously avoiding any competition with other child-placing professionals willing to find permanent families for children who are or who should be available for adoption, but offering assistance whenever those families cannot be found.

18

Working With Judges and Court Staff

THE ROLE OF THE COURT

The court's role in the child welfare system is vital, for only the court has the legal power to sever parent's rights and make a child legally available for adoption. The court may not only hold or share custodial responsibility for the child within its jurisdiction, but also make the ultimate decision which allows a child to be adopted by a specific family.

In Michigan, juvenile courts rely upon adoption programs to find and prepare potential adoptive parents and to secure the documents necessary to make a legal adoption possible. They also depend upon adoption programs to supervise new placements and to make periodic reports and recommendations prior to confirmation of the new parent-child relationship. It is the contention of the Spaulding staff that the successful adoptive placement of older and handicapped children requires workers who aggressively work with judges and court staff on behalf of children to overcome legal hurdles to permanent placement.

The Need for Attorneys

The Spaulding staff are convinced that the best interests of the child will be insured if courts continually exercise the option of assigning an attorney to the child. It is their belief that the presence of a knowledgeable attorney acting as an advocate for the child brings added balance and a vital perspective to the legal complexities of the placement.

Parents and social workers involved in a potential adoption typically develop a deep emotional interest in the child because of the nature of their relationships with him. In the excitement of the adoption, therefore, each may have difficulty concentrating on the specific courtroom procedures which are affecting the child's future. Under these circumstances, an attorney, in possession of what is ideally an objective frame of reference, can help clarify legal terminology and effectively communicate legal information to judges.

An attorney can also function as a safeguard to help insure that all important matters which pertain to the child have been objectively examined and resolved (such as the appropriateness of specific strategies for the child's immediate care or the viability of potential long range plans.) As an impartial observer, an attorney can be particularly helpful as a mediator in those instances where parents, social workers, or judges champion different alternatives for the child.

In addition, parents and even some placement professionals are frequently unaccustomed to working within the legal system. As a result, problems may arise when courts make requests of workers or recommendations to parents which are not followed. In many cases, the problem exists because these individuals do not know how to implement what is being asked of them. When this occurs, an attorney can assist parents in following court recommendations which would, for example, enable them to retain custody of their child. He can help workers by clarifying information or procedures.

An attorney can also help formulate the questions which need to be answered by the parents and the agency before the rights of the parents are affirmed or terminated: "What is being done to reestablish the child within his previous family?" . . . "What is the agency (or institution) doing to help the family?" . . . "Are the agency's expectations of the family realistic?"

Once such questions have been formulated and responded to by the parents, workers, and judges involved in the adoption, the court has fulfilled its legal responsibilities. If parents' rights are to be terminated, the court knows this action is being taken on solid legal grounds.

Finally, an attorney aggressively representing the child's best interests can also benefit the judge and the court. The actions of an effective attorney will help remind courts and judges that it is not just the responsibility of the family and agency to constructively reach out to help the child so that he does not become "caught in" or "lost within" the system. Sometimes, too, judges are not able to become familiar enough with the details of a case to know that certain areas or questions should be pursued more vigorously than others. Occasionally, judges may also focus too closely on judicial technique or procedure and lose sight of the case's essential ingredients or the child's special needs.

In nearly all instances, an effective attorney can assist children, families, and social workers, as well as courts, in his role as an advocate for the child. With his more objective perspective and his legal training, an aggressive attorney can almost always help families, workers, and judges provide a child with his greatest opportunity to receive the decisions and services which will enable him to achieve his most approriate available placement.

The Need for Periodic Reviews

Courts alone are able to provide an objective due process forum where any conflicting interests can be aired and legally resolved. As a result, courts are in the most ideal position to assume the increasingly important (and necessary) task of periodically reviewing the legal status of children within their jurisdiction.

Although most courts are usually to be commended for the way in which they use the law to bring children within their jurisdiction into care, many of these children are left to needlessly drift within the foster or institutional care system without meaningful planning and review. A large number of such children should and can become legally available for adoption. However, many are not placed with permanent families because the courts either have no adoption service of their own, do not see it as their responsibility to ensure that plans for permanent placement are developed or facilitated, or do not work effectively with public or voluntary adoption programs which might offer such plans. Unfortunately, many courts also do not have accurate knowledge of the needs, or even the numbers, of children within their jurisdiction.

The problem of children becoming "lost" within the child care system would be considerably lessened if mandatory, periodic, and objective reviews of the status of all children in foster care homes, group homes, and institutions was assured. Mandatory reviews of all children in care would do a great deal to help each child receive adequate planning for a permanent future. Such reviews would not only give courts and judges better understanding of these children, but would help the public become more aware of children in need of adoption. This knowledge would enable the public to assist both the legal system and the child care system in achieving the most appropriate placements possible.

As of this writing, only temporary wards of the court are required to be reviewed by judges in Michigan. In addition, only one Michigan court, the Kent County Juvenile Court, in Grand Rapids, has been positively identified as having instituted a comprehensive review system of the

type under discussion. (This review process, the refinement and extension of an earlier Spaulding project in Kent County, is described more
fully in the section entitled, "Training and Consultation," p. 265.)

It is clear that a law requiring mandatory review would be needed
before children in care would benefit on a large scale. However, even
though laws existed which would demand that a child's status be reviewed, it could not be assumed that the recommendations which result
from individual reviews would be implemented. Some courts and judges
are not aware of the crucial need to follow up their recommendations to
assure implementation. Others believe they have done their job by
making the child a ward of the court and assume that appropriate plans to
resolve the child's future will be vigorously persued simply because the
court has taken jurisdiction. As a result, many of these courts regard the
remaining responsibility for the care and future of the child as belonging
exclusively to agency placement workers.

The intention of legislated court review goes beyond the creation of a
review process to include the quality and implementation of that process. Such an achievement is possible only when a court staff is sensitive
to the needs of children who are or who should be available for adoption
and is acting assertively and knowledgeably on the child's behalf. A
court staff cannot relax their vigilance just because a review statute exists
or because requested agency documents have been received and filed.
They must have proof that an appropriate plan has been initiated.

THE ROLE OF THE AGENCY

In working with courts and judges, it is critical for adoption workers to
do their legal, political, and psychological homework before they
approach the court. In most instances, competent preparation of the case
being filed and straightforward descriptions of the child, the prospective
family, and the reasons for this specific choice of child-parent combination will result in a prompt and positive action by the court. Occasionally, however, and particularly in instances where the proposed placement involves children formerly considered hard-to-place or "unadoptable," a court will be opposed to the plan. This situation is often further
complicated by the sheer complexity of the law and the intricacy of the
procedures accompanying it.

Adoption workers in contact with various county courts find little
consistency in required procedures from one court to another among
Michigan's 83 counties. Nevertheless, workers in those states in which
such variety still exists must possess a comfortable working knowledge

of the variable procedures and requirements of the system within which they work. The mastering of such extensive knowledge is difficult, time-consuming, and challenging, yet workers must be aware of these differences if they are to avoid potentially harmful delays and make appropriate decisions.

Workers who are naive about adoption law and its variable interpretations are at a distinct disadvantage when working with judges and court staff. Uninformed workers will not know whether the procedures a court is using meet legal requirements, and since they do not understand that other alternatives or interpretations exist and are practiced in experienced and effective courts, they frequently will have no choice but to accept the opinion of the first voice of authority they encounter.

For example, a court staff may rigidly apply antiquated, inappropriate, or even illegal procedures to the adoption process, thus preventing or delaying the permanent placements of some children with some families. Without the ability to differentiate between statutory requirement and interpretation, placement workers lose much of their effectiveness because they cannot use the complex legal system to help individual children. They cannot make the most appropriate choices and seek the best solutions for each child.

It is unfortunate that so many professionals responsible for the welfare of children believe the legal system is inflexible. They are quick to point out that "the law says . . . ", "that judge has never . . . ", "this court doesn't . . . " and assume that knowledge of these apparent obstacles exempts them from further efforts to meet their responsibility. The key to the ability to aggressively defend an appropriate placement decision is the realizaton that adoption law is a complex mixture of broadly defined procedures, poorly detailed intentions, and all too often uninformed interpretations. Although it is true that some parts of the adoption law are more flexible than others, even those portions which could have been legitimately interpreted to more greatly benefit children have often been ignored by adoption workers. This has occurred either because workers lack the initiative, the interest, or the tenacity to prepare well and then fight for what they believe in, or they have not developed the competence to challenge the attitudes and philosophies underlying inappropriate legal practices and interpretations. Similarly, they do not realize that their personal efforts, supported by logic, knowledge of the law, and placement practice alternatives, could produce desirable changes in a judge's attitude and specific action beneficial to children.

Spaulding workers have realized the necessity for learning how to work within this complex judicial system. A particularly effective Spaulding technique for minimizing conflict and error has been to establish a relationship with one person within each court who they have found to be particularly knowledgeable and competent. Since the children the staff place have traditionally been considered hard-to-place or "unadoptable," it has been important to indentify a court staff member who understands the problems of such placements and has developed confidence in the knowledge, commitment, and integrity of the Spaulding worker.

As each case is prepared, a Spaulding placement worker makes contact with a court staff member to validate legal procedures specific to that court. In some cases, these contact people have been judges themselves. Such contact has frequently allowed the agency's workers to influence the court to accept adoptive placement for children whom they formerly considered "unadoptable." Occasionally, this has made it possible for the agency to help a court establish a new precedent for later cases and provide a base of positive experiences upon which to build substantial constructive change in juvenile court interest and practice.

WORKING WITH JUDGES

The Spaulding staff have also had to learn to overcome the sense of trepidation and awe which many workers feel when they work with judges. Workers who have not yet learned they can appropriately and positively influence judges' decisions can often do no more than bemoan a particular judicial policy or the attitude of a given judge. Spaulding workers feel they are best able to benefit children in need of adoption by being aggressive, forceful, and knowledgeable enough to diplomatically offer the most appropriate placement plan available and reinforce their choice with a good grasp of the law. They frequently persuade judges to concur with their recommendations because they take the trouble to prepare sensible arguments to support their position. Good adoption advocacy is rare, and many courts have never been approached by placement workers who are armed with a sophisticated knowledge of the legal alternatives to the child's current placement plan.

The agency's placement staff have learned that the decision judges make are based upon a complex combination of factors. One of the most significant of these is the judge's perception of his political situation. Because Michigan juvenile court judges are elected, there may be some who are reluctant to make decisions which they feel might be contrary to community opinion and which might weaken their political support. Judges are more apt to risk changing tradition if they know they can count on strong support from influential citizens or community groups. They are less likely to misread community opinion or assume opposition if they are aware of the best current thinking regarding adoption philosophy and practice. For this reason, adoption workers are wise to use every opportunity to discuss adoption issues and problems with community groups and judges. Groups of voters or taxpayers, including active and well-informed foster and adoptive parent organizations, make excellent allies for placement workers and progressive judges.

Frequently, the well-being of children is a strong enough argument for extending the placement policies of the court. When this is not the case, workers who are backed by groups of voters and taxpayers may be able to convince conservative county commissioners and judges of the considerable financial savings of adoption. They can readily point out, with the aid of references to the higher costs of other forms of child care, that it is simply bad business practice not to place children into adoptive families. Few politicians can afford to be fiscally irresponsible when human savings and tax savings coincide.

Adoption workers should also familiarize themselves with the legal precedents for any controversial positions they may take. Some judges are not hesitant to be local trail-blazers as long as they are convinced there is enough precedent to back up their decision. Consequently, it is helpful for workers to be able to refer to at least one other judge (hopefully, one the judge in question knows and respects) who has previously made a decision similar to the one they desire. Some judges simply need to be reassured they are not the first to take such a position. Other judges prefer to know that they have been farsighted in accomplishing something worthwhile in a specific case, that they have had a positive impact on the life of a child, or that they are in accord with national standards or positions of child welfare or legal organizations.

Another important factor influencing judicial decisions is that many judges are seriously overworked and consider adoption cases to be only a small part of their work responsibilities. As a result, there is usually not enough preparation time available for them to acquire expertise in the psychological implications of their decisions. However, most judges are responsive to the viewpoint of competent placement workers who can present information in ways relevant to the legal system. Most also welcome the opportunity to make use of knowledge acquired or reinforced while workers are presenting a case. For this reason, placement workers should always be ready to take full advantage of the opportunities they have to discuss adoption issues and implications with judges.

Although it may be difficult to reach judges when their schedules are extremely full, there are other avenues such as meetings and conferences for talking with them about specific issues. Broadening the horizons of judges may also be accomplished through a general, rather than a specific, approach. Most judges are eager to attend meetings as speakers and many will agree to lunch with parents' groups or professionals or meet to talk with agency staff about the implications of philosophical differences or general problems in the field of child placement.

Judges may even be amenable to discussing case-related problems. However, they will usually decline to discuss individual cases, partly because of the legal and ethical implications of sharing case-specific information, and partly because such discussions put them at a tremendous disadvantage because they often have not had time to obtain all facts or understand the complexities of the case. Nevertheless, discussions with judges may well help staff significantly improve themselves as court witnesses and assist them in making better legal presentations.

In addition to their political situation and the size of their workload, a third factor in judicial decision-making is the personal attitudes of judges concerning adoption. Placement workers must realize that there is a most effective way to present the facts and implications of available placement alternatives for every case. They should determine which information to emphasize with each judge and become sensitive to the best time to pursue an issue as well as when to wait for a more opportune moment. It is also helpful to know if a specific judge is generally comfortable with more traditional or more innovative positions, and whether he is primarily interested in benefiting individual children or in minimizing child care costs and saving tax dollars. With some judges, the overall financial benefits of a proposed adoption should be emphasized. With others, the emotional benefits to a child in a permanent placement are perceived as being most important.

Although most judges in Michigan are on the bench because they have special talents or interests, and all have been exposed to family problems in seminars, publications, and judge's training, Spaulding workers have learned that judges, like almost everyone else, can benefit from information concerning the current realities of adoption and the needs of children who are older and handicapped. Many judges still believe the hallmarks of a good and deserving family are or should be an adequate income, church membership, and regular habits of a temperate nature. Judges may need to learn more about the problems of parenting a child not born to a family, or the difficulties of learning to adjust to a child with a chaotic history, a child old enough to remember his past, or a child who is physically or mentally handicapped.

Spaulding's most effective technique for working with judges has been attempting to persuade them to consider a decision "which may not be a traditional one, but is one which will benefit children." If this approach does not resolve the problem, they then devise alternative strategies through brain-storming sessions with other members of their placement team (more fully described in "Teamwork and Collegial Supervision," p. 41). Devising alternative strategies with which to again approach the judge is an important part of placing older and handicapped children. If workers are to obtain the legal opportunities to successfully place children with available families they believe can best meet those children's needs, additional efforts to persuade unconvinced judges are often required.

If workers are unable to personally convince judges of the propriety of a proposed placement, they may be able to obtain helpful assistance from other local sources. No matter where assistance is sought or what approach is used, the purpose is consistent. It is to find a practical solution to the difficulties inherent in the placement situation and to persist in looking for the means to make the solution acceptable to the court. Workers may ask the advice of community volunteers or elicit a supportive statement from the state office of the Department of Social Services or its equivalent. They may enlist the aid of a supportive judge or make use of press clippings which offer examples of successful cases or other judges' successful decisions. They may draw attention to the newest national standards or resolutions which demonstrate acceptance of positions which support the judge in constructively resolving the issue. They may also impress upon the judge the unpleasant consequences of gaining community notoriety or losing public esteem when good practice is not followed.

If the judge is still not convinced that the worker is acting in the best interest of the child, it may be possible for the worker to present the case to another judge. Under Michigan law, a legal adoption action can be filed in either the county where the prospective family resides or in the county where the child is in care. Thus, for a Michigan child, the alternative course of action consists of filing the adoption petition in another county. However, for a child from another state who is being adopted by a Michigan family, there is no alternative: the worker must work through the difficulties in the county court where the prospective adoptive family resides. Rules concerning the geographic location in which the case may be filed vary with each state according to statute and court rule.

If all else fails (that is, when workers who have done their homework are convinced that the legal and factual justification for the placement they have chosen has been presented adequately, and the legal decision is still contrary to what they consider to be the best placement for the child), the worker is obligated to move to the next step in the legal process and pursue an appeal.

Such action might create an enemy, however, and could be disadvantageous to an agency who must work with a specific judge again and again. At this point, an attorney for the child can greatly strengthen the agency's position that a wrong decision has been made by the court. As with all other aspects of adoption, the decision to appeal is a calculated risk based upon all available information and experience, and the stakes are high. Yet, whether or not the judge's decision is reversed, great gains may be made. His philosophy may change, or he may begin to see how children are endangered by unsympathetic legal decisions. Of equal importance is the possibility that he may also begin to realize that certain agencies or adoption professionals are willing to fight for what they believe in and, as a result, gain new respect for such persistence, competence, and dedication.

SUMMARY

In working with courts and judges, it is critical for adoption workers to do their legal, political, and psychological homework before approaching the court. In most instances, competent preparation of the case being filed and straightforward descriptions of the child, the prospective family, and the reasons for this specific choice of child-parent combination will result in a prompt and positive action by the court. However, when this does not occur, workers who have a thorough knowledge of the variable procedures and requirements of the system in which they work, who are not naive about adoption law, and who can take advantage of the flexibility of that law will be more effective in using the complex legal system to benefit individual children.

Placement professionals who have not yet learned they can appropriately and positively influence judges' decisions can often do no more than bemoan a particular judicial policy or the attitude of a given judge. The Spaulding staff feel they are best able to benefit children in need of adoption by being aggressive, forceful, and knowledgeable enough to diplomatically offer the most appropriate placement plan available and reinforce their choice with a good grasp of the law.

The agency's placement staff have learned that the decisions judges make are based upon a complex combination of factors. These include the judge's perception of his political situation, the usually enormous number of cases over which he must preside, and his personal attitudes concerning adoption. Spaulding's most effective technique for working with judges has been attempting to persuade them to consider a decision "which may not be a traditional one, but is one which will benefit children." If this approach does not resolve the problem, they then devise alternative strategies through brain-storming sessions with other members of their placement team. Devising alternative strategies with which to again approach the judge is an important part of placing older and handicapped children with appropriate adoptive families.

If workers are unable to personally convince judges of the propriety of a proposed placement, they may be able to obtain helpful assistance from community volunteers and parents' groups, elicit the aid of a supportive judge or the state office of the Department of Social Services or its equivalent, or draw attention to the most current national standards or resolutions which demonstrate acceptance of positions which support the judge in constructively resolving the issue. They may also impress upon the judge the unpleasant consequences of gaining community notoriety or losing public esteem when good practice is not followed, present the case to another judge, or pursue an appeal.

The appointment of an attorney for the child may also offer children a greater opportunity to receive the decisions and services best able to help them achieve their most appropriate available placement. In the excitement of the courtroom, attorneys are often more effective than parents or workers in asking the most pertinent legal questions or focusing on the most essential details regarding the best interest of the child, the family, and the requirements of the legal system.

Although the probability of a child in need of adoption finding an appropriate placement is increased significantly by the presence of a knowledgeable worker and the assignment of an attorney, the problem of children becoming "lost" within the child care system would be even further reduced if mandatory, periodic, and objective reviews of the status of all children in fosfer care homes, group homes, and institutions was assured. Such reviews would not only give courts and judges better understanding of these children, but would help the public become more aware of children in need of adoption. This knowledge would enable the public to assist both the legal system and the child care system in achieving the most appropriate placements possible.

19

Working With Physicians and Other Health Professionals

It is important for agency and court workers placing older and handicapped children for adoption to realize that family physicians, pediatricians, nurses, and other health professionals frequently have extensive influence over a family's decision to adopt. Many potential adoptive parents consult the opinion of a respected health professional for assurance that their decision to adopt a specific child, particularly a child with a handicap, is a good one.

In many cases, the advice of these individuals can prove very useful. Those health professionals who know the family well are in a good position to counsel parents on their ability to understand and successfully cope with the child's medical problems. They may also be effective in preparing the family for the difficulties they must face in living with a child with a handicap and in providing parents with considerable emotional support in their follow-up care of the child after adoption. In addition, medical consultants are able to provide both adoptive parents and placement workers with essential information concerning diagnosis, prognosis, future hospitalization possibilities, the availability of specialized services and devices, and the extent of potential family involvement in treatment and therapy.

Although the adoption advice dispensed by health professionals is based upon their appraisal of both the parents' care-taking abilities and the physical and mental characteristics of the child, it is also a reflection of their personal attitudes toward adoption in general. If they are supportive of the adoption, they may be able to prevent considerable parental and child distress by providing the family with the encouragement and support they need, both before and after the child is placed. If they do not believe the adoption should occur, they frequently have sound reasons for their decision.

In some cases, however, it has been the personal opinion of professionals, specifically physicians, which has been responsible for a family not adopting a child. Parents may be advised to avoid some children, usually those who are older or handicapped and who are believed to be either too difficult to parent or too costly to care for. These suggestions may be based upon their experiences with families who have had problems with similar biological or adopted children, and they may wish to protect their patients or friends from personal hardship.

It is imperative that placement workers do everything they can to convince physicians and other health professionals that children traditionally considered hard-to-place or "unadoptable" can be successfully adopted. Physicians, in particular, have tended to spend their careers as advocates for adults rather than children, and must often be helped to be more aware of the needs of the many older and handicapped children who are available for adoption. In addition, many health professionals fail to realize the degree of risk some adoptive parents are willing to voluntarily assume. They may not realize that it is one thing to be forced by natural circumstances to accept a handicapped child, and quite another to voluntarily accept a similar condition when given the option adoption provides.

There are a few health professionals who oppose all adoption of older and handicapped children. Once presented with evidence of adoptive success, however, some can be convinced of the feasibility of adoption for these children with certain parents. Others can be similarly convinced only by fellow professionals. Unfortunately, those who are consistently opposed to adoption seldom change their minds. In these cases, placement workers can only recommend to potential adoptive parents that they seek supplemental consultation services from other medical sources.

The opinion of health professionals that older and handicapped children can and should be adopted is one of the most valuable resources for any child welfare program interested in changing public and professional attitudes toward the definition of adoptability. It is most desirable, too, for placement workers to have access to consulting physicians and other health professionals who can help them understand medical conditions and the relevance of those conditions to the lives of the children who have them. Consulting physician-to-family communication regarding medical information is generally preferable to less direct routes, for this approach risks far fewer errors in translation than the same information about a child transmitted through adoptive families or placement workers.

Good medical support is required for the family of a child with a handicap. It is the responsibility of both the child's and family's worker to assist the family in finding the best medical service available. It is also the worker's responsibility to add more adoption-minded health professionals to the growing group of informed adoption consultants.

20

The National Strategy:

The Clark Project

THE CLARK PROJECT AND SPAULDING FOR CHILDREN

In July 1974, Spaulding for Children began participating in a national strategy designed to stimulate the development of additional specialized adoption services for older and handicapped children. This effort, funded by the Edna McConnell Clark Foundation of New York City, has enabled Spaulding to have a much broader impact on the child welfare system as a whole than the agency's size and influence might normally command.

Funds provided to Spaulding in Michigan, which will continue until 1978, are meant to assist the agency in meeting general operating expenses in order to maintain existing services and allow key staff to provide training and technical assistance in the implementation of the national strategy.

To understand the role of Spaulding for Children in a "national strategy" requires knowledge of the various projects funded by the Clark Foundation in its efforts to improve the adoption/foster care service of this nation and strengthen the future of children in care outside of their biological families. These projects include the creation of a "Family Builders" network of specialized placement agencies (of which Spaulding is a member), the establishment of the North American Center on Adoption, the development of advanced training programs for placement workers, the implementation of the Children in Placement Project of the National Council of Juvenile Court Judges, and the design of a case management and tracking information system for placement workers (CYCIS).

Specifically, the Clark Foundation aims to accomplish these improvements by fulfilling the following six goals:

1. Determine where children in need are and who is responsible for helping to meet their needs
2. Increase public awareness of the needs of these children and the high human cost of ignoring their needs
3. Plan sensible strategies for financing the placement of older and handicapped children with permanent families using primarily those child welfare funds now being spent to serve and maintain children outside of such family settings
4. Develop a small group of specialized referral adoption programs to place the children for whom other programs have not been able to find permanent families
5. Raise the awareness of judges, lawyers, and legislators concerning the need for new laws and procedures to untangle the complicated legal issues of custody and adoption which obstruct the rights of children to have the love and protection of permanent parents
6. Develop curriculum packages to be used in conjunction with graduate and undergraduate programs in leading colleges and universities to train social work practitioners in the skills and attitudes needed to find permanent families for children.

PROJECT DESCRIPTIONS

The "Family Builders" Network

"Family Builders" is a name given a new program created under the auspices of the North American Center on Adoption to establish a coordinated network of referral agencies specializing in the adoptive placement of older and handicapped children. At present, there is a network member in each of nine states or areas (Michigan, New Jersey, New York, Ohio, Florida, Washington, D.C., California, Washington, and Georgia). These are:

Spaulding for Children
P.O. Box 337
Chelsea, Michigan 48118
(313-475-2500)

Spaulding for Children
321 Elm Street
Westfield, New Jersey 07090
Mr. John Boyne, Executive Director, (201-233-2282)

New York Spaulding for Children
24 West 45th Street
New York, New York 10036
Ms. Kathryn S. Donley, Executive Dir., (212-869-8940)

Spaulding for Children — Beech Brook
3201 Euclid Avenue
Cleveland, Ohio 44115
Mr. John Cowles, Director (216-432-0025)

Project CAN
2960 Roosevelt Blvd.
Clearwater, Florida 35530
Ms. June Fountain, Project Dir., (813-536-9427)

Peirce-Warwick Adoption Service
5229 Connecticut Avenue, N. W.
Washington, D.C. 20015
Ms. Johnnie Penelton, Executive Dir., (202-966-2531)

Children's Home Society of California Family Builders
3200 Telegraph Avenue
Oakland, California 94609
Ms. Patricia A. Montgomery, Program Dir., (415-655-7406)

The Adoption of Special Children
Medina Children's Service
123-16th Avenue
Seattle, Washington 98122
Ms. Betty Higley, Director, (206-324-9470)

Child Service & Family Counseling Center, Inc.
1105 W. Peachtree Street, N. E.
Atlanta, Georgia 30309
Ms. Mildred F. Clark, Director, Adoption Unit, (404-873-6916)

"Family Builders" agencies share Spaulding for Children's philosophy and focus on the placement of children traditionally considered hard-to-place or "unadoptable." These common principles are:

1. Adoption is the sole service of the agency or project
2. Children are referred for placement on a purchase of service basis from other public or private agencies which have not been able to place them for adoption
3. Services must be in accordance with accepted high professional standards

4. Fees and donations are neither charged nor requested from adoptive applicants

5. The agency or project must make a commitment to participating in a significant expansion of services to meet the needs of waiting children

6. The agency or project must vigorously pursue financial reform in specialized adoption services including full-cost purchase of service

7. Child advocates and adoptive parents committed to meeting unmet adoption needs for children should be a significant part of the policy-making process of the program or project

8. The agency or project must make a commitment to cooperate among network agencies to strengthen the pace of progress toward mutual goals

Agencies using the full name "Spaulding for Children" or any part of that name must, in addition to sharing the above principles, also agree to the following:

1. Under normal circumstances, network agencies will not assume legal custody of children referred to them for placement planning, but may in fact accept commitment responsibility at the time of placement[1]

2. They will assume a leadership role in the field of adoption through demonstration of successful placement technology and technique concerning older, handicapped, and minority race children.

3. They will not use those funding sources in competition with existing agencies to cover the difference between purchase of service fee income and total budget needs

4. Exceptions to these standards may be made in isolated conditions upon consent of the local Board of Directors. Other agencies and projects using the "Spaulding" name must be notified of and agree to these exceptions in order that a pattern of noncompliance not develop.

All of these network agencies are, in theory, placing the hardest to place older, handicapped, and minority race children legally available for adoption. In practice, however, wide variations occur among the pro-

---

[1]Under normal conditions, most network agencies are exclusively referral agencies that act only on behalf of other placement programs. However, some network agencies and projects operate under different legal requirements and must assume total legal and fiscal responsibility for the child — called "commitment responsibility" — before they are allowed to carry out a placement plan.

grams regarding the referred children's mental and physical characteristics. These variations result from demographic differences (urban vs. rural, Black vs. Caucasion or Indian, etc.) as well as diversity in the kinds of children which the referring programs using these specialized agencies perceive as "hard-to-place."

Current planning seeks to expand the "Family Builders" Network to between 10 and 12 agencies by the latter part of 1977. By that time, it is intended that each specialized referral agency will be able to serve specific geographic areas which have a large population of children, specific problems in working with their "hard-to-place" child population, and an established citizen support base.

In addition to associating themselves for purposes of mutual support and assistance, the "Family Builders" network of agencies has agreed upon two initial areas of focus:

1. The development and promotion of a new purchase of service formula which is based upon a full-cost reimbursement principle and the use of a single step, hand-written, worker-managed cost and time accountability system, and
2. The development of a practical means of solving the financial problem created because the actual cost of placing children who are older, handicapped, or minority race is often greater than the reimbursement available. One possibility is the Family Builders by Adoption support program, a national project designed to solicit monthly contributions from individuals and groups wishing to support the search for permanent adoptive families for waiting children in a pattern similar to Spaulding for Children in Michigan's original Child of the Month Club (see p. 20)

Of the money that is raised by Family Builders by Adoption for specialized adoption efforts, 10 percent of the proceeds will be used for the support of the North American Center on Adoption and the balance distributed (essentially *pro rata*) among network agencies and projects, not to exceed 15 percent of each member's operating budgets. The remainder of each program's support is expected to come from purchase of service fees or other support generated individually by each network member.

The North American Center on Adoption

The North American Center on Adoption was established in New York City on January 1, 1975 as a special project of the Child Welfare League of America to deal with the problems preventing the placement of children legally available for adoption. The Center focuses on these problems in five ways: by increasing public awareness, by improving training and staff development, by offering placement programs the services of ARENA (The Adoption Resource Exchange of North America), by concentrating on needed financial and financing reforms including more efficient and wide-spread use of inter-agency purchase of service agreements, and by providing the facilitating staff support for the "Family Builders" network of specialized placement agencies.

Through its public education efforts, the Center works with all media to increase broad citizen knowledge of and supportive concern about older, handicapped, and minority race children who are or should be available for adoption and about the steps which can be taken to promote their permanent placement. The Center adds to the extensive information and consultation services already established by the Child Welfare League, thus making an even wider range of adoption materials and assistance available to adoption professionals and the interested public. A large number of films and video tapes are available for loan at a nominal fee from the Center. In addition, a quarterly newsletter, entitled *Adoption Report,* is published and distributed to all adoption agencies and citizen advocate groups in North America.

Helping agency staff and other child welfare professionals to improve their skills in placing children traditionally considered hard-to-place or "unadoptable" is also viewed as an essential task. The Center provides training materials, technical assistance, and consultation. A library of recruitment materials has been created and work has begun on a manual explaining how families can be recruited for children who need permanent families. Publicity and recruitment kits containing materials and explanations of techniques which have proven successful will be shared with local placement programs and citizen's groups who wish to launch their own campaigns.

Workshops on recruitment techniques have also been presented and a booklet entitled "How to Use Title XX to Provide Permanence for Children" has been commissioned, published, and distributed to every state planner, adoption agency, and adoptive parent group in the country. In addition, the Center has collaborated in the design of a model purchase of adoption services system which is being implemented by all agencies in the "Family Builders" Network.

In January 1975, the Center assumed coordinating responsibility for ARENA, the Adoption Resource Exchange of North America. This organization was created by the Child Welfare League of America in 1967 to mobilize national action toward helping placement programs exchange child and family resources to facilitate more adoptions. During its first nine years of operation, ARENA assisted in the placement of more than 1,600 children, with an ever-increasing proportion being older, handicapped, or of minority race.

ARENA operates a free clearinghouse achieved by maintaining a registry of "waiting" children and available parents and by making referrals of specific children and families whose needs and interests correspond. In addition to assisting in the placement of children, ARENA has gathered extensive information about state, provincial, and regional exchanges, offered consultation aimed at more efficient and effective exchange operations, promoted the development of additional exchanges, and identified policy barriers to permanent placement.

Future ARENA plans include improvement and expansion of its information and referral services, the design of a model adoption resource exchange system for state, provincial, regional, and national use, and the creation of a national network of adoption resource exchange directors. ARENA is also involved in the establishment of a forum for the sharing of information and resources and the implementation of an "Outreach" project intended to select several agencies across the country to recruit and study families for the children known to ARENA and remaining unplaced the longest.

Leadership Training

The national strategy also includes the development and implementation of special programs providing advanced training to experienced social work practitioners which are designed to significantly expand the base of highly qualified leadership in the specialized adoption field. The completion of these programs can lead to a "Certificate of Advanced Training," Continuing Education Units, and possible graduate credit. These course experiences were implemented with the help of the North American Center on Adoption, "Family Builders" Network professionals, and three graduate schools of social work (the University of Michigan, Columbia University, and the University of Southern California). Begun during 1976, each program drew participants from both their own geographic area and from various other parts of the country. The three schools developed their own approach to training as a part of the national strategy to determine how to best meet practitioners' needs.

The curriculum of all three schools has focused on increasing leadership and problem-solving skills and improving services in adoption and foster care for children traditionally defined as hard-to-place or "unadoptable." Content areas have included child and family development, communication skills, parenting styles, legal and legislative issues, the special problems of older, handicapped, and minority race children, post-placement services, improving supervision and inter-agency relationships, the implementation of purchase of service fee systems, program expansion, and staff training. The curriculum offers participants a better understanding of the child welfare system, the negative impacts upon children caught within it, and the skills necessary to help those children experience family permanence and stability.

This multi-disciplinary approach to training has included representatives from a wide range of professions (law, public health, education, social work, psychology, and medicine) as well as practitioners actually placing older, handicapped, and minority race children. Means of instruction have included mini-lectures, video tapes, simulations, problem-solving seminars, decision experiences, skill workshops, independent study, and individual guidance.

Throughout 1976, Spaulding served as "Family Builders" Network liaison to Project CRAFT (Curriculum Resources in Adoption and Foster Care Training), the largest of these leadership training projects which was located at the University of Michigan.

The approximately 80 graduates of these programs are eligible to apply to become "Fellows" of the North American Center on Adoption. Ten trainees will be chosen by a committee to receive expense stipends to continue their leadership involvement and development. This program, ideally intended to be a two year commitment undertaken in addition to their regular employment, asks each participant to advance child welfare knowledge and the national strategy through writing or practice in an area related to their own interest and to participate in important national meetings and Center activities.

A second grant request will make possible a second round of training as well as the further development of curriculum materials suitable for wide-spread use by other schools. Although no direct grants to additional schools are anticipated, Michigan, Columbia, and Southern California may well offer similar leadership training programs in cooperation with other colleges and universities.

The Children in Placement Project

The Children in Placement Project is sponsored by the National Council of Juvenile Court Judges (NCJCJ), the oldest and largest judicial organization in the United States. This investigation was initiated following a 1972-1973 court review project in the Kent County Juvenile Court, Grand Rapids, Michigan, which had been funded by the Grand Rapids Foundation and the Keeler Foundation and conducted under the auspices of Spaulding for Children. The NCJCJ recognized that courts as well as agencies not only have a responsibility to make appropriate placement plans for children, but are accountable to the general public for the results of their orders and actions. The NCJCJ also recognized the need to document the nature and extent of the problems inherent in planning for children in placement by reviewing the status of children in the custody of, or committed by, a representative sample of courts. It was agreed that if such documentation was available, a national focus on both the problem and its proposed resolution could and should be undertaken.

Because the enthusiasm and commitment of judges was regarded as vital to a successful project, judges were asked to volunteer their juvenile court systems for participation. By using only willing judges and trained community volunteers, it has been possible to avoid the risk of an unsuccessful project due to participant disinterest or outright opposition.

The selection of project courts was made so that a wide variety of geographic regions would be represented. Other selection considerations were the receptivity of the court, the availability of community support and cooperation, and the demonstration of the court's interest as measured by their willingness to invest their own court personnel, time, and equipment. Twelve courts were finally chosen and included those in:

Greenville, Mississippi
Providence, Rhode Island
Columbia, South Carolina
Wausau, Wisconsin
Portland, Oregon
El Paso, Texas
Santa Barbara, California
Honolulu, Hawaii
Ravenna, Ohio
Denver, Colorado
Lincoln, Nebraska
Salt Lake City, Utah

The pilot project court in Grand Rapids, Michigan, has remained involved by providing two training consultants to the NCJCJ who are experienced in the concepts of systematic court review. Leadership of the project committee is furnished by Judge John Steketee of the Grand Rapids Juvenile Court.

This project began as a two year systematic case review program in September 1974, and was designed to improve the care of neglected and dependent children in court-ordered institutional and foster care placement. It was created as a nation-wide effort to find those children either "lost" within the child welfare system or no longer benefiting from a specific placement and to devise for them an appropriate placement plan. It was intended that this program of court review, together with the policy of including a review hearing date on all court orders, would do much to safeguard such children.

Each project court has developed and implemented a program for reviewing cases under their jurisdiction which have been given either "dependent" or "neglect" court status. In addition to providing better service for children, this project has compiled important information about each child in placement in an effort to facilitate professional staff and judicial action. Included is information concerning whether the child is a temporary or permanent ward, the length of wardship, the number of moves the child has made, and the frequency of contact between the child, parent(s), and caseworker(s). Appropriate statistics have been tabulated in order to produce a composite picture of children in court care.

The project has also created and made available informational materials including a video tape aid to judicial understanding of the project, training tapes and guidebooks for project coordinators and volunteers, and a promotional slide presentation with sound track to be used for public education with a wide variety of community groups. As of this writing, these materials may be obtained through the Children in Placement Project, NCJCJ, Box 8978, Reno, Nevada, 89507, or by calling (702) 784-4945.

It is hoped that the results of this project will encourage other courts to undertake a systematic review of the children in their care. Each of the thirteen current project courts plan to continue their review process on an on-going basis and are capable of serving as regional models for other interested courts.

An additional grant has been awarded for a second phase of the project which is designed to expand the number of courts participating in the reviewing and monitoring process and, through a wide-spread series of training and conference activities, extend the influence of the NCJCJ in safeguarding the future of children who come within court jurisdiction at any point in their lives.

The project's second phase will also test a new concept of "dual guardianship" to reduce the possibility of neglect for children in placement. Based upon programs successfully implemented in Denmark, the concept of "dual guardianship" consists of recruiting and training individual volunteers to work with social workers to help accomplish appropriate goals for specific children in care. This program is an effort to replace the impersonal "corporate" agency atmosphere within which children become "lost" (because worker, supervisor, and program priorities may not focus primarily on the child) with a personalized, individual, responsible process.

The CYCIS Project

CYCIS (Child and Youth Centered Information System) is a project developed under a grant from the Clark Foundation to the Child Welfare League of America to establish a model case management inventory system for all children in care outside of their own homes. Based upon the most successful features of the several computerized state and county child welfare systems now in operation, CYCIS is designed to bring together the judicial, public, and private sectors concerned with child care in a united effort to regularly monitor where children are in "the system," who is responsible for them, and what plans are being made for their permanent placement. Current plans include the implementation of CYCIS, by late 1977, in approximately six states representing both state-administered and county-administered programs and chosen for their wide geographic diversity and differing public agency/private agency "mix."

SUMMARY

For many years it has been clear to advocates for children that if the low priority given to achieving permanence for children was to change, a multitude of problems would first have to be solved. The Edna McConnell Clark Foundation has played a major role in assisting agencies, courts, and child advocate groups in meeting these challenges by establishing a multi-faceted national strategy to improve services to children in temporary care. Because of the exceptionally high cost-benefit ratio inherent in these reforms, it is hoped that broader governmental support will emerge to sustain existing efforts.

Specialized referral services in adoption are an integral part of a national strategy. However, agencies and projects created for this purpose cannot be expected to carry the entire burden of required placement responsibility and must be supported by the other aspects of reform discussed here.

The children wait, but a broad-based effort has now been implemented to remove the obstacles which keep them waiting and to stop the needless waste of human and financial resources which occur while they wait. Hopefully, the momentum created by the commitment of the Clark Foundation will be great enough to begin reversing the current apathy and skill lag which has traditionally hampered attempts to provide permanence for children. Hopefully, the Clark Project is only the beginning of the massive and continuous effort which is essential if this country seriously intends to help its children develop to their fullest potential.

In Conclusion: 21
The Present
and Future of
Adoption

ADVANCES IN ADOPTION

During the last ten years, steady and significant progress has been made in the field of adoption. Children who were once thought to be so difficult to place as to be considered by all but a few placement professionals as "unadoptable" are now secure family members. More and more placement programs, in almost all parts of the country, are becoming convinced that they, too, can successfully place older, handicapped, and minority race children, and are doing so. New casework techniques, recruitment tools, and a significant decline in the number of healthy babies and toddlers available for adoption have contributed to these advances. Changes in social attitudes and family planning practice, increased social responsibility on the community level, and a heightened public interest in the welfare of children (as shown by the emotional impact of the airlifts of Vietnamese and Cambodian "orphans") are apparent throughout the country.

SPAULDING'S CONTRIBUTIONS

Spaulding for Children has contributed to this progress through its continuing efforts to expand the definition of adoptability, through the example it has set regarding the permanent placement of "unadoptable" children, and through its efforts to help other programs begin placing similar kinds of children. But has Spaulding really been successful? The answer to this question depends upon how large a success has to be before it is considered a success. For specific children and parents, the agency's success is often measured by the arrival of a long-waited place-ment. For other children and parents, success is sometimes measured by the helpful support of a social worker after the placement has been made.

On a somewhat larger scale, Spaulding's success may be measured by the improvements which have occurred in the field of adoption within Michigan as a result of the agency's example and its willingness to share attitudes and techniques. The increased responsiveness of other Michi-gan placement programs to the problems of hard-to-place children in need of adoption, and Spaulding's expanding schedule of training and consultation outside of Michigan, have led the agency's staff to accept an increasing number of appropriate out-of-state referrals during the last several years.

PROBLEMS IN ADOPTION

In actuality, Spaulding's success has just begun to influence the field of adoption. They have just begun to scratch the surface of the problem they set out to help solve. Children are still unplaced because they require services and commitment more difficult to provide than those commonly offered by workers, supervisors, and administrators. Potentially capable applicants are frequently not allowed to adopt children in need of per-manence because they fail to meet the eligibility requirements imposed by placement programs intent upon finding perfect families for a di-minishing population of available infants and toddlers. Not only is the focus of these programs directed away from the majority of available children, but their screening practices all too often fail to consider par-ent's capabilities or the child's need for nurturance.

Though some placement programs and, therefore, some parts of the country are slowly becoming more responsive to those children who are or who should be available for adoption, large pockets of resistance remain. Many programs and individuals in the field are still not only trying to deny the need for specialized placement programs, but are continuing to ignore the children who have always remained unplaced.

As a result, there are many children legally available for adoption or, for all practical purposes, totally without family ties, who are not yet considered adoptable by the agencies and courts having responsibility for them. These include young children and adolescents of white and minority race, both handicapped or non-handicapped, and children who have spent most of their lives in foster care homes or institutions. As these children grow older, the normal aging process, coupled with the high risk of emotional difficulties created by the insecurity of repeated foster care or institutional placements, make it increasingly likely that the agency or court who retains legal custody and the responsibility for placement will gradually come to consider such children as "lost causes."

In addition, there will always be children who, from the point of view of their parents, grow too emotionally disturbed, too large, or otherwise too difficult to be cared for on a continuing basis in the home. The existence of these children, added to those who will someday enter the child welfare system because of abandonment, neglect, or abuse, means there will always be older children and handicapped children waiting to be adopted.

ADOPTION IN THE FUTURE

Although progress is slowly being made, the real tragedy is that both waiting children and waiting parents exist in substantially greater numbers than do the current services or commitment to bring the two together. Fortunately, some solutions are available. They are not easy, quick, one-step solutions, but they will slowly and steadily improve the future of adoption in many areas of practice. When implemented on a wide scale, these changes will enable the entire child placement profession to provide more thorough, efficient, and rewarding services to children. These solutions require changes in program attitude and procedure and improved program communication. They also require the implementation of a periodic review of children in temporary care, the development of a nation-wide tracking system, the implementation of coordinated research efforts, and the inauguration of supportive services to separating families.

Attitude and Procedure
THE RECOGNITION THAT OLDER, HANDICAPPED, AND MINORITY RACE CHILDREN ARE ADOPTABLE, BUT THAT TRADITIONAL ATTITUDES, METHODS, AND TECHNIQUES MUST BE CHANGED IN ORDER FOR PLACEMENT TO OCCUR.

The first benefit for children resulting from improvements in the field of adoption will be that more and more placement professionals will realize that the vast majority of children who are now or who should be available for adoption cannot be successfully placed by programs determined to use the attitudes, methods, and techniques that successfully place healthy white babies and toddlers. As a result, placement professionals will begin focusing their attention on meeting the needs of all children in their custody, broadening their range of "acceptable" parents, actively recruiting parents for specific children, and thoroughly preparing children and parents for adoption in general and for their own adoption in particular. Greater numbers of placement workers, supervisors, and administrators will also realize that the stability of a child's future depends upon their success in building a relationship with families which allows those families to request help without fear of jeopardizing the adoption.

To provide stability for children, placement programs will furnish post-placement services whenever necessary, help the child and family through their separation experience should their adoption disrupt, and replace the children whose adoptions have disrupted with other adoptive families. Agencies and courts will also find ways to repair the staff morale problems which result from confrontation, crisis, bizarre behavior, and disruption.

In addition, child welfare professionals will gradually help society alter its views of adoption. The placement of older, handicapped, and minority race children remains difficult, in part, because the current concept of adoption is still based upon an attempt to duplicate or replace biological reproduction. In the future, both "adoption" and "parenting" will be redefined, "parenting" will be distinguished from "reproduction," and the importance of "nurture" in parenting a child will be emphasized. In this way, the blond blue-eyed child, the child of minority race, and the handicapped child will be regarded as individuals in their own right, and the latter will be adopted out of pity or duty.

Communications
THE DEVELOPMENT OF BETTER COMMUNICATION AND SHARED RESPONSIBILITY BETWEEN CHILDREN, FAMILIES, AND PLACEMENT PROFESSIONALS.

The second important improvement in the future of adoption will be better communication: better communication between professionals and children, between professionals and families, and between placement programs. Communication between placement professionals and children who are waiting to be adopted is now too often non-existent. In the future, increasing numbers of placement workers will realize that children who are old enough to share their attitudes, beliefs, and expectations can provide valuable information during the search for appropriate parents. More importantly, workers will realize that failing to discuss and take into consideration the thoughts and feelings of the children themselves significantly decreases the probability of a successful adoption.

Communication between placement professionals and families is now too often limited to:

a. presenting a battery of requirements, in no way related to parenting ability, for the purpose of reducing the number of applicants to a manageable number.

b. seeking to obtain honest descriptions of personal attitudes, activities, and problems from applicants who have learned from the experiences of others that they will almost certainly lose their chance to adopt if they are found to be "imperfect" in any way.

c. moving applicants who want to adopt one or more of the program's hard-to-place children through the adoption process as quickly as possible, but leaving them uninformed concerning any information which cause them to change their mind.

In the future, more placement professionals will begin to help applicants focus on the kinds of skills and capabilities essential to provide adequate parenting for children who have special needs. Workers, supervisors, and administrators will gradually realize that in order to help applicants achieve or expand these skills, it is vital to create a relationship in which it is repeatedly emphasized that parental imperfection is normal and does not jeopardize an applicant's chance to adopt.

Placement professionals will also realize that applicants must be fully informed concerning the needs and level of functioning of both the kinds of children whose adoption they are initially considering and the specific child they may eventually prepare to adopt. In this way, child, family, and worker will benefit greatly, for the applicant will be able to share in the process of accurately accessing his ability to parent a specific child.

More and more workers, supervisors, and administrators will realize that once a child is placed, post-placement services must be provided whenever necessary. They will understand that the success of many placements involving older, handicapped, and minority race children is tied directly to a relationship between parents and placement worker which allows the parents to feel comfortable asking for help — a relationship which must include repeated emphasis by the worker that it is normal to have post-placement problems and that the presence of such problems does not mean the child must be removed from his family. However, should the existence of serious, unsolvable post-placement problems cause the adoption to disrupt, workers will also be able to help the child and family through their separation experience and work to replace the child with another adoptive family.

It is imperative that feelings of competitiveness between adoption programs decrease in the future. Feelings of competitiveness and elitism, rather than shared responsibility, still form the foundation of the majority of relationships which exist between placement programs. Both staff pride and definitions of program success among child welfare professionals are still predominately linked to the easily measurable "number of placements," not to the much more difficult to measure, but more important "quality of placement."

In addition, competition between the public and private sectors of the child welfare system continues on such a large scale in every state that examples of cooperation are still exceptional departures from typicl conditions. In all but the most unusual circumstances, the private sector has retained its capacity to pick and choose the children it serves, and to protect itself from assuming the financial and emotional responsibility of caring for children whose placements require extended worker time and commitment.

The public sector, which cannot restrict the types of children in its care, must assume the responsibility for the older, handicapped, and minority race children left behind by the private agencies' selection process. This division has created the current imbalance between available children and aspiring applicants which constitutes one of the major problems in the field of adoption today. So many applicants are now seeking the relatively small number of generally young, white, healthy children in the custody of private sector agencies that even those "appropriate" parents who manage to satisfy strict eligibility requirements often wait between five and seven years to adopt. The public sector, on the other hand, has had to assume custody of so many older, handicapped, and minority race children that its workers have not usually had the time to find permanent families for more than a few of them.

The future of adoption will see an increase in inter-program contact and cooperation to enable placement professionals to build the level of trust in each other required to work together to benefit these children. Such cooperation will do much to bring together children currently waiting to be adopted and applicants waiting to adopt.

Permanent Planning

THE DEVELOPMENT OF A PROGRAM OF PERMANENT PLANNING AND PERIODIC REVIEW FOR ALL CHILDREN IN TEMPORARY CARE.

Current child placement practice is now generaly little more than a series of hasty reactions by overworked staffs to a series of placement crises involving first one child, then another. The replacement of casework by "crisis work" because no specific plan has been developed for the child's future often forces children into the frequently more emotionally devastating position of having to cope on their own wih repeated, poorly understood separation experiences.

In the future, child placement professionals will gradually recognize that that successful movement of children out of temporary care requires the identification and monitoring of those children as well as the development, implementation, and periodic review of specific permanent planning for each child. This move toward thorough permanent planning for all children will be stimulated both by lawsuits filed by child advocates and by increased judicial involvement as increased numbers of juvenile courts come to terms with their responsibility to the children within their jurisdiction.

Tracking

THE DEVELOPMENT OF A THOROUGH AND EFFICIENT TRACKING SYSTEM TO KEEP CHILD PLACEMENT PROFESSIONALS INFORMED OF THE CHARACTERISTICS AND PLACEMENT HISTORY OF CHILDREN AND FAMILIES.

Present tracking systems which focus on children in temporary care currently provide only information concerning local trends or an approximation of the number of children in a specific category. Attempts to ensure anonymity make children statistics rather than individuals and totally eliminate the possibility of using computerized information to benefit specific children.

In the future, the growing effort among child placement professionals to remove children from temporary care will lead to the development of local, regional, and national computer tracking systems which contain an up-to-date inventory of children currently availale for or needing adoption. Such a data bank will include a description of the child (as well as attitudes toward the child and expectations of adoption), a description of the child's special needs, a listing of the city or town and type of temporary placement in which the child is waiting, the length of time the child has been available, and a description of the permanent plan which has been developed for that child. These tracking systems will also store description of applicants and the kinds of children they are capable of considering for placement.

Finally', the data bank will provide description of the local, state, and national resources available to help parents who adopt, as well as collect and provide the cumulative results of placement activities on local, state, and national levels.

Research

THE IMPLEMENTATION OF COORDINATED RESEARCH EFFORTS FOCUSED ON THE ADOPTIVE PLACEMENT OF OLDER, HANDICAPPED, AND MINORITY RACE CHILDREN.

Presently, only infrequent research is being conducted involving the children, families, workers, and problems associated with the process of adoption. In the future, both child welfare professionals and social scientists will realize the need to obtain and coordinate the vast amount of knowledge now lacking in the areas of child and family attitudes, expectations, and needs. Research is needed on the improvement of various recruitment techniques, child and family preparation, placement and maintenance, and replacement methods. Further information should be obtained on worker morale and efficiency, and how to best organize and coordinate the entire child placement system to better serve children.

Biological Families

THE DEVELOPMENT OF REHABILITATIVE PROGRAMS TO HELP DECREASE THE NUMBER OF CHILDREN REMOVED FROM THEIR FAMILY OF ORIGIN AND TO INCREASE EFFORTS TO REPLACE CHILDREN WITH THEIR BIOLOGICAL FAMILIES.

Many of the children who currently are or who should be available for adoption have been separated from their biological origins for years in foster care placements or institutions. Despite the obscurity of those origins, some child placement professionals are currently espousing returns to the biological parents as the most appropriate placement solution for many children. The fact of the matter, however, is that most such placements require exceedingly complex social work techniques and extensive cooperation between one or more placement programs and the family. These placements are also often emotionally demanding experiences for the worker. For actual "returns" to become a reality on anything more than an accidental basis, much more commitment and cooperation is required than is now commonly available.

In the future, not only will child welfare professionals begin working earlier with biological families in danger of separating, but increased worker commitment and cooperation will permit the development of the techniques necessary to return children to the families they have left. In some cases, the children will come from extraordinarily fractured families where there have been deeply-rooted and complicated social problems, and even intensive work with these families may not bring improvement. However, in some cases where the child has reached an age of self-care and has such strong attachment to his biological family that he either cannot or will not form attachments anywhere else, child placement professionals will gradually come to realize that the most appropriate placement may well be a supported return to what has traditionally been considered a less than adequate family.

Yet with all these improvements, child welfare professionals must realize that it will never be possible to totally predict adoptive success. For reasons which are not known at the time of placement, or which later develop, there will always be children and families whose adoption disrupts. Inappropriate attitudes, inadequate skill, insufficient effort, and lack of judicial uniformity will always lead to the inability of some placement programs to find permanent families for some of the children in their custody. There will always be a need for some programs to pick up the pieces that others leave or to resolve new issues. Despite these conditions, however, it will still be possible to bring order out of chaos and sanity out of madness if child placement professionals make the welfare of the child their highest priority, learn to work together, and achieve and maintain the deep level of commitment which the placement of older, handicapped, and minority race children requires.

Appendices

Appendix A

The Early History of Spaulding For Children

The creation of Spaulding for Children in February, 1968 was the result of the combined effects of four major elements. The first of these began as adoptive parent dissatisfaction on the part of Peter and Joyce Forsythe and evolved into the creation of the Council on Adoptable Children in Ann Arbor, Michigan, in the early 1960's. The second element which helped create Spaulding began as a dream in the mind of Warren Spaulding, a farmer in the small southeastern Michigan town of Chelsea, who was to eventually provide the physical facilities which gave hope to the new agency. The third component was the establishment of a concerned and active Board of Directors who took upon themselves the difficult task of articulating a new philosophy of adoption which would serve as the foundation of the new agency's approach to adoptive placement. The fourth factor was the adoption philosophy, skill, and commitment provided by Kay Donley, the agency's Director.

Spaulding for Children could not have been established and could not exist in its present form or function had not all of these forces been recognized, available, and capitalized upon.

PARENT DISSATISFACTION

In large measure, Spaulding for Children came into being through the conviction and planning of Peter and Joyce Forsythe of Ann Arbor, Michigan. Peter Forsythe, a lawyer, and Joyce, a young woman of enormous energy, were biological parents of two children. They had become dissatisfied with current adoption philosophy and practice when, after several years of study by two different agencies, one refused quest for a "waiting" child but cheerfully offered to find them one who was "normal."

The agency's negative reaction to their willingness to adopt an older, handicapped, or mixed race child led the Forsythes to share their anger and frustration with several friends who had also tried to adopt "waiting" children. The negative experiences also encountered by their friends confirmed the Forsythes' belief that something had to be done if children in need of the love and security of permanent families were to have a chance of finding such placements.

In the Spring of 1966, the Forsythes and several other adoptive parents formed the Council on Adoptable Children (COAC). The group hoped to publicize their difficulties with adoption programs and to work cooperatively to change adoption policies. Their major goal was to help make the community more aware of the number of children who were available for adoption but were not being placed.

At that time, area adoption programs were typically reporting that they did not have children like those requested by the Forsythes.COAC had evidence that this was not the case, however, and to support its position relied upon figures in a 1960 Master's thesis written by Fred Wight at the School of Social Work, University of Michigan, Ann Arbor.[1] This thesis was a complete 1959 inventory of permanent state wards in Michigan who had been available for adoption for more than three months. It indicated there were more than 700 of these children, many of them older, handicapped, or of minority race, who were waiting to be adopted. Many had been in care for years with no plans made to find them families.

COAC's efforts to inform the public of the problems of adoption had little immediate effect on professional practice, for public opinion was not yet well enough informed to significantly affect child placement programs. Although agencies and courts, when questioned, maintained that changes in their adoption programs were taking place, very few improvements were visible.

In a further attempt to meet what its members were beginning to see as a critical need for change, COAC decided to concentrate its efforts on adoption agencies and to directly challenge the basic ideas which had led to complacency in meeting children's needs. This attempt to produce improved adoption services resulted in meetings with agency Boards of Directors and social workers during which COAC hoped to determine what practices were used and how workers viewed the needs of children. It was COAC'S plan to first identify the practices and attitudes which

[1]Wight, Fred E. "Unadopted Adoptable Children . . . Under the Care of the Michigan Children's Institute as of June 1, 1959 . . . (A Study To Determine Why These Children Have Not Been Adopted, And What The Agency Might Do To Provide Adoptive Planning For This Group)." University of Michigan School of Social Work, 1960.

prevented children from finding permanent families. Then, by citing practice reforms from other parts of the United States and Canada, the group would try to convince agencies and courts to remove these obstacles from the child placement process.

In its attempts to change the restrictive policies of adoption programs, COAC itself faced a number of obstacles. Agency supervisors felt that they did not have enough time to share information with COAC or to "study" the families found by COAC in the Ann Arbor area who were interested in adopting older or minority race children. The group also found there was a high turnover rate of adoption workers. Because the workers frequently left their jobs for new or better positions, COAC soon learned that it was unable to simultaneously influence enough workers to cause change in policy within an agency or court. Workers felt their supervisors were the problem and the supervisors blamed executive directors and Boards of Directors. There seemed no way to break through a tight "buck-passing" circle surrounding children in need of parents.

In an effort to work around these problems, Joyce Forsythe recruited a qualified, trained social work supervisor and eight trained social workers to volunteer their services to adoption programs in the Ann Arbor area. They offered to help find and study families willing to accept the children waiting for adoption. They also agreed to be supervised by the programs to whom they were volunteering. They felt their volunteered services would help the adoption programs by providing, at no cost, a stable corps of dedicated workers. The addition of these trained social workers would also give the programs' regular workers time to provide additional services. In this way, more families would receive children and more children would find permanent families.

Of all the adoption programs approached, only the Muskegon Children's Home was receptive to the COAC offer. All others refused to accept the volunteer help. COAC members found that most supervisors in local agencies denied that there were problems in placing older, handicapped, and minority race children. Those few who did admit to a problem felt that lack of interest from applicants, not the programs' current placement practices, was primarily responsibile for the failure to find adoptive families for these children.

After several months, the volunteers recognized that their efforts had failed to change program operations and policies. Adoption programs were still not actively seeking parents for many of their available children. The children were being held in temporary care indefinitely because no permanent plans or efforts were being made for their future, and placement professionals in agencies and courts still assumed that "nobody *wanted* to adopt these kids."

At this point, COAC concluded that their only real alternative for bringing about program change lay outside the existing agencies and courts. The group developed a new strategy and began to concentrate on helping families. They quickly found they could provide families with a valuable service by sharing with them their information about the type of children each adoption program had in its custody. That is, they could direct families to the programs having custody of the kinds of children the families wanted to adopt. This referral activity did not mean that COAC was "playing agency," as some adoption programs asserted. No license was required to suggest to families that they apply to a given agency to adopt a child or to provide other information to create informed applicants.

Lack of significant cooperation or enthusiasm by almost all Michigan agencies had, by 1967, convinced some of the leaders of COAC of the necessity for establishing a new type of adoption agency. The group still believed that agencies could, should, and indeed must change. But now, based upon their past experiences, they also knew that without more effort the pace of change acceptable to most adoption programs would be far too slow to benefit the large numbers of waiting children.

COAC knew that it needed many laymen and professionals to support its innovative ideas before it could ever hope to be successful. Fortunately, the group's efforts had begun to stimulate broader public and agency interest. In order to take best advantage of this growing awareness, COAC decided to bring together child welfare professionals and interested citizens (including those who wanted to adopt older, handicapped, and minority race children) to discuss the changing adoption climate and to learn more about each other. COAC hoped that support from nationally known child welfare professionals would make its position more acceptable and serve to convince other professionals of the directions in which the group felt adoption program reform needed to proceed.

In the autumn of 1967, a conference organized by COAC and known as "Frontiers in Adoption" was held in Ann Arbor. It was co-sponsored by COAC, The University of Michigan School of Social Work, the Michigan Department of Social Services, The Michigan Probate and Juvenile Judges Association, and other key civic and adoption organizations within Michigan. Participants discussed the development of current adoption practices and the problems these practices had caused. The focus was on "finding homes for the hard-to-place child."

The effect of "Frontiers in Adoption" was tremendous. By publishing its proceedings, this conference sharply focused attention on Michigan's increasing number of children who were waiting to be adopted. Much of this success was also due to the presence of Muriel McCrea, at that time Executive Director of the Children's Service Centre, Montreal, and Clayton Hagen, then Supervisor of the Adoption Unit of the Lutheran

Social Services of Minnesota. Each described their agency's innovative placement practices.

By focusing the attention of child welfare professionals on the adoption problems highlighted at its conference, COAC was finally able to establish its credibility and to initiate a major impact upon the adoption system. Equally important was the effect the conference had on non-professionals. As a result of their contact with various agencies and adoption workers, adoptive parents and other interested citizens became much better informed about the field of adoption.

They learned, for example, that children other than infants were not being placed in large numbers by agencies and courts, and that placement programs, in many cases, did not have adequate enough records on children in foster care to determine which, or even how many, children were in need of adoption. Larger numbers of persons became better acquainted with such practical matters as the sequence of events in the adoption process and the attitudes held by specific judges, supervisors, and workers which were not conducive to the placement of waiting children.

Many of the conference participants arrived at the same conclusion COAC had reached earlier: without external stimulation, changes in existing adoption practices that would benefit children would be slow in coming. There was a clear need for a new specialized agency that could serve as a model for other programs by placing children in need of permanent families.

Happily, other events were occurring in the nearby town of Chelsea that would eventually make this possible.

WARREN SPAULDING

Warren Dennis Spaulding, was born March 1, 1883, in Chelsea, Michigan, a small town eighteen miles west of Ann Arbor. Warren was the last of nine children and outlived his one brother and seven sisters. He was truly a native of Chelsea. His whole life centered around the sixteen room farmhouse where he was born and reared. Warren never married, but he and Bertha, the sister with whom he shared the family home, had a great love for children. They often brought Sunday School children out to visit their farm and, as a result, a close bond developed between the Chelsea townspeople and the Spaulding family.

The townspeople still speak fondly of their childhood memories of the frequent picnics and hayrides held at the Spaulding farm. They remember Bertha as the organizer and the provider of honey and peanut butter sandwiches. They remember Warren as the smiling driver of the haywagon.

After Bertha died, many of the townspeople began to believe that the outings to the Spaulding farm had become too great an imposition, and the children began to visit much less frequently. Only his closest friends could detect the loneliness Warren felt without the laughter and scattered toys which identified his house as a home frequented by children.

Two of Warren's friends, Dorothea Pielemeier and her brother, Albert, were among the few who knew Warren's true feelings. They also knew that Warren's dream of helping children included turning the farm he loved so much into a home for needy children where they could spend their childhood as happily as he had spent his. When Warren reached the age of 84 without having put his plan into action, Dorothea wondered whether there would be any way in which she could help him. In her thought and meditation about the problem, the name of a young family friend, Richard Schneider, came to mind and she wrote to him immediately. Here was a man who had been a member of her church, had grown up in Chelsea, and had later gained a Master's degree in social work. He and his wife had adopted older children and he had directed a children's program in Kentucky.

Miss Pielemeier called on Warren Spaulding to ask if he would welcome a call from a friend of hers who might be able to help him with his plan. With this agreement, Miss Pielemeier then sought the support of Warner Siebert, then pastor of St. Paul Church in Chelsea. He was very interested in becoming involved and offered whatever assistance might be helpful.

Eventually, a mutual friend, a COAC member, was instrumental in introducing Richard Schneider to the Forsythes and the idea of a new agency gradually began to take shape based upon the Forsythes' ideas and strategies and Richard Schneider's sensitive feel for Warren Spaulding's dream.

ESTABLISHING THE AGENCY

A Board of Directors was formed, primarily composed of Chelsea area residents sympathetic to the idea of an alternative and innovative adoption agency. Peter Forsythe was an initial member of that Board, but Joyce chose to continue working with the COAC group and to help Spaulding "from the outside" as a volunteer. Articles of Incorporation, approved by the Board, were filed in February, 1968.

Although the people of Chelsea were aware that a new agency was being established, not everyone clearly understood its goals or its place in the community. Many area residents knew of Warren Spaulding's original intent to turn his farm into an orphanage, but were not aware of his more recent understanding that there was no demand for more institutions for children and his agreement that he could do more for children by helping to establish an adoption agency. Consequently, they were surprised to find that Spaulding for Children was not an orphanage, since that had been the expectation in the community.

Richard Schneider made early attempts to interpret the purpose of Spaulding to groups of Chelsea residents, especially through his articles in the town newspaper, *The Chelsea Standard*. Other events, including ill health following an automobile accident and the mounting duties of his full-time employment as an assistant director of the Chelsea Methodist Home, led him to resign from his voluntary duties at Spaulding in May of 1968, just as the Board was attempting to obtain a license to operate a child placing agency. (Such licensing by the Michigan Department of Social Services is legally required for any agency to begin placing children in Michigan.) As a result, the task of clarifying both Warren Spaulding's support and the intent of the agency remained incomplete in the midst of efforts to begin placing children.

To qualify for a license as a child placement agency, the new agency had to meet five requirements. First, it needed to show that a proven need existed for the agency itself. A need existed for Spaulding if it could be shown that other agencies and courts had custody of, but were not placing, certain types of children for adoption. The agency produced information that children legally free for adoption were being cared for in foster homes and institutions. The Board also had in its possession a copy of a special report presented to the Michigan legislature in 1967[2] which indicated that there were 8,000 Michigan children in need of permanent families. Twenty percent, or approximately 1,600, were considered hard-to-place. The report also stated there was no existing avenue in

---

[2]"Report of the Committee on Adoption Procedures" (created by 1966 House resolution no. 417), 1967 *House Journal*, no. 36, pp. 668-670.

Michigan through which permanent families could be found for these children who had been left to grow up in temporary foster homes.

The second requirement for licensing was that the agency establish a sound financial plan which would indicate that it could ensure sufficient and regular funds. Although their funds were neither sufficient or regular, Spaulding had received sufficient donations (as "seed money") to begin operations and, at the time of licensing, was receiving some additional donations to keep the agency operating. The agency also had use of the Spaulding farmhouse and the resources from the rental of some of its farmland which helped provide a small amount of financial support.

The third requirement was the employment of a professionally qualified Director which was filled, following the resignation of Richard Schneider, by the hiring of Kay Donley. The last two requirements, that the Board who received the license in their name be of "good character," and that the agency's program be "conducive to the welfare of children" were characteristic of the participants and the program.

Spaulding's license was granted July 8, 1968, and enabled the agency to begin seeking referrals and recruiting parents as soon as the new Director could begin work.

THE DIRECTOR

The responsibility for finding a Director for the young agency was assumed by Board President, Warner Siebert, and Board Vice-President, Peter Forsythe. They undertook an extensive search for a hightly qualified and innovative social worker who would be able to take the risks the new venture would entail. Kathryn S. (Kay) Donley was identified to the search committee by a faculty member of the University of Michigan School of Social Work where she had received her Master's degree in Social Work in 1965. Her history included the establishment of a pilot project in protective services, a lengthy foster care placement career, and extensive juvenile court practice. Her experience as a child welfare worker, supervisor, and administrator helped convince the Board to hire her.

Initially, the fledgling agency was only able to afford the full-time Director and one part-time social worker with a Bachelor's degree (Sue Schroen, who is still a Spaulding placement worker). When the two social workers arrived at the farmhouse, they faced a considerable amount of physical work to be done before they could begin to place children. The most immediate task was to clean the farmhouse and turn some of its rooms into office area. Work parties using Board, community, and COAC volunteers were orgainzed to help with this task. Once completed, the staff began concentrating on transforming Spaulding's basic philosophy into an innovative and practical program of child placement.

Appendix B

The Structure and Later History of Spaulding For Children

The history of the structure of Spaulding for Children is included here to provide a brief picture of the administrative framework upon which the agency's approach to adoption has been built. As Spaulding evolved from an initially avant-garde adoption agency begun by citizen volunteers into one of the major forces behind the current national movement to find permanent families for children traditionally considered hard-to-place or "unadoptable," so, too, did the pattern of responsibilities for maintaining its operation.

Out of a need to keep pace with changes in the growth of agency activity, the administrative structure of the agency has passed through three significant phases of development. The earliest phase lasted approximately two years. Core leadership was provided by the original members of the Board of Directors. The middle phase, lasting approximately four years, was characterized by continuing expansion of agency reputation and influence within the field of adoption, and the steadily increasing leadership role played by the Director and placement staff. The current phase, the result of a total reorganization and clarification of responsibility for the functions of the agency, evolved out of the need to begin removing total administrative responsibilities from an overburdened placement staff to enable them to concentrate on meeting their ever-increasing placement, post-placement, and training and consultation commitments.

INITIAL ORGANIZATION

As indicated earlier, the agency was founded by two small groups of citizens — one group who felt a need for a small, private adoption agency specializing in placing the kinds of children for whom other agencies were not then finding permanent families, and one made up of friends and acquaintances of Warren Spaulding who wanted to do something special for children. The agency's first Board of Directors was composed of representatives of these two groups and other local residents sympathetic to the interests of waiting children.

The newly established Board created five standing committees: Executive, Planning and Personnel, Finance, Property, and Nominating. (A Public Relations committee was added in 1970.) During the period of the agency's initial organization, the Board of Directors (and particularly its Executive Committee) was the dominant force behind Spaulding policy and activity. The Executive Committee met once each month and occasionally even more frequently. The group articulated an initial philosophy concerning all aspects of the agency's approach to adoption and hired a Director who, in turn, began to hire staff and organize the agency's professional activities.

A five-member Advisory Board, composed of local child-welfare professionals, was also organized by the Board of Directors early in the agency's first year of operation. While it existed, the Advisory Board served a valuable function. It provided the means through which established child welfare professionals became associated with the new agency. The credibility added by their support was significant in increasing Spaulding's acceptance within the child welfare profession. However, after approximately a year, the Advisory Board was dissolved, for more people with professional experience in the child welfare field were elected to the Board of Directors and the existence of a separate but similarly skilled group became unnecessary.

Much of the activity of the Board and staff during this time was directed toward the gradual creation and implementation of a practical working relationship. During most of the agency's first two years of operation, the staff was comprised of the Director and one worker. These individuals necessarily focused their energies on improving their skills in finding and placing the kinds of older and handicapped children not then being placed for adoption by other agencies. Since they did not have the financial resources to hire additional staff, the initial Board of highly committed community and church leaders assumed early responsibility for management activities not directly relaed to the placement of children. The responsibilities of Board and staff were clearly defined and each combined their efforts to improve the quality of all aspects of agency service. Together they determined the desired qualifications of staff, monitored agency programs, assessed program results, and determined and altered program goals. They also determined salaries and fringe benefits and worked to balance the agency's financial affairs. When skills beyond those held by available staff or Board members were needed, the Board recruited volunteers.

Throughout its history, the agency's vitality has always been dependent upon the commitment of its volunteers. This was especially true for the initial fulfillment of clerical and bookkeeping requirements and for the generating of operating expenses during the time when the agency did not have sufficient income from purchase of service fees, donations, and other sources to support its increasingly requested services. Fund-raising projects, organized and carried out by volunteers, became an early and essential part of Spaulding's operation.

The agency's volunteers have ranged from individuals and groups who have undertaken single projects to those who have offered their services on an on-going basis. The most formally organized volunteer group was the Women's Auxiliary, established during the winter of 1969 and composed of a small group of women from the local communities. The Auxiliary was originally organized to help raise money for office supplies, but their function gradually evolved into broad fun-raising and public relations activities. They organized spaghetti suppers, fashion shows, rummage sales, garage sales, and social events for Spaulding families. They also developed the Holiday Card Sale Project, a major source of income for the group. Through these activities they helped sponsor the redecoration of Spaulding's offices, the printing of some of the agency's brochures, the painting of a series of signs marking the way to the agency, and the creation of the agency's parking lot. The Auxiliary's activities also helped establish the agency library and made it possible for staff to attend regional and national workshops. Before they disbanded in December 1972, the group met a major mortgage payment on the farm property and contributed $1,000 to the agency's operating budget.

Despite the dissolution of the Women's Auxiliary, volunteers are still an important part of Spaulding's approach to adoption. Two of the projects begun by the Auxiliary have developed into the agency's most widely known annual social events, involving families, staff, and volunteers. These are the Ice Cream Social, held each summer, and the annual Tree Trimming Party. The Holiday Card Sale, once a major source of income for the agency, continues to serve as a means of widely circulating knowledge concerning the specialized service provided by Spaulding. Holiday and note cards are sold both by direct mail and in specific retail outlets in the Ann Arbor area. Service groups or college students also often take on direct sales responsibilities.

Many local people interested in Spaulding continue to find time to help the agency. Since 1972, the most organized form of volunteerism has been provided by Beta Sigma Phi, an Ann Arbor women's service group which has packaged the Christmas cards and helped with the Ice Cream Social. These volunteer efforts have provided invaluable assistance in carrying out agency activity, have significantly added to public interest in Spaulding, and have further strengthened the agency's credibility in the surrounding communities.

GROWTH

Spaulding's first four years of operation were concentrated on efforts to develop the knowledge and skills needed to place older and handicapped children for adoption, to establish an ever-widening basis for agency credibility, and to develop public and professional awareness of the need for the agency's specialized services. An essential staff task was the creation and maintenance of working relationships with adoption professionals, judges, parents' groups, and local and state child welfare groups. Out of these efforts came the referral of children (some who had been waiting years to be adopted) and the gradual acceptance of the concept of "purchase of service" (whereby the referring agency or court shared some of the costs of Spaulding's specialized adoption services).

As a wider network of working relationships developed, knowledge of the agency spread and increasingly older and more handicapped children were referred to Spaulding. Through accumulated experience, the staff grew more knowledgeable and competent, and continued to refine the process of recruitment and preparation they considered so necessary to the successful establishment and maintenance of adoption placements for such children.

During this time, the staff became more comfortable in their role of confronting and overcoming the attitudes and bureaucratic obstacles hindering adoptive placement. As they did so, a natural but unplanned shift of major responsibility from Board to staff for the day-to-day management of the agency began to occur. Although the staff continued to operate entirely within the philosophy and activity established by the Board, and the high degree of cooperation between Board and staff remained unchanged, the Board gradually assumed less of a guiding function and began supporting and assisting the expanding long and short-term activities of the professional staff. The agency's middle phase of development had arrived.

The next four years were on a time continued growth. Growing awareness of the agency's success among adoption professionals outside

Michigan led to increasing referrals from surrounding states and Canadian provinces. Michigan adoption workers, stimulated by Spaulding's example and the creation of a special project within the Michigan Department of Social Services, began to feel that they, too, might be able to place some of the hard-to-place children on their own caseloads. As these workers moved in the direction of placing older and handicapped children, referrals to Spaulding from within the state logically moved in the direction of increasingly older and handicapped children.

Rapidly increasing demands for Spaulding's services required that a major role of the Board include making contact with individuals and groups in the surrounding communities who might be interested in financially supporting the agency. Since the geographic area served by the agency included the entire state of Michigan, the Board realized that donors in Ann Arbor and Chelsea could not be expected to continue providing total support. A wider financial base was essential. The Board had previously expanded primarily to obtain members who could offer vital management skills but now responded to the agency's financial needs by recruiting members who were willing and able to contact a broader range of potential donors from previously unrepresented parts of the state. By 1971, the original Board of nine members had grown, through several stages, to number 21 members.

The Spaulding Staff
Left to right: Kathy Cavanagh, Mary Jane Dettling, Kay Donley, Sue Schroen, Gerry Sullivan, Jayne Kidney, Ann Feeney, Marty McClatchey.

During this time, the staff also grew in size, reaching their greatest number. By 1973 the staff consisted of a Director, two full-time and one part-time placement workers, a bookkeeper, a case-aide secretary, and a part-time Director of Agency Development responsible for enlisting financial aid in the form of donations and grants from individuals, service groups, and foundations.

Still further growth occurred as the result of crisis conditions within specific placements. During 1971, Spaulding workers seeking to place children found themselves forced to cope, for the first time, with significant numbers of disruptions. In response to the emotional trauma disruption created in workers, the Spaulding staff gradually replaced their more traditional supervisor-supervisee relationships with a system of shared responsibility which they came to call "collegial supervision." This gradually led to a more complete sharing among staff of all major decisions regarding all placements, disruptions, and replacements, and Spaulding's team approach to adoption was born. (For more information on "Teamwork" and "Collegial Supervision," see p. 41.)

The consequence of this total sharing among the social work staff of all placement decisions was a greater feeling of comradery, higher staff morale, and a significant increase in the probability that the most appropriate placement decisions would be made. The resultant improvement in the agency's operations also meant the more tightly-knit and smoothly functioning staff was able to assume even more responsibility for service as well as administrative activities.

With more frequent referral of increasingly older and more handicapped children, and the recognition that the more time-consuming process of sharing responsibility for major decision-making was a necessity when placing such children, the Spaulding staff realized they could never place sufficient numbers of waiting children to meet demand. Neither did they expect their experiences to be spontaneously communicated to others in the field of adoption and thus guarantee the significant changes in attitudes toward the adoptability of these children that were necessary before large numbers of them could be placed with adoptive families.

As a result, Spaulding began, in 1971, to actively seek opportunities to provide training and consultation in the form of workshops, conferences, and seminars. As word of their success spread, more and more agencies requested explanations of "how these kinds of children are placed." In response, the agency's commitment to training and consultation as the most appropriate means of sharing their successful approach to adoption has grown steadily and has reached the point where training and consultation on a national scale now constitute a major portion of the agency's activity.

During this period, the agency's income was supplemented by reimbursements for training and consultation (in addition to income from purchase of service fees, the Child-of-the Month Club, donations, special projects, and an annual holiday appeal for funds). The day-to-day responsibility for Spaulding's budget now rested with the agency's Director and the Finance Committee. Involvement of the total Board for fund-raising activities occurred only in those cases (usually approximately once a year) when the agency's expenses threatened to outdistance cash reserves.

REORGANIZATION

During this period of growth, there was an unspoken acceptance on the part of each Board member that the staff had proven, by their actions, that they could be trusted to adhere to the agency's philosophy and aggressively perform along the lines of the highest professional standards. As long as this remained the case, Board members appeared content to let the staff continue to assume overall responsibility for maintaining the effectiveness of the methods proven successful in the placement of older and handicapped children. There was no clear definition or understanding of the Board's function beyond the agreement that the staff ran the agency, would keep the Board informed of staff activities, and would come to the Board for advice on important issues.

As more and more responsibility for an increasingly larger, more complex, and well-known agency was being assumed by the Director and placement staff, their resources of time and energy became thinly stretched. The theoretical solution to this problem was to reorganize agency responsibilities. Although this was clearly what had to be done, serious practical obstacles existed. With a Board of Directors representing all areas of the state and a team of workers struggling to meet continuously increasing demands on their time, the Board and staff had lost their capacity to meet often enough to provide active commitment to, and shared responsibility for, the operation for the agency.

By early 1974, the Director and the placement staff were not only directing the agency, but shepherding the Board through its affairs, meetings, and agendas. Consensus began to grow among Board and staff that some changes had to be made. After some talk of the need for better committee organization, the issue of change and, more specifically, the clear determination of who had what responsibilities, was referred to the agency's Planning and Personnel Committee for study and recommendations. In early 1974, that committee began what became a yearlong analysis of the various functions of the agency. The intent was two-fold:

to clarify existing responsibilites and to reorganize those responsibilities to produce a more logical, efficient, and equal sharing of the efforts required to plan, implement, and administer agency policy and service. All agency functions were defined and grouped into the eight larger categories of finance, personnel, advocacy/public relations, business operations, placement services, special projects, policy development, and training/consultation.

The analysis, completed in late 1975, underscored what the staff already knew: that they had more responsibility than they could handle and that the Board could and should handle much more responsibility than it had. The recommendations were to create an activist Board of increased size and representation, to increase the coordination between Board members and staff (as well as between the Board members themselves), and to provide the new Board with a thorough orientation to the agency. Recommendations were also made which would limit the responsibilities of the staff to administration and implementation of placement and training activities. It was also indicated that the agency should hire a full-time Director of Agency Development to assume those public relations and 'fund-raising coordination responsibilities supportive of Board and staff.

To increase the size of the Board of Directors while ensuring the close coordination which was necessary if reorganization was to be successful, the old Board structure was replaced by a Council and an Executive Board. The Council Members were made responsible for promoting interest in and support for the agency and for serving on various committees. Continuous and coordinated efforts were made possible by the provision that Council members must represent all major geographic areas within Michigan and that responsibility for each area would belong to "clusters" of 3 to 5 individuals who combined a variety of interests and skills. The Council must meet twice each year. (There are currently 43 Council members serving staggered three year terms. New members are chosen once a year at the agency's annual meeting, vacancies may be filled by appointment, and there is no limit to the total number of members or "clusters.")

A special meeting, organized by the Planning and Personnel Committee, was held in October 1976 to serve as a formal orientation meeting for Council members. Presentations included a history of Spaulding, a review of current grants and special projects, consideration of Council and Executive Board responsibilities, an explanation of the agency's reorganization process (including new job descriptions, added positions, and a clarification of the relationship between Executive Board, Council, and staff), a description of proposed committees and their responsibilities, and a summary of the different kinds of funding sought by the agency.

The Executive Board continued as the policy-making and corporate governing body of the agency. The 11 member Executive Board includes the President (who is also Council President) and ten additional members elected from the Council. (Three non-elected charter members who are original members of the Board, all listed in the Articles of Incorporation, are also members of this Executive Board.) The President and other elected members serve two year renewable terms, one-half of the membership being elected in alternate years. Other executive officers (Vice President, Secretary, and Treasurer) serve for one year renewable terms. Regular Executive Board meetings are held bi-monthly, but special meetings may be called at any time.

Elections occur at the Agency's Annual Meeting now held during the second quarter of the year.[1] Each individual who has contributed financially to the operation of the agency is eligible to vote on Board membership, executive officers, and agency policy. This technique of involving the public in agency policy-making is written into the Spaulding Constitution and By-laws. However, few members have taken advantage of this opportunity and policy-making has been almost totally left up to Board members and agency staff. This has occured in spite of a conscious effort on the part of agency planners to devise a means of offering entry to dissident views from the community.

Redesign of the Executive Board also involved a reorganization of its committee structure, a move which has produced clearer and more specific descriptions of committee responsibilities. Current committees include Planning and Personnel, Finance and Fund-Raising, Membership-Nominating, Public Relations, and Property. Each committee is made up of Council members and other volunteers, and all committees are expected to work closely together whenever necessary. Committee chairmen are appointed by the President of the Executive Board. Temporary or *ad hoc* committees may also be formed as the need arises. (Specific committee responsibilities are listed in the agency's Constitution and By-laws.)

The reorganization of Spaulding for children, effective June 30, 1976, and actually implemented with the first meeting of the new Council and Executive Board on July 28, 1976, leaves the Director free of primary

---

[1]Two of Spaulding's annual meetings have been combined with special programs of public interest focusing on some important aspect of adoption. In 1972, the staff sponsored a workshop, entitled "Discovery," which focused on the problems and efforts of revealing a child's biological heritage to him and his adoptive family. In 1975, the annual meeting included an open forum on "Adoption Disruption." More than 100 people attended, including public and private child welfare agency staff and adoptive parents, some of whom had experienced a disrupted adoption. Both annual meeting programs were planned and conducted by staff and adoptive parents.

responsibility for matters not directly related to the organization and coordination of agency services. Placement staff concentrate on recruiting families, evaluating children, making placement decisions, providing post-placement services, and offering training and consultation.

The reorganization has also resulted in the creation of an additional full-time position, Director of Agency Development. The responsibilities of this position include coordinating public relations and funding efforts and expanding the base of interest and financial support for the agency with the assistance of Council "clusters," Executive Board members, staff, and community volunteers.

Organizational Chart of Spaulding for Children

CONSTITUTION AND BY-LAWS OF SPAULDING FOR CHILDREN

Article I

Name

The name of this corporation shall be Spaulding for Children, a name duly registered by the U.S. Patent Office.

Article II

Purpose

The agency shall seek to undertake by casework and related services the following:

1. To care, treat, and protect children whose parents are unable or unwilling to carry out their child rearing responsibilities.
2. To locate, establish, and maintain foster homes and/or agency homes.
3. To locate, study, and counsel with adoptive parent prospects.
4. To place children in permanent homes through adoption.
5. Other services to children and families as may be deemed appropriate and in keeping with professionally accepted child care philosophy and practices, and without regard for race, color, or creed.
6. Promote activities for quality adoption and related care services.

Article III

Membership

Section 1. The membership of this agency shall consist of interested citizens and organizations who contribute to its support annually. Membership shall be classified according to the annual fiscal contribution to the agency.

A. Regular Membership
B. Contributing Membership
C. Sustaining Membership
D. Supporting Membership
E. Life Membership
F. Sponsoring Organization
G. Charter Member

Section 2. The size of the contribution qualifying for each category shall be set by the Executive Board and may be revised as needed. Charter Members shall be the original members of the Board of Spaulding for Children as listed in the Articles of Incorporation.

Section 3.   The annual business meeting of the agency shall be held in the second quarter of the year at a date and time determined by the Executive Board. A quorum shall consist of those members present, provided that ten (10) days written notice shall have been given the membership.

Article IV

The Council

Section 1.   The Council shall be responsible for promoting interest in and support for Spaulding for Children, related adoption issues, and Spaulding concepts and practices.

Section 2.   Members of the Council shall be elected from representative local areas in Michigan with 3 to 5 members from each area in a balanced variety of membership including adoptive parents, community and civic groups, professionals and interested individuals. Designation of areas and members shall be established and may be altered by the Executive Board in its discretion from time to time.

Council Members shall be elected to serve three year staggered terms.

Council Members shall be elected at the annual meeting from a slate of nominees presented by the Membership-Nominating Committee. Vacancies on the Council shall be filled for the remainder of the unexpired term by appointment of the President with approval of the Executive Board.

Section 3.   Functions of Council members shall be as follows:
  A.   To attend orientation and informational meetings regarding Spaulding for Children.
  B.   To serve individually and with other area members in public relations, community information and development of local community support.
  C.   To attend the Annual Meeting and at least one general membership meeting to advise the Executive Board and bring local interest information to Spaulding.
  D.   To serve on Spaulding committees and the Executive Board upon election or appointment.
  E.   To elect the Executive Board and the Council President, who shall also serve as President of the Executive Board.

Article V

The Executive Board

Section 1. The Executive Board shall be responsible for conducting the affairs of Spaulding for Children, with full power and responsibility as the corporate governing body.

Section 2. The Executive Board shall be the policy making body of the agency.
It shall implement its policies by selecting and hiring an Executive Director to serve as the administrative staff director. The Executive Board shall offer continuing confidence or relieve the Executive Director of duties as necessary.

Section 3. The Executive Board shall be responsible for the fiscal affairs of the agency. It shall approve the operating budget and all capital expenditures. It shall approve a general policy for the investments of the funds of the agency. It shall designate depositories for all funds of the agency. It shall provide appropriate bonds for those officers and employees handling Agency funds. All checks, drafts, or other orders for the payment of money, notes, or other evidences of indebtedness shall be signed by such officers, agency or agents of the agency, and in such manner as such shall from time to time be determined by resolution of the Executive Board. The Executive Board shall be responsible for the program and financial affairs of auxiliaries, organizations, subsidiaries and groups related to their agency.

Section 4. The Executive Board shall be composed of:
  A. The President
  B. Ten (10) additional members to be elected at the annual business meeting from Council membership from a slate presented by the Membership-Nominating Committee. The President and Executive Board Members shall serve two years renewable terms, one-half the members to be elected in alternate years.
  C. The Charter Members, who shall serve with full Executive Board privileges and responsibilities, in addition to the eleven (11) elected members.

Section 5. Vacancies occurring between annual business meetings of the agency shall be filled by the remaining members of the Executive Board at any regular or special meeting from names placed in nomination by Membership-Nominating Committees.

Section 6. Regular meetings of the Executive Board shall be held bi-monthly at a time and place that it shall designate. Special meetings may be called by the President or on request of any three members of the Board provided that five (5) days written notice is given prior to the meeting. Only such business as is stated in writing in the call may be transacted. Such notice may be waived in writing or by the unanimous vote of the Board. Six (6) members shall constitute a quorum.

Article VI

The Officers of the Executive Board

Section 1. The officers of the Executive Board shall be a President, a Vice-President, a Secretary, and a Treasurer, and such other officers as the Executive Board shall from time to time determine, all to be elected by the Executive Board, except the President, elected by the Council to serve as President of both the Council and the Executive Board. Terms of office for all officers except the President shall be one year. Officers may be elected to succeed themselves, as long as they are members of the Executive Board.

Section 2. Duties of the President shall be as follows:
  A. To preside at all meetings of the Council and Executive Board.
  B. To be a member ex-officio of all committees.
  C. To present a report on the work of the agency at the annual business meeting.

Section 3. The Vice-President of the Executive Board shall serve as chairman when the regularly elected President is unable to perform such duties.

Section 4. Duties of the Secretary shall be:
  A. To keep for permanent record all minutes of Council and Executive Board meetings.
  B. To accept and file all committee minutes.
  C. To notify all members of the Executive Board in writing of regular and specially called meetings of the Executive Board at least five (5) days in advance of the meeting, and in case of special meetings, the purpose for which the meeting is called.
  D. To notify all members of the Council in writing at least ten (10) days in advance of the annual meeting and such other

meetings as shall be set for the Council by the Executive Board or by the Council at the annual meeting.

Section 5. Duties of the Treasurer shall be as follows:
  A. To keep an account of all receipts and expenditures of the agency.
  B. To submit, at the close of each fiscal year, a financial statement to the Executive Board which shall be audited by a Certified Public Accountant.
  C. To collect interest, rents, fees, and other income or credits to which the agency is entitled.
  D. To make expenditures in accordance within the provisions set forth by the Executive Board.
  E. At the discretion of the Executive Board to have the authority to sign for the Executive Board the transfer of all stocks, bonds, mortgages, and other evidences of indebtedness bought or sold in transaction concerning the endowment portfolio of the agency.

With consent of the Executive Board, the Treasurer may delegate any of the above duties to a properly bonded agency or individual.

Committees

Section 1. Committee Chairmen shall be appointed by the President with approval of the Executive Board. Committee members shall be selected by Committee Chairmen from Council membership and interested individuals. Committees are responsible to the Executive Board to recommend activities, programs, projects, etc. for Board consideration and approval. The President shall act in timely fashion to insure necessary communication and action, and may request committee chairmen to present reports or attend Board meetings as appropriate. Committees shall record minutes of all meetings which shall be presented to the Executive Board to become part of the permanent record.

Section 2. Planning and Personnel Committee:
shall be responsible for general planning and direction for Spaulding and shall keep the Executive Board and Council apprised of trends in the field, and issues in related child care matters. They shall be responsible for maintaining current personnel policies and salary ranges, and the preparation of job descriptions. The Executive Director shall serve ex-officio on the Planning and Personnel Committee.

Section 3. Finance and Fund-Raising Committee:
shall be responsible for general financial guidance in preparation of

budgets, fiscal reports, financial projections, and other pertinent documents. They shall be responsible for fund-raising, including guidance as to feasible sources or projects to raise necessary monies to carry out agency plans. The Treasurer shall serve ex-officio on the Finance and Fund-Raising Committee.

Section 4.　Membership-Nominating Committee:
shall be responsible for Council, Executive Board and general membership development. The Committee shall present appropriate slates of nominees as established by the Executive Board.

Section 5.　Public Relations Committee:
shall be responsible for community information and advocacy relating to issues of concern to Spaulding and shall prepare information on Spaulding for Children, adoption and related issues for agency use and dissemination.

Section 6.　Property Committee:
shall be responsible for property maintenance and matters regarding general farm concerns and local relations.

Section 7.　The President, with the approval of the Executive Board, may appoint such ad-hoc committees and advisory committees as from time shall be necessary.

Article VIII

Staff

Section 1.　The Board shall employ an Executive Director, who, subject to the control and direction of the Executive Board, shall have general charge, oversight, and direction of the affairs and business of the agency, and shall be its responsible managing head. The Executive Director shall have authority to sign on behalf of the organization all necessary papers in connection with guardianship, placement, or adoption proceedings; and shall have authority to make expenditures within the approved agency budget that have been delegated by the Executive Board. The Executive Director or a delegate shall attend all meetings of the Executive Board and its committees. The Executive Director shall be the liaison between the Executive Board and the staff.

Section 2. The Executive Director's responsibilities are as follows:

A. To plan and participate in the formulation of policies and procedures.

B. To organize the agency's services and coordinate the work of the Executive Board and the staff.

C. Either directly or by delegation, to employ and direct staff, provide supervision, training, and give professional leadership in the field of the agency's service.

D. To prepare budgets and reports, and keep the Executive Board informed of the agency's operations and programs.

E. To represent the agency professionally in the community and to interpret the agency's services.

F. To help the Executive Board members appropriately perform their roles.

Article IX

The Executive Board shall provide a proper corporate seal.

Article X

The Fiscal Year

The fiscal year shall be the calendar year.

Article XI

Amendments

These By-Laws may be amended by a two-thirds vote of the members present at any stated meeting of the Executive Board, provided that a ten (10) day notice of the proposed change has been given to every Executive Board Member.

Article XII

Parliamentary Authority

All meetings shall be governed by Robert's Rules of Order, Newly Revised, in all matters not inconsistent with provisions of the Articles of Incorporation, this Constitution and By-Laws, or appropriate law.

Article XIII

Spaulding Auxiliaries and Local Interest Groups

Any local auxiliary or Spaulding interest groups shall present minutes of all meetings to the Executive Board. These interest groups shall conduct only such programs and projects for the benefit of Spaulding for Children as shall be approved by the Executive Board. Proceeds of all projects shall be deposited with the Treasurer of the Spaulding Executive Board, who shall maintain records, and such necessary special accounts as the Executive Board shall from time to time determine, and shall make only those disbursements approved by the Executive Board.

Article XIV

Dissolution

Upon dissolution any remaining assets of Spaulding for Children may be sold or transferred in kind and such assets or their proceeds thereafter transferred to any successor corporation or other organization, provided that any organization to which assets are transferred be non-profit and qualified under Section 501 (c) (3) of the Internal Revenue Code as amended as tax exempt; such money, property, or other assets to be used solely to provide care, counseling, homes, education, training, or other social services to children.

Effective date: June 30, 1976

Appendix **C**

Outlines of Spaulding Inquiry Materials

Since the inception of Spaulding for Children, its placement staff have conducted adoption inquiry meetings in order to present up-to-date general and specific information about adoption to the public. At various times in their history, the agency's workers have combined, separated, and re-combined the general and specific aspects of adoption into either one meeting or two. Included here are samples of the comprehensive topical outlines used by the Spaulding staff for their Public Adoption Meetings (PAM), their more specific Spaulding Adoption Meetings (SAM), and their Day Long Group Meetings (DLGM).

These outlines were developed by Spaulding staff to ensure consistent coverage of information from one meeting to the next. The outlines for PAM and SAM are no longer used in the form presented here. The information from both meetings is now presented by Spaulding workers at single group sessions called Spaulding Public Adoption Meetings (SPAM). The Day Long Group Meeting (DLGM) is no longer part of the Spaulding preparation process.

PUBLIC ADOPTION MEETING (PAM)

PAM materials were presented at the Spaulding farm on Sunday afternoons to provide general adoption information to families who had either responded to agency newspaper recruitment efforts for specific children, called the agency for general information about adoption, or been in personal contact with a Spaulding worker who had suggested they attend.

Public Adoption Meeting Outline

I. Introduction: Welcome to Spaulding for Children.
   We will be telling you about different kinds of adoption, the various adoption agencies, and the kinds of children who are available through these agencies.

   A. Why are we having this meeting?
      1. You need to know the kinds of children who are available so that you can make a good decision about adoption.
      2. We are a small agency and have few caseworkers to cover the entire state. We have done a lot of thinking and planning and have decided this is the best and fastest way to give you the information you will need to decide about adoption.
   B. The Adoption picture has changed.
      1. There are very few babies available.
      2. There are an enormous number of children needing families but they are not healthy pre-schoolers.
   C. At the end of this meeting, we will give you some material to take home and read.
      1. Send back the enclosed card if you are interested in coming to our second meeting.
      2. The second meeting will be on a Wednesday evening in 2½ weeks and we will spend about two hours describing the kinds of children we place and how families work with these children.
      3. If you decide to come to our second meeting but cannot come to the next one, tell us that on the card or ask to be seen individually if that is what you wish.

II. Building a family
   A. What is a parent?
      A person responsible for the loving care and guidance of a child. It is the loving care that makes a child one's own.
   B. There are two ways to bring a child into your family.
      1. Birth
      2. Adoption
   C. What is adoption?
      Accepting as your own a child not born to you.
   D. Why do people adopt?
      1. They may not be able to have children of their own.

2. They may wish to provide a home for a child who might not otherwise have one.
3. They may be concerned about over-population but still like to have a family.

III. Why fewer babies now?
  A. Fewer released to agencies
    1. Changing culture — more unwed mothers keeping babies.
    2. Birth control methods better known and used.
    3. Abortion reform has changed the picture.
  B. More families interested in adoption
  C. No foreseeable change in this pattern

IV. Who are the "available" children?
  A. Those *released* by their parents:
  A parent or parents asks an agency to plan for the adoptive placement of their child. (This legal release of the child to the agency is witnessed by the court.)
    1. Most are young; a few are older.
    2. Some are not placed due to physical and mental handicaps.
  B. Those available through court action:
  The Juvenile Court permanently terminates all parental rights when that action is found (by a full investigation of the facts) to be in the best interest of the child.
    1. Most enter the foster care system during their school years.
    2. Many have special problems as a result of their life experiences.

V. Why are children removed from their parents?
  A. *Released* children are not removed; the parent(s) have *voluntarily* decided to give up their parental rights. Most of these released children are given up in infancy and are quickly placed with waiting families. Only a few released children will remain unplaced because of physical, mental, or emotional handicaps.
  B. Children who are available through court procedures are usually removed because of neglect or abuse by their parents (being left without food, clothing, or supervision repeatedly, not being given medical attention, being physically mistreated, etc). They usually go to foster homes where a family licensed

by an agency agrees to provide temporary care for the child. The family usually receives some form of payment. Thus, a foster child may live with a family for any length of time, but is not adopted by them, and may be removed from the home by agency plan or at the family's request.
C. Most of the children waiting for adoption in Michigan are living in foster homes. Some have been there for several years. Most have moved repeatedly from foster home to foster home. It isn't unusual for us to see a boy of 12 who has lived in four different foster homes over the past five years of his life.
D. Some of the available children waiting for adoption are in institutions or group care homes. Many times this is because the agency has run out of foster homes, or because the child needs very special care that is available in this kind of facility.

VI. What are those children like?
  A. Some are like the children you have at home or know in your neighborhood, but there is a difference — they have life experiences other children have never known.
  B. Some are confused by many moves.
  C. Some distrust adults.
  D. Some feel they were separated from their families because they were bad. Like children who experience death, they believe they were bad and their parent(s) left them because that was what they deserved.
  E. Some have a "spotty" kind of maturity, being either "little old people" or immature "babies."

VII. What is adoption?
  A. For the child it means:
    1. I belong to someone
    2. I have a family and a home (they belong to me)
    3. Same last name as the rest of the family
    4. No one can take me away
    5. We're stuck with each other
  B. For the family it means:
    1. A permanent relationship — unlike foster care — no one can take the child away.
    2. The child and parent(s) have the same rights as a biological family.
       a. inheritance
       b. permanence

c. can make decisions regarding their lives and their future together
3. Similar to marriage
   a. adjusting takes time
   b. there are good times and bad times
   c. it is a commitment that is total

VIII. Myths about adoption
   A. First some facts:
      1. Policies are not laws.
      2. Most agencies have radically changed their policies in recent years.
      3. Many still have rigid policies, however.
         a. some designed to assure that they place the child with the "best" family ("correct" spacing of children, no working mothers, etc.).
         b. some designed to reduce the vast numbers of parents looking for children (must be infertile, must have been married a specific length of time, and in some cases must be of a certain religion).
      4. Above all, remember that policies change and vary — call and ask.
   B. Myths:
      1. Must be of a certain religion
      2. Must have a certain level of income, amount of savings, debts, etc.
      3. Must be married a specific length of time
      4. No working mothers
      5. No apartment or trailer living
      6. No handicapped parents
      7. No problems in past or present family group
      8. A need to match the age of the child within the age range of the parents' other children
   C. Agencies have also changed ways of dealing with families:
      1. Housekeeping standards — there are now fewer snoopy social workers.
      2. Contacts with workers are not as formal as they once were.
      3. Contacts with other agencies are encouraged prior to actual application.

D. Myths and fears about the status of the adopted child:
1. Biological parents can "snatch" him back at any time.
2. The adoptive family cannot move after adoption.
3. The agency will conceal important information about the child.

IX. General adoption process
A. Application to a licensed agency.
An application may be filed with any licensed agency that serves your area. A medical examination and certain other documents will be necessary.
B. Interviews between the family and an adoption worker.
Some interviews will be held in groups, some individually. During the interviews, people discuss their feelings about adoption, their own experiences, and talk about being parents. Interviews are held over a period of a few weeks to a few months.
C. A decision about adopting a specific child.
The adoption workers locate a child the family may be interested in adopting. The workers tell the family about the child and his background. The family decides whether they want to consider adopting the child.
D. Filling out the legal papers.
1. *The Petition to Adopt* is a legal document requesting that the Court place a specific child with the adoptive family. It includes the name given to the child by the adopting family.
2. *The Consent* is a legal document filed by the agency in which the agency agrees to the adoptive placement.
3. *The Order Terminating Rights.* After the Court examines the Petition and Consent papers, finds them in order, and agrees to the placement, the judge signs the Order Terminating Rights (OTR) which ends all the rights of all prior persons and agencies and makes the child a ward of the Court in the county of residence of the adoptive family until the adoption is confirmed. Now the child may be placed in his new home.
E. Service and consultation by the placement agency to the family (usually for a period of one year).

The placing agency will maintain routine contact with the family until the adoption is confirmed.

F. Recommendation by the agency to the Juvenile Court that the adoption be made final.

After a time (usually between six months and a year after the placement), the family's adoption workers, in the name of the placing agency, recommend that the adoption be finalized.

G. Signing of the Order of Confirmation by the judge.

The Order of Confirmation makes the child permanently and legally a member of the adopting family.

X. Where do you apply?

A. Private agencies (for infants)

1. The chief source of children; those released by unwed mothers.

2. The vast majority of available infants are found here.

3. They usually charge fees which vary according to the agency, the income of the family, and the kind of child being adopted.

4. There is usually a long waiting list.

(Hand out the brochure "Adopting a Child in Michigan").

B. Public Agencies (for older and handicapped children)

1. Some Juvenile Courts have placement programs.

2. Every county has a local office of the Michigan Department of Social Services (MDSS).

3. No fees are charged parents through MDSS or Juvenile Courts.

4. Children available through court action.

a. usually of school age.

b. history of family problems.

C. Direct Consent or "Private" adoption

(Note: eliminated as a legal possibility in Michigan except for close relatives as of January, 1976)

Families need:

1. An attorney

2. A home study by an agency (sometimes done by a court worker).

Although families have successfully adopted in this way, it entails risk because the biological mother may change her mind

356 *Chaos, Madness, and Unpredictability*

before, during, or after the placement. It also entails technical risk because it is easy for people to unknowingly break the law regarding how contact with the biological mother is made, who made the specific arrangements, and when those arrangements were made. Families need good advice from the court or agency doing the home study and competent legal counsel. Always check with your own local Juvenile Court for details.

XI. Fees

Fees charged by adoption agencies vary. Some make no charge. All agencies will ask the adopting family to pay the Court filing fee which varies from $14 to about $30 (in Michigan) depending upon the family's county of residence.

XII. Similarities and differences
   A. Whether families are built through birth or adoption, there are similarities:
      1. Full legal rights.
      2. Full responsibility for raising a child.
      3. The satisfaction of helping a child grow.
   B. There are also differences:
      1. From the time the child joins the family, he must know he is adopted. He has that right.
      2. The family must recognize and accept the child's past.
      3. The family must take the responsibility for helping their child feel comfortable with and proud of his heritage.

XIII. Post-placement services

All agencies are available for consultation if any questions arise after placement. Adoptive parents may wish to join one of the various adoptive parents' clubs or organizations available throughout the state.

XIV. Spaulding For Children
   A. Do children live at the agency?
      Children are not housed at the agency but are referred for placement with Spaulding families.
   B. Where do we get children?

1. Children are referred by agencies who have not found families for them.
2. Children are referred by public agencies and are either older children (over 11 years) or handicapped.

C. Why does Spaulding exist?
  1. To be sure that an agency exists which focuses its entire attention on the placement of older and handicapped children waiting for adoption.
  2. To apply pressure to the existing child placement system and to convince agencies that a family exists for nearly every child if enough time, energy, and commitment are used to find that family.

D. Who should apply?
  1. The agency needs families for children already known to us or who will probably be referred to us.
  2. The agency doesn't accept applications from families interested only in the kinds of children we never see.
  3. We discourage people from asking many questions about the children presently waiting. We hope you will be interested in serveral of the children recently placed (use examples below).
     a. Many of our children presently available will be adopted by families we are already working with.
     b. An example:Tommy, age 12; handsome, affectionate, acts like a typical 8 year old. He will probably be headed for a specific family while you are yet deciding if you are seriously interested in adopting an older child.

E. Describe some children who were adopted in the past six months.
  1. Use balanced examples.
  2. Use photographs.

XV. Wrap-up
  A. Review procedure to follow if they are interested in adopting through Spaulding.
  B. Help them reach any other agency if they decide Spaulding does not have the kinds of children they are interested in adopting.

SPAULDING ADOPTION MEETING (SAM)

The SAM was developed as a body of follow-up information for families who had previously attended a Public Adoption Meeting or who were already aware of the more general PAM information, but needed specific information about Spaulding's operation and placements.

Spaulding Adoption Meeting Outline

I. Introduction:
   A. Why we don't talk with you today about *all* the children who are available.
      1. Most children now needing placement will hopefully be placed even before you are ready for placement. There is a lot yet to think about.
      2. There may be some specific children we are currently recruiting for. Now is the time to talk about them.

II. Why do parents adopt?
   A. Out of a sense of uniqueness: doing a job few others can do.
   B. Because children are available: they are . . . they live . . . they need parents.
   C. Because some parents feel special things about certain children.
      1. Some parents know a child who needs special help and feel comfortable in the presence of that child.
      2. Some parents feel they have something to offer such a child.
   D. To fill a gap in their family.
      1. To balance the sexes.
      2. To fill age gaps.
   E. To fulfill a humanitarian impulse
      1. Concerned about over-population
      2. "Do-gooders"
   F. Because they like children and want more than they have.
   G. Because something is lacking in their lives.
   H. (Can the audience think of other reasons?)

III. The rewards of adoption:
   Motivation and needs can fit together.

IV. Common expectations of rewards for the parents:
   A. Gratitude . . . change . . . improvement . . . affection.

    B. Stengthening a marriage.
    C. Completing a family.
    D. Getting community or family approval.
    E. Self-satisfaction . . . heirs . . . companions . . . .
    F. Other rewards?

V. Common reactions of parents:
    A. "We will love the child."
    B. "We won't get angry with the child."
    C. "We won't make the same mistakes as the child's biological parents."
    D. "We won't make the same mistakes as the child's foster parents."
    E. "We will feel the same way about this child as about our other children."
    F. "What will happen if it doesn't work out?"
    G. "How can we avoid being disappointed?"

VI. Description of the kinds of children Spaulding places:
    A. Most of the children are multiply handicapped.
    B. Not many of our children are only physically handicapped.
    C. Their handicaps often prevent accurate psychological testing.
    D. They are as different and diverse as other children.
    E. We can't be sure of what you can handle . . . how can you know? . . . how can you help us know?
    F. There is no guarantee of success, just as with biological children.

VII. Children we have recently placed:
(Note: These children were used at different times in Spaulding's history as "current" examples of actual placements. The effort was always to use specific examples of individual children placed within the previous six months to assure that the children were representative of children then available.)
    A. Timmy, age 9
       — handsome
       — potentially dependent as an adult
       — educationally handicapped
       — physically handicapped
       — hyperactive
       — brain-damaged
       — learning problems
       — resources needed: special education; psychological testing

B. Donnie, age 10
   — background of neglect; removed from home at age 5
   — emotional problems
   — importance of permanence
   — commitment needed
   — rewards available
   — resources needed: supportive Spaulding worker (previous adoption disrupted); parents' own strong convictions about themselves as competent; previous adoptive experience helpful, but no guarantee.
C. Morgan, age 4
   — very physically appealing
   — partially dependent as an adult
   — cerebral palsy
   — educational handicap: slow and non-motivated
   — resources needed: Crippled Children's Commission; University Hospital (University of Michigan); Rackham Program for Pre-School Physically Handicapped Children (Ann Arbor).
D. Meg, age 15
   — immature — acts much younger than 15
   — minor physical problems
   — educational problems — mildly retarded, is a "question-mark" child with both emotional and educational problems
   — requires integrated classroom
   — potentially independent as an adult
E. Tom, age 11
   — emotional problems: shy, insecure, immature
   — slow; requires an integrated classroom
   — uncoordinated
   — probably brain-damaged
   — hyperactive
   — his previous foster home placement was very problematic which may be predictive of future difficulties
F. Ann and Carl, ages 8 and 9
   — school problems
   — "borderline" functioning (culturally deprived? slow?)
   — foster home problems (over-protective parents assumed children were incapable of learning)
   — may be partially dependent in adulthood

VIII. Wrap-up
   A. Where do you go from here?
   B. What do you do next?

THE DAY LONG GROUP MEETING (DLGM)

For approximately three years, the Day Long Group Meeting constituted Spaulding's final phase of family preparation. The meetings, usually between a Spaulding worker and four or five prospective adoptive families, served to allow workers to re-cap important information presented earlier in the preparation process. In addition, the meetings gave parents the opportunity to hear the attitudes and responses of other families and to ask questions.

Day Long Group Meeting Outline

I. Adoption
   Similarities and differences between biological and adopted children.

II. Questions adoption raises for children:
   A. "Where did I come from?" (This is a concern for both the adopted and biological children of an adopting family).
   B. "What happened to my first parents?"
   C. "Were they bad people?"

III. Telling history
   A. "Cover stories:" children's versions of who they are, where they came from, and why they are in a specific family; prepared with the help of their parents or workers for family members, neighbors, school staff, and playmates.
   B. In telling history, workers and families must consider how much the child knows, how much he should know, when and where to get missing information, and who should provide help.

IV. Presentations
   A. What kind of information you will get.
   B. A discussion of when and how biological children should be involved in the early stages and later.
   C. A description of "showings" in which the child may know or may not know what is going on ("blind" and "known" showings).

V. Placement problems
   A. Separating "kid" problems from adoption problems.

B. The bicycle syndrome: a discussion of what really happens when an adopted child does not express more than superficial gratitude or momentary interest in the material objects adoptive parents buy to convince the child that they love him and see him as a part of their family.

C. Old ghosts remembered and revered: how to handle the child's remembered past.

D. Heredity: a discussion of the child's and family's fears that the child will turn out like his biological parents.

E. A lack of affection from the child.

F. A lack of attachment on the part of the child.

G. How to deal with problems created by gaping holes in the child's past history.

H. Ambivalence: helping the child, family, and worker deal with the fact that they may feel differently about the same event (like the adoption itself) at different times.

I. Dealing with the parents' naive expectations of instant and uninterrupted love from the child.

J. Dealing with the school: helping parents with registration, records, with negotiation for classroom placement; with personality or achievement tests.

VI. Messages and meanings to and from parents:
  A. "I hate you . . . I hate Billy . . . Ann . . . the social worker . . ."
  B. "I'm ready to go to a new family now."
  C. "He doesn't really seem to care."
  D. "I seem to be telling her the same thing over and over again."
  E. "If I could only know what he is thinking."

VII. Getting and giving help (making best use of):
  A. Friends
  B. Relatives
  C. Other adoptive parents
  D. Workers

VIII. Disruption possibilities:
  A discussion of the causes of adoption disruptions; worker and family panic reactions.

IX. Measuring success:
  A discussion of when and how the child and the parents will know if the adoption is working.

Appendix D

Resources
for Adoption
Workers and Parents

RESOURCES FOR ADOPTION
WORKERS AND PARENTS

The following resource section is included for agencies and families who would like further information or assistance with parenting children with specific handicaps. These organizations may be able to help families solve specific problems, and frequently are able to provide up-to-date lists of parents who are able and willing to help other parents or adoption programs with mutual problems. The national headquarters of each organization is included. It is also suggested that individuals consult the white pages of the telephone book for state and local chapters of these organizations, and the yellow pages under "Social Service and Welfare Organizations" for other locally available resources and organizations.

GENERAL ADOPTION INFORMATION

AASK (Aid to Adoption of Special Kids)
3530 Grand Ave.
Oakland, California 94611
(415) 451-1748

A non-profit organization which promotes the adoption of older and handicapped children throughout the United States by serving as an information exchange between licensed adoption agencies and adoptive parents. Although it must rely upon contributions from private citizens for financial support, AASK also tries to meet requests for financial aid from parents who adopt "special" children.

COAC (The Council on Adoptable Children)
125 E. 23rd St.
New York, N.Y. 10010
(212) 677-6830

COAC is a citizen's group with many local chapters which assists interested people in adopting older and handicapped children. The group refers prospective parents to adoptive agencies, helps them cut through red tape, acquaints them with the requirements of caring for a child with a specific handicap, and introduces them to others who have adopted similar children.

North American Center of Adoption
67 Irving Place
N.Y., N.Y. 10017
(212) 254-7410

The North American Center on Adoption, a project of the Child Welfare League of America, was established in 1975 to address, on a national level, those obstacles which have traditionally prevented children from being placed for adoption. The Center exists as a major information bank for many aspects of adoption, including publicizing children, recruiting families, training staff, supporting legislation, and establishing funding sources. In addition, the Center provides rental films on the adoption of older and handicapped children and offers examples of successful fund-raising and publicity efforts. Other assistance can be offered to parents' groups and adoption professionals.

Since early 1975 the Center has also housed ARENA, The Adoption Resource Exchange of North America. More information on ARENA may be found in Chapter 20.

Specific information about adoption laws, requirements, and procedures can be obtained by writing to your Department of Social Welfare, Adoption Division. With few exceptions, these offices are located in your state capitol.

SPAULDING PUBLICATIONS

Older and Handicapped Children are Adoptable: The Spaulding Approach

A short handbook describing the methods used by Spaulding for Children for placing older and handicapped children for adoption, preparing families to adopt these children, and providing services to these families after placement. Copies of this handbook are available from Spaulding for Children, Box 337, Chelsea, Michigan 48118, for $2.00. (313) 475-2500.

Looking Back on Disruption

A short handbook originally produced by Spaulding for Children for adoption workers describing the child's, family's, and worker's reactions to disruption and the worker's responsibility before, during, and after the disruption occurs. Copies of this handbook are available from Spaulding for Children, Box 337, Chelsea, Michigan 48118, for $1.00. (313) 475-2500.

SPECIFIC HANDICAPS

Blindness

National Federation of the Blind
218 Randolph Hotel Building,
Des Moines, Iowa 50309
(515) 243-3169

Local organizations for the blind usually provide job placement, training, physical restoration, rehabilitation, teaching, and counseling for persons over 16 years of age. Information regarding children under 16 years and special services such as leader dogs are also available. The Social Security Administration (check telephone book for local office) also provides financial assistance to the blind.

Cancer

National Headquarters,
American Cancer Society
77 3rd Ave.
New York, New York 10017
(212) 371-2900

Local Cancer Society units must provide information, counseling, and transportation to and from treatment centers, as well as cancer dressings and a loan program of hospital equipment such as beds, wheel chairs, and walkers. Local units may also provide medication, visiting rehabilitation programs (such as a "Reach to

Recovery" program for breast cancer patients, usually staffed by mastectomy volunteers), Pap smear clinics, nursing evaluation visits, home health visits, and public and professional educational programs and literature to communities. They may also conduct self-help groups for patients and their families.

Some states also have Leukemia Societies or Children's Leukemia Foundations. Although services offered vary widely, they may include counseling, out-patient prescription medication programs, blood distribution programs, equipment loan programs, X-Ray therapy programs, and hospital emergency programs. Local parents' groups, in many areas known as "Lamp Lighter," provide peer support counseling for other parents or friends of young people with leukemia.

Cerebral Palsy

United Cerebral Palsy Association, Inc.
66 East 34th St.
New York, N.Y. 10016
(212) 481-6300

Services provided by local centers (either directly or through referral) may include medical care, therapy, recreation, social activities, parent guidance, psychological testing, counseling, day care, and group play experiences.

Cleft Lip and Palate

Children with this disability need extensive and well coordinated medical services. It is advised that these children be enrolled in the cleft lip and palate clinic at the nearest leading university affiliated medical center. County health departments and other organizations such as National Easter Seal Society may offer assistance to low income families for whom necessary medical treatments create financial hardship. Contact local speech or cleft palate clinics for addresses of parents' groups, or contact:

Dr. Gary Smiley
Secretary, American Cleft Palate Assn.
School of Dentistry
University of North Carolina
Chapel Hill, North Carolina 27514

Crippled Children/Birth Defects

National Easter Seal Society
for Crippled Children and Adults
2023 West Ogden Avenue
Chicago, Illinois 60612
(312) 243-8400

Local chapters may provide information, consultation, and referral for physically handicapped children and adults. Services may also include a summer camp for children, club and recreational programs for all age groups, loan equipment, assistance with transportation, and payment of diagnostic fees. However, handicaps served can vary in each center.

National Foundation — March of Dimes (Birth Defects)
P.O. Box 2000
White Plains, New York 10602

The March of Dimes is concerned with the prevention and treatment of congenital malformations or defects of body function or chemistry present at birth. They also fund programs for general research and patient care, as well as provide public and professional health education. Local chapters may provide direct or referral assistance, direct aid, prenatal care, genetic counseling and diagnosis, and treatment. They may also sponsor scholarships in related health fields.

Cystic Fibrosis

Cystic Fibrosis Foundation
3379 Peachtree Road, N.E.
Atlanta, Georgia 30326
(404) 262-1100

The Cystic Fibrosis Foundation supports research and public education and assists parents of cystic fibrosis patients to obtain equipment and drugs. Local offices are located in most counties.

Deafness

International Association of Parents of the Deaf
814 Thayer Avenue
Silver Spring, Maryland 20910
(301) 585-5400

Local Hearing and Speech Centers usually offer educational programs, parent and professional workshops, hearing aid evaluation, otological screening, therapy, and counseling to the hard-of-hearing.

Diabetes

American Diabetes Association
1 West 48th St.
New York, N.Y. 10017
(212) 541-4310

Juvenile Diabetes Foundation
7525 N.W. 74th Ave.
Miami, Florida 33132
(305) 888-3437

Both the Association and the Foundation disseminate scientific knowledge concerning diabetes to the medical profession and diabetics. Local chapters may identify individual diabetics so they may be properly treated. They may also promote medical research, counsel diabetics, sponsor public educational programs, and support summer camps for diabetic children.

Emotional Disturbance (also Emotionally Impaired)

Resources available for these children do not generally specialize in just the problems of the emotionally disturbed child. Local, country, and state public and private mental health centers, treatment centers, child guidance centers, and psychiatric hospitals can usually help with these problems. Local and university libraries usually have directories of services available to children and adults within their area.

There is no national organization presently established to cover all aspects of emotional disturbance. As of this writing, the state level Association for Emotionally Disturbed Children, in Michigan, offers perhaps the most complete list of available national resources.

Michigan Association for Emotionally Disturbed Children
23555 N. W. Highway
Southfield, Michigan 48075
(313) 356-2566

A citizen's organization which provides public education, community planning, assistance to children's facilities, support for training, and service to parents.

National Society for Autistic Children
169 Tampa Avenue
Albany, New York 12206
(518) 489-7375

This group assists families in the care and education of their autistic children, promotes public awareness and diagnosis of autism, and supports training and education for teachers and professionals.

National Association for Mental Health, Inc.
1800 North Kent Street
Arlington, Virginia 22200
(703) 528-6405

The Association seeks continuous improvement and the expansion of services for the mentally ill at federal, state, and community levels; holds conferences and workshops; publishes newsletters, bulletins, and pamphlets; provides referral services for treatment and information; and is a source of information for professionals.

Epilepsy

Epilepsy Foundation of America
1828 L. Street, N.W.
Washington, D.C. 20036
(202) 293-2930

Local chapters may offer research, diagnostic, and information resources.

Heart Disease

American Heart Association
7320 Greenville Ave.
Dallas, Texas
(214) 750-5300

Local chapters are usually able to provide information, counseling, and referral services to cover the surgical, nutritional, vocational, rehabilitation, and educational (home teaching) needs of children with congenital heart disease or rheumatic fever.

Learning Disabilities

Association for Children with Learning Disabilities
4156 Library Road
Pittsburgh, Pennsylvania 15234
(412) 341-1515

Local chapters are usually able to provide general information and consultation as well as a child advocate and referral service for parents whose children need services beyond those mandated by Special Education laws.

Mental Retardation (Also Mental Impairment)

National Association for Retarded Citizens
2709 Avenue E. East
Arlington, Texas 76011
(817) 261-4961

Local chapters may provide educational, social, recreational, and rehabilitational services, as well as diagnostic assessment and treatment services to the mentally retarded. They may also provide counseling, parent volunteer "buddy systems" for parents wishing assistance, nursery schools, and assistance for mentally retarded adults.

Multiple Sclerosis

National Multiple Sclerosis Society
205 E. 42nd St.
New York, N.Y. 10010
(212) 986-3240

Local chapters may operate a multiple sclerosis clinic and may provide information, counseling, referral, and transportation services, medical supplies, an orthopedic equipment loan program, and funds for research. They may also offer educational, social, and recreational programs to individuals with multiple sclerosis, including a volunteer program to help these persons become aware of available services and "contact" persons in their community. Although not generally considered a childhood disease, some cases have been reported under age 20.

Muscular Dystrophy

Muscular Dystrophy Association of America, Inc.
810 7th Ave.
New York, New York 10019
(212) 586-0808

Local chapters may support research, public education, and patient services, as well as provide medical care and supportive services.

Renal (Kidney) Failure

National Kidney Foundation
116 East 27th Street
New York, N.Y. 10016
(212) 889-2210

Local chapters may establish and maintain steroid-type drug banks, provide grants for research, promote professional, public, and parent education, and provide diagnostic and referral services.

MANDATORY SPECIAL EDUCATION

Many states now have mandatory special education laws. For example, Michigan's 1971 law requires the State Department of Education to provide special education programs for all handicapped persons from birth to age 25 who have not completed a regular high school program. For purposes of this law, a handicapped person is one who has been diagnosed:

A. Educable, Trainable, or Severely Mentally Impaired
B. Hearing or Visually Impaired
C. Physically or Otherwise Health Impaired
D. Speech or Language Impaired
E. Hospitalized or Homebound
F. Learning Disabled
G. Severely Multiply Impaired

In Michigan, the local school district has primary responsibility to provide programming and planning, transportation, and room and board where necessary. The local district must also evaluate the needs of its students. The main function of the intermediate school district remains one of coordinating services at the county level and maintaining a record of every handicapped person in the district age 25 and under.

Parents of any child in any state who may benefit from, but are not yet receiving special education, should contact their local school district, intermediate school district, and State Department of Educaton. Districts usually have information regarding other specialized services or programs available in the community.

MISCELLANEOUS

The Goodwill Industries and the Salvation Army are two other organizations able to offer help to handicapped persons. They are usually able to provide a number of social services and some on-the-job training. They are also usually familiar with other available resources in surrounding communities. Their addresses are available in your telephone directory.

Information concerning services available from the Social Security Administration, The Department of Vocational Rehabilitation, and the Veterans Administration may be found in Chapter 3. United Community Services, which exist nation-wide, are local citizen planning organizations committed to the identification and solution of social problems. Most United Community Services organizations offer direct public services in the form of county-wide information and referral services as well as client advocacy programs. Most also offer a community services directory for public sale. In addition, these organizations usually engage in public planning, public relations, and research activities, work to improve agency relations, and distribute the proceeds from annual fundraising drives to a wide range of community service groups.

United Community Services, as well as the individual community service organizations they represent, are usually listed in telephone directories under "Community Information," "Volunteer Bureaus," or "Social Services."

SELECTED READINGS

The following are recommended for further reading. Some are quite general in content; others apply to specific concerns or handicaps. Some are more appropriate for workers; others are more appropriate for parents. Some are better read before placement, some after.

Annotated Adoption Bibliography, Department of Health, Education, and Welfare, Social and Rehabilitation Service (Washington, D.C.: 1976).

Axline, Virginia. *Dibs – In Search of Self*. New York: Ballantine Books, 1964.

Berman, Claire. *We Take This Child – A Candid Look at Modern Adoption*. New York: Doubleday and Company, Inc., 1974.

Bernstein, Basil. "Social Structure, Language, and Learning." *Educational Research*, 3 (1961), 1-15.

Blank, Joseph. *Nineteen Steps Up the Mountain: The Story of the DeBolt Family*. Philadelphia: Lippincott, 1976.

Carney, Ann. *No More Here and There: Adopting the Older Child.* Chapel Hill: University of North Carolina Press, 1976.

Clark, Kenneth. *Dark Ghetto, Dilemmas of Social Power.* New York: Harper and Row, 1965.

Comer, James and Oliver Poussaint. *Black Child Care.* New York: Simon and Schuster, 1975.

Donley, Kay. *Opening New Doors.* London: Association of British Adoption Agencies, 1975.

Ferman, Pat and Bruce Warren. *Finding Families for the Children.* Ypsilanti, Michigan: Eastern Michigan University Press, 1974.

Fisher, Florence. *The Search for Anna Fisher.* New York: A. Fields Books, 1973.

Forsythe, Joyce, ed. *Frontiers in Adoption: Finding Homes for the "Hard-to-Place."* Lansing: Michigan Department of Social Services, 1969.

Geiser, Robert. *The Illusion of Caring: Children in Foster Care.* Boston: Beacon Press, 1973.

Ginott, Hiam. *Between Parent and Child. New York:* Macmillan, 1965.

——————— *Between Parent and Teenager.* New York: Macmillan, 1969.

Goldstein, Joseph, Anna Freud, and Albert Solnit. *Beyond the Best Interests of the Child.* New York: The Free Press, Macmillan Publishing Co., Inc., 1973.

Gordon, Thomas. *Parent Effectiveness Training.* New York: Peter H. Wyden, Inc., 1970.

James, Howard. *The Little Victims – How America Treats its Children.* New York: David McKay Co., 1975.

Killilea, Marie. *Karen.* New York: Dell Publishing Co., 1952.

Kravik, Pat, ed. *Adopting Children with Special Needs.* Ossing, New York: North American Council on Adoptable Children, 1976.

Klukholn, F.R. "Variations in Value Orientations as a Factor in Educational Planning," in *Behavioral Science Frontiers in Education.* Eds. E. Bower and W. Hollister. New York: Wiley, 1967.

Levison, Andrew. "The Working Class Majority." *The New Yorker,* Vol. L, No. 28, (Sept. 2), 1974.

Lifton, Betty Jean. *Twice Born: Memories of an Adopted Daughter.* New York: McGraw-Hill, 1975.

Littner, Ner. *Some Traumatic Effects of Separation and Placement.* New York: Child Welfare League of America, 1956.

Lund, Doris. *Eric.* Philadelphia: Lippincott, 1974.

McNamara, Joan. *The Adoption Advisor.* New York: Hawthorn Books, Inc., 1975.

Massie, Robert and Susan Massie. *Journey.* New York: Alfred A. Knopf, 1973.

Miller, S.M. and Frank Riessman. "The Working Class Subculture: A New View." *Social Problems,* 9 (1961), 86-99.

Pringle, M. L. *Adoption – Facts and Fallacies*. New York: Humanities Press, 1967.

Rainwater, Lee. "Crucible of Identity: The Negro Lower Class Family." *Daedalus*, 96, (1967), 172-216.

Rose, Anna Perrot. *Room for One More*. Boston: Houghton Mifflin, 1950.

Rose, Anna Perrot. *Gentle House*. Boston: Houghton Mifflin, 1954.

Rowe, Jane and Lydia Lambert. *Children Who Wait*. London: Association of British Adoption Agencies, 1973.

Wheeler, Candice. *Adopting Older Children*. Oregon Department of Human Resources, 1977.

Wooden, Kenneth. *Weeping in the Playtime of Others*. New York: McGraw-Hill Book Co., 1976.

Authors and Friends

Lee Ridley, Elizabeth Johnson, Christopher Unger, Nancy Unger, Gladys Dwarshuis, Ken Ridley, Kathrine Anne O'Sage, Irish Muffin O'Sage

Mr. Unger is Research Director for Spaulding for Children and refinishes furniture. He received his graduate training at the University of Michigan. The Irish Setters are his. Mrs. Dwarshuis is married, the parent of three sons, and received her graduate training at the University of Chicago. Ms. Johnson sings and sews. She, too, received her graduate training at the University of Michigan. All three are psychologists.

Copies of
Chaos, Madness, and Unpredictability
may be purchased from

Spaulding for Children
Box 337
Chelsea, Michigan 48118

1 copy: $4.00 plus .50 postage and handling
5 copies: $15.00 plus $2.00 postage and handling
10 copies: $25.00 plus $3.50 postage and handling

Print Name_____
Address_____
City_____
State_____ **Zip**_____